387
W9-CFA-454

Ship to Shore

A dictionary of everyday words and phrases derived from the sea

Peter D. Jeans

illustrated by
Ross H. Shardlow

ABC-CLIO
Santa Barbara, California
Denver, Colorado
Oxford, England

Library of Congress Cataloging-in-Publication Data

Jeans, Peter D.
Ship to shore : a dictionary of everyday words and phrases derived from the sea / Peter D. Jeans ; illustrated by Ross H. Shardlow.
p. cm.
Includes bibliographical references and index.
1. English language—Etymology—Dictionaries. 2. Seamen—Language (New words, slang, etc.)—Dictionaries. 3. Naval art and science—Dictionaries. 4. English language—Terms and phrases. 5. Seafaring life—Dictionaries. 6. Figures of speech. I. Title.
PE1583.J33 1993b 422'.03—dc20 93-28533

ISBN 0-87436-717-4 (alk. paper)

00 99 98 97 96 95 94 93 10 9 8 7 6 5 4 3 2 1 (hc)

ABC-CLIO, Inc.
130 Cremona Drive, P.O. Box 1911
Santa Barbara, California 93116-1911

This book is printed on acid-free paper ⊗.
Manufactured in the United States of America

For Judith, Romony, and Simon

"No man will be a sailor
who has contrivance enough
to get himself into a jail;
for being in a ship is being in a jail,
with the chance of being drowned."

—Dr. Samuel Johnson

Contents

Preface

My aim in this work is to illustrate what I believe is the astonishing debt that our idiomatic speech owes to the nautical language of the past. English is extraordinarily rich in metaphor, and it is the intention of this book to show that many of the figures of speech that we use from day to day derive from the language and customs of the sea.

Some of these expressions are very clearly nautical in origin, such as "to come adrift," "beachcomber," "to lose one's bearings," "to blow over," and so on. The remainder, by far the most interesting in this collection, have more or less successfully concealed their nautical background from the light of day: such expressions as "bowing and scraping," "by and large," "off and on," "the devil to pay," "to rummage," and "to flog a dead horse."

I have also included a relatively small number of nautical terms that in themselves are not part of our daily idiomatic coinage, yet because of their prevalence and importance in the literature of the sea are reasonably familiar to the general reader as belonging to matters maritime, such as "flensing," "mutiny," "marooned," and "Davy Jones's Locker."

Some older nautical expressions have lost their currency in our figurative speech and for the most part I have excluded them, but it would be an unfeeling person indeed who could reject out of hand such gems as "to be stabbed with a Bridport dagger," "all Harry Freeman," and "black's the white of my eye"; hence I have included a selection of these phrases because of their metaphorical impact and their historical importance to the language of the seafarer.

This project began through an almost accidental meeting with the nautical origin of the expression "Between the devil and the deep blue sea," which refers clearly enough to the situation where a person is faced with a choice between two risky or undesirable courses of action. What with being menaced by the devil on the one hand and the perils of the sea on the other, the phrase seemed perfectly self explanatory; but when I happened to come across an account of a ship's crew engaged in recaulking the seams of their leaky vessel, with great emphasis being laid on the difficulty of paying and pitching the two seams known as the devil seams, I was intrigued: perhaps the devil in the metaphor was not Old Nick himself, as I had otherwise always believed.

And indeed, this proved to be the case, as the reader will discover in the two entries under *Devil:* "Between the devil and the deep blue sea," and "The devil to pay."

Putting aside the expressions that were quite obviously nautical in origin, I then began to pay particular attention to the language used by such writers as Richard Henry Dana (*Two Years Before the Mast*), Frank Bullen (*The Cruise of the Cachalot),* and the contemporary novelist Patrick O'Brian (the "Jack Aubrey" series), to name but a few. In them I discovered that such ordinary, everyday expressions as "to skylark about," "to rummage," "to flog a dead horse," "to break new ground," and hundreds of others discussed in this dictionary were in fact born at sea as part of the jargon that English-speaking seamen have used for many hundreds of years.

How many other words and phrases that we use in our own daily life, I wondered, are in fact coinages from the very different world of the professional seaman? With this in mind I began a search, first through the literature that deals exclusively with nautical expressions (such as Rogers and Lind), and later through those books that treat the seafaring life in all its many aspects (such as Falconer, Harland, Hakluyt, and Kemp).

Armed with a very lengthy list, I then checked each term that was not obviously nautical against the best general and etymological dictionaries to which I had access. A decision to admit any particular term into this present work (or, of course, to exclude it) depended on a combination of what these reference works had to say and what I had learned over a lifetime of teaching English and, in particular, reading very widely in the nautical field.

Some of the most useful texts that I consulted were *The Country Life Book of Nautical Terms under Sail* by Whitlock and others; Falconer's *Universal Dictionary of the Marine,* Smyth's *The Sailor's Word Book,* Dana's *Two Years Before the Mast,* Hakluyt's *Voyages and Documents,* Harland's *Seamanship in the Age of Sail,* Kemp's *The Oxford Companion to Ships and the Sea,* Masefield's *Sea Life in Nelson's Time,* and Morton's *The Wind Commands.*

There are several books available that deal with nautical terms as they are used in our daily speech, but with the exception of Rogers they tend to be shallow in range, superficial in treatment, and rarely do they treat the language background of their subject. This is where, I believe, this present work has something to offer; it is a serious attempt to document a portion of the linguistic heritage that has been passed down to us by whole generations of seafarers, and it offers a clear indication of where the word came from, hence the inclusion of etymologies for most of the terms in this dictionary.

Examples are provided of how these nautical expressions might be used in our ordinary daily speech, together with citations from our literature showing their usage at some particular era in history.

I have tried to position this work for a readership that has an interest in language not necessarily as linguists or language specialists, but as reasonably informed readers who sometimes wonder about the words and expressions that they use in their daily speech. I have also endeavoured to write for those readers who have an interest in the sea, perhaps the professional seafarer, or the sometime voyager, or that much-maligned species, the armchair sailor.

Language has always been of concern and interest to people; it is my hope that this dictionary will encourage an even greater interest in what I consider to be a rich and fascinating topic: the idiom and metaphor that, over the centuries, has been passed on from ship to shore.

A Note on the Organization of This Book

The entries in this dictionary are arranged in alphabetical order (the terms appear in large, bold roman type in the left-hand column of the page). In many cases, various phrases and expressions in which a particular term is used are treated in subentries following the main term (such phrases and expressions are in bold, italic type in the left-hand column). Thus, for example, the term **About** is followed by subentries for ***To bring about, To come about, To go about,*** and so forth.

Cross references often appear at the end of entries to direct the reader to terms that are related by their meaning or etymology. The cross references give the main term to which the reader is directed, and are followed, where appropriate, by a phrase or expression separated from the main term by a semicolon. Thus, for example, the cross reference "See also *About, To come about*" directs the reader to the subentry ***To come about*** under the main term **About.**

Many examples of the modern usage of terms and expressions occur in the text of the entries. In addition, occasional examples from various historical and literary sources appear in the left-hand column, adjacent to the terms they illustrate.

The bibliography includes selected works that were consulted, including such standard references sources as dictionaries; books on the language of seafaring, such as Rogers and Lind; general reference books for those who are interested in various aspects of sailing and seamanship, such as Chapman, Harland, and Whitlock et al.; social histories of the Royal Navy, such as Garrett and Lloyd; first-hand accounts of sea-going experiences, like Dana and Gaby; and seafaring novels that have become classics of their kind, such as Marryat and Smollett.

There are four appendixes. Appendix 1 deals with some two dozen or so prepositional phrases that begin with the Old English *a,* for *on, in, into, to,* or *toward;* a group of words rather peculiar to nautical speech, but not wholly so. They represent the economy of words that is so typical of orders given aboard ship.

Appendix 2 is a sampling of the many words that have had their form and pronunciation altered and modified over centuries of use at sea.

Appendix 3 indicates the extent to which the seaman named the various parts of his ship from the human anatomy, and Appendix 4 similarly lists the words taken from his domestic environment, general environment, and the animal world.

Acknowledgments

I would like to record my deep appreciation to my family for their encouragement and forbearance during the four years that I worked on this book. It takes a certain kind of understanding to be able to live with a person whose passion of the moment demands that the family home be endlessly littered with dictionaries, histories, novels, and the like—anything and everything, as long as it has to do with the sea.

For rather similar reasons I thank my colleagues of the '80s in the English Department at Willetton Senior High School, Perth, Western Australia, each of whom maintained a stoic patience far beyond the demands of duty and loyalty when their every utterance was subjected to an immediate litmus test for nautical parentage.

I warmly thank my original typist, Mrs. Pat Bishop, whose personal interest and professional concern with the original draft made my task of editing so much easier. My daughter Romony has earned my everlasting gratitude for her cheerfulness and skill in keyboarding the whole of the large typescript into the family computer. The title of this book is the result of a brilliant flash of serendipity on the part of my wife Judith.

Various friends have read through parts of the manuscript for me and have made a number of valuable suggestions as to how it might be improved. I am indebted to the following people for their interest and specific ideas: Donald Burnside, Rob and Denise Main, Brendan Mulvey, David Price, and Judy Semple. Terry Woodings went to painstaking lengths in tracking down information about conditions of life in the sailing navy of Olde England, and I thank him here most warmly for his enthusiastic help.

The illustrations that greatly enhance this book were done by Ross Shardlow. His beautiful line drawing of the *Edwin Fox,* which graces the dust jacket, is reproduced here by the kind permission of Challenge Bank Limited, which commissioned the illustration as one of a series of prints depicting vessels with historical connections to Fremantle and Perth. The drawing of the clipper *Flying Cloud* on the endpapers is also from Mr. Shardlow's pen. Ross has given me many hours of his time in enlightening me on some of the finer points of ship design and construction; he has also suggested the inclusion of a dozen or more of the main dictionary entries, and I will always remain grateful for his friendship and for the fact that he so readily shared his extraordinary maritime knowledge with me.

Finally, I gladly acknowledge the encouragement given to me very early in the project by my friend Dr. Andrew Ong, whose enthusiasm for hard work helped to keep me going at my own task.

I would be pleased to hear from readers who have comments, corrections, or contributions that would enhance any possible future edition of this book.

Peter D. Jeans
Perth, Western Australia

Introduction

Words are not simply distilled from the air that we breathe whenever we need them. Rather, language is a living entity, ever-changing to suit different circumstances, moulded not only by its own internal laws of development but also by the influences and demands of the human society that it serves. We are constantly inventing new words and borrowing old ones from other languages, then reshaping them to suit our own needs. As a consequence English is by far the most flexible and fertile of tongues, and its force and variety reflect the character of those individuals and classes of people who have helped create it.

One such group that has profoundly influenced the development of English as a living language are the seafarers—the masters, mates, and matelots—who spent their lives wresting a precarious living from the sea in tall ships driven by the four winds across the oceans of the world. We shall not see their like again, but as a reminder of their passing they have left behind them—those "iron men in wooden ships"—a rich heritage of the metaphor and idiom with which they have written so much of the world's history. It is this *lingua franca* of the sea that has contributed so significantly to the ebb and flow of the landsman's daily speech, a sea-flavoured manner of phrase which it is the purpose of this book to celebrate.

What manner of man was it, then, who had such an impact on the language that we shore-bound folk speak? Where did he come from—unlettered, of obscure birth, and possessed of the most meagre of aspirations? What sort of life did he lead, such that the English-speaking world has raised to him that most noble and enduring of monuments, an honoured place in the ranks of English idiom?

He was many men.

He was the hardy British seaman who ventured into the ice-bound waters of Greenland in the early 17th century to hunt the whale, and a hundred years later he was the seafarer from New England and Newfoundland who pursued the same great beast south to the Antarctic and thence into the Pacific and Indian oceans; he was the grizzled fisherman from Maine and Massachusetts and Nova Scotia, cold and alone in his dory, adrift on the fabled cod grounds of the Grand Banks; he was the maintopman in the South China Sea, driving his tea clipper under a full press of canvas across the heaving oceans to the impatient markets of London; he was the British tar who roared with excitement when ordered to engage the enemy at Trafalgar, and he was the American foremast jack who, serving under John Paul Jones, rejoiced at the victory of the *Bon Homme Richard* over the British frigate *Serapis* in the war that won independence for his country; he was the mate of the slaver slanting its way across the Atlantic from the Gold Coast to the Caribbean with its cargo of human misery; and he was to be found in the fishing smacks of the Dogger Bank in the North Sea, in the stately full-rigged grain ships working up to Port Pirie in South Australia, in the nitrate and guano carriers beating across the remorseless Pacific, and in the steamers, tramps, and coasters, and thousands of other vessels that since time began have fought their battles or laboured for a livelihood across the seven seas.

He was the man who long, long ago lashed some logs together and paddled out to the distant horizon, where he has remained from that time to the present day patiently practising that most demanding of arts, the conduct of a ship at sea.

This, however brief and ill-told, is the story of all those seafarers who left the English-speaking world a priceless legacy—their language.

During the many conflicts that have engaged the maritime nations of Europe in the past thousand years or more, naval authorities experienced the greatest difficulty in finding crews to man their warships. For one thing there was no such notion as an established, permanent naval force; for another, conditions of service were generally so appalling that having once tasted the rigours of naval life very few men were eager to reenter that service; and finally, when hostilities had ceased, governments had no further use for their seamen so they were then cast ashore in their thousands, to fend for themselves as best they could.

If a man survived his service at sea, and if somehow he did get into port before peace was declared, he still had to run the gauntlet of the much-feared press-gangs.

In England these gangs—groups of ruffians for the most part but given official sanction by the authorities and usually under the command of a naval lieutenant—scoured coastal towns and villages for suitable men to make up the desperately needed ships' crews in time of war. Often these press-gangs operated far inland, and many a country lad enjoying an ale in his local public house after a day in the fields found himself in the clutches of the press gang that evening and on board the naval tender a few days later.

For many such a recruit (he was usually rated as *landsman* until he had acquired the necessary skills of a seaman) this was his first sight of the ocean, let alone a ship, and his introduction to the seafaring life was immediate, usually rough, and often brutal. The bosun's mates would literally beat a certain raw understanding into the newly pressed man with their hated ropes' ends and rattan canes. Every order was accompanied by a curse and a blow to the seaman's shoulders in the belief that each man needed instant corporal encouragement to go about his appointed tasks. Thus to a greater or lesser extent the pressed seaman, and with him the apprenticed midshipman, the fisherman's son, the greenhorn newly shipped into the grain trade, and all those countless other men and boys for whom the sea beckoned—each of them learned the art of seafaring. The vast majority of them came to accept the life and some perhaps to enjoy it, despite the often galling and frequently despotic conditions under which they lived.

Ever since the epochal discoveries of Christopher Columbus (who in 1492 discovered an astonishing new world in the Caribbean and set the scene for later Spanish hegemony in that part of the hemisphere); of Bartholomew Diaz (who rounded what is now called the Cape of Good Hope in 1488); and of Vasco da Gama (who, following the route pioneered by Diaz, reached India in 1498), the world's trading nations have understood that mercantile—and therefore political—power lay in their ability to maintain some measure of strategic control over their sea lanes. Within a decade of Diaz' first tentative foray into the Indian Ocean, the need for dominance at sea assumed an importance in world affairs that has been challenged successfully only in the second half of the 20th century by the superior technology of air power.

In the American War of Independence, for instance, fought between Britain and the 13 American colonies that had opted to sever their ties with England, naval power was of crucial importance in determining the outcome of the conflict. It is an interesting comment on the social forces at play in England and America at that time to note that the American ships were for the most part manned by volunteers, whereas the crews of the British vessels were frequently made up of men who had been forcibly pressed into the king's service.

The merchant marine, however (with one exception, noted below), never had any need to adopt the press-gang practices that so characterised the navies of the European maritime nations. The British tea traders that raced each other to be first home from China to the London Docks—vessels such as *Cutty Sark* and *Thermopylae*—had crews that were, on the whole, composed of volunteers who for one reason or another preferred that kind of life.

The same can be said of the American whaling ships that scoured the oceans of the world for whale oil, and of the British and American grain ships and nitrate ships—the magnificent square-riggers that have now almost disappeared forever—that added so much to the development of Australia and the Pacific coast of South America in the 19th century: all of them were crewed by men who for the most part had chosen to go to sea.

The fishing fleets of the North Sea and the Atlantic—the drifters, cod-bangers, smacks, schooners, and trawlers that put out in every weather from Hull, Grimsby and Bristol, Halifax, Boston and St John's, and a thousand other ports in between—were manned by men and boys who were fishermen by vocation as were their fathers before them.

The American whalers, too, were a tough breed who went to sea by choice on long voyages that could last up to three years; Herman Melville's novel about Captain Ahab's hunt for the white whale "Moby Dick" is based on his own earlier experiences on the whaler *Acushnet* in the 1840s, and it describes accurately and vividly the hard and unrelenting life that these men led in the whale fishery.

There were, of course, some exceptions to this generalisation about the relative democracy of life in the merchant service of the English-speaking world.

For instance, conditions on many of the 19th century American clippers that plied the Cape Horn route between the American east and west coasts were so brutal (in a livelihood that was already dangerous to begin with), that many a master or his agent had to resort to "shanghaiing"—kidnapping—men into their ships, usually by means of strong liquor or drugs. Only in this way could shipping owners secure a full complement of men who would otherwise never have chosen to serve in these hard-driving a nd hard-driven hell-ships. Some captains and their officers (the infamous "bucko mates") drove their men with a tyrannical ruthlessness that is difficult to match elsewhere in the annals of the sea. Richard Henry Dana's classic *Two Years Before the Mast* details the horrors that he endured on the brig *Pilgrim* on a voyage from Boston to the Pacific seaboard in 1834.

The shanghaiing of men was in effect little different from the press-gang methods so notably pursued by the British Navy in earlier times; but vicious though it might have been, the system flourished for only a relatively short period in the 19th century when sailing ships, in order to compete efficiently as cargo carriers against tramp steamers, had to acquire crew by any possible means so as to keep up their sailing schedules.

But life on board a sailing ship—whether under the relentless discipline of a naval code or as a result of the usually more benign (but rarely slack) rule of the merchant service—was still one dominated by the pressing needs of war or commerce, and often both at the same time, as well as by the ever-present dangers of the sea.

It was an intense, cheek-by-jowl existence.

In the naval service each man was allotted about fourteen inches of space in which to sling his hammock from the deck beams overhead; for his part the merchant seaman found rest and refuge of a kind on a thin straw palliasse in a bunk, one of a series of narrow wooden shelves arranged in tiers in the forecastle, the dark and dingy and reliably damp quarters assigned to seamen in the ship's bows.

The naval seaman messed in a group of four to eight men in the narrow spaces (known as berths) between the guns; the merchant seaman took his meals in the only space that was specifically allotted to him—the fo'c'sle, his sleeping quarters. In these cramped areas, lit only by a stinking candle or a smoky oil lamp and hemmed in on all sides by the tools of his trade, the seaman ate and drank, made merry, danced, got drunk and, in port, entertained his female acquaintance. He whiled away his off-watch hours by sleeping, yarning with his mess-mates, or by repairing his usually pitiful store of clothing and other personal effects.

The seaman was, above all, a social being, a gregarious animal. He had to be; the conditions of his day-to-day life demanded it. On board a sailing ship it was quite impossible for a man to be alone, to enjoy a private moment of peace or solitude. He necessarily shared with his fellows all the rigours of shipboard life: the wretched food, the sometimes oppressive discipline, and the ever-present dangers of the sea. It is no accident that the concept of male fellowship, what the seaman might have called "mateship," found its greatest expression in the intense confines of the mess and the fo'c'sle.

In a man-o'-war the noise, heat, stench, and violence of a sea-fight was enormous and the labour prodigious. The slaughter was often horrific and it was common for a hard-pressed ship to have her decks running rivers of blood. This was known as the "butcher's bill," the "Price of Admiralty." The merchant seaman, on the other hand, though rarely confronted with exigencies of this kind, nevertheless faced other pressing problems.

On board a grain ship or a nitrate ship, for example, tracking across the wastes of the Indian or Pacific oceans, or a tea clipper racing for home in a bid to be first to market, or a Cape Horner battling the Southern Ocean carrying miners and mails to California, the search for speed and more speed pushed men, ships, and gear to the limits of endurance and sometimes beyond. Ship owners, beset by rising costs and increasing competition from steamships, sought to offset the one and meet the other by cutting down on food rations, engaging the smallest possible number of men to work their vessels, and demanding even shorter passage-making times from their captains.

These sorts of constraints, coupled with the ever-present threat of fire in such cargoes as grain and coal and wool, made life in the merchant marine just as demanding and dangerous as it was in the naval service; indeed, frequently more so because of the unrelenting pressure of the dictates of commerce on the one hand and, on the other, the smaller crews that were employed, thus placing great burdens on their capacity to handle their ship in time of emergency.

Broadly speaking, sailing ships were worked under a two-watch system (port watch and starboard watch) of four hours each, so that half the ship's company was on duty while the other half was below sleeping or relaxing. In an emergency all hands would be called on deck. The ship's working day began at noon, and the following 24-hour period was divided into four-hour segments of duty. However, the evening watch from 1600 to 2000 (4:00 P.M. to 8:00 P.M.) was broken into two-hour watches so that the men did not have to keep the same watches every day.

The men in each watch were further subdivided into several divisions whereby each group was allotted a particular task, such as working the mainmast, overhauling and cleaning various items of gear and rigging, and so on. Many of the crew did not stand a watch but instead worked at special crafts and tasks about the ship; these people were known as "idlers," although no scorn or contempt was implied by the name.

The men were generally fed abundantly but badly. For hundreds of years nothing was known about the art of preserving food other than the age-old practice of using salt. Consequently the bulk of the provisions taken aboard a sailing ship consisted of salt beef, salt pork, and salt fish. Ship's biscuit—a kind of bread known as hard tack and baked ashore, sometimes many years earlier—was the other staple of the seaman's diet. Weevils soon infested the whole stock and it was necessary to tap each biscuit vigorously on the mess table so as to dislodge the maggots and casts. Quite often the biscuit was yellow and stinking from the urine of rats. Fresh food was rarely obtainable, certainly never on a daily basis; hence the prevalence of scurvy, which was otherwise so easily cured with the vitamin C of fresh fruit and vegetables.

Drinking water was kept in casks where it soon became foul and slimy. Vast quantities of beer were carried to offset the water problem, but it too soon suffered the same fate because of the unreliable means of storage.

Peas, cheese, butter, sometimes raisins, oatmeal, and a few other items also formed a part of the seamen's diet, but in many instances he was defrauded of his proper allowance by dishonest victuallers ashore and a scheming ship's cook afloat. Many a cask of foul green meat, crawling with maggots and swimming in the ooze of putrefaction, had to be thrown overboard within only a week of a ship's setting sail from port. Other foodstuffs were often so old and stale that they were inedible long before they became part of the ship's stores; indeed, one of the seaman's hobbies was carving dry, iron-hard cheese into serviceable buttons and other knick-knacks for his own use. Occasionally livestock was carried on a long voyage and slaughtered for fresh meat.

It was a hard life—harder, perhaps, than any life ashore. All seamen, whether serving in their country's navy or in the merchant marine, understood the absolute need for discipline afloat. They knew that a slovenly run ship was a hell-ship, where each tier of authority was permitted by default to bully and tyrannise the echelon next below.

Ship-board life was certainly hard and often degrading, but insofar as the men themselves (often referred to by their officers as "the people") were concerned, theirs was not a gratuitous cruelty. Confronted by the unrelenting elements and the dangers of disease and battle, the seaman was forced to adopt a certain hard-nosed attitude toward his lot. Sometimes his life was barbarous and disgusting: he got drunk whenever possible and he conducted his social life aboard on the lowest level of humanity. But for all his ignorance, superstition, simple-mindedness, and brute-like attitude to life, society at sea was never artificial. In at least this one great respect the seaman differed from, and became superior to, his fellow man ashore.

One of the curious things about the seaman of the age of sail—and one comes across this frequently in the literature of the sea—was that no sooner was he ashore, often after a hateful voyage in an unhappy ship, than he was longing to be away to sea again. For the most part they loved their calling, or if "love" is too strong a term, at least they took an inordinate pride in their skills, in their ability to "hand, reef and steer"; and in their own grudging and inarticulate way they respected the sea and could know the beauty of a ship under a full press of canvas.

What brought the seaman low was his love of liquor and his need for female society, both available in endless quantity and variety throughout the bars and bordellos of every seaport in the world. When they had sated themselves what else was there for them? They were different—not of the land. People marked them and pointed them out and took advantage of them. The seaman spoke in the only language he knew, which was the sometimes incomprehensible jargon of the sea. His dress was outlandish, his manners coarse, and he embraced life with a touching but foolish naivete. He did not belong to the society of men ashore. He yearned to be away at sea, and was even willing to accept the rotten food, poor pay, and frequently brutal, man-killing conditions, because then and only then could he be among people he understood.

He was a simple soul: superstitious, God-fearing, profane, uncouth, and often illiterate, gentle with his fellow men on occasion, and strangely moralistic and conservative in his attitude (considering his own prodigious physical appetites), with a strict code of honesty that enabled him to endure the privations of the sea and the fearsome impositions of close-quarters living that marked his life as being so very different from that led by men ashore.

The essential simplicity of the seafaring man (an astonishing trait, considering that many of these seamen were literally men of the world) made him an easy prey for the swindlers, the sly-grog sellers, and the good-time girls, all of whom constituted the only society that he knew, or could possibly know, ashore. He hated these people but he couldn't avoid them. His training and his background—his very life and nature—made him unfit for any but the most basic levels of human society.

His was a different life. He valued above all else the openness and simple if crude honesty of his shipmates. At least he knew where he stood with them. It was a mateship that he never achieved with men who lived ashore.

The would-be seaman brought aboard with him customs, attitudes, and dialects that often were in marked contrast with those of his fellows. In a relatively short space of time he began to fathom the rudiments of seafaring. The bosun and his mates saw to that. What he learned was the art and sometimes the science of managing ("conducting") a ship at sea. What he contributed in return was a particular kind of speech, a jargon that marked it as being utterly different from the occupational discourse of any other livelihood. Because he was personally so close to the exigencies of life (or death: the two are so nearly the one at sea) he named and peopled his environment with the things that were known to him.

This is a natural reaction. When a man is engaged upon an enterprise—"doing business in great waters" as Psalm 107:23 puts it—that might very well (and frequently did) spell his ruin, he tends to surround himself with the familiar, as a sort of talisman of hope and security.

Hence he sought to interpret events at sea in the light of his previous experiences. He named names from what he already knew. He invented a language and an idiom within that language, and when necessary adapted his own vocabulary so as to enable him to maintain his connections with his past and the now very different present. Various parts of the ship were named from the human body: waist, buttocks, cheeks, eyes, ribs, belly, and dozens more. Gear and rigging were given the names of things from the earlier familiar environment of farm and manor, hearth and village: shoe, floor, hog, lizard, feather, castle, yoke, crown, and many other such homely words.

The jargon of the sea still contained much that was esoteric and just plain gibberish to the landsman newly entered in the ship's books; what, for example, was he to make of "Stand by to wear ship!," "mains'l haul!," "pass the earring!," and a hundred others like these? But he mastered it and in the process of doing so gave to the English tongue perhaps the world's most colourful and expressive idioms.

When he went ashore he spoke in the only way he knew; consequently his discourse was a salty distillation of the sea-going phraseology that came so naturally to him. The oft-quoted story of the sailor's visit to the dentist is not as apocryphal as it might seem; when asked which tooth it is that hurts he replies, "'Tis the aftermost grinder aloft, on the starboard quarter."

The influence of the nautical experience on the English language has been enormous. Whenever seamen forgathered to share a drink or to swap a yarn, and in all their ordinary daily social intercourse with the rest of society, the vernacular of the sea—though it necessarily had to change and adapt to varying circumstances—slowly found its way into everyday speech.

The enduring greatness of the seafarer over the centuries is best typified by the fact that the very coinage of his working life, the verbal warp and weft of his everyday existence, is firmly embedded in the fabric of our native tongue. It is hoped that in some small measure this book will contribute toward an understanding and appreciation of that greatness.

A

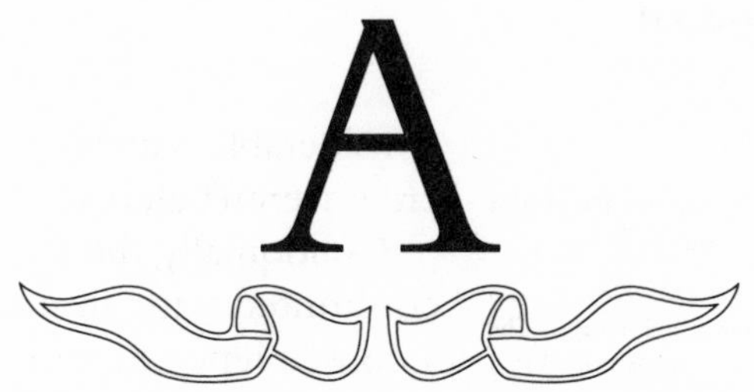

A1
To be in A1 condition

A1 is the old and famous classification given by *Lloyd's Register of Shipping* to vessels as an indication of their state of seaworthiness. The letter refers to hulls that meet Lloyd's requirements concerning materials and method of construction. The numeral refers to a vessel's ground tackle; if her anchors, cables, and such meet Lloyd's standards, then they are given the classification *1.* Thus, to be "A1" was to be first rate, the very best. The more modern system uses the notation *100 A1,* but the older classification is still widely used and has since the eighteenth century gone into colloquial usage to designate anything that is of the best quality, first class: "The material to be used in the tenting has to be A1 quality if we are to endure the rigours of our proposed expedition."
(See also *Lloyd's of London. Lutine Bell.)*

A.B.

The abbreviation for the term *able-bodied;* it is not the initials of the two words, as is often thought, but originally was simply the first two letters of *able.* To be rated able-bodied in the old sailing days, a man had to be able to hand, reef, and steer; that is, he had to be skilled in all the facets of handling sails, and had to be able to steer with skill in any weather. In the modern navy, of course, a seaman must have many more skills than that. There were three rates of seaman: A.B., Ordinary Seaman, Landsman.

The term came to be used ashore to refer to anyone who was healthy and strong, fit enough to carry out the task intended for him or her. Froude's *History of England* (1856) has the term in much the same way that we would employ it today: "For the able-bodied vagrant, it is well known that the old English laws had no mercy."
(See also entries under *Rate.)*

Aback
To be taken aback

"I don't think I was ever so taken aback in all my life."
—Charles Dickens (1812–1870), English novelist, *American Notes* (1842)

The sails of a square-rigger were said to be "aback" when the wind was blowing directly on the wrong or foremost side of the sails. In certain ship-handling manoeuvres, putting the sails aback was deliberate; at other times, it could create a dangerous situation, because a sudden shift in the wind, especially a gale-force wind, could cause considerable damage to spars and rigging if the officers and crew weren't alert to the threat.

"Brace the foremost yards aback . . ."
—William Falconer (1732–1769), Scottish poet, lexicographer, and seaman, "The Shipwreck" (1762)

Colloquially, the term means to be surprised or to be confronted with an unexpected situation or development, as a consequence of which one is at a loss as to what to do or say next.

Able-bodied See *A.B.*

Aboard
To go aboard

In or within the ship; on board. Originally nautical, from the French *a bord,* in turn from the Anglo-Saxon *bord,* meaning plank or side. Now extensively used to describe being on or within a bus, train, wagon, or other conveyance, as well as a ship.

About A direction across the wind with reference to the bow of a ship; a vessel goes about when she swings her bows through the eye of the wind (called "tacking"). From the Old English *abutan,* from *on butan,* on the outside of.

To bring about To cause to happen, to accomplish, as in "He hopes to bring about a change in his fortunes." Nautically, the expression means to turn a vessel on to the opposite tack.
(See also *About; To come about.)*

"... to bring about all Israel unto thee."
—2 Samuel 3:12

To come about A vessel comes about when she goes from one tack to the other, so as to move off in a new direction with the wind coming over the other side. The essential meaning consists of a change in direction.

"The wind came about and settled in the West for many days."
—Francis Bacon (1562–1626), English philosopher and essayist

Figuratively, the term means to come to pass, to happen, to arrive in due course, just as the vessel comes about to head onto its new course; also rendered by *to bring about.*

To go about *To go about* means to go from one tack to the other to change direction, so that the wind is now blowing on the other side of the vessel. This is the same as *to change tack* and is sometimes rendered by the sailor as *to put about.* As a metaphor, *to go about* is to change direction, to change one's angle of attack (or defence) in an argument or discussion. The colloquialism more commonly used is *to change tack.*
(See also *About; To put about. Tack; To change tack.)*

"Why go ye about to kill me?"
—John 7:19

To put about To change the direction in which the vessel is moving. Figuratively, to change one's own position, to shift one's attack to another quarter; to make publicly known: "The ship put about and returned to port"; "It was put about that the Cabinet was in disagreement."
(See also *About; To go about.)*

Abraham
To sham Abraham

"An Abraham-man is he that walketh bare-armed and bare-legged, and fayneth himself mad, and caryeth a packe of wool, or a styck with baken on it, or such lyke toy, and nameth himself poor Tom."

—*Fraternitye of Vacabondes* (1575)

To malinger, to pretend to be sick to avoid unpleasant or arduous duties. Sometimes spelled as "Abram" and known as an Abram-man or Abraham cove; frequently referred to in literature as Tom of Bedlam.

In the fourteenth century, Bethlehem Hospital began to receive lunatics; it later degenerated into a public place of spectacle and disgrace (the word *bedlam* is a corruption of *Bethlehem).* Inmates of Bedlam—Bethlehem Hospital—who were not dangerous were kept in a section of the building known as the Abraham Ward. Occasionally they were allowed out into the street, in distinctive dress, and permitted to beg. This gave an opportunity to many imposters, who would adopt the dress and manners of the genuine inmates in order to impose on the public at large as licensed beggars belonging to the hospital.

There is also a suggestion that the Abraham Ward was given over to the care of insane naval patients. It is interesting to note that in Admiral Horatio Nelson's time (1758–1805) the incidence of insanity among sailors was about eight times the national average; it has been suggested that one of the reasons for this high figure was the fact that seamen frequently smashed their heads against the very low deck beams in their ships.

Sham in this expression means, of course, to imitate, to do a spurious counterfeit.

Abreast
To keep abreast of; to keep abreast with

"... two men could hardly walk abreast."

—Thomas Babington Macaulay (1800–1859), British essayist, historian, and politician, *History of England* (1848)

To the sailor, *abreast* means side by side, parallel to. If two ships are lying side by side and parallel, with their sterns more or less level with each other, then they are said to be "abreast." "Abreast" is the position of one thing in relation to some other recognisable mark or place; it means exactly the same as *to be abeam of.* Colloquially, to be abreast of, or with, is to keep up with, as in "to keep abreast of developments in computer technology," or "to keep abreast of the times in clothing fashions." Derived from the Old English *breast;* the verb *to breast* is to keep up with, to bring the breast (upper chest) up to the tape, mark, wall, or such.

Abroad
To be abroad

"In one house shall it be eaten; thou shalt not carry forth ought of the flesh abroad out of the house. . . ."

—Exodus 12:46

Out at sea; as in "The wind is getting abroad the night," a once-common expression to mean that bad weather is coming. Now it means out of doors, as in "at large"; also to be in a foreign country. From the Middle English *on brede,* on breadth, widely scattered, out of doors. The sense of travel suggested by this word is characteristic of a seafaring people.

Account
To be on the account

An old phrase meaning to sail off on a piratical expedition; the term was often used by buccaneers to describe their rather irregular way of life at sea. The phrase is intended to sound a little more polite than "turning pirate," and probably derived from the fact that a would-be pirate so arranged his affairs that he would be able to account for his actions if caught and charged with illegal practices. More loosely, *to be on the account* means to be ready to benefit from any situation that arises.

Action Stations!

The action station is the place of duty assigned to every man on board when the ship goes into battle. These action stations are listed on the ship's Quarter Bill; this is the origin of the naval order to "beat to quarters," when the ship's drummers would beat a particular rhythm on their drums to indicate that action was imminent and that the men must go to their assigned Quarter Bill stations. The order in the modern navy is simply "Action Stations!" The expression is widely used in everyday colloquial speech, to mean "take heed," "get ready": "Action stations! The concert is about to begin!"

Adam's Ale

Sailors' slang for fresh drinking water, which was cherished on board sailing ships that might make a voyage of 200 days or more, during which the drinking water was sure to turn foul or be in dangerously short supply. Ale, or indeed any alcohol, was heaven to the sailor; how much more so was potable water in his time of need. The expression is used facetiously, as in "We have no wine left; you'll just have to drink Adam's Ale."

Addle

The seaman's name for water that had gone stale or putrid in the cask. This occurred so frequently that many ships carried large quantities of beer, which kept much longer than did fresh water. The expression came to mean muddled or confused, spoiled or rotten. From the Old English *adela,* liquid filth. Colloquially, anything that is addled is muddled or confused, as in "His mind is addled over the new woman in the office."

"Yet thy head has been beaten as addle as an egg."
—William Shakespeare (1564–1616), *Romeo and Juliet,* act 3, scene 1

Admiral

The title of the commander of a fleet, or a subdivision of it. From the Arabic *amir,* prince, leader; thence to the French *amiral.* The English word *admiral* is an artificial spelling of the French term. The Arabic word in full would be *amir-al-bahr,* commander of the sea; hence the clipped English form *admiral.* It was common practice in the fifteenth and sixteenth centuries for the man himself to be called the general, or general-captain, with the word *admiral* being reserved for his flagship.

There are four active ranks of admiral in the Royal Navy today: admiral of the fleet, admiral, vice admiral, and rear admiral, all known as flag ranks. In the U.S. Navy, there are four grades of admiral: admiral of the fleet (insignia five stars), full admiral, vice admiral, and rear admiral; these grades have been in use since the American Civil War (1861–1865).

Adrift
To come adrift

To be at the mercy of the elements, especially wind or tide, usually as a result of something breaking or being carried away, such as an anchor cable or mooring line. The sailor who has come adrift is one who, for whatever reason, is late, overdue from leave, or absent from his or her place of duty. Colloquially, the phrase means to be confused, to be wide of the mark, to be last, to come undone. "Since his wife left him he has come more and more adrift."
(See also *Adrift; To turn adrift. Moorings; To lose one's moorings.)*

To turn adrift

"... As I have said, it was A time of trouble; shoals of artisans / Were from their daily labour turn'd adrift / To seek their bread from public charity."
—William Wordsworth (1770–1850), English poet, *Excursion,* Book 1 (1814)

A vessel is adrift if it is floating without control wherever the winds and current may take it. Captain Bligh and his 18 companions were turned adrift by the *Bounty* mutineers in 1789. They were set at large by Fletcher Christian and the remaining crew with very little food and water, and only the barest essentials in sails, rigging, and navigation instruments—that is, they were cast out to wander where they would. It was only because of Bligh's outstanding seamanship and navigation that they did not all come adrift.

Adventure

"I am no pilot, yet, wert thou as far as that vast shore washed with the farthest sea, I would adventure for such merchandise."
—William Shakespeare (1564–1616), *Romeo and Juliet,* act 2, scene 2

A commercial term, long recognised in maritime usage, to denote consignments of cargo sent abroad in a ship to be sold or traded by the master to best advantage, as the opportunity arose. Such merchants were called "venturers" and later "adventurers." The Merchant Venturers' School in Bristol, England, preserves the fame of the Elizabethan venturers. The word and the ground-sense (no pun intended with respect to the following remarks) are found today in commercial enterprises such as the Argyle Diamond Mine Joint Venturers, in the far north of Western Australia. An adventure is now regarded as an undertaking of uncertain outcome, a hazardous enterprise, a commercial or financial undertaking of any kind. Ultimately from the Latin *adventura,* the future, a thing about to happen.

Afterguard

The afterguard were the seamen responsible for working the gear in the after part of the ship, that is, toward the stern. Their station was on the poop or on the quarterdeck. The term today refers to the racing yacht helmsman and his advisers on tactics and navigation, all grouped in or near the stern. By extension, the afterguard in any enterprise is that person or group of persons whose task is to provide support or protection to the leadership. "The sales manager delegated the intricacies of billing to the afterguard in the accounts branch."

Ahead In front of the ship, in the direction toward which her bow is pointing. From the Old English prefix *on,* meaning on, in, into, to, toward; and the Old English *heafod,* head (of the body).

All clear ahead The allusion is obvious: there is no obstacle in the direct path of the vessel, it is safe to proceed. Similarly, the metaphorical usage implies the same, that there are no obstacles or other sources of interference to the course of action planned: "The bank has given us the all clear ahead for our plan to buy that house."

To go ahead Originally a purely nautical word, and one of many that has the preposition *a* as prefix so as to indicate, precisely and economically, direction and amount—a consideration of particular importance to sailors who are required quickly and efficiently to handle a vessel under all conditions of sea and battle. Other examples of such peremptory orders are "abaft," "abreast," "ahoy," "a-lee," "avast," "astern," and "aloof." (See appendix 1 for more on such terms.)

"... it was necessary that a man should go ahead with a sword to cut away the creepers."
—Charles Darwin (1809–1882), English naturalist, *Voyage Round the World* (1870)

Ahead, of course, means in front of the ship, in the direction toward which she is pointing. To go ahead means just that: to move forward. As an expression it means to proceed (often with permission implied), to take the lead, to be in the forefront, as in "The foreman was told to go ahead with his plans for improved production."

Ahoy! The standard hailing cry of the sailor to attract attention. From the interjection *a* + *hoy,* a small coasting vessel, sometimes called a sloop or a smack. A coasting vessel is one that keeps the coast in sight when sailing from one port to another; such vessels use coastal landmarks by which to navigate, rather than stellar navigation. Often used in everyday idiomatic speech, as in "Ahoy there! What do you think you're doing with that spade?"

When a small naval craft approaches another naval ship at its mooring, the gangway sentry challenges the smaller vessel with the standard cry "Boat ahoy!" The coxswain of the visiting boat replies in one of a number of ways: if his boat is carrying any member of the royal family, he would cry "Standard!," a reference to the royal standard that his boat would be wearing (by day, of course, such a challenge would be unnecessary, as the gangway sentry would see, and would certainly know beforehand of, the royal personage's approach).

Should the boat have a member of the Admiralty aboard, the coxswain would reply "Admiralty!" With an admiral or commander-in-chief aboard, the coxswain answers the challenge with "Flag!" followed by the name of the flag officer's ship. With a captain on board the visiting small craft, the reply is merely the name of the ship that the captain commands. If the passengers are officers other than the captain, the coxswain replies "Aye, aye!" and if there are no officers at all the reply is "No, no!" Strictly speaking, even the Archbishop of Canterbury as a passenger would merit only a "No, no!" from the coxswain, but in fact the coxswain would reply "Aye, aye!" to ensure that the distinguished visitor was received aboard the warship with proper courtesy.

American usage adopted many of the practices of the Royal Navy, which one might reasonably expect given the common language and background of the two nations. In the U.S. Navy, the responses to the hailing of a boat include cries similar to those previously detailed. For example, "No, no," "Aye, aye," and the ship's name are used if its captain is in the boat.

All aboard!

"And finding a ship sailing over unto Phenicia, we went aboard, and set forth."
—Acts 21:2

Of nautical origin in the sense of the word *aboard,* and used as a cry, an exhortation, for passengers and crew to get onto or into the conveyance, whatever it might be—ship, train, bus, ferry, or the like. *All ashore!* follows the same pattern of use.
(See also *Aboard; To go aboard.)*

Aloof
To keep aloof

"Thy smile and frown are not aloof / From one another."
—Alfred, Lord Tennyson (1809–1892), English poet, *Madeline*

To keep the ship's head as close as possible to the wind, to keep away to windward; from the Middle English *lof.* Now rendered as "luff," "to luff up," "to keep your luff." From this nautical usage is derived the modern meaning of *aloof:* to keep at a distance from, to stand apart from, to keep away from, as in "She is a very aloof sort of person; I find it difficult to talk with her"—yet another interesting example of how a purely nautical expression has found its way into everyday language.

Anchor

From the Anglo-Saxon *ancor,* a very early loan word from the Latin *ancora* and the only nautical word from Latin that has been adopted by the Teutonic languages. Used colloquially, as in "She keeps me firmly anchored in reality whenever I start dreaming about the future."

One's best bower anchor The bower anchors are the two largest anchors in a ship, carried one on each bow in such a manner that they are always ready to be let go in an emergency. They were known as "best bower" and "small bower," not from any difference in size or weight (both anchors were identical), but rather from their placement: the best bower was on the starboard side and the small bower on the port. Starboard is always the preeminent side of a vessel for the purposes of tradition, particularly in the *Rules of the Road for Preventing Collision at Sea;* hence the terminology for these two anchors.

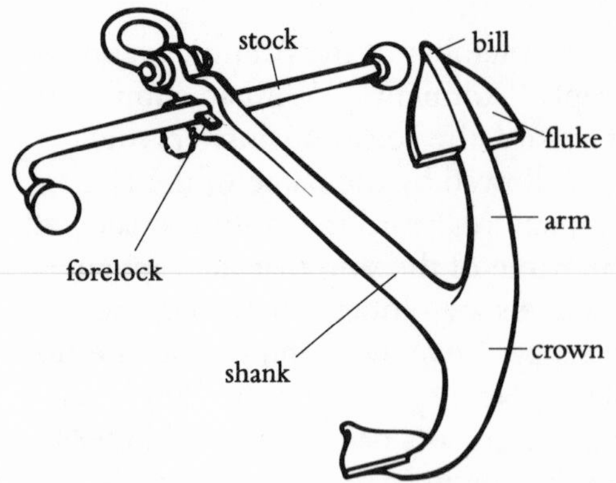

The metaphor follows the literal meaning: to be prepared for every event by having everything in its proper place, ready for immediate use: "I was sorry to learn that my secretary was resigning; she had proved to be my best bower in many difficult situations." (See also *Anchor; One's sheet anchor.)*

One's sheet anchor One's last hope or refuge, one's mainstay. The sheet anchor was once the heaviest anchor carried aboard the vessel after the bower anchors, but the distinction is now academic because all a vessel's working anchors have long since been the same weight. In the days of sail, the sheet anchor was carried abaft (astern of) the fore rigging (i.e., abaft the bower anchor) and was always ready to be let go in an emergency if), for example, the bower anchor was dragging in heavy weather on a lee shore.

The term *sheet anchor* is used as a synonym for security generally; one's business partner, helpmate, offsider, etc., may be termed one's sheet anchor if that person is utterly dependable, always to be relied upon.
(See also *Anchor; One's best bower anchor. Mainstay.)*

To swallow the anchor To retire from a life at sea and settle down to living ashore. (See also *Beach; To be on the beach.)*

Andrew Derived from the term *Andrew Miller,* which in turn is the seaman's traditional name for the Royal Navy. It is said to come from an eighteenth-century press-gang operator of that name, who impressed so many Portsmouth men into naval service during the wars of that period that he was said to own the whole Royal Navy. The name stuck, so that in the nineteenth century *Andrew Miller* also meant a warship or government authority. In fact, there is no record of anyone named Andrew Miller being responsible for pressing men into naval service, but he may have been

a civilian employed by H.M. Impress Service, as were a good many naval officers, including Lord Nelson himself at one time.
(See also *Press; Press gang, to press.)*

Ardent

"Ardent and intrepid on the field of battle, Monmouth was everywhere else effeminate and irresolute."
—Thomas Babington Macaulay (1800–1859), British historian and politician, *History of England* (1848)

A very old term from seafaring days; it referred to a ship's propensity for rounding up to (i.e., turning into) the wind unless firm control was kept on the tiller or wheel. Light weather helm is a desirable characteristic in sailing vessels, because if the helmsman falls overboard the craft will repeatedly round up into the wind, thus losing way and giving him at least a chance of climbing back on board.

The word found its way into English metaphor to mean earnest, passionate, and fervent, from the apparent desire of a ship to seek the wind. It comes from the Latin *ardere,* to burn.

Argosy

"Your argosies with portly sail . . . do overpeer the petty traffickers."
—William Shakespeare (1564–1616), *The Merchant of Venice,* act 1, scene 1

A large merchant ship, especially one with a rich cargo; also, a fleet of such ships. The word is perhaps a corruption of the Italian *Ragusea,* a vessel of Ragusa, an ancient port in the Eastern Mediterranean (Ragusa is the original name for Dubrovnik). Other authorities claim that *argosy* is from *Argo,* Jason's famous ship, in which the Argonauts sailed from Greece in search of the Golden Fleece *(argo* is from the Greek *argo,* swift).

Armada

A Spanish word, from the Latin *armata,* a fighting force; the word *army* is also from this source. *Army* later displaced the native English word *her,* fighting force, still found in such terms as "Hereford," "harbour," "harbinger," and "Hereward the Wake." Used now to refer to any fleet of warships, and more loosely to describe any large number of conveyances such as ships, boats, airplanes, and other vehicles.

The word is most closely associated with the Spanish Armada, a fleet of 130 vessels assembled in 1588 to attempt the invasion of England. The Spanish ships sailed from Lisbon and made their way up the English Channel, thereby disturbing, the story tells us, Sir Francis Drake at his game of bowls on Plymouth Hoe. After a series of battles with the English, the Spanish fleet anchored off Calais to embark the Prince of Parma's troops, which were to be used in the invasion. The English ships (commanded by Lord Howard of Effingham and not, as many people believe, by Drake himself) anchored nearby and sent in a number of fireships, causing great havoc and confusion among the Spanish. The Spanish left their anchorage

"They melt into thy yeast of waves which mar
Alike the Armada's pride or spoils of Trafalgar."
—George Gordon Byron (1788–1824), English poet, *Childe Harold* (1818)

without taking on the promised army, and, after losing many ships to the fire hulks, English guns, and the worsening weather, they were forced to return to Spain by way of the North Sea. Many of the Spanish ships were wrecked on the coasts of Scotland and Ireland and their crews slaughtered mercilessly by the local people as they struggled ashore. Of the great fleet of 130 ships, only 67 returned to port, their crews broken and starving and the vessels battered by the fierce storms of the North Sea. Never again did Spain contemplate an invasion of England.
(See also *Run; To cut and run.)*

Arrive

"At length a ship arriving brought / The goods so long desired. . . ."
—William Cowper (1731–1800), English writer, *A Tale* (1793)

Like *rummage,* the term *arrive* has very successfully concealed its nautical parentage from the public gaze. It came into English from the French *arriver,* and in turn from the Vulgar Latin *adripare* or *ripa,* shore (we see this source reflected in the word *riparian,* pertaining to the bank of a river or lake). The earliest sense of this word meant to bring something ashore, to land, to come ashore.
(See also *Rummage.)*

Arsenal

Another example of how words originally nautical in application have become much broader in meaning and usage. *Arsenal* was a sixteenth-century word for the docks and wharves in many of the great seaports of that time, for example, the arsenal of Venice and that of the London waterside area. The term later came to be applied to a storehouse for munitions. It comes from the Italian *arsenale,* wharf, but derives ultimately from the Arabic *al-cinaa'h,* workshop.

Articles
Ship's Articles

The "Articles of Agreement" formed the contract between the merchant shipowner and the crew. It detailed a code of conduct, the disciplinary measures and penalties to be expected, and the pay, rations, leave, and living space to be provided. Most Ship's Articles contained a clause allowing the master to call on the crew for extraordinary labours in time of distress or danger.

The "Thirty-Nine Articles of War" (the number was reduced to 36 in the Georgian navy, ca. 1714–1820) was a code of discipline adopted by the Royal Navy in 1661, in which severe penalties were specified for errors, incompetence, and infractions that led to the loss of a ship or for failure to carry out one's proper duties; for example, Admiral John Byng was executed by firing squad under the Articles in 1757 for failing to recapture Minorca from the French in 1756.
(See also *Broke; To be broke. Mayonnaise.)*

The Articles, which were the legal basis for discipline in the Royal Navy, covered four groups of offences:

1. Offences against God and religion.
2. Offences against the executive power of the king and his government, such as espionage, treason, mutiny, desertion, and striking an officer. Readers may remember Herman Melville's novel *Billy Budd,* published posthumously in 1924. Billy is a very fine British navy seaman, but he accidentally kills the malevolent Claggart, who has been persecuting Billy. Captain Vere, despite his awareness of Billy's innocence, has no alternative but to invoke the Articles and hang him.
3. Offences that violate the rights and duties men owe to one another, for example, the commission of murder, theft, or sodomy.
4. Battlefield actions, such as giving in to the enemy ("yielding and crying for quarter"), retreating ("withdrawing or keeping back from fight"), and failing to give chase ("forebearing to pursue an enemy").

For any infractions not specifically covered by the Articles, the captain could make recourse to the catch-all clause, "All other crimes, committed by any person or persons in the fleet, which are not mentioned in this act, or for which no punishment is hereby directed to be inflicted, shall be punished according to the laws and customs in such cases used at sea" (from B. Lavery, *Nelson's Navy,* 1989, personal communication).

The maximum number of lashes from the cat-o'-nine-tails was fixed at 48 in 1866; before that, the severity of punishment was usually left to the captain. (For example, "flogging around the fleet" was a court-martial sentence in which the offending seaman was lashed face-down to a grating in a boat, and then rowed alongside each ship lying in harbour, where he was given 12 strokes of the cat by the bosun's mate of that ship.) It is worth noting that the death penalty was mandatory for contravening 8 of the Articles, and optional for 20 more; all the Articles carried with them severe punishments at the least. Well might seamen refer to their captain as "master under God."

The American experience was considerably different. Naval seamen signed on for a period of two years (they were known as "enlisted men," a term still in wide use in the U.S. armed forces); there was no such thing as conscription or the press gang, which was in keeping with the egalitarian principles of the new nation that emerged from the American Revolution of 1775–1783. Indeed, many a captain in the Royal Navy was astonished and aghast at what seemed to him the insupportable air of "Jack's-as-good-as-his-master" that permeated the crew of most American naval vessels.

The expression is used now in such phrases as "an article of faith," the essential points of faith or belief held by a person, as in religion or a code of personal conduct; and "articles of agreement," particulars in a contract, treaty, or some other kind of formal agreement, wherein conditions of the contract are clearly stated or delineated.

(See also *Haze; To haze someone. Press; Press gang, to press.)*

Australia From the Latin *terra australis,* known to the French as *terres australes,* and to other navigators of the early eighteenth century as *Australiasia* (note spelling), from *Auster,* the ancients' name for the south wind, and *Asia;* hence "land to the south."

The continent was also known variously as New Zealand; New Holland; Eendrachtsland (from the name of Dirk Hartog's ship the "Eendracht"); The Great South Land (called "terra Australis" by the ancient philosophers and astronomers); Terra Australis Incognita; La Austrialia del Espiritu Santo (named by the explorer De Quiros in 1606, when he thought—mistakenly—that he had at last reached the Great South Land; his name for it means South Land of the Holy Spirit); Beach; The New South Land; and Davis' Land (this last name later being given to Easter Island, which was the land most probably sighted by John Davis, the navigator, in his circumnavigation in the late sixteenth century). The Malays also apparently knew Australia as The Land of the Dead.

The present name, *Australia,* was suggested by Matthew Flinders (1774–1814) in 1814.

Average A word of primarily nautical origin; possibly derived from the Arabic *awar,* damaged goods, and *awariya,* damages. The intermediate connection with English is probably the French *avarie,* customs duty (a twelfth-century usage). Its maritime usages included customs duties, extraordinary expenses of shipping damage at sea, and the equitable distribution of a resulting loss (the last still current in modern insurance practice).

"Defendants said that as by what had happened they lost their freight, they were entitled to claim a contribution, by way of General Average, on account of the loss of freight."

—*The Shipping Gazette* (London), March 29, 1881

The modern mathematical sense, an arithmetic mean, occurs in English only. More loosely, the word has also come to mean ordinary, normal, typical, the common run of things.

Away
To be squared away

When a ship was "squared away," she was ready for her voyage proper; she had left the harbour, the tow was dropped, her decks were cleared, and all yards were properly braced for that point of sailing. Everything was ready and shipshape for what lay ahead. As a figure of speech, to be squared away is to be complete, fixed up.

To square away one's account is to settle it, to pay it, to arrange an accommodation or an understanding. "Before I resigned and went overseas, I squared everything away with my firm's accountant."
(See also *Shipshape; All shipshape and Bristol fashion.)*

To clear away

To clean up and stow gear in its proper place after some manoeuvre, such as weighing anchor. Now widely used to mean to remove, to tidy up, to put to rights, as in "I'll clear away all this rubbish in the garden shed."

Awning

"... wee did hang an awning (which is an old saile) to ... trees to shadow us from the sunne."

—Captain John Smith (1580–1631), English sea captain, *The General History of Virginia, New England, and the Summer Isles* (1624).

A rooflike shelter of canvas or other material, hung before a window or door, or over a deck, as a protection from the weather; used mostly as a shade from the sun. The word first occurs in English in 1624. Its etymology is obscure, but it is certainly nautical in origin; it may derive from the French *auvent,* a covering of cloth in front of a shop window.

Aye aye

"Heard the voices of men through the mist, the rattle of cordage / Thrown on the deck, the shouts of the mate, and the sailors' 'Ay, ay, Sir!' "

—Henry Wadsworth Longfellow (1807–1882), American poet, *The Courtship of Miles Standish* (1858)

The correct and seamanlike reply on board ship when given an order; an affirmative or confirming response to a question or an order. Its origin is unknown, but it may be related to an early Greek word meaning "ever."

B

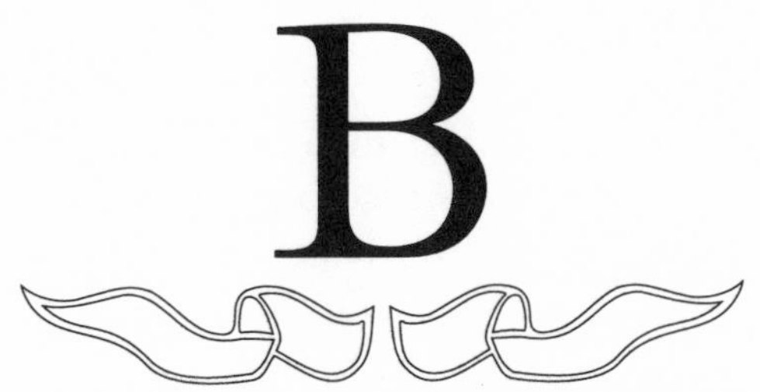

Back
To back and fill To trim the sails of a vessel so that they are alternately aback (with the wind on the forward face) and filled (with the wind blowing onto the aftermost face), so that the vessel maintains her relative position, as in taking on a pilot, mail, or stores; or so that she can be manoeuvred through very narrow passages or out of a congested anchorage, generally using the tide to help her. Colloquially, the phrase means to be irresolute, infirm of purpose, denoting the backward and forward movement of the vessel previously described. "Her persistent questioning caused him to back and fill repeatedly on the nature of his liability for the accident." The term is also used to describe the movements of a vehicle in alternatively going forward and then reversing and using the steering to best advantage to turn around on a very narrow track or roadway.

(See also *Aback; To be taken aback.)*

To put one's back into it To do something with all one's energy and strength; to give the task all of one's effort. A phrase in wide use at sea, especially in encouraging a pulling boat's crew to work hard. From the fact that pulling on an oar requires, among other things, a strong back.

Back water To row backward in order to check the way of the boat, or to go astern. Colloquially, to back down in an argument, to withdraw a statement or charge; as in "She challenged him to substantiate his claim that he had been dismissed because of his religious beliefs, and he was forced to back water and retreat in confusion."

Backwash Originally, the water thrown back by the motor, oars, or paddle wheels of a small boat or other vessel. Now also a figure of speech meaning a condition that lasts after the event that caused it, as in an argument, debate, political matters, and the like: "He breezed into the bank manager's office, only to find himself enmeshed in the backwash of a heated exchange between the manager and the branch accountant."

Backwater

"Mr Temple, on reaching the backwater of a river which had been quite shallow in the morning, found it ten feet deep."

—*The Reader,* vol. 2, no. 47, November 21, 1863

A body of water unaffected by tidal or other forces, usually stagnant, always quiet and peaceful; hence the figurative application to a small town or village that is off the beaten track, a place not affected by what is happening in the world outside, usually because of its isolation. Used as in "The country town to which he was posted has always been considered a backwater."

Bad hat

A rascal or good-for-nothing (also, a "bad egg," a "bad lot"); someone who is a dishonest, disreputable person, usually considered a failure in life. Originally a sailor with an unsavoury reputation; an interesting transfer of meaning from the days when sailors wore hats, almost always of their own manufacture from tarred canvas or woven straw. An ill-fitting hat was known as a "bad hat," and the expression came to be applied to people, possibly because the sailor who could make only a poor piece of headgear was not much of a sailor at all. Used as in "I knew her husband was a bad hat long before he was sent to prison."

Bale
To bale out

A bale (often spelled "bail") is a bucket or other vessel used for baling or scooping water out of a yacht or ship's boat, when the pumps are not working. Commonly used as an order to make a parachute jump from an aeroplane; it also means to abandon a dangerous position or course of action, as a member of a diving group might decide to withdraw from a proposed expedition to a wreck on a dangerous reef. The ground-sense is from the idea of emptying or evacuation, as in the original usage. From the French *baille,* bucket, and deriving from the Latin *aquae baiula,* water-bearer. "The government refused to bale out the foundering travel agency with public funds."

Balk

"The thorny ground is sure to balk / All hopes of harvest there."

—William Cowper (1731–1800), English writer, *Olney Hymns: The Sower* (1779)

An old term for naval timber imported from the Baltic countries as large, squared beams. From the Anglo-Saxon *balca,* ridge, and the Old Norse *balkr,* hedge, boundary. *To balk* is to put an obstacle or stumbling block in someone's path, to check another's freedom, in the same way that a timber (a beam, a frame, or some such) can be a hindrance or act as a boundary to one's sphere of movement. Found, for example, as the "balk line" in the game of billiards. "I had intended to transfer that responsibility to the branch accountant, but the manager balked me."

Ballast Originally any heavy material carried by a vessel to ensure proper stability and avoid capsizing; the usual forms of ballast were sand, gravel, stone, ironpigs, and so on. A vessel that has discharged her cargo usually needs to take on ballast to stabilize and trim her while sailing empty; she is then said to be "in ballast." In the past, many vessels foundered when their ballast shifted to one side or the other as a result of heavy weather and improper ballast stowage. Ballast is used in ballooning for controlling the rate of ascent and is packed around railway ties, or sleepers, to give stability, provide drainage, and distribute the load.

"There must be middle counsellors to keep things steady, for without that ballast the ship will roll too much."
—Francis Bacon (1561–1626), English jurist, *Essays* (1597)

Colloquially, anything that gives mental, moral, social, or political stability or steadiness can be termed "ballast"; as in a cave-exploring party taking with it an experienced doctor, or a teachers' curriculum review committee inviting representatives of parents and employers to join in the deliberations. Perhaps from the Low German *bal,* bad, and *last,* load; but the earliest form of the word appears in the Old Swedish and Old Danish *bar,* mere (simple, unmixed), and *last,* load.

Bamboozle A slang word that many people believe to be American in origin, but in fact it seems to have begun life as a cant word in England, probably in the purlieus of London in the late seventeenth century (it is attested in print as early as 1703), and is among what Jonathan Swift called, in the *Tatler* (no. 230; November 1710), "certain words invented by some pretty fellows, such as Banter, Bamboozle." *(Pretty fellows* is itself a term from that period, meaning flash folk, thieves, robbers, and the like.) *Bamboozle* meant then, as it does now, to cheat, to swindle, to deceive: "The artful young man bamboozled his friends into believing that he had no intention of ever getting married."

"Let no one be bamboozled by this kind of talk."
—Edward A. Freeman, *Times of London,* February 10, 1877

What is certain is that the word *bamboozle* was used by British seamen to describe the Spanish practice of hoisting false colours (flags) to deceive the enemy. Any note of indignation from the British of that period should be ignored, as they were just as assiduous as every other maritime nation in following this hallowed custom of the sea.

Bandana See *Bandanna.*

Bandanna Also "bandana." A cotton neckerchief or scarf, usually brightly coloured (white designs on a bright red or blue background being the most popular), worn by seamen in the nineteenth century as a head covering, head band, or neck cloth; sometimes also as a waist band. A Hindi word, introduced into English by British seamen and the military. From the Hindustani *bandhnu,* a mode of dyeing in which the cloth is tied in such a way as to prevent parts of it from receiving the dye.

Bang-on Sailors' slang meaning "right on target" with reference to their big guns. Now a colloquialism meaning correct, right on the mark: "He was very pleased with himself: his assessment of the gold market trend had been bang-on." (See also *Bang-up time.)*

Bang-up time Seamen's slang for celebration of a special occasion; probably from the fact that a successful hit with the ship's guns was cause for much loud cheering among the crew. Now a metaphor to mean first-rate. "We had a bang-up time at the party as soon as the official guests left." (See also *Bang-on. Rate; To be first-rate.)*

Banyan day Any day when crew members are given a treat, such as extra food, grog, or an unexpected day's shore leave. Specifically, a banyan day was originally a meatless day, a custom introduced in the Elizabethan era as a means of economizing on the cost of meat. Instead, fish or cheese were issued to replace the meat lost thereby. The expression is still in use in the Royal Australian Navy, and in fact was part of the language when the great sheep and cattle stations were being established in the early days of Australian pioneering history: a banyan day occurred in the out-camps or mustering camps whenever the meat supplies were exhausted, and was so called by the stockmen who were involved.

From the Portuguese and Arabic *banyan,* and ultimately the Sanskrit *vany,* merchant; these were men of the trading caste who abstained from eating any flesh. The banyan tree took its name from the "banians" who venerated it and built temples and pagodas as close to it as possible.

It is typical of nautical usage that the term *banyan,* which originally denoted a time of hunger and deprivation, has undergone a complete inversion of meaning, so that now it stands for a feast, a party, or any kind of a good time, preferably with everything being provided free.

Barbecue This is the well-known method of cooking food outdoors, popular particularly in Australia, America, and New Zealand; in all these countries the word can refer to the informal social event that usually accompanies this kind of outdoor cooking (also called a "cookout" in America). Essentially, a barbecue is a metal frame or grill for cooking meat above an open fire of coals, wood, or the like.

"Oldfield, with more than harpy throat endued,
Cries, Send me, gods, a whole hog barbecued."
—Alexander Pope (1688–1744), cited in the *Universal Dictionary of the English Language* (1897)

The word is from the Spanish *barboka.* The connection with maritime usage is that, in the early days of piracy in the Pacific and the Caribbean, these privateers became known as "buccaneers" from the French *boucan,* grill, or the cooking of dried meat over an open fire. Buccaneers (later known as "pirates") became closely involved with the illegal trading in such meat throughout the Caribbean. Thus, the innocent and enjoyable pastime of having a barbecue in one's own backyard owes its origin to the bloody history of piracy on the Spanish Main.

Barge Colloquially, to move aggressively, with undue energy, to bump or collide, as in to barge one's way through a crowd; also "to barge into," to collide with. Ultimately from the Greek *baris,* boat; also related to the Latin *barga* and *barca,* a ship of burden. The word is also found in *barque* (or *bark),* an evolved type of ship-rig. A barge today is a quite different kind of vessel from a bark, though both have the Latin *barca* as their common ancestor. There are also other vessels to be found today called "barge," of specialised use.

The metaphor *to barge ahead* derives from the ability of the earliest barges to carry a substantial cargo, making them more squat and cumbersome than most other vessels, and therefore less easily and delicately managed: "She barged ahead with her plans for a reconstruction of the firm's finances before she realised that her views were not welcome."

Barge pole
Would not touch with a barge pole

A barge pole is a long, heavy pole, tipped with iron at one end and used aboard barges for fending off from other vessels and obstructions.

The colloquialism is an extension of the original usage: it means to not go near someone or something, to have nothing to do with; as in "She was offered the special class for the remainder of the year, but she said that she wouldn't touch it with a barge pole." The expression is one of intensification: the barge pole itself is an indicator that the speaker doesn't want even first-remove contact, let alone personal contact.

Barrel
Over a barrel

Sometimes expressed as "over the barrel." To be in a predicament, a jam, from which there is no apparent way out. The term originates from the days when a seaman under punishment was spread-eagled over a gun barrel for a flogging (also known as "to marry the gunner's daughter"). To have someone over a barrel is to be in a position to get whatever one wants from that person: "I wouldn't help her if I had any choice in the matter, but at the moment she's got me over a barrel."

Barricades The well-known defensive barrier hastily erected, as across a street, to stop an enemy; witness the historical cry, "To the barricades!" Not, of course, of nautical origin, but included here because of the source. Barricade is from the Spanish *barricada* or *barrica,* a barrel or cask filled with earth for the purpose of defence. Casks were the all-important item on board sailing vessels, without which no voyage of any length or duration could be undertaken, and it is highly likely that the seaman's development of the cask led to its adoption and use ashore.
(See also *Shakes. Stave.)*

"Fast we found, fast shut,
The dismal gates, and
barricadoed strong. . . ."
—John Milton (1608–1674),
English poet, *Paradise Lost* (1667)

Battleship The only colloquial use is a derogatory one, referring generally to the size or appearance of some particular person, usually a female.

The phrase is a shortening of the term *line-of-battle ship,* from the days when fighting sail went into battle in a fleet formation that ranged from the largest ships in the forefront (the first-rates), with the smaller vessels (the sixth-rates) bringing up the rear.
(See also *Rate; To be first-rate.)*

Baulk See *Balk.*

Bay
Over the bay From the days of square-rigged ships, a description of officers who had taken a few extra tots of spirits to keep themselves going for the remainder of the watch.
(See also *Sun; The sun over the yardarm.)*

Beach From the Anglo-Saxon *bece,* brook, with a transfer of meaning from the pebble bottom of the brook to the pebble or shingle shore of most of England's beaches. Sea-worn shingling was often used for building paths and roads; the operation was called "beaching." In the mariner's language, "to beach" is to haul a boat up onto the land or shingle, just beyond the reach of the waves. A larger vessel may be deliberately run ashore to prevent her from foundering in deeper waters, or to carry out repairs on her underwater hull.

To be beached, as a metaphor, is to be left high and dry, stranded and penniless. *To beach* is to cause this to happen (to someone): "When my business partner disappeared with our company's funds I was left beached, completely high and dry."
(See also *Beachcomber. High; High and dry.)*

To be on the beach

"Hailt to the welcome shout!
—the friendly speech!
When hand grasps hand uniting
on the beach. . . ."
—George Gordon Byron (1788–1824), English poet, *The Corsair* (1814)

To be retired from naval service, or to be out of a job, as often happened to commissioned officers in the British navy in peacetime. To retire voluntarily is to *swallow the anchor.* From the fact that a vessel, when driven ashore, is said to be "beached" or to be "left high and dry," and that while in this condition she is of no use to anyone. Colloquially, to be broke, without a job.
(See also *Anchor; To swallow the anchor.)*

Beachcomber

Originally a word to describe waves that habitually crash onto the shore, such as the long-crested waves to be found in many parts of the Pacific, particularly around the islands of Hawaii; the action of the wave was likened to that of a comb as it thundered onto the sand and withdrew again into the sea (a comber is any long curling wave; *beachcomber* described those waves that reached the shore). The word became a metaphor for seamen who preferred to hang around ports and harbours, living on the charity of others rather than work; such a person often wandered up and down the beaches looking for flotsam and jetsam that might prove saleable.

"Here was a change in my life as complete as it had been sudden. In the twinkling of an eye I was transformed from a sailor into a 'beach-comber' and a hide-curer . . ."
—Richard Henry Dana (1815–1882), *Two Years Before the Mast* (1840)

The term now more generally describes any loafer around the waterfront, particularly in the "lotus" islands of the Pacific; many followers of the surfing craze were also called beachcombers because they seemed to do no useful work. The word in this form is said to have originated in New Zealand in about 1844.

Beach is from the Anglo-Saxon *bece,* brook. The word for what we call the beach today was the Anglo-Saxon *strand,* found in cognate forms in the other Teutonic languages, for example, the Dutch *strand,* and Icelandic *strand. Bece* then became *-beach* in many English place names, such as Wisbech and Holbeach, and gradually the meaning was transferred from pebbly brook to the pebbly shore (one needs to remember that many of the beaches of England are composed of pebbles or shingle).

"The waves combed over the vessel."
—William Clark Russell (1844–1911), cited in *Shorter Oxford English Dictionary* (1962)

Comb is from the Anglo-Saxon *camb,* German *kamm,* Old Norse *kambr,* a common Teutonic word that derives ultimately from the Sanskrit *quambas,* tooth. The application of *comber* to describe the typical Pacific wave drew attention to the notion of the breaking wave's lip seeming to be like a comb in action as the wave reared a foaming crest, was flung forward, and then crashed down into itself.
(See also *Beach.)*

Beaker

Any cylindrical drinking vessel with a flat bottom, commonly made of plastic or glass and usually provided with a wide mouth, and (in laboratories) fitted with a pouring spout. The word comes from the Spanish *barrico,* a wooden cask filled with fresh water and kept permanently stored in a ship's boat as an emergency ration should the vessel be wrecked.

The seaman pronounced the word as "breaker," although it was always given the Spanish spelling *barrico,* having been used by seamen in this form since the sixteenth century. It possibly stems from the earlier Spanish *bareca,* a small wooden keg. The Anglicised form *beaker* is still in common use, the first *r* having disappeared because of the fancied resemblance of the pouring spout to a bird's beak.

Beam

To be on one's beam ends

A vessel is on her beam ends when she has been laid completely on her side by very heavy weather, such that her deck beams are vertical or nearly so. The beams are the transverse timbers stretching across the vessel from side to side at right angles to the keel. To be on her beam ends is a particularly dangerous position for any vessel. The colloquialism is used to describe the situation in which a person finds himself when driven to his last shift, his final resources; when she is broke, down and out, and with little hope of succour. "I'm sorry, I can't lend you any money at all—I'm on my beam ends myself."
(See also *Hard; Hard up. Poles; Under bare poles.)*

"For many a busy hand toiled there,
Strong pales to shape and beams to square."
—Sir Walter Scott (1771–1832), Scottish man of letters, *Lay of the Last Minstrel* (1805)

Bear

"If I bring him not unto thee, then I shall bear the blame to my father for ever."
—Genesis 44:32

From the Anglo-Saxon *beran* and the Sanskrit *bhar,* to hold or support, also to remain firm. All the intransitive senses (for example, "to bear with") are originally nautical: "Bear with me for a moment and I will explain my scheme in detail."

To bear a hand

To come and help, to lend a hand. Nautically, *to bear* means to lie off in a certain direction from any particular point; thus, to bear a hand means to apply physical effort, *hand* being the traditional term for a seaman. "Could you bear a hand? We have to unload this truck before nightfall."

To bear away

Nautically, to fall further off from the wind, or from some designated object, such as another vessel. Colloquially, to keep away from.

To bear down upon

To approach from the weather side, from upwind, from the position of advantage (for sailing ships, the weather gage). Colloquially, the phrase suggests intimidation, as from a position of superior advantage; to bear down upon somebody is to bring all one's guns to bear upon that person, so to speak.

To bear in with When a vessel sails so as to join or accompany another vessel, she is said "to bear in with" it; to come closer to, to sail in company. Also used when approaching land or a certain landmark: to bear in with the land, to sail closer to it so as to pick up identifying marks. The colloquialism is much the same: to bear in with someone, a crowd, etc., is to join with. "We asked her to bear in with us so as to improve our chances in the competition."

To bear off To stand further off from, as in a vessel's bow being shoved off from a wharf. As an expression, to move away from something or some person, for any reason.

To bear up

"A religious hope does not only bear up the mind under her sufferings, but makes her rejoice in them."

—Joseph Addison (1672–1719), English poet and essayist, cited in the *Universal Dictionary of the English Language* (1897)

Colloquially, to keep one's spirits up, to not lose one's courage in the face of adversity. From the order to the helmsman to "bear up," to bring the vessel even closer to the wind. Such a course always means a much wetter and generally more difficult thrash to windward; hence the metaphor of gritting one's teeth for the duration: "She's bearing up well after the shock of her husband's criminal conviction."

(See also *Brace; To brace oneself, To brace up.)*

To bring to bear Colloquially, to bring about, to cause to happen, to bring into effective operation: "He brought his considerable talents for objectivity to bear in the debate about the club's future." From the nautical usage connected with distance and position.

Bear (direction) To tend in course or direction, to move or go with respect to some other object; to be located or situated, as in "This remark bears closely on the subject," or "The ship bears due west." From the seaman's use of *bearings,* to establish position and direction. The word comes to us via Latin and the Teutonic languages and ultimately from the ancient Sanskrit *bhar,* movement. Common phrases such as "to bear to the left" are originally nautical in origin (for example, "to bear to port").

Beard
To singe his beard Words uttered by Sir Francis Drake in April 1587, after he had destroyed several Spanish ships and a vast quantity of stores being assembled in Cadiz, an important seaport on the south coast of Spain, for the projected invasion of England. Philip II planned to attack the English after having embarked the army of the Prince of Parma, who at the time was campaigning in the Low Countries. Drake is reported to have said that the operation at Cadiz had "singed the King of Spain's beard."

Drake, with the support of Elizabeth I, went on to become one of England's greatest sea captains; certainly his qualities of leadership and personal courage made him a legend in his own day. The heroic quality of his exploits—particularly against the Spanish, whom he loathed—laid the foundation for the British naval tradition. He was the first captain to command his own ship on a complete circumnavigation, and he became the most successful privateer of all time, having brought back enormous quantities of Spanish booty to the English treasury.

Drake died of yellow fever on January 28, 1596, after an unsuccessful raid on Spanish settlements on Puerto Rico, and was buried at sea off Porto Bello, Panama.

To singe anyone's beard is to deal a telling and impertinent blow, usually metaphorically: "We have certainly singed the beard of the opposition—they have little hope of winning the Davis Cup now."
(See also *Armada. Drake's Drum.)*

Bearing
To have no bearing on

To have no connection with; to be irrelevant to the matter at hand. A colloquial usage taken from the nautical *bearing,* which has to do with the angular distance between an object and true north, or between an object and the vessel from which the bearing is being determined. Used as in "Your explanation has no bearing on what we are discussing at the moment."

Bearings
To find one's bearings; to lose one's bearings; to take one's bearings

The term *bearing* refers to the horizontal angle between the direction of true north and the direction in which an object is moving. It is the means by which the relative position of an object is determined, and is an essential element of all forms of navigation. To lose one's bearings, then, is to be off course, to be lost, bewildered. The application of the colloquialism, in all its variations, is quite obvious: "He has confused me so much that I have quite lost my bearings."
(See also entries under *Bear.)*

Beat
To beat about

"I am always beating about in my thoughts for something that may turn to the benefit of my dear countrymen."

—Joseph Addison (1672–1719), English poet and essayist, cited in the *Universal Dictionary of the English Language,* (1897)

Nautically, to tack first one way and then the other against a foul or contrary wind. Such an operation of sailing to windward is called "beating." The allusion is to the type of person who cannot make up his mind, who heads first in one direction of thought and then the other; not to be confused with the hunting term "to beat about the bush," which now has the same figurative meaning as the nautical expression.
(See also *Wind; In the wind's eye.)*

Bell
To warm the bell An old seafaring dodge, which enabled the crew to stop work or to finish their watch duties before the proper time; to do something unjustifiably early. From the fact that in the days of sail, time was measured by a half-hour sandglass. Each time the sand ran through the glass, it was turned, usually by the midshipman of the watch, and the ship's bell was struck: once for the first half hour of the watch, twice for the next, and so on up to eight bells, which then marked the end of that four-hour period of watch-keeping duty.

It was supposed—probably correctly—that if the glass could be kept warm it would expand a little and allow the sand to run through the neck more quickly, and thereby end one's period of duty a little sooner. Logically, this dodge ought to be called "warming the glass," but nautical usage is nothing if not whimsical in its adherence to logic. One twentieth-century commentator on the jargon of the sea states quite solemnly, "Old sailors believed that warming the bell with their hands would cause it to strike early" (Lind 1982)—but even the most desperate seaman could not bring this about.

Bell-bottomed trousers Many readers will be familiar with the old music-hall song that began,

> "Bell-bottomed trousers, coats of navy blue,
> She loves a sailor and a sailor loves her too."

After the establishment of a standard uniform for sailors in 1857, it became possible for the men to buy their own lengths of blue serge (of the navy-pattern colour) so that they could have their own best shore-going clothes (their number one suits or "rigs") made up by the "jewing firm," the group of sailors who were authorised to do tailoring on board ship.

By using the whole width of the bolt of serge, and thereby avoiding waste, the Royal Navy seaman was able to introduce the full, bell-bottomed trouser that has long since been a mark of his naval uniform. The distinctive crease that the seaman gave to his bell-bottomed rig was achieved by a method of folding each leg inside to outside in concertina fashion, dampening them with water, and pressing them between stiff cardboards, large books, or other heavy objects.

Bells See *Bell; To warm the bell.*

Bend
To go round the bend Another seaman's phrase of old; now a well-known slang expression in the Commonwealth countries meaning to be a little bit mad or crazy, but not in any serious sense: "You must be round the bend to want to marry the boss's daughter; her mother will nag you to your grave!"

The expression is a twentieth-century one and probably derives from the fact that the curve or bend in the waste pipe of a toilet (the "head" on board ship) represents the end of the matter, so to speak; for anything to be round the bend is for it to be beyond recall, as a person's wits may be said to be when driven beyond endurance.

Bender The famous drinking spree that a person will embark upon to celebrate some noteworthy occasion; it usually involves an expedition that encompasses every public house within reach, with the sole object of getting as drunk as possible. Workers employed in hazardous jobs (such as putting out dangerous oil-well fires) might go on a bender to relieve the considerable stresses of the job: "He went on a bender for the whole weekend when he learned that his wife had run off with the milkman, taking the children with her."

The expression, which is nautical in origin, may reflect a seaman's pun: to get drunk is to be "tight," and a "bend" is a shipboard knot that is tight.

(See also *Booze. Tight.*)

Berth Probably from the seaman's use of *bear,* in the sense of direction. In its oldest sense, *berth* means convenient sea room, and all later meanings of the word have evolved from this original nautical usage. This is a good example of how our everyday language has willingly accepted nautical metaphor.

(See also entries under *Bear.)*

A good berth; a snug berth; an easy berth A "good berth" is where a ship can be safely anchored or moored; a berth is also the seaman's allotted space for sleeping, either in a bunk or a hammock. Also, by extension, the word means a job or position on board a ship. The metaphorical application is obvious: "He has fallen into a good berth by marrying the boss's daughter."

To give a wide berth The place where a vessel is moored or anchored is called its "berth." *To give a wide berth* is to not come near a person, to keep at a safe distance from him or her; literally, it means to give a ship plenty of room in which to swing at anchor while lying at her moorings. This is the oldest meaning of the expression; all others derive from this usage: "When you are in New York, it is wise to give Central Park a wide berth at night."

To seek a berth A berth is the space allotted to a seaman; his living quarters. To have a berth is thus to be part of the crew; to belong. To seek a berth means to look for a position or a job—on a ship, on a football team, and so on. When a seaman sought a berth, he literally was looking for a job, to be signed on as a member of the vessel's crew.

Bilge
Bilge-water; load of old bilge

The bilge is the lowest part of the vessel's interior space, immediately above the keel. This name is also given to the sides of the vessel where they curve upwards. Naturally, it is the space where rain and seawater inevitably collect and become foul.

"To ply the pump,
and no means slack,
May clear her bilge,
and keep from wrack. . . ."
—*Olia Sacra* (1648), cited in the *Universal Dictionary of the English Language* (1897)

In the older sailing vessels of the seventeenth and eighteenth centuries, it was not unknown for men to be asphyxiated by the foul gases emitted from the bilges. In slang usage, *bilge* means worthless stuff, rubbish: "The story that he told us about his innocence in the affair was a load of old bilge."

It is an alteration of the word *bulge,* found in the French *bouge,* the bilge of a ship or cask. The bilge of a cask is its belly or bulge; casks were always stowed in the hold "bung up and bilge free," i.e., laid lengthwise on timbers that kept the staves of the cask out of contact with the decking of the hold, and with the bung uppermost so as to reduce leakage.

Billboard

One is sorely tempted to suggest that the billboard of theatrical fame (the boarding that advertises coming attractions and the like) is a direct descendant of the nautical billboard, which is the covering on each side of the ship's bow to protect her planking from being gouged by the anchor bills when the anchor is being catted home after weighing. In the absence of evidence more compelling than the one word's being identical to the other, however, the matter must be left in abeyance.

Binge

To binge means to rinse out, or "bull," a cask to prepare it for new contents. Casks were an essential part of a ship's equipment for they were the only means of carrying food and water over lengthy voyages; hence, great care was taken of them.

Binge is also a colloquialism for a spree, a period of excessive indulgence in drink especially, or food. Probably derived from the sailor's love of spirits, which he might occasionally have been able to steal when bingeing a cask. From the Lincolnshire dialect word *binge,* to soak. "The football players had a thorough binge at their end-of-season party."

(See also *Knock; To knock down.)*

Bitter
To the bitter end

Relentlessly, unceasingly, as in "He saw it through to the bitter end," to the last stroke of adverse fortune. The phrase is from the sailor's name for the inboard end of rope or cable that is secured or belayed to the bitts to prevent it being lost overboard: this is literally the bitter end. The bitts were very strong timbers especially constructed for securing anchor cable inboard of the vessel; they were also used for securing some of the rigging. When a vessel is riding to her anchor, the part of her anchor cable that lies abaft the bitts is the bitter end; to pay a rope or chain out to the bitter end means that all of it has been paid out and no more remains to be let go.

From the Old Norse *biti,* cross-beam. The expression is not in any way connected to *bitter* in the sense of evil, sour, or unpleasant.

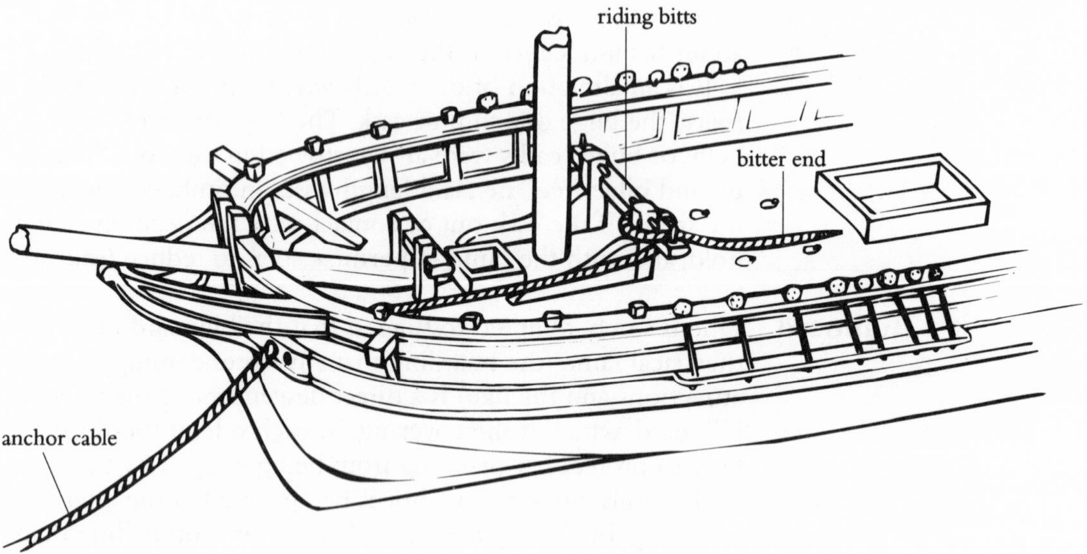

Black books
To be in one's black books

To be in disgrace, out of favour. A black book today is one supposedly recording the names of those who are in disgrace or who have merited punishment of some kind. From the *Black Book of the Admiralty,* the English codification of the ancient Laws of Oleron, a charter for seamen that was introduced into England by Eleanor of Aquitaine in 1154 when her husband, Henry of Anjou, succeeded to the English throne as Henry II. Sir William Blackstone in 1769 wrote of the origin of the laws that they were "compiled by our King Richard the First at the Isle of Oleron on the coast of France." Among other things, the Laws of Oleron attempted to protect the sick sailor; the code also contained an authoritative description of the ancient customs and usages of the sea.

The *Black Book* itself took its apparently sinister name from the fact that the colour of the earliest edition's binding was black. Black books for the recording of offenders' names are mentioned in the literature of the sixteenth century. In colloquial use today as in "Ever since he forgot about the party, he has been in her black books."

Black list
To be on the black list

A list of those in disgrace, or those who have incurred censure or punishment. Originally a list of sailors undergoing punishment; probably deriving from the term *black books,* which, because of their close association with the laws, customs, and usages of the sea, came to be associated with the awarding of punishment. Used as in "The waterside workers voted to blacklist the foreign vessel because of the poor state of its safety gear." (See also *Black books; To be in one's black books.)*

Blackstrap

An old sailing-ship term for molasses, and also for any strong dark liquor, especially dark red wines. Blackstrap in North America is a mixture of molasses and rum or whisky, with vinegar sometimes added.

"The seething blackstrap was pronounced ready for use."
—Allan Pinkerton, *Molly Maguires* (1882)

Blackstrap was also the contemptuous name given by seamen in the British navy to a type of cheap Mediterranean wine that was served out to them with their rations as they passed through the Straits of Gibraltar into the Mediterranean. No doubt it was so named because it was the thick, dark lees or dregs left over from the fermentation process and thus bought cheaply as shipboard supplies; the element "strap" may be the sailor's way of describing its appearance as it was poured or its effect when it was drunk.

Blame
To sheet home the blame

A sheet is a rope (or chain, in the case of the large, square-rigged grain ships of the late nineteenth century) used for trimming a sail to the wind. A square sail has two sheets, one at each lower corner; a fore-and-aft sail has only one sheet. *To sheet home* is to haul on the sheets until the sail is setting as required, when it is drawing fully and there is no more slack to haul in. The essence of a sheet is that it is attached to the sail; thus, in the metaphor *to sheet home the blame,* the meaning lies in the fact that blame or responsibility for a certain event is to be laid on (attached to) some person. "It was impossible to sheet home the blame for the scratch down the side of my new car; it could have been done while we were parked at the supermarket."

Blazer

The jacket or coat well known by school children, members of teams, and others as an element of a uniform. Originally it was an item of dress devised by Captain Washington of HMS *Blazer* in 1845, who dressed his crew in special blue-and-white striped jerseys or guernseys. Accordingly, the crew became known as the "Blazers," from which is derived the term used for the garment today.

Blighty Originally the soldier's name for England. Once widely used in Britain, Australia, and New Zealand, but, because of vastly changed geopolitical considerations in the postwar era, the term would be remembered now only by the older generation. The word was adopted by the men of the British army who served in India during the period known as the "British Raj," which began with Queen Elizabeth the First's granting of a charter to the "Governor and Company of Merchants of London trading with the East Indies" and which finally came to an end when India gained its independence in 1947 *(raj* is the Hindi word for sovereignty).

Blighty is from the Urdu *bilati,* foreign, which in turn is from the Arabic *wilayate,* distant government. *To get a blighty* was to sustain a wound serious enough to be shipped home to England.

Blockade *Blockade,* from the archaic German *blocquada,* is a declaration by a belligerent power in maritime warfare, forbidding seaborne trade with the enemy. Originally, the blockade was of a close-range nature, with the blockading power patrolling off an enemy port so as to prevent all movement in and out. With later developments of the torpedo, the mine, and the long-range gun, close blockade soon gave way to distant blockade.

"The approaches were closed, and the town effectively blockaded."
—James Anthony Froude (1818–1894), English writer and historian, *History of England* (1870)

International maritime law recognises blockade as a belligerent right, but the law also stipulates that for a blockade to be binding, it must be effective; that is, the blockading nation must be physically capable of enforcing the blockade. A ship that breaks the blockade by escaping the blockading force is said to "run the blockade." The writers Joseph Conrad (1857–1924) and Erskine Childers (1870–1922) were blockade runners at some time in their careers, both dealing in gun-running. Childers was caught and subsequently shot for his trouble.

The word has come to mean any obstruction of passage or progress; for example, the upper house of a bicameral political system may choose to set up a blockade against a bill sent to it from the lower house.

Blood
Blood is thicker than water Not in itself a nautical expression, but said to have been uttered as the result of a naval bombardment, when the British were attacking the Peiho River forts on the China coast during the Second China War (1856–1859). A number of British seamen who survived the attack on the forts were towed offshore in their boats by Commodore Josiah Tattnall, USN, flag officer of the small steamer *Toeywan* on the American Asiatic station. Tattnall used this phrase when

explaining his actions the next day to the British commander-in-chief, Sir James Hope. Commodore Tattnall (1795–1871) joined the Confederate side during the American Civil War (1861–1865) and later became commander of its naval forces.

"Blood, as all men know, than water's thicker, But water's wider, thank the Lord, than blood."
—Aldous Huxley (1894–1963), English novelist and essayist, *Ninth Philosopher's Song* (1920)

The metaphor implies that one should express greater loyalty to one's relatives than to other people. In the incident referred to here, Tattnall was simply acknowledging the fact that he felt a greater kinship with the British than with the Chinese; the shared Anglo-Saxon heritage of the Americans and the British counted for more than expressions of duty toward strangers. The saying apparently did not originate with Tattnall, but his action certainly made it popular.

Blood money

Originally money paid to an agent, such as the keeper of an inn or boardinghouse, for the procurement of men to fill vacancies in a ship's crew. The expression has gained a number of wider meanings in colloquial speech: a fee paid to a hired murderer; compensation paid to the relative of a slain man; and small remuneration earned by great effort, as in the old days of sweated labour in factories. The expression is also said to derive from the bounty paid by the British Admiralty for the capture of smugglers and their boats in the nineteenth century. The payment was 20 pounds for each smuggler captured and convicted.
(See also *Press; Press gang, to press. Shanghai.)*

"It is not laufull to put them into the God's chest, for it is bloudmoney."
—Matthew 25:6, Miles Coverdale Bible (1535)

Blow

Found in many nautical expressions, *blow* is from the Anglo-Saxon *blawan,* to blow, and ultimately cognate with the Latin *flare,* to expand. A "blow" in the nautical sense is a strong, sustained wind, perhaps of half-gale strength.

Blow me down!

Like *Shiver me timbers!,* an expression with obvious nautical elements but of very doubtful nautical authenticity. The sailor's own figures of speech were generally more colourful than is suggested by this example; however, it still may have originated within the seaman's milieu. It means to be so surprised, so taken aback, as to be easily felled by a puff (or blow) of wind. "He was so stunned at winning the lottery that all he could mutter was, 'Blow me down!'"
(See also *Timbers; Shiver me timbers!)*

"Blow the Man Down"

"Blow the Man Down" was perhaps the best known of all ship's shanties (or chanteys), which were sung on board to lighten the labour of working the ship. There were two broad classes of song: *capstan shanties* for the continuous effort required in heaving up the anchor with the capstan;

and *halyard shanties,* where the effort required was more rhythmic, as in hauling up a yard or a sail to its proper place on the mast. The idea of the shanty was to coordinate the physical efforts of the crew as they bent to the allotted task. (See also *Shanty.)*

I'll be blowed! An expression from the early nineteenth century, used by a seaman to mean that he had spent all his money; he was broke. It was used as a mild imprecation or expletive, and probably derives from two sources: the action of the wind in sweeping things away, as one's funds sometimes seem to be swept off by sudden events; and the blowing of the whale as it expels its air—to be done with it. Colloquially, the expression now means to lose one's chances of success, usually through one's own fault, as in "I had an opportunity to win my tennis match, but I blew it by playing to the grandstand."

To blow from another quarter A squall or storm may suddenly change its direction of assault and thereby present a new danger for the unwary seaman; similarly, a person in the middle of an argument may suddenly be assailed from another quarter by someone who has just joined the fray. "The attack on the firm's financial investment performance began to blow from another quarter when the general manager released his annual report."

To blow off From the days when the navy was propelled by steam; *to blow off* was to release excess steam from the boilers via a relief valve usually fitted on the funnel. Colloquially, the expression means to show off, to exaggerate, to make a lot of noise. "She was always blowing off about her daughter's musical ability."

To blow over Something "blows over" when it is finished or done with. As a storm will eventually die down—blow itself out—so a disturbance in one's personal affairs will, in time, die a natural death. The allusion is to the fact that storms are travelling centres of atmospheric disturbance; hence, if a person remains more or less stationary, the storm will, quite literally, blow over. Used as in "Pay no attention to him—his wrath will soon blow over."

To blow the lid off Originally, to be drunk and disorderly; an old Dutch nautical expression. The exact origin is obscure; it may derive from the fact that the Dutch usually drank from pots or mugs with a small hinged lid at the top. Nowadays, *to blow the lid off* something is to expose a scandal or to reveal a sorry state of affairs. "The television report blew the lid off the union's illegal political contributions."

Blower A common colloquialism for the telephone, and widely used as such in Australia and the United Kingdom. The term is derived from the voice pipes in use in the navy of the mid-nineteenth century and later. The person speaking (say, an officer on the bridge wishing to pass an order to the engine room) would remove the cover of the voice pipe and blow down it. A whistling sound at the other end would attract the attention of a nearby person.

When the telephone came into widespread use (after Bell's patent of 1876), the similarity between speaking into a long metal tube and speaking into a telephone apparatus was sufficiently great to enable the term *blower* to be applied to the new invention with ease. Used as in "When his wife went off to her mother's place for the weekend, he was quickly on the blower organising a night out with the boys."

Blowhard Sailor's slang for a wind-bag, a talkative show-off who sets out to impress his audience with tales that reflect only credit on himself. In British and Australian slang, a "skite" (from the Scottish *blatherskate* and the Old Norse *blathra,* to talk stupidly). The allusion was to the windy words of self-praise, as if the speaker were all wind, hot air, without substance, in the way that the wind often blows endlessly at sea; also, the insubstantiality of the wind itself. An expression still common in Australia: "He was widely avoided at social gatherings because of his reputation as a blowhard."

Blubber To weep, to shed tears; an allusion to the way in which oil ran in small globules from whale blubber or fat. The language of the whalers is an important source of metaphor in our own daily speech, although it did not contribute as freely as did the merchant service and, particularly, the British navy during its supremacy of the global seas between the sixteenth and twentieth centuries.

Blue ensign See *Red, white, and blue.*

Blue Ribbon Also "Blue Riband." The ad hoc trophy awarded to the passenger vessel that made the fastest crossing of the Atlantic; the contest was unofficial but nevertheless various national lines competed earnestly for it because of the status gained by winning. The first vessel to hold the Blue Ribbon was a Cunard liner, the *Acadia,* built in 1840; the last was the *United States* in 1952, with a speed of nearly 36 knots.

So prestigious was this award that the blue ribbon became the emblem of supremacy in all sorts of contests. It is, for example, given as a kind of laurel to winning exhibits in agricultural shows, horse shows, and other contests. The main event in a competition is often called the "blue ribbon event."

The colour blue was almost certainly chosen because of its long association with royalty and nobility. The expression *blue blood* denotes high or noble birth; the notion originated in Spain from the fact that the veins of the pure-blooded Spanish aristocrat appeared to be more blue than those of other Spaniards of mixed ancestry, especially those with a Moorish connection.

Bluff

"Bluff Harry broke into the spence. . . ."

—Alfred, Lord Tennyson (1809–1892), English poet, *The Talking Oak,* cited in the *Universal Dictionary of the English Language* (1897)

Bluff, probably from the obsolete Dutch *blaf,* flat, was originally used to describe the appearance of a ship with a broad and clumsy bow, which pushes through the water rather than cuts through it (familiarly known as "apple-cheeked bows"). Now used to mean somewhat abrupt and unconventional in manner; hearty, frank, and bold. "The old fisherman's bluff manner was a refreshing contrast to the politician's studied charm and smooth tact."

Board

From the Anglo-Saxon *bord,* meaning board, plank, table, side of ship. Related forms are also found in the Dutch *boord,* German *bort,* Old Norse *borth,* and Gothic *baurd.*

Board is the old name for the side of a ship and is the source of the following terms:

Board and board: Alongside another ship, side-by-side and touching.

Boarders (or boarding party): A body of men detailed to board a ship.

Close aboard: Close to the ship's side.

Inboard: Between the sides of a ship.

Larboard: An old name for the opposite side to starboard, originally spelled "ladeboard" because this was the loading and unloading side for seamen and cargo (now called the "port side," from the Latin *porta,* gate, opening).

On board: Anywhere within or on the ship.

Outboard: Outside the ship.

Starboard: The side on which the steering oar or "steer-board" was located before the invention of the rudder (the right-hand side of the vessel when facing forward).

To board: To enter a ship by force or authority.

"Our captain thought his ship in so great danger that he confessed himself to a capuchin [priest] who was on board."

—Joseph Addison (1672–1719), English poet and essayist, cited in the *Universal Dictionary of the English Language* (1897)

To go aboard: To enter a ship.
To go by the board: To fall over the ship's side.
To make a long board: To make a long tack.
To make a stern board: To sail backwards.
To run aboard of: To run foul of another vessel.

All above board Above the deck and therefore open and visible; hence the term's use to denote open and fair dealing. Someone who is above board is honest and straightforward: "Take it from me, that used-car dealer is quite above board."

To go by the board When a mast is shot away at close to deck level, or when it is carried away by parted rigging or very heavy weather, it is said to have "gone by the board," over the ship's side. Similarly, when something is gone for good, when it is quite finished and done with, it is said to have gone by the board. "All my plans for an early retirement went by the board when the stock market crashed."

Boat
To be all in the same boat To a seaman, a boat is a specific kind of vessel, not to be confused with a ship. A boat is a small open craft without decking and usually propelled by oars or a small engine. A ship is a seagoing vessel, whereas a boat is for estuary and coastal waters. Curiously enough, in the British and Australian navies, submarines, patrol boats, and destroyers, as well as fishing vessels of whatever size, are boats (note also the German "U-boat," for *Unterseeboot).*

To be all in the same boat, then, means to be forced into more or less close confines, to be forced to share the same dangers and discomforts, and to have to work together to a common purpose, as in a boatload of survivors from a shipwreck. "It's no good complaining about it; we're all in the same boat as far as low wages are concerned."

To miss the boat Literally, to be too late to the pier or dock, so that one misses embarkation. Figuratively, to miss an opportunity, to be too late to participate in something: "I meant to send her a birthday card but I missed the boat—her birthday was two weeks ago."
(See also *Boat; To be all in the same boat.)*

Boats
To burn one's boats To take an irrevocable step; to cut oneself off from all chance of retreat. When invaders or attackers burned their boats (either by accident or design), they were thereby impelled to conquer or die; there could be no going back. Analagous to the crossing of the Rubicon by Caesar in 49 B.C. "She burnt her boats by resigning from her job and going overseas."

Bolster

To bolster up

A bolster, as used in the older sailing ships, was a rounded piece of wood (usually hardwood, but occasionally softwood was used) used in various places to prevent chafe or nip, i.e., to stop rigging from chafing against the sharp edges of some structure, such as the cross-trees and trestle-trees in the masts. Sometimes these bolsters were covered with layers of canvas so that rigging, spars, and such would have a softer surface against which to rub. In modern vessels, wooden bolsters are often fitted around the hawseholes to prevent the anchor cable from rubbing against the hawsehole cheeks.

"... and put a pillow of goats' hair for his bolster, and covered it with a cloth."
—1 Samuel 19:13

The sense of support and cushioning is clearly expressed in the colloquialism *to bolster someone up,* to prop up or uphold someone who needs that support. The usage is generally in the moral sense of support rather than the literal or physical. "Her family gathered around to bolster up her crushed spirits when she learned that she had failed her entrance examination." The word is from the Anglo-Saxon *bolster,* support.

Bolt

A bolt of cloth

"Saying, he now had boulted all the floure."
—Edmund Spenser (?1552–1599), English poet, *The Faerie Queene* (1596)

Originally the standard measurement of a length of canvas that was supplied by the makers for sail-making. It was 39 yards in length, and usually between 22 and 30 inches (56 to 76 centimetres) in width. It gets its name from the fact that, in its original rolled shape, it resembled an arrow (slightly thickened, with a heavy head for stunning). Widely used today in the cloth trade; from the Old French *buleter,* Italian *buratto,* fine cloth, at one time used for such things as sifting meal.

Bombshell

Also "bomb," "bombard," and "bombketch." *Bomb* is from the Latin *bombus,* humming; bombs were so named from the humming sound associated with their passage through the air. A bombketch (sometimes called a "bomb vessel") was a ship in the old sailing navy with a mortar fitted to the foredeck; they were used for shelling places ashore. The mortar was in a fixed position, and the vessel was warped about on her anchor cables until the mortar was brought to bear on the desired target. The projectile fired was called a "bombshell." As the science of gunnery and gunpowder developed, so the bombshell became a fused device, set to explode on impact or following a set period of time.

Colloquially, a bombshell is an unexpected event, a sudden or devastating action or effect: "Her resignation from the mathematics staff came as a complete bombshell to her friends"; "He dropped a bombshell at the meeting by advocating a total ban on lobster fishing by amateurs."

Bone To scrounge or pilfer, to come into possession by subterfuge. The term *to bone* derives from a particular Royal Navy petty officer of the Napoleonic Wars period; his name was Bone and he was notorious for his ability to acquire ship's stores from other vessels in order to replenish his own supplies. When Bone's commission in the flagship ended and he departed the vessel, Admiral Cornwallis is said to have remarked, "I trust, Mr. Bone, that you will leave me my bower anchors."

To have a bone in her teeth A "bone" is the foam formed at the bow or cutwater as the vessel moves through the water. When the foam is quite marked, the ship is said to have "a bone in her teeth." More loosely, it is applied to a person or conveyance of some kind that is moving along very freely and briskly, with an air of determination and purpose.
(See also *Snore; To snore along.)*

Boobs Seaman's slang term for a woman's breasts; from *booby,* a large, robust seabird that was remarkable for its inability to take fright at the approach of a human. The seaman regarded a woman's breasts in much the same light as he regarded everything else in the world about him: Was it functional? Did it work? Clearly, insofar as his own needs were concerned, the female mammaries were a useless article; to this end they were "stupid," and so shared similar traits with the booby bird. The expression has firmly established itself in everyday speech.
(See also *Booby.)*

Booby The well-known tropical seabird. It prefers to rest out of water at night, often perching on the yards of ships. The name is from the Spanish *bob,* fool; the bird was considered stupid because it allowed itself to be so easily caught by seamen, it having no apparent sense of danger. The word is used aboard in *booby hatch,* a small hatchway with a sliding cover; and ashore in expressions such as "booby prize" and "booby trap." A booby (sometimes "boob") is a stupid person, a fool.

"Then let the boobies stay at home."
—William Cowper (1731–1800), *The Yearly Distress,* cited in the *Universal Dictionary of the English Language* (1897).

Books
To be on the books

To be on the books is to be officially a member of the crew. The word *book* at one time had a wider meaning, to include a single sheet or even just a list; thus, to be on the books was to be listed as part of the ship's muster or complement. The names in the ship's books were the basis upon which daily provisions were issued, pay given, and prize money calculated. Colloquially, to be on the books is to be known, admitted, recognised: "She was told that she wouldn't be getting any share of the annual bonus because officially she wasn't on the firm's books."
(See also entries under *Muster.)*

Boom

From the Dutch *boom,* meaning tree, beam; related to the Anglo-Saxon and Modern English *beam,* tree, spar. On board a vessel, a boom is a long spar or pole run out for the purpose of extending the bottom of a particular sail, such as the jib-boom, spinnaker-boom, or, in older sailing ships, the studding sail boom (pronounced "stun's'l"). In everyday speech, a boom is a spar or beam used as a derrick, or like a crane; a fixed or movable arm for holding things aloft or for guiding things from one place to another.
(See also *Booming; To boom along.)*

To boom something up

Colloquially, to sing the praises of, to advertise, to promote a cause or product; as in "He was always ready to boom up his daughter's musical talent." Connected with the Middle English *bommen,* to hum, but it is likely that the phrase derives from an earlier nautical metaphor, as in "The ship came booming."
(See also *Booming; To boom along.)*

Booming
To boom along

To boom along or *to be booming along* is to sail, move, crack on at a great pace, "to have a bone in her teeth." A sailing ship under full sail and with studding sails set (additional fair-weather sails set out on special booms) was said to be "booming along." Colloquially, the phrase means to be moving along in some enterprise at a fast pace, without hindrance. "Her dried-herb business is booming along nicely now."
(See also *Bone; To have a bone in her teeth. Bowling; To be bowling along.)*

Bootlegger

Bootlegging was the practice of trafficking illegally in alcoholic liquor so as to avoid paying duty on it. This became a major racket in the United States during the years of Prohibition (1920–1934), with the criminal element seeing to it that the universal desire for alcohol would always be met—at a price. The original bootlegger was the seaman who smuggled ashore items such as liquor (especially brandy), tobacco, and perfume, by the simple expedient of stuffing them into his long and capacious seaboots.

Bootneck A marine, known in earlier days as a "leatherneck," and at one time as a "turkey." The nickname *leatherneck* derives from the leather tongue that they once wore as a stock at the collar of their tunics; *bootneck* followed by analogy. (See also *Nicknames.)*

Booty A very old word, connected to the Old Norse *byti,* plunder, profit, spoils of war. From the days when the plunder on a ship captured at sea was immediately distributed among the captors. Booty used to be defined as everything that could be picked up by hand above the main deck. The word is closely linked with the plunder seized by pirates. Today, the term *booty* applies loosely to anything that comes one's way as a result of enterprise of some kind, usually—but not always—illegal. "The children ran home happily clutching their booty from the Christmas party." (See also *Filibuster.)*

"When the booty had been secured, the prisoners were suffered to depart on foot."
—Thomas Babington Macaulay (1800–1859), English writer and historian, *History of England* (1848)

Booze A well-established expression in the English-speaking world for any alcoholic drink. There is a strong presumption that this word was brought into our everyday language by seamen. It is from the Dutch *buizen,* to drink to excess, and was probably introduced into English in the sixteenth century as a result of the commercial intercourse that was typical of two seafaring nations such as England and Holland. A Middle English word, *bouse,* to drink deeply, is recorded for the thirteenth century; the two words may ultimately be related.

One authority suggests that there is some evidence to support the story that the phrase derives from one Colonel E. Booze who, at the beginning of the nineteenth century, marketed a popular brand of whisky in bottles shaped like log cabins, but the word was in use long before the supposed Colonel Booze presented his wares to the world. (See also *Jib; To bouse his jib.)*

"And in his hand [Gluttony] did bear a bouzing can,
Of which he supt so often, that on his seat
His dronken corse he scarse upholden can. . . ."
—Edmund Spenser (?1552–1599), English poet, *The Faerie Queene* (1590–1609)

". . . a boozing clown who had scarcely literature enough to entitle him to the benefit of clergy."
—Thomas Babington Macaulay (1800–1859), English writer and historian, *History of England* (1848)

Boss Not ever used nautically in English, but some hundreds of years ago Dutch seamen referred to their captain as "boss" *(baase,* from the Dutch *baas,* uncle). The English spelling and current sense are from the American colonies. (See *Dutch; I'll be a Dutch Uncle.)*

Bosun See *Coxswain.*

Bottler For something to be described as a "real bottler"—often in terms of grudging admiration—is indicative of its remarkable qualities peculiar to itself, as perhaps in a description of an argument or a party that went with a bang, or an unknown horse that beat the field, and so on. The emphasis is upon the unexpected.

The phrase is widely used in Australia. It stems from the old naval term for a reprimand or criticism delivered by someone in authority; originally, a "bottle" was a purgative given in all cases of sickness on board ship, the results usually being dramatic, often painful, and always to be remarked upon. Another possible origin of the expression is the fact that seamen who were caught sleeping on watch were usually lashed to the mast with arms overhead; buckets of cold water were then dowsed over the culprit's head and down his sleeves, thus filling his clothing and thoroughly soaking him and, presumably, waking him up. In this sense he was said to be "bottled."

Bottom Usually the sea bed; also, figuratively, a ship, specifically its cargo-carrying facilities (i.e., its hold), as in "goods imported in British bottoms." *Bottom* is from the Old English *botom,* probably related to the German *Boden,* Dutch *boden,* keel.

Never venture all in one bottom Don't put all your eggs in one basket. *Bottom* in this usage refers to the hull, the ship itself, with intended reference to its hold, which is at the bottom of the ship's structure.

To have no bottom *To have no bottom* is to be unfathomable, as a body of water that appears to be bottomless cannot be plumbed with a deep-sea lead line. Similarly, an argument that has no bottom is one that is baseless or groundless.

To hit rock bottom The nautical allusion is obvious: as a vessel is in danger when she bottoms on the sea bed, especially on rocks, so a person is in danger of foundering, metaphorically, when she is at the lowest level of her fortunes, at her lowest ebb; sometimes rendered by "to touch rock bottom." "When his business collapsed and his wife left him for another man, he was convinced that he had hit rock bottom in his fortunes."

To knock the bottom out of The "bottom" is the part of a ship that is under water when the ship is laden; the part of the hull in direct contact with the sea. The word is found in such commercial phrases as "goods imported in British bottoms." Literally, "to knock the bottom out" of something is to render it useless, as to stave in a cask or the hull of a ship's boat. Figuratively, it is to confound, to bring to naught, to show that some theory or argument is invalid and won't hold water: "The opposition leader knocked the bottom out of the government's argument concerning the legal age for drinking." (See also *Stave; To stave in.)*

Bound
To be bound for

In the sense of movement, determination, and obligation, the word is from the Old Norse *buinn* and *bua,* to get ready. It is worth noting that many of the strong English verbs denoting action, basic tools, and the like come from the North European languages, reflecting the enormous impact that maritime trade and warfare (for example, the Vikings and the Hanseatic League) had on early life in Britain.

The sailor speaks of being "outward bound," when his vessel is leaving port; "homeward bound," when heading back; "Fremantle-bound," when specifying a destination; and "weather-bound," "wind-bound," and "tide-bound" when these elements are hindering his vessel's progress (these last three are from the Old English *binden,* to tie, make fast with a bond). To be bound to do some (particular) thing is one of the figures drawn from the nautical usage. The word *bound* in the original sense of "ready" (as above in "homeward-bound") is still found today in some northern dialects in Great Britain: "I have packed my bags and am bound for Bangkok on the next plane."

Bow

The bow of a ship; another basic nautical word taken into English from the Teutonic and Scandinavian tongues: for example, Dutch *boeg,* Danish *bov,* Swedish *bog,* all meaning shoulder, and ship's bow. The word is closely related to *bough,* from the Anglo-Saxon *bog* and then *boh,* shoulder (but the sense of tree is peculiar only to English). As every landlubber knows, the bows of a vessel are the forward part from where the planks or plates begin to curve inward to where they meet at the stem. Found in such colloquialisms as "to put a shot across his bows" and "to be up in the bows" (to be angry, enraged).

Bowing and scraping

In the Royal Navy, an officer's cocked hat was nicknamed a "scraper"; hence the origin of the colloquial expression "bowing and scraping." *To bow and scrape* originally meant removing one's headgear in salute to a superior officer and then bowing to express even greater respect; it now means to be servile toward someone, to show humility: "It really is most embarrassing: she's always bowing and scraping to the new manager, and in fact he was appointed to the position only on trial."
(See also *Hat; To take one's hat off to someone.)*

"... bowing and scraping and rubbing his hands together."
—Anthony Trollope (1815–1882), English novelist, cited in the *Universal Dictionary of the English Language* (1897)

Bowling
To be bowling along

Bowling is probably a corruption of *bowline* (pronounced "boe-lin"), which in the early days of sail was a bridle of ropes leading from the vertical edge of the square sail to a point on or near the bow. This was hauled taut to keep the leading edge of the sail steady when the vessel was sailing close-hauled to the wind. Such a vessel would be said to be "sailing (or standing) on a (taut) bowline," and would in that case be going along at a good clip; hence the figurative usage, to move smartly and efficiently.

It is possible that there is also a connection with "Tom Bowling," a very famous sea song of the late eighteenth century, by Charles Dibdin, English dramatist and songwriter (1745–1814). The name was originally used by Smollett in his *Adventures of Roderick Random* (1748) to refer to a type of naval officer much to be admired. "I was bowling along down the main street when I suddenly happened to see an old school friend."

(See also *Boom; To boom along.)*

Bows
To be up in the bows

Sailor's slang meaning to be angry or enraged; from the fact that a person in this state tends to thrust forward in a determined manner, as a ship is said to do when she is shouldering the sea aside with her bows: "He was a bit up in the bows when I told him that his girlfriend had been out with another fellow."

To cross one's bows

In naval custom, it is considered a grave breach of etiquette for a junior ship to cross the bows of a senior vessel; such an action would be considered a deliberate affront. The colloquial usage follows the same path: *to cross someone's bows* is to cause annoyance to another and to incur that person's displeasure: "I am afraid that I crossed his bows when I suggested that his sales team was far short of the firm's target figure for the year."

To put a shot across his bows

Colloquially, a verbal warning to someone who is treading on dangerous ground in a conversation; it may also involve a physical warning of some kind to deter someone from carrying out a particular action.

Literally, in the days of fighting sail, the phrase meant what it says: one vessel wishing to stop or examine another (in time of war, for example, or for suspected smuggling operations) would fire a shot just ahead of the suspected vessel, so that the shot passed close enough to its bows to give it pause for thought. The implication was that the next shot would be delivered into that vessel's hull. This tactic is still used in twentieth-century naval warfare. Used as in

"I think the solicitor's letter we received was merely a shot across the bows."
(See also *Bow.)*

Brace
To brace oneself

To prepare oneself for a shock, disappointment, or onslaught of some kind; to get one's nerves and possibly one's body into a state of readiness, to be firmed up for the blow. The brace is the rope or chain that controls the horizontal movement of the yard from which a square sail hangs. By means of braces, the sail is firmly set to receive the wind from a particular direction. Each mast is also braced fore and aft by stays, shrouds, and—in the forward direction—a brace, a very heavy and strong cable that helps to support the mast. "His accountant told him to brace himself for some bad news."
(See also *Bear; To bear up. Brace; To brace up.)*

To brace up

"And every moral feeling of his soul / Strengthen'd and braced, by breathing in content."
—William Wordsworth (1770–1850), English poet, *Excursions* (1814)

Figuratively speaking, to prepare oneself for the worst, to face the music. From the act of swinging the yards, by means of controlling ropes or chains called "braces," so that the sail is presented at a more efficient angle of attack to the wind: "He braced himself to receive the judge's sentence."
(See also *Bear; To bear up. Brace; To brace oneself.)*

Bracer

A drink following a long or arduous spell of duty; a stimulating drink or tonic. A colloquialism derived from the shipboard gear that controls or steadies the yards from which the square sails hang.
(See also *Brace; To brace oneself.)*

Brass
As bold as brass

From the appearance of the highly polished brasswork on a ship, which of course served no real purpose in the working of the vessel; it was for show only. Colloquially, the expression means very bold, usually impertinent; used as in "She walked into the office late as usual and as bold as brass."

To part brass rags

Seamen in the Royal Navy were once required to provide their own cleaning equipment. Because maintenance of shipboard gear was of paramount importance, sailors placed a high value on splicing tools, mending kits, cleaning rags, and protective coverings. It was considered a sign of trust and friendship if two seamen shared their cleaning gear with each other, and they were then known as "raggies" (friends or chums). If their friendship broke up in anger, they were said to "part brass rags"; i.e., to give back the rags and other gear that they had been sharing. This is also probably the source of the common colloquialism *to be*

brassed off, to be fed up, unhappy, disillusioned. "I was thoroughly brassed off at the news that we were not to be given any overtime for our weekend work."
(See also *Pigtail* in appendix 4.)

Brass tacks
To get down to brass tacks

To get down to the basics or fundamentals of a problem or situation; to deal with basic principles. Lind (see bibliography) states that linoleum was often used to cover the deck, and that brass tacks were employed to nail it down to the planking. This writer has never encountered any reference to linoleum being used at sea for this purpose, but it does not seem unreasonable—at least for cabins, the tween-decks, the flats, and such. It would be unthinkable to have "lino" as a surfacing on the main deck of any vessel. The expression may also owe something to Cockney rhyming slang, in which brass tacks are facts.

The expression would have appealed to seamen because brass did not corrode at sea as did iron, and also because sailors took considerable pride in keeping the ship's brightwork (brass fittings, varnished railings, and so on) in good condition. A widely used metaphor throughout the English-speaking world, as in "Let's stop arguing about the theory of teaching and instead get down to the brass tacks of classroom practice."

Brassbounder

An apprentice midshipman in merchant sail, so named because the apprentices wore caps decorated with a thin gold lace binding around them. Probably the source of the phrase *to be brassbound,* to be governed by one's restrictive code of behaviour; to be unbending; perhaps from the fact that brassbounders were frequently underpaid and badly treated during the late nineteenth and early twentieth centuries, when merchant sail was in dire straits in competing with steam for paying cargoes.

Brassed
To be brassed off

See *Brass; To part brass rags.*

Breach
A clean breach

Breach is from the Middle English *breche,* the action of being broken, and is cognate with *break.* A breach is a clean break in a sea wall or the hull of a vessel, so that the sea is let in directly. A "clean breach" occurs when the sea breaks completely over the vessel. "When I left prison I was determined to make a clean breach with my criminal friends."

Colloquially, when something untoward or unexpected happens, so as to take one by surprise and quite unprepared, it is said to be "a clean breach"; as in a breach of etiquette, when the expected observance of good manners is inexplicably thrust aside. The word is also used by whalers to describe a whale's action of leaping from the water (when a whale dives it is called "sounding").

Breakers
To have breakers ahead; to see breakers ahead

"Old sailors were amazed at the composure which he preserved amidst roaring breakers on a perilous coast."
—Thomas Babington Macaulay (1800–1859), English writer and historian, *History of England* (1848)

Breakers in an open sea always mean danger, hidden rocks, reefs, sandbanks, etc. For obvious reasons, seamen fear submerged rocks and a lee shore more than they do storms at sea. In this sense the expression has become part of our figurative language. "Breakers ahead" in daily life are dangers at hand, warnings not to be ignored, such as severely reduced profits in a business, domestic problems, marked signs of ill health, and so on: "We could see breakers ahead when his wife began coming home later than usual after work."

Breakfast
A donkey's breakfast

Something that is very badly performed; a task bungled, so that the result is a mess. From the name for a seaman's straw-filled mattress, found in crew quarters when bunks were used in preference to hammocks. The reference is to the untidy, every-which-way nature of straw and the mess it seems perpetually to be in: "The farmer was angry because the contractor had made a donkey's breakfast of putting up the new fence."

Breeze

Originally a wind from the north or the northeast; from the French *brise* and the Spanish *brisa,* and altered by seafarers from the earlier French *bise,* northeast wind. Hawkins speaks of the "ordinary brise" in the Atlantic, in 1564, as a light wind from the northeast or northwest.

To breeze along

"We find that these hottest regions of the world, seated under the equinoctial line, or near it, are so refreshed with a daily gale of easterly wind, which the Spaniards call breeze, that doth ever more blow stronger in the heat of the day."
—Sir Walter Raleigh (?1552–1618), English poet, sea captain, and explorer, cited in the *Universal Dictionary of the English Language* (1897)

Breeze is originally the name (from the French *brise)* for a north or northeasterly wind in the Atlantic. To the sailor, a breeze ranges from a light breeze of about 4 knots to a strong breeze of about 27 knots. So essential is wind to the life of a mariner at sea, it is not surprising that we find elements such as sail, sea, wind, and so on, peopling his figures of speech. Some metaphors on breeze are: "to breeze along" (to move off quietly but smartly), "it's a breeze" (an easy task), "to bat the breeze" (idle talk), "to have the breeze up" (to be afraid), "to put the breeze up" (to make afraid), and "to breeze through" (to do something without undue effort).

Bridport
To be stabbed with a Bridport dagger

Bridport, a small seaport on the Dorset coast, was famous for its hempen goods; one of the best-known naval ropeworks of the seventeenth and eighteenth centuries was situated there. For many years the Navy Board stipulated that all anchor cables for British warships had to be made at Bridport; the rope was of such excellent quality that all cables used for anchor work were known to British seamen as "Bridports." *To be stabbed with a Bridport dagger* was to be hanged, a nautical witticism referring to the fact that the hangman's rope was of Bridport manufacture.

Brigand

"Besides two thousand archers, and brigans so called in those days of an armour which they wore named brigandines."

—Rafael Holinshed (d. 1580?), English writer and historian, cited in the *Universal Dictionary of the English Language* (1897)

Originally a name for "pirate," especially in the Mediterranean, where the vessel most favoured by pirates was the oar-driven galley. As sea brigandage became more widespread across the world's oceans, so the type of ship used became better adapted to sail power alone. The favourite vessel of brigands was known as a "brigantine," a very handy two-masted craft, square-rigged on the foremast and fore-and-aft rigged on the mainmast.

The word *brigand* derives from the Italian *brigare,* to quarrel; *brigade* is also a direct descendant. Commonly, the term *brigand* is now used to describe, perhaps somewhat archaically, a robber, cheat, ne'er-do-well, its nautical origin having long since been lost in the mists of time.

Brine

A well-known word for the ocean. Brine is water that is strongly impregnated or saturated with salt. Ship's stores or provisions of meat were steeped in brine, this being for hundreds of years the only known method of preserving flesh. The word (which is from the Old English *bryne)* came to be associated with the sea, for obvious reasons. *Briny* is both an adjective, as a description of brine, and a noun, as another word for the sea.
(See also *Junk.)*

Bring
To bring up

To cause the vessel to come to a standstill by letting go an anchor, by fouling an obstacle or the sea bottom, or by throwing the ship aback, thus quickly taking the way off the vessel (i.e., causing her to lose forward momentum). The normal practice, particularly in small ships or vessels under sail, is to bring up head to tide, steering the vessel so that she is pointing in the direction from which the tide is coming. If the sails are loosed, the vessel will then lose way (come to a standstill); but if not checked with an anchor or a mooring line, for example, she will begin to drift back with the tide.

If there is little or no tide, a vessel would bring up head to wind, a manoeuvre usually called "rounding up" in smaller sailing craft. The vessel would be steered so that she faced in the direction from which the wind was blowing; on a square-rigged ship the sails would then be set aback. If it was a fore-and-aft rigged vessel, such as a modern-day yacht, the sails would luff in the wind (i.e., spill their wind and flap loosely).

"... we close-reefed the topsails trysail, furled the courses and jib, set the fore-top-mast staysail, and brought her up nearly to her course."

—Richard Henry Dana (1815–1882), American writer and jurist, *Two Years Before the Mast* (1840)

To bring up also means to make adjustments to the sails, sheets, and helm to align the vessel more closely on the desired course.

In colloquial usage the phrase means to stop, to cause to slow down and come to a halt. "After a riotous evening in the casino, our party of revellers brought up in a quiet bar off the main street and assessed our losses for the night." (See also *Aback; To be taken aback.)*

To bring-to

To head a ship close to, or into, the wind, and kill her headway (her forward movement) by manipulating the helm and sails; to stop a vessel's motion through the water by bringing her head to wind. Also to force another vessel to stop by firing a shot across her bows.

"We brought-to in a narrow arm of the river."

—Charles Darwin (1809–1882), English naturalist and author, *Voyage Round the World* (1839)

Thence, as a metaphor, to bring a person back to consciousness or to his senses; to bring about a change in condition, usually for the better. "This police report on his conduct ought to bring him to his senses."
(See also *Bring; To bring up. Heave; To heave, to heave to.)*

Briny

See *Brine.*

Broach
To broach a subject

"Barelle ferrers they brochede, and broghte theme the wyne." ("They broached various[?] barrels and brought them the wine.")

—*Mort d'Arthur,* cited in the *Universal Dictionary of the English Language* (1897)

The term *to broach* means to introduce, mention, bring about; from the French *broche,* a spit, and derived from the Latin *brocchus,* a projecting of teeth. *To broach a subject* means to open up a subject or start a topic in conversation. From the fact that the crew's victuals were kept in casks; to get to the supplies of water, spirits, and beer the seaman had to tap the cask with a peg or gimlet. "He was very cautious about broaching the subject of buying a new car."

To broach-to

To broach is to bring a vessel suddenly broadside to the sea when running before a heavy wind. This always puts the vessel into a very dangerous situation, and many ships have been, and still are, lost at sea through careless ship-handling of this kind.

Figuratively, the phrase means to stop someone in his tracks, to suddenly arrest his flight or argument. "She made him broach-to with her tart comment concerning the amount of liquor he had been drinking recently."

Broad arrow

The mark, well known in the countries of the British Commonwealth, in the shape of a broad arrowhead placed on British government stores, and once widely used on clothing worn by the convicts of the Australian colonial days. It was sometimes incorporated into architecture of the day; an excellent example is the Town Hall of Perth, Western Australia, built by convicts in the nineteenth century; the windows or slits of the tower are in the form of broad arrows, as a wry sign of authorship.

The mark is thought originally to have been an anchor, used as early as 1609 on timber reserved for the Royal Navy; in 1698, the law provided for heavy fines for anyone found in possession of naval stores marked with the broad arrow. It is possible that its use goes back even further. Henry, Viscount Sydney, Earl of Romney and Master-General of the Ordnance (i.e., government property), in the period 1693 to 1702, used the device of the broad arrow on all military stores under his control. It is also the mark used by the Ordnance Survey to indicate the exact points from which trigonometrical measurements have been made.

Broadside
To fire a broadside; to give a broadside

A vessel "fires a broadside" when she discharges all her guns on one side simultaneously into the enemy. Figuratively, a person fires or sends off a broadside when she delivers a forceful rebuke, or marshalls the points of her argument or criticism in a vigorous and telling manner: "She gave him a broadside as soon as he stepped inside the front door."

"The crash reverberates like the broadside of a man-of-war through the lonely channels."
—Charles Darwin (1809–1892), English naturalist, *Voyage Round the World* (1839)

Broke
To be broke

When a sea officer was deprived of his commission as a result of a court-martial, he was said to be "broke" (occasionally expressed as "broken"); the full wording of the sentence was "to be broke and rendered unfit to serve His Majesty at sea." Today we would say, "dismissed the Service." Officers broken in this manner found themselves "on the beach," and in short order many of them had serious financial problems, as their training (and inclination) had fitted them for a life at sea rather than one ashore. Hence the origin of the metaphor *to be broke:* to be bankrupt, short of funds, quite out of money. "He desperately wanted to go to the pop concert but he was too broke to afford even the bus fare into town."
(See also *Rocks; To be on the rocks.)*

Bucket
To kick the bucket

An old colloquialism, susceptible of at least three explanations, only one of them being nautical. *To kick the bucket* is to die, or to involve oneself in serious trouble. Used in expressions such as "They were all waiting for the old man to kick the bucket so that they could finally get their hands on his money."

According to one explanation, the beam from which pigs were suspended for slaughtering was called a "bucket," from the Old French *buquet* and the later French *trebucket,* a balance; the pig, in dying, literally kicked the bucket. Another version is that the would-be human suicide often used a bucket to stand on, which he then kicked away from under him the better to hang himself.

The third explanation rests on the well-known seafaring superstition that to lose, or accidentally kick, a bucket overboard was a serious mishap, not to be lightly dismissed. The reason for this is that, as a receptacle, a bucket is of great importance to the seaman: it is his bailer when his vessel is taking in water, and it is of great use for catching rainwater when shipboard supplies are low. It also has many other day-to-day uses in the routine of life at sea. It would seem that this last is the most likely explanation behind the expression if only because, as a body, seamen have over the centuries had the profoundest effect upon our language, an effect greater, I believe, than any other occupational class of people in the history of our tongue.

Bucko *Bucko,* or *bucko mate,* was the nickname given to the brutal mates often employed aboard American merchant ships of the late nineteenth and early twentieth centuries. Crews on these ships were worked cruelly hard to complete the Cape Horn passage in the shortest time possible. Such ships were widely known as "hell ships," and many a seaman met his death on the East Coast–to–California voyages as a result of the relentless drive for speed, enforced by captains and mates who spared neither force nor fury in their efforts to work the crew to a record-breaking passage.

Today the term *bucko* refers more to a young man, an upstart perhaps, rather than a brute and bully; sometimes addressed to a friend or acquaintance, as in "Now, my young bucko, let's sort out this matter of the dent in my car."

Bullocks The name formerly given to the men of the Royal Marine Artillery, because of their magnificent physiques.
(See also *Grabbies. Jollies. Pongo. Turkeys.)*

Bully beef Well known to twentieth-century British and Australian soldiers; it is the name given to tinned corned beef. Originally the seaman's name for salt beef, from the French *boeuf bouilli,* boiled beef. Not related to the other meaning of the word *bully,* which is from the Dutch *boll, boel,* lover, sweetheart, and loosely used in this sense by seamen ("Well, my bully boy, where are you off to?"); it later came to take the more modern meaning of blustering, overbearing; a bully.
(See also *Sweet Fanny Adams.)*

Bulwark
A bulwark against

A bulwark is the solid part of a ship's side extending like a fence above the level of the deck. Later it came also to mean any protection against annoyance, attack, or injury from outside, as a fort, or wall of earth situated around a defended place.

"... and thou shalt build bulwarks against the city that maketh war with thee."
—Deuteronomy 20:20

The colloquialism is usually a phrase such as "My optimism is my bulwark against the ills of the world." From the Middle English *bulwerk* and the German *bollwerk,* bole work, i.e., tree work, tree "thing," mass (a "bole" is the stem or trunk of a tree).

Bumboat

A small boat used for carrying vegetables, fruit, and other provisions to ships lying in harbour or at anchor offshore; familiar to passengers who passed through Suez, Panama, etc., in the great days of steamship travel earlier this century. These small vessels were also used as scavenging boats for removing a ship's waste, slush, and so on, in the days when shipboard hygiene was a very rudimentary affair. From the Dutch *boem, bodem,* bottom, and originally rendered in English as "bomb-boat," from *bombard,* a small vessel used to carry beer to soldiers on duty.

Bumpkin

An awkward, clumsy sort of person (a "country bumpkin"); the archetypal country yokel. From the diminutive of the Dutch *boom,* tree, spar, and found in the nautical word *bumkin,* a short boom projecting outwards from the stern. The connection lies in the stolid "woodenness" of both the boom and the clumsy yokel.

Bung up and bilge free

A method of stowing casks so that the stave with the bung in it is uppermost, with the bottom tier or layer of casks resting on special beds so that the bilge, the widest part of the cask (the middle), is clear of the deck. Colloquially, the sailor's term to describe the position adopted when he is relaxing.

Bunk
To do a bunk

Colloquially, to disappear quickly, often to abscond with someone's money, spouse, property, etc.: "The accountant did a bunk when he learned that the police wanted to question him about some missing funds." A bunk is a built-in bed, as found on a ship or a train, a sleeping berth; "to do a bunk" was to ship oneself away as quickly as possible, usually to avoid facing one's creditors, spouse, or other troublesome persons. Probably from the Dutch *bank,* bench.

Bunting

A coarse, open fabric of worsted or cotton used for flags, signals, general decoration, and the like; nowadays most festive bunting, such as that used to decorate Christmas trees and car yards, is made from plastic. Widely used aboard ship, especially in the days when all communication at sea was by signal flag. Oceangoing ships today, such as naval vessels and passenger liners, still carry large stocks of bunting for "dressing ship overall," i.e., decorating it for some occasion. From the German *bunt,* particoloured. Once known as "bewpars" or "bewpers."

"The bridges, the private houses had broken out in bunting."
—*Daily News* (English newspaper), September 24, 1870

Samuel Pepys, who in 1664 was an official at the Navy Board, had his fingers burnt when—unofficially and illegally—he became a supplier of flags to the navy. He used calico, which proved to be quite unsatisfactory because it was heavier than bunting and frayed rapidly in the wind.

Buoy
To be buoyed up (in spirits)

". . . wherever there was heat enough in the air to continue its ascent, and buoy it up."
—Woodward, *Natural History,* cited in the *Universal Dictionary of the English Language* (1897)

A buoy (pronounced "boo-ee" in North America, "boy" elsewhere) is a floating mark used mainly for navigational purposes to mark a channel, bank, rocks, and the like. It is used for many other purposes as well. The essential element is that a buoy is strongly borne up by the water it displaces; hence the allusion to one's spirits rising to the surface, of being borne up despite adverse circumstances. The word is from the Latin *boia,* fetter, chain; thence to the Dutch *boei,* buoy, float. Used as a metaphor in expressions such as "He was buoyed up by the knowledge that his daughter would soon be with him."

Burden
To burden, to be burdened down

"For I mean not that other men be eased, and ye burdened."
—2 Corinthians 8:13

The term *burden* refers to the number of tons of cargo a vessel can carry. The original term was *burthen* (still in poetic use today), and it was based on the number of tuns (casks) of wine that a ship could carry in her holds, the total number being her burthen or burden. This system of cargo-carrying capacity is still found in contemporary literature. *To be burdened down,* or *to carry a burden,* is to be under an obligation or responsibility, something that is borne with difficulty: "The knowledge that I had failed him will remain a burden with me to the end of my days."

By and by

Also "bye and bye." To sail a vessel "by the wind" is to sail her as close to the wind as she will go, with all sheets hardened in and the bow pointing into the wind as much as possible. A seaman says that his vessel is sailing "by and by" when she is making very slow progress against the wind; the doubling of *by* in the phrase is an intensifier, to indicate the degree of difficulty encountered and the slowness of the ship's progress.

By and by as a colloquialism means after a short time, soon, in the near future. Like *presently,* this phrase used to mean immediately—when the Elizabethan said, "I shall be there presently," she meant that she would attend at once. The expression has since been influenced by the nautical usage so that now it has been quite altered in its application (testimony to the enormous importance of the navy in the daily life of England).

> "Nature did yeeld thereto; and by-and-by Bade Order call them all before her Majesty."
>
> —Edmund Spenser (?1552–1599), English poet, *The Faerie Queene* (1596)

Used in such expressions as "The result of the delegates' vote will be available to the convention by and by."

By and large Taking one thing with another; all things considered; generally speaking. From the fact that when a vessel is sailing into the wind (i.e., when she is close-hauled), if she sails a little off the wind—that is, frees her wind a point or so—she is said to be sailing "by and large." She is near the wind but not fully on it, so that the leading edge of each sail is still setting almost as close to the wind as it will go, but yet just sufficiently free that it maintains an efficient shape. The colloquialism derives its meaning from the idea of compromise inherent in the nautical usage: "Things at the office are going quite well, by and large."

It is interesting to note that the nautical usage itself has undergone a shift in meaning among seamen. To sail "by the

wind" is to sail on a bowline, that is, with the yards braced up sharp so that the vessel is pointing as close into the wind as possible. *To sail large* is to have the wind not quite over the stern but rather over the quarter, so that the yards are braced more or less square; an easy and pleasant point of sailing, in contrast to the hard flog that pinching up (sailing by the wind) usually means. Strictly speaking, it is quite impossible to sail both "by" and "large" at the same time; it is a contradiction in terms. Nevertheless, nautical language is nothing if not adaptable, and the expression still lives in good standing.

Bye and bye See *By and by.*

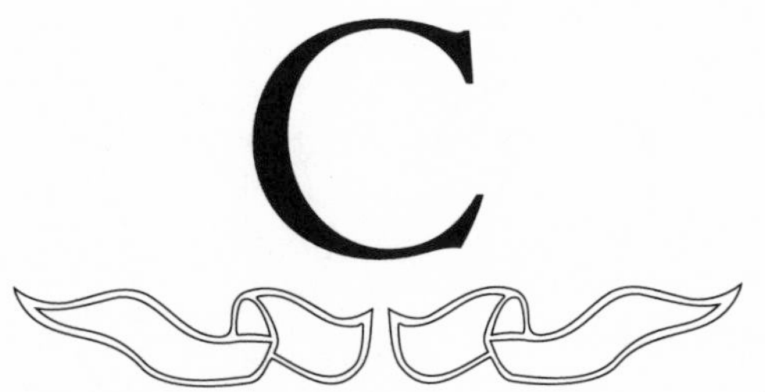

Caboose The seaman's name for the galley or cook house on a small vessel, often resembling a sentry box in shape; it was located on deck, rather than between decks as in larger vessels. Sometimes called a "cuddy," although in larger sailing ships a cuddy was generally the compartment where the officers had their meals. *Caboose* is from the German *kabuse,* a small hut or dwelling; hence the usage in the United States meaning the last wagon on a goods train, which accommodated the guard, the brakesman, and any chance passengers; what the English would call the "guard's van."

On American whaling ships in the early nineteenth century, *caboose* was also the word for the try-works, the very large iron pot set up on deck for boiling down whale blubber; a variation of this was *cambouse.*
(See also *Cuddy. Try; To try, to try out.)*

Cannibal From the Spanish word *Canibal, Caribal,* which was the Spanish rendition of *Caribe,* for the fierce and warlike Indians first encountered by Columbus in what is now known as the Caribbean Sea. The word entered Europe by way of the *conquistadores,* the Spanish explorers who discovered and then colonised much of what we today call Central America. The Carib people were noted for their practice of eating human flesh; the name probably means "strangers."

Cannibalism is one of humankind's greatest taboos. The idea of eating one of our own kind fills us with horror and revulsion. The fact is that most of us have never experienced the true extremities of thirst and starvation; we have been hungry, even famished, but never starving enough to contemplate seriously the prospect of eating human flesh to permit ourselves a chance of survival. The literature of the sea is well signposted with accounts of decent, God-fearing men and women who, in extremity, have done this very thing.

One of the most famous of these stories is that of the Nantucket whaler *Essex,* which on the morning of November 20, 1820, was repeatedly rammed and then sunk by an enraged sperm whale in the empty wastes of the South Pacific. The crew of twenty took to the sea in three open boats, but only eight men in two of these boats survived the ordeal; the third boat under the second mate disappeared. The captain, George Pollard, commanded one of the boats and Owen Chase, first mate (who told the story of this sinking), commanded the other. On February 18, Chase and his men were rescued by the English brig *Indian.* Captain Pollard and one other survivor still in his boat were picked up by the American whaler *Dauphin;* both sets of survivors arrived at Valparaiso, Chile, within three weeks of each other.

Such was the suffering of the men in Chase's boat in the ensuing 90 days that when one of their number died, they agreed immediately with the first mate's agonised decision that they should eat their comrade's flesh, as recorded in Chase's 1821 account: "I addressed them on the painful subject of keeping the body for food . . . it was without any objection agreed to."

"The cannibals that each other eat / The anthropophagi."
—William Shakespeare (1564–1616), *Othello,* act 1, scene 3

Captain Pollard's account of his experience was even more chilling. After having exhausted their meagre supplies, they too ate the bodies of the men who died; when these were consumed, it became obvious to the remaining men that lots would have to be cast to determine who would be sacrificed for the sake of the others. "The cabin boy, Owen Coffin, was chosen. He was sixteen years old and happened to be Pollard's first cousin. The captain shouted to him, 'My lad, my lad, if you don't like your lot, I'll shoot the first man that touches you. . . .' The poor emaciated boy hesitated a moment or two; then, quietly laying his head down upon the gunnel of the boat, he said, 'I like it as well as any other'" (quoted from Edward E. Leslie's *Desperate Journeys, Abandoned Souls* [1988]).

Such were the conditions faced by men whose livelihood was founded in and bounded by the sea, when the drawing of lots for cannibalism was, of necessity, one of the customs and usages of the sea. The story of the ramming of the *Essex* became the basis for the climax in Herman Melville's *Moby Dick* (1851), when the great white whale turns his fury on the whaler *Pequod* and sinks it.

Cannon
A loose cannon

A loose cannon on board a sailing ship is a very dangerous object indeed; given its great weight and mass, a cannon that has come adrift of its tackles (the ropes that control it and secure it to the ship's sides) during heavy weather presents a serious threat to the safety of the vessel and to life and limb of the crew. It could quite easily crash through the side of the ship (if it were a cannon from one of the lower decks, this would open a large breach close enough to the waterline to put the vessel in danger of foundering). To somehow bring it under control calls for extraordinary luck and seamanship on the part of the crew.

Metaphorically, a loose cannon is a person who happens to be in possession of certain knowledge, facts, information, etc., and who for any of a variety of reasons is in a position to reveal these facts to another party, thus causing commercial, social, personal, or political distress to someone or some organisation. For example, a computer programmer in a firm that is under contract to a defence department, and who has been dismissed for some reason (such as drunkenness or persistent lateness), may be in a position to cause considerable harm to the firm by revealing commercially sensitive information to a rival company, to the press, and so on. Such a person is called a "loose cannon," both because of the potential damage he or she could bring about, and because of the difficulty of legally preventing that person from becoming a threat to the firm's stability: "My ex-wife has become a loose cannon because she knows of my secret arms contracts in the Middle East and she is vindictive enough to seek revenge for what she sees as my poor treatment of her."

Canvas

"With such kind passion hastes the prince to fight, / And spreads his flying canvass to the sound."
—John Dryden (1631–1700), English poet, *Annus Mirabilis* (1667)

From the Greek *kannabis,* hemp, the plant fibre from which canvas was originally woven. Hemp is a tall-growing herb that yields drugs such as "bhang," "cannabin" (cannabis), and "hashish" (whence we derive the word *assassin).*

To be under canvas

A ship under canvas is one that has set her usual working sails; to be under sails generally. To have too few sails for present conditions is to be "under-canvassed"; to have too many is to be "over-canvassed." *To live under canvas* is to be camping out in tents.

To carry too much canvas

To spread more sail than the vessel can safely carry under the prevailing conditions. Figuratively, to attempt to carry out a task that is far too big for one's resources: "She said that she would supervise the production of the school play, but it soon became obvious that she was carrying too much canvas."

Cap

To set one's cap at/for

Originally a nautical metaphor, but today no longer recognised as such. Usually rendered as a maid "setting her cap at" the man she admired; the explanation being that she would wear her most becoming cap to attract the attention of the favoured gentleman. However, in this expression, *cap* is Provençal (the language spoken in southeastern France) for head, from the Latin *caput,* head, as in the French expression *mettre le cap sur,* to turn the ship's head toward. The colloquial expression is a folk etymology of what was once purely a sailing direction.

Cape Horn Included here because of its great significance in the history of seafaring, and its prominence in the literature of the sea, past and present.

Cape Horn is in fact an island, Horn Island, off the southernmost tip of Tierra del Fuego ("Land of Fire"). Here, south of the continent, enormous swells roll eastward with a fetch of thousands of miles, driven by the fierce winds of the Southern Ocean. Even in the summer season of November to January, it is a cold and forbidding place, with fog, rain, snow, and changeable winds. In the winter season, as experienced by many of the old-time sailors (later called the "Cape Horn Breed" in the more romantic literature), it was sheer hell to make a passage in either direction.

Two Dutch vessels—the *Eendracht* and the *Hoorn*—were the first recorded ships to reach the Pacific from the Atlantic by way of Horn Island; this was in 1615–1616. Schouten, the pilot of the expedition, named the island after his native town of Hoorn. In fact, the *Hoorn* was lost on the Patagonian coast, but the *Eendracht* carried on, naming the strait through which she passed after Isaac Le Maire, the head of the trading company that was sponsoring the expedition. The *Eendracht* continued across the Pacific to the Dutch East Indies where, for some reason or other, she was confiscated by the authorities. Some time later, during another voyage, the *Eendracht* was wrecked on the West Australian coast, about 400 miles north of Perth.

"It's North you may run to the time-ringed sun,
Or South to the blind Horn's hate;
Or East all the way into Mississippi Bay,
Or West to the Golden Gate."
—Rudyard Kipling (1865–1936), *L'Envoi*

Schouten's discovery opened the way for further voyages in this region. The English mariner Drake had much earlier sighted what is now called Cape Horn in 1578, but in his westward passage through the Straits of Le Maire he was blown east again in a terrible storm. He eventually recovered and doubled the cape into the Pacific, where he wrought great havoc among the Spaniards.

The Cape's fame dates from the 1850s, when American clipper ships, speeding to the California goldfields, braved the vicious westerly gales—among the worst in the world—rather than take the shorter but far more treacherous route through the Straits of Magellan, discovered by that great voyager in 1520 (it was Magellan who gave the Pacific its name, from the gentler weather with which it greeted him).

After the collapse of the west coast goldfields, square-riggers continued to use the Cape Horn route in the guano, nitrate, and grain trades, but the opening of the Panama Canal in 1914, and the already widespread use of steam instead of sail, brought the era of the Cape Horner to an end. The route still figures, of course, in modern-day deep-sea yachting races, and no yachtsman or yachtswoman can claim to have achieved some circumnavigational record or other without rounding the fearsome cape at least once. It is known to sailors as "Cape Stiff" because of its often fierce gales and fearsome cold.

Capsize

The earlier term was *overset;* this was replaced by *capsize* in the eighteenth century. Originally the word was *capacise,* ultimately from the German *koppseisen.* It means to upset or overturn in connection with a vessel at sea or in harbour; usually due to natural causes, such as high winds or heavy seas, but it can also occur because of human error (for example, faulty stowage of cargo causing instability).

"It is a pleasant voyage thus to float, / Like Pyrrho, on a sea of speculation; / But what if carrying sail capsize the boat?"
—George Gordon Byron (1788–1824), English poet, *Don Juan* (1820)

One of the best-known examples of capsize through human error was that of HMS *Royal George* in 1782. She was being heeled over for repairs to an underwater fitting; the sea entered through her open gunports and she turned over and sank very quickly, with the loss of some 900 men, women, and children. In 1848 Augustus Siebe, a German inventor, was able to demonstrate his new diving suit while helping to remove the wreck. He was so successful that the Royal Navy adapted his close-diving helmet dress as the pattern for all future underwater work. This suit later became famous on the pearling grounds at Broome, on the northwest coast of Western Australia.

The term *capsize* has come to be applied to any notion of overturning or upsetting other than the nautical, although the ground-sense of a physical upending is still retained: "The chair capsized under his great weight."

Caravan

Immediately from the French *caravane,* but ultimately from the Persian *karwan,* a company of ships or merchants travelling together for a common purpose; hence the term *caravanserai,* from the Persian *sarai,* inn or mansion. The nautical application of the word has long since disappeared. The modern usage derives from the seventeenth century, when certain vehicles for carrying passengers to and from London were called "caravans." The lifestyle of gypsies has no doubt also influenced the current sense of the word.

"When Joseph, and the Blessed Virgin Mother, had lost their most holy Son, they sought him in the retinues of their kindred, and the caravans of the Galilean pilgrims."
—Jeremy Taylor (1613–1667), English cleric, *Eniautos* (1653)

Caravel

A Mediterranean trading vessel of the fourteenth to seventeenth centuries, often used by the Spanish and the Portuguese for voyages of exploration. Its hull construction was much simplified for the times, having neither forecastle nor sterncastle in most instances, and no beakhead at all. The average length was about 80 feet, and for the most part a caravel carried a combination of square rig and lateen rig.

Columbus's small fleet of 1492 consisted of three caravels, and the ships of Diaz and Magellan were also of this type. The word *caravel* is from the French *caravelle,* through Spanish and Italian from the Late Latin *carabus,* coracle. *Caravel* did not give rise to the word *carvel,* although in time the two words became hopelessly confused because of the extreme similarity of their spelling and pronunciation.

(See also *Carvel-built. Clinker-built.)*

Careen From the Latin *carina,* keel. To cause a ship to heel over wholly or partly on its side, so as to clean the under portions of its hull, or to carry out repairs.

Careen is occasionally used in colloquial speech when in fact *career* is probably intended: "When she heard that the store had already opened its doors for the summer sales, she careened off down the street in her car."

Captain James Cook careened his vessel HMS *Endeavour* after she was holed on the Great Barrier Reef off the Queensland coast of northeastern Australia on the night of June 11–12, 1770. A large lump of coral had broken off and become wedged in the hull, otherwise the ship would certainly have sunk immediately. Cook stemmed the inrush of water by fothering his ship. Fothering is a method of stopping a leak by quickly stitching old yarn and rope ends across the surface of a sail or suitable piece of canvas and dragging it to cover the hole in the hull, when the pressure of water will hold the patch close to the vessel, thus allowing it to be sailed to some safe haven while the pumps are coping with the water that will inevitably enter.

"He could not prevail on them to careen a single ship."
—Thomas Babington Macaulay (1800–1859), British historian and politician, *History of England* (1848)

Cook careened his vessel for some three weeks in the mouth of the Endeavour River, which was named by him: "To the harbour which we had now left [after the repairs], I gave the name of Endeavour River." Cooktown was some time later established on the banks of this river, close by Cook's original careenage, and named to commemorate his visit.

Having got his vessel in seagoing trim again, Cook continued up the east coast, only just escaping disaster once more when the *Endeavour* was becalmed on the seaward edge of the Great Barrier Reef, the coral rampart that stretches for 1,200 miles along this coast. The late but fortuitous arrival of a breeze saved the ship and crew from being wrecked on the savage coral, and Cook decided to continue his voyage using the channels on the inner edge of the reef.

His earlier discovery, in 1770, of Botany Bay on the southeastern coast of Australia led eventually to the establishment of the colony of New South Wales in 1788, when the American War of Independence (1775–1781) made the American territories no longer available to England as penal settlements. Sydney Town, as it became known, was located in Port Jackson, some six miles north of Botany Bay, by Captain Arthur Phillip; it boasted one of the finest natural harbours in the world and the colony gradually flourished to become a major trading centre. Sydney today is still the focal point of Australian history.

Cook met an untimely death during his third voyage in 1779 when his ship, the *Resolution,* was forced to return to the Sandwich Islands (present-day Hawaii) because of problems with her foremast. The natives, having already exhausted their food supplies in entertaining Cook and his men (who were regarded as Polynesian gods, foretold by age-old legends) became sullen and troublesome. As a result of a number of misunderstandings and cases of petty theft, Cook and some of his men were attacked while ashore. In the subsequent fight, Cook was overwhelmed and stabbed to death.

"The fleet careen'd, the wind propitious filled
The swelling sails."
—William Shenstone (1714–1763), English poet, *Love and Honour,* cited in the *Universal Dictionary of the English Language* (1897)

Charles Clerke, captain of the *Discovery* (which was accompanying the *Resolution* on this voyage) took command of the two vessels and sailed off to continue exploration in the Bering Sea. However, within a month he was dead of consumption; Lieutenant Gore, Cook's subordinate in the *Resolution,* then took over and finally, in October 1780, the two vessels returned to England.

Cook has long been revered by the maritime world as a superb seaman and a brilliant navigator, and as a commanding officer with enlightened views on how to manage a crew with firmness tempered by justice.

Cargo The lading or freight of a ship; its load; from the Spanish *cargar,* to load. Also applicable to aircraft freight, but not, interestingly enough, to the freight for any other form of transport.

Carry From the Old Northern French *carier* or *charrier,* vehicle (whence "car," "chariot," "charabanc").

To be carried away *To carry away* is to break away, to part, usually through the stress of storm or battle; particularly applicable in the case of masts or yards. Used also to describe ropes and hawsers when they break as a result of sudden violence, such as a heavy wind, a clumsy mooring attempt, and so on. Objects that have broken or parted in this fashion are said to have been "carried away." Colloquially, *to be carried away* is to lose one's self-control, to be greatly influenced (usually beyond one's ability to remain in reasonable control): "She got carried away by the duty-free shopping facilities at the airport."

To carry all before one To succeed, to triumph, to carry the day, to overcome adversity. From the naval usage, meaning to capture a ship by coming alongside her in battle (known as "laying her aboard," the term *board* being an old word for the ship's side), and then taking possession of her by boarding parties: "In his last year as a runner he carried all before him and won all the championships."

To carry on To increase sail when the wind is still strong, despite the risk. As a metaphor, it means to continue, to keep up without stopping, to pursue an activity from a point already reached; also, to behave in an excited, foolish, or improper manner, to go somewhat beyond the bounds of reason: "The children always carry on noisily when the teacher leaves the classroom."

"The internal government of England could be carried on only by the advice and agency of English ministers."
—Thomas Babington Macaulay (1800–1859), British historian and politician, *History of England* (1848)

To carry the day The expression *to carry the day* means to win the contest, to carry off the honours of the day, to achieve final success: "Their greater skill and experience eventually carried the day in the bridge tournament." From the days when sailing navies engaged the enemy by day because so much depended upon visibility; only occasionally was an action begun at night. The outcome of the engagement by daylight determined which side it was that "carried the day."

Cartel Originally of nautical origin, but not now used at sea; instead, the word has a wide application in the modern world of commerce. A cartel today is an international syndicate or trust, usually formed to regulate prices, production, marketing, or other concerns in some field of business.

In the days of sailing navies, a cartel was an agreement, usually documented, between belligerent countries concerning the exchange of prisoners during the actual progress of the war. Such cartels were widely used by the American and British navies during the American War of Independence. The word came to be applied to the ship that carried out the required negotiations with the enemy; such vessels displayed a white flag, which was a universally recognised sign that gave immunity from gunfire when approaching the enemy. Occasionally it was necessary to

"As this discord among the sisterhood is likely to engage them in a long and lingering war, it is the more necessary that there should be a cartel among them."
—Richard Addison (1672–1719), English writer and essayist, *Freeholder*, cited in the *Universal Dictionary of the English Language* (1897)

exchange messages with the enemy during battle, and ship's boats, acting as cartels and flying the white flag, would be used for this purpose, again being granted safe passage. From the Italian *cartello,* which derives from the Latin *carta,* card. The ground-sense is related to the written agreement that formed the cartel proper.
(See also *Flag; To show the white flag.)*

Carvel-built A type of construction in wood in which the side planks (or sheets of marine ply) are all flush, laid edge to edge and then caulked to make them watertight. The word derives from the Dutch *karviel,* in reference to the name of the nail used in the process and not, as is commonly thought, from *caravel,* a small trading vessel common in the Mediterranean from the fourteenth to the seventeenth centuries.
(See also *Caravel. Clinker-built.)*

Case oil See *Trane oil.*

Cast
To cast a look Formed on the nautical term *cast.* As a figure of speech, the expression means to direct a glance, to cause the eyes to fall upon: "He cast a wary look at the angry dog."

To cast adrift To set loose, to get rid of, to free oneself of. In the literature of seafaring, the most famous example of being cast adrift is that of William Bligh, captain of HMS *Bounty,* who was put into an open boat with 18 other men, near Tonga in the South Pacific. Bligh's 3,600-mile voyage to Timor, off the northwest coast of Australia, stands as one of the greatest epics of small, open-boat journeys in the history of seafaring. Used colloquially in expressions such as "She tired of his attentions and cast him adrift at the first opportunity."

To cast anchor To drop the anchor in order to bring the vessel to a halt. Metaphorically, to put down roots, if even only temporarily; to stay awhile in one spot.

To cast off; cast-offs "Casting off" is the action of letting go the cable or rope that secures the vessel to a buoy, wharf, or other ship, so that the vessel may move to another berth or proceed on her way to sea. The sense of letting go, or giving up, is echoed in the colloquial usage, which refers to making use of clothing that has outlived its usefulness and is then used by someone else: "For many years he had to be satisfied with the cast-offs from his older brother."

Castaway Originally said of a ship that had been deliberately wrecked, or of a shipwrecked person, or a sailor who had been

"Why do you look on us,
and shake your head,
And call us—orphans,
wretches, castaways?"
—William Shakespeare (1564–1616),
Richard III, act 2, scene 2

marooned. More loosely, anything or anyone who has been abandoned or rejected, overlooked, or made redundant. The best-known castaway in English literature is Robinson Crusoe, from Defoe's novel of that name, published in 1719. The story is based on the experiences of one Alexander Selkirk, who was marooned for nearly five years on Juan Fernandez Island in the southeast Pacific in 1704.

Cat

No room to swing a cat

The ground-sense is of confined space; it conveys the idea that a room, house, or other area is very restricted and too small for a particular purpose. The origin of the phrase is nautical. *Cat* is the sailor's abbreviation for the cat-o'-nine-tails; as a punishment, it was administered on deck, generally in the space between the poop and the mainmast. This was itself a quite restricted area, and to swing the cat effectively required some skill on the part of the bosun's mate.
(See also *Cat; To let the cat out of the bag. Cat-o'-nine-tails.)*

To let the cat out of the bag

Cat was the short name by which the cat-o'-nine-tails was known. It was traditionally kept in a bag made of red baize; naturally, when it was taken out of this bag, it was for the ominous purpose of punishment by flogging.

The expression is probably an example of the sailor's penchant for grim humour, with an allusion to the fact that a domestic cat kept in a bag is usually a flailing ball of fury when let out. Hence, "to let the cat out of the bag" was to put an unpleasant state of affairs into motion. The metaphor carries much the same meaning in colloquial speech: to allow a secret to escape, to disclose information, usually unintentionally.

The expression may also owe something to the old practice of fraudulently selling a cat trussed up in a bag as a suckling pig; the noises made by both animals in their confinement were presumably similar. If the buyer opened the sack, he literally let the cat out of the bag, and the trick was disclosed. A blind bargain such as this is known as "buying a pig in a poke."
(See also *Cat-o'-nine-tails.)*

Catamaran

Strictly, not a nautical term in the English language, but included here because of its widespread use in the everyday speech of people who otherwise have only the barest acquaintance with matters maritime. A catamaran is a twin-hulled sailing yacht connected by an above-water deck that carries the mast, rigging, cockpit, and cabin. It is also the name given to the small rectangular raft used in dockyards to keep a vessel's hull from surging against a mole or jetty.

The word is from the Tamil (South India) *katta,* to tie, and *maram,* wood; in English it is frequently mispronounced as "catamarang." The earliest catamarans consisted of a raft-like structure of two or more logs or tree trunks lashed together, and used as a means of local transportation. A similar primitive but effective vessel is still built and used by the coastal aborigines of Northern Australia. The first catamaran recorded in European boat-building history was constructed in 1662 by Sir William Petty; she measured some 30 feet overall and was named *Simon and Jude.*

Cat-o'-nine-tails A nine-lashed whip widely used for flogging seamen on the bare back in the old days of sail. The cat-o'-nine-tails was made of nine lengths of cord, each about 18 inches long, some with three knots at the end and others with a single knot worked into the cords, usually at different distances (nine cords each with a knot at the very end would present a formidable mass after only a few lashes, and could do too much damage to the seaman's back). All the cords were seized to a thicker piece of rope that served as a handle. This handle was often painted red, and the cat was kept in a bag made from red baize.

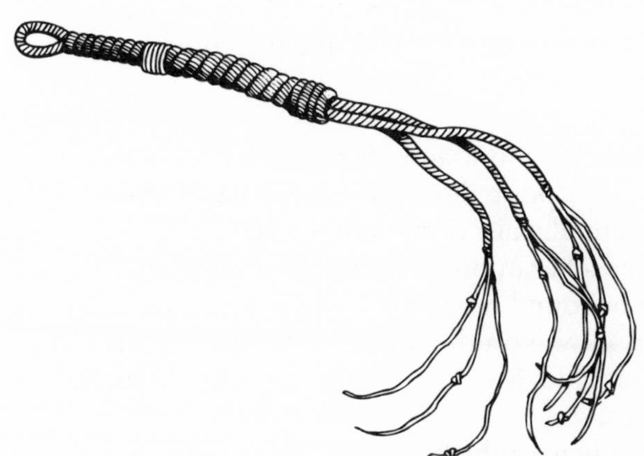

Curiously, most ships' cats were works of art, considered solely from the point of view of design and workmanship. They weren't just a few bits of rope tied together for the purpose of hitting someone with—rather, many of them were beautifully crafted examples of fine ropework on which the seaman could exercise his skill and ingenuity during his time off-watch.

Very often the lash used for punishing cases of theft on board was a sturdier and more utilitarian device, usually with more than one knot to each cord and larger and harder ones at that, reflecting the seaman's abomination of this crime in a shipboard society that threw so many men together for long periods of time. It was common, too, for a dozen lashes from this "thieves' cat" to be given at the beginning and at the end when a seaman was punished by running the gauntlet.

Regulations in the British navy limited the rigour of a captain to award up to 12 lashes, but this was so frequently abused that, as in *Hamlet,* the custom was more honoured in the breach than in the observance. On occasion, as many as 500 or 600 lashes were awarded for crimes that were insufficiently serious to attract the death penalty. If this seems a savage state of affairs, one must remember that malefactors in the army of that day could be given as many as 1,500 lashes.

"You dread reformers of an impious age,
You awful cat o' nine tails, to the stage."
—*Prologue to Yanbrugh's False Friend,* cited in the *Universal Dictionary of the English Language* (1897)

Curiously enough, virtually all seamen approved of the cat and of the naval system of discipline in general. They knew that the ship where discipline was lax was likely to be a real "hell-ship" where everybody suffered, regardless of who was innocent and who was guilty. The cat was officially abolished in 1879.

Colloquially, *cat-o'-nine-tails* could be a description of a particularly scathing or savage argument or verbal attack by one person on another. It is curious to note that Smollett, who wrote so graphically of shipboard conditions in his early novel *The Adventures of Roderick Random* (1748), refers to the lash as the "cat *and* nine tails."
(See also other entries under *Cat. Gauntlet; To run the gauntlet.)*

Cat's whiskers A slang expression from the navy, meaning just perfect. Its precise origin is obscure, but it may be related to the fact that many ships from the nineteenth century onwards carried a cat, usually for the purpose of keeping down the rats. Used colloquially as in "He thinks he's the cat's whiskers now that his wife has presented him with a baby."

Catwalk A catwalk is a narrow fore-and-aft passageway or walkway connecting a ship's poop deck with its forecastle, thus avoiding the central waist of the ship, or no-man's land, which could be a hazardous place in heavy weather. Catwalks can be found on bridges, where a narrow, safety-railed walkway on the outer edge of (or underneath) the roadway provides access to certain areas for inspection or maintenance.

In colloquial usage, which mirrors the nautical usage, almost any narrow path or walkway may be called a catwalk.
(See also *Gangway.)*

Chantey See *Shanty.*

Chink A slang term for a Chinese person; originally a nautical expression from the nineteenth century, and not derogatory, as it is now.

Chock-a-block Describes the position when two blocks (or "pulleys," in landlubber's terms) have come together so that no further movement between them is possible. Technically, this is "choking the luff" of each block, whence the term *chock-a-block* derives (from *choke-the-block,* also found as *chock and block).* To increase the distance between these blocks is to "overhaul" them.

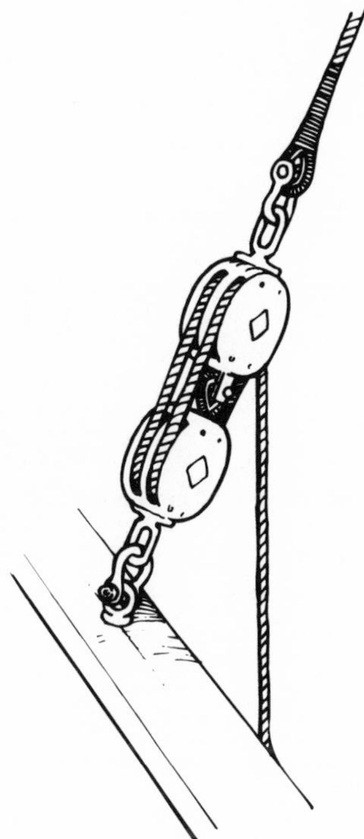

Chock-a-block is also a slang term meaning full up, to be bored or fed up, to be unable to take any more. Also, to be "chockers," a very common colloquialism in Australia. "By the time we got there, the pub was chock-a-block with raging teenagers." (See also *Overhaul.)*

Chockers See *Chock-a-block*.

Chop-chop An order to do something quickly, to hurry up; to bring something immediately. From the pidgin English *chop,* quick, and brought into everyday English by sailors who served on the China Station in the nineteenth century. "Bring me that book right now, chop-chop!" (See also *Chopsticks.)*

Chops of the Channel Well known to every sailor of old; the western entrance of the English Channel when approaching from the Atlantic. It was here that seamen returning home to England after a long voyage experienced "channel fever," a state of excitement at the prospect of a period of shore leave and freedom from ship's discipline for a while.

Chopsticks Not, of course, a nautical term, but in itself the seaman's rendering of the Chinese *k'wai-tsze,* nimble ones. *Chop* is pidgin for quick; hence, to do something "chop-chop" is to do it quickly, straightaway. The term *chop* used in this sense is recorded by Dampier in the seventeenth century. (See also *Chop-chop.)*

Chow The American seaman's word for food; also widely used in the American army, and understood and sometimes used by

other English-speaking armed forces. The word comes from the pidgin Chinese *chow,* food, a shortening of *chow-chow,* a dish of mixed pickles and preserves. It was probably picked up when Commander Perry of the U.S. Navy opened up the Western Pacific—particularly Japan—to American influence in the 1850s; merchant vessels would subsequently have spread its use. *Chow* is an early Australian slang term for a Chinese person, and also the name of a dog of Chinese breed.
(See also *Pidgin.)*

Chowder

"My head sings and simmers like a pot of chowder."
—Tobias Smollett (1721–1771), English novelist, *Sir Launcelot Greaves* (1762)

A kind of soup or stew made of clams, fish, or vegetables, with potatoes, onions, and other ingredients added, together with appropriate seasoning. Shark meat at one time formed a common ingredient, especially for British seamen, who added it to salt pork and ship's biscuit. Now widely known only in the United States and Canada, particularly the clam chowder version introduced into Newfoundland by Breton fishermen. From the French *chaudiere,* cauldron, in which the stew was made.

Chunder

To chunder is to vomit. It is widely used in Australian colloquial speech and is said to derive from the fact that a seasick passenger on an upper deck would (it was hoped) cry out "Watch under!" as he leant over the rail while succumbing to the rigours of sea travel. *Chunder* is the laconic shortening of an otherwise heartfelt cry.

Clanger
To drop a clanger

A colloquialism for a glaring error or mistake, an embarrassing remark; from the supposition that such an horrendous incident would be enough to cause the ship's bell to clang. "You certainly dropped a clanger when you mentioned Jack to her—they were divorced two years ago!"

Clap

Originally the sailor's word for venereal disease; now a widely used colloquialism for any form of VD, but especially gonorrhea; from the old French *clappoir, clapier,* brothel.

To clap on

"Clap on more sails."
—William Shakespeare (1564–1616), *The Merry Wives of Windsor,* act 2, scene 2

To add something temporarily to an already existing part, such as when adding a whip or purchase to a line when additional hauling power is required. Similarly, extra sail is "clapped on" so as to take advantage of a fair wind. Colloquially, *to clap on* is to add more, something extra, to achieve greater speed or power from the prevailing conditions; often expressed as "Clap a hand on to this!" Found also in "to clap eyes on," "to clap on speed," "to clap into gaol." From the Middle English *claeppettan,* to throb.

Clear Most of the compounds with clear are of early (sixteenth-century) nautical origin: "to steer clear," "to stand clear," "the coast is clear," "clear the decks," "to clear away," "to clear for action," "to clear customs," "to clear the land," "to clear out for Guam" (this from the heyday of shipping, when vessels leaving Australian ports on their return voyage to the northern hemisphere were required to specify a port when clearing outwards; it became the habit of captains to nominate Guam, in the Pacific, as their hypothetical destination, when in fact they would search for cargoes wherever they could), and so on.

A ship is "cleared" to sail when all the formalities in connection with the ship's papers at the customs house have been observed, before the vessel sails from that port. From the Middle English *clere,* and deriving from the Latin *clarus,* clear. (See also *Steer; To steer clear.)*

To clear for action See *Deck; To clear the deck.*

To clear out Colloquially, to disappear, to go away, to decamp, usually in haste; also to empty out.

Cleat Nautically, a small wedge-shaped block, or a horn-shaped fitting, both used for securing lines to prevent them from slipping. From this we get the stud, sprig, bar, etc., attached under a shoe or boot so as to afford better traction, as in football or golf shoes. From the Middle English *clete,* wedge.

Clench Also "clinch," a later variation. It means to secure a nail, spike, rivet, or the like by flattening over or beating down the point; thus, to fasten firmly together. Hence the nautical description of a boat's being clincher- or clinker-built, fastened together by overlapping the planks or strakes and securing them with rivets (usually copper). This method is often called "lapstrake," especially in the United States. The term arose to differentiate this construction method from carvel-built, which is a method of planking a hull by laying the planks close together, rivetting or nailing them through to the frames, and then caulking them by driving oakum into the seam and pouring hot pitch over this caulking.

"Thou hast hit the nail on the head, and I will give thee six pots for't, though I ne'er clinch shoe again."

—Francis Beaumont (1584–1616) and John Fletcher (1579–1625), *Martial Maid,* cited in the *Universal Dictionary of the English Language* (1897)

Clench, from the Middle English *clenchen,* to hold fast, is used in phrases such as "He clenched his fists" and "He clenched his teeth at the screeching sound." *Clinch* is used in the more material senses, as in clinching a rivet; colloquially, as in "to clinch an argument," to win it, to settle the point. "He clinched the dispute by producing new evidence of his innocence in the affair." (See also *Carvel-built. Clinker-built.)*

Clewed See *Clued; To be all clued up.*

Clinch See *Clench.*

Clinker-built Sometimes called "clinch" or "clincher-built"; a method of boat-building in which the adjacent edges of the planks are slightly overlapped, exactly as in constructing a weatherboard house. Often called "lapstrake," a "strake" being one of the planks on the side of a ship. This method of construction contrasts with carvel-built. From the Anglo-Saxon *clencan, beclencan,* to make to cling; found in the Dutch as *klink,* a latch or rivet.
(See also *Caravel. Carvel-built. Clench.)*

Close
To close with

"If I can close with him, I care not for his thrust."
—William Shakespeare (1564–1616), *Henry IV, Part 2,* act 2, scene 1

From the French *clos, clore,* to close, and ultimately from the Latin *claudere,* to close. *To close with* is to come near to; a vessel that "closes the land" is one that draws near to it. Similarly, *to close with the enemy* is to engage, to grapple with; a "closed" space on shipboard was originally where a last stand could be made against boarders. The ground-sense of the term implies a physical quality to the engagement rather than an abstract one. Colloquially, the phrase means to come to grips with, to encounter, to come to terms with: "The delegate at the company meeting closed with the secretary over the thorny matter of annual dividends."

Close quarters
To be at close quarters

"Close-quarters" were strong, very sturdy barriers of wood set across the decks of sailing merchant ships. They had loopholes cut into them through which muskets could be fired to repel or fight off boarding attacks from pirates. The essence of the phrase *to be at close quarters* is that one is closely confined, shoulder-to-shoulder, with one's fellows, with the enemy only a short distance away, all fighting furiously for possession of the deck. Colloquially, *to be at close quarters* carries with it the same nautical meaning of direct and close contact, often in a small, cramped place or position. "He was staying at our hotel for the conference, so I had an opportunity to observe him at close quarters."
(See also *Fights.)*

Clued
To be all clued up

A "clue," often spelled "clew," is the aftermost corner of a fore-and-aft sail. In a square sail, it is the name of the two lower corners to which the sheets are attached. "Clew lines" are lines by which the corners of these sails are hauled up to the yards from which the sails are suspended. This is one of the first steps toward furling or final trussing of the sails. In such a situation, the sail is said to be "clued up."

"Their he shuld fynd in certeyn a clew of yern."
—*Nugae Poeticae,* cited in the *Universal Dictionary of the English Language* (1897)

Colloquially, the phrase means to be very knowledgeable, to have everything at one's fingertips, to have the situation in hand. The allusion derives directly from the sailor's task of furling sails on the yards, getting them organised and under complete control. *Clew* is from the Old English *cleowen,* a ball or skein of thread or yarn (the word *clew* is still current in the northern parts of Great Britain in this sense).

Coast

The land immediately bordering the sea; the seaside. From the Latin *costa,* rib, side, in the sense that the coast or shore resembles a long strip or rib, a narrow band between the sea proper and the hinterland; what geographers call the "littoral." We recognise the Latin source in *costal cartilage,* the cartilage that connects the ribs to the sternum.

The coast is clear

Probably from the days of smuggling; if the coast was clear, the implication was that there were no coast guards or revenue and excise agents about who might otherwise interfere with the smugglers' activities. The phrase carries a closely similar figurative meaning: there is no apparent likelihood of interference, there is no enemy in sight: "The lookout for the illegal gambling den signaled that the coast was clear."

To coast along

"... coasting upon the South Sea."
—Edmund Spenser (?1552–1599), English poet, *View of the Present State of Ireland* (1596)

To coast is to sail along the line of the coast; also "coasting," or navigation along a coast by reference to landmarks. A "coaster" is a vessel that plies between the harbours of a particular coast or adjacent coasts, usually in pilotage waters and seldom out of sight of land (older readers may recall John Masefield's "Dirty British coaster with a salt-caked smoke-stack"). Such vessels generally encountered few serious obstacles to a safe passage, since they were always within sight of land and therefore could fix their position with great accuracy. In bad weather, such a vessel could readily put into a nearby haven.

Colloquially, then, *to coast along* is to carry out a task with minimal effort, without unnecessary fuss or bother: "He had a good grounding in mathematics and was able to coast through the navigation course."

Cock up

A "cock up" is any mess, any disturbance to the ordinary state of affairs; "to cock something up" is to bring it to a near state of ruin. Very commonly heard in the Commonwealth countries as part of the indigenous slang: "Despite his confidence in his abilities as a public speaker, the president made a right cock up of his welcoming speech to the visiting dignitaries."

The source of the expression is *cockbill* or *a-cockbill,* a term that referred to the state of the anchor when it had been hoisted to the cathead, hanging "up and down" ready for letting go. The "bill" is the pointed end of the fluke of the anchor, the part that digs into the sea bed. Because the anchor is hanging from the cathead, the two bills are naturally cocked up, i.e., pointing to the sky.

The metaphor takes its force from the fact that a square-rigged sailing ship would set its yards a-cockbill—trimmed at an angle to the deck—for the purpose of loading and unloading cargo. A ship would also deliberately set its yards a-cockbill as a sign of mourning for a death on board. At any other time, a vessel with its yards a-cockbill would be regarded as presenting a very sloppy appearance, as having made a mess of things.
(See also *Scandalise. Spanish [Spanish reef].)*

Cockboat A small boat, especially one used as a ship's tender, and usually towed behind while at sea. In the fifteenth century this was also called a "cogboat." The oldest form of this word is *cok* or *cokbote,* probably from the Old French *coque,* vessel, and related to the Modern French *coque,* shell of an egg, walnut, etc.
(See also *Coxswain.)*

Cockpit Originally, the "cockpit" in a man-of-war was the compartment under the lower gundeck where the wounded were attended to during battle. This space was near the after hatchway and was at one time used as the mess for certain of the officers on board.

"Can this cockpit hold
The vasty fields of France?"
—William Shakespeare (1564–1616), *Henry V,* act 1, chorus

Nowadays the cockpit is the well or sunken recess of a small sailing vessel where the steering wheel or tiller is located, the place from where control is exercised. Nowadays it is also the pilot's space in an aeroplane and the driver's seat in a racing car. The "cockpit" was also the pit used for cockfighting; the "pit" (or "pits") in the theatre also takes its name from this source.

Cockswain See *Coxswain.*

Codswallop Nonsense, worthless rubbish; now a colloquial expression, said to derive from the contents of a cod's stomach, hence its passage into nautical slang. Another possible source of the term is the fact that one Hiram Codd marketed a mineral water in a bottle with a marble stopper in 1875. At that time, the word *wallop* was (and still is, in England) a slang expression for beer; hence, *Codd's wallop* is said to have become a term of disparagement, among beer drinkers, for mineral waters and other weak liquid refreshments. The expression then gradually acquired a more general application.

Colour
To put a false colour on a matter

To give a false impression, to hide the truth of a matter. (See also *Sail; To sail under false colours.)*

Colours
To come in with flying colours

Colours is the name given to a vessel's national flag flown at sea. It is the means by which ships establish their nationalities. Such flags are of particular significance and importance to all maritime nations, and there are long-established customs and expectations regarding the flying of ensigns, national flags, and courtesy flags.

Sailing navies relied primarily on flags, not only for means of recognition, but also for the transmission of signals, orders, and the like. In battle a ship signified surrender by lowering its colours; a ship or fleet that had been victorious would sail into port with all flags flying at the mastheads. Colloquially, the phrase means to be completely triumphant, to win hands down. "She passed her final nursing exams with flying colours."
(See also *Colours; To show one's true colours. Flag; To nail one's flag to the mast.)*

To lower one's colours

See *Sail; To strike sail/to strike the colours.*

To show one's true colours

To reveal one's true character, shorn of all falsehood. The *colours* is the name given to the national flag flown by a ship at sea. During the days of fighting sail, it was a common *ruse de guerre* for one vessel to fly some other national flag when being challenged by a vessel of unknown nationality. Naval men-o'-war always revealed their true colours at the moment of going into battle, but it was not unknown for some privateers to continue to sail under false colours for purposes of deception.
(See also *Colours; To come in with flying colours.)*

Comb

See *Beachcomber.*

Come
To come at

Nautically, to be able to get to the cargo or the ballast; to delve into, to rummage. *To come* has a number of meanings in maritime usage. When the helmsman of a sailing vessel is ordered to "come no nearer," he is to hold the vessel as close to the wind as she already is, and no closer (that is, he is not to point any higher into the wind). A ship "comes to an anchor" when she lets it go (usually rendered as "she came to anchor"). "Come up the capstan" is the order to

"Then came to him his mother and his brethren, and could not come at him for the press."
—Luke 8:19

walk (or release) the anchor cable out a bit so as to ease the strain, or to veer (let out) some of the cable. An anchor is said to "come home" when its flukes are no longer holding in the ground and it is dragging.

Colloquially, *to come at* is to reach: "The gear is up there on the shelf—can you come at it?" Alternatively, it means to undertake or to agree to: "Your expense account is far too high; the boss won't come at that."
(See also *Rummage.*)

Commission
To be in commission; to commission

The word is from the Latin *committere,* to entrust, and the oldest sense of its meaning is a written instrument or warrant. A commission, first found in the early Royal Navy, is a document specifying the status of an officer in a naval vessel. In the days of fighting sail, when a newly appointed captain boarded his ship, the crew were mustered aft and the captain "read himself in," that is, he read his commission to the assembled officers and crew. This was the visible form of the new captain's authority to be there and to act in the name of the sovereign.

"So also were the apostles solemnly commissioned by him to preach."
—*Decay of Piety,* cited in the *Universal Dictionary of the English Language* (1897)

When a vessel is assigned a period of service while on a particular assignment or in a particular part of the world, she is said to be "in commission." After she has been commissioned, she continues in that state until she returns to her home port to pay off, at which time she may be decommissioned or recommissioned. The expression is widely used in figurative speech; for example, "to commission a generating plant" is to put it into productive operation. *To be in (or out) of commission* indicates a state of active service or use of something; a severe hangover could put one "out of commission" for some time.
(See also *Pay; To pay off.*)

Commodore

A well-known naval rank dating back to the early days of sail, and now widely used to refer to the president or head of a yacht club or boat club. In the navy, commodore is the intermediate rank between captain and rear admiral; it is not a promotional step, but rather a term that pertains to the responsibilities of the position. When the duties of the commodore have been discharged, the incumbent reverts to his substantive rank of captain. Earlier rendered as "commandore," possibly from the Dutch *kommandeur,* but the *dore* ending suggests a Portuguese influence.

Companion

One's friend or messmate. The term is from the Latin *com,* with, and *panis,* bread: to share bread together, which is the oldest meaning of *companion.* The structure known as a "companion" on a ship is a wooden cover over a cabin hatchway. In the early days of sail, the companion was a hatch or sash arrangement that permitted light to enter the cabins below the quarterdeck. The more common term *companionway* means the stairway or ladder leading from the deck to the accommodation below. The word is from the Dutch *kampanje,* quarterdeck.

Companionway See *Companion.*

Company
The ship's company The whole crew of a ship, including all officers, men, and boys; the usual term for such. The ground-sense of the word is sharing; literally, to share bread, to eat together, which also translates the seaman's term *messmate.* Extended usage gives us a number of individuals assembled or associated together; a group of people. Used in expressions such as "to keep company" and "to part company"; said of ships and vehicles as well as of people.
(See also *Companion.)*

Compass
Every point of the compass A well-known metaphor, used to describe something that seems to be occurring in every direction at once, as a fitful breeze will often seem to blow from every which way, or an excited tracker dog will cast in every direction for the scent of its quarry.

The compass (from the Latin *compassus,* equal step), or more strictly the "mariner's compass," as it was called by the early seafarers, was in use in the Mediterranean as early as the twelfth century. Its origin almost certainly lies in the pre-Christian era of China, when sailors of that period were navigating with a primitive instrument known later to western seafarers as the "lodestone."

The modern-day magnetic compass is divided into 360 degrees, from north through the cardinal points east, south, and west, back to north. The intercardinal points are north–east, south–east, and so on; and the card is further divided into intermediate points. However, this point system (where 1 degree was equal to 11-1/4 points) is now obsolete; compass bearings are now given as so many degrees relative to magnetic north, i.e., from 0° to 360°.
(See also *Lodestone.)*

To box the compass A nautical phrase meaning to name the 32 points of the compass in correct order, both clockwise and anticlockwise, starting from any given point. Now that most navigation at sea is by gyroscopic compass, satellite readouts, long-range radio and radar, and so on, the ability to box the compass is very nearly a lost art. A wind is said "to box the compass" when it blows from every quarter in rapid succession.

Figuratively, the expression means to go right round in one's political, social, or philosophical views and end up at one's starting point; to shift one's position frequently: "He became notorious for his ability to box the compass on the question of whether women should remain at home instead of joining the workforce."

Contraband

"The law severely contrabands
Our taking business
off men's hands."
—Samuel Butler (1612–1680), English essayist and dramatist, *Hudibras* (1678)

Goods imported or exported illegally; that which is smuggled. The English use of the word dates from the illicit maritime trade that England conducted with the Spanish possessions in South America in the seventeenth century. From the Spanish *contrabanda* and the Italian *contrabando,* against the law *(contra,* against, and *ban* from the Anglo-Saxon *bannan,* proclamation).

Convoy
To be in convoy

"That through the fear of the
Algerines,
Convoys those lazy
brigantines."
—Henry Wadsworth Longfellow (1807–1882), American poet, *The Golden Legend* (1851)

The word is from the French *convoyer,* to convey. It means to accompany, to escort, generally for mutual protection. The original use was at sea, particularly when supply ships and vessels carrying bullion, specie, treasure, etc., needed safe passage to their destination. Military vehicles now frequently travel in convoy, and persons are colloquially said "to be in convoy" when they accompany each other for some mutual purpose.

Copper-bottomed

Sailor's slang to mean very (doubly) safe and sure, secure; to be trusted; that which cannot fail. The expression derives from the practice, first officially begun in 1761, of sheathing the underwater portion of a vessel's hull with thin sheets of copper to prevent the teredo worm from eating into the planks. The sheathing also helped to limit the buildup of weeds and barnacles on the ship's bottom. Nowadays most small craft are protected by a layer of copper-based antifouling paint, put on the vessel's bottom every season or so. The word *copper* is from the Anglo-Saxon *coper,* which in turn derives from the Latin *cuprum,* from the old name for Cyprus where the metal was first mined and where it was known as "Cyprian bronze."

Corsair

"Joining a corsair's crew,
Over the dark sea I flew. . . ."
—Henry Wadsworth Longfellow (1807–1882), American poet, *The Skeleton in Armour,* cited in the *Universal Dictionary of the English Language* (1897)

A well-known maritime term from the days when piracy was rife in the Mediterranean. A corsair was a privateer, especially one on the Barbary Coast of North Africa; it was also the name given to the fast and very handy vessel used by these pirates, who were in fact usually legitimate privateers licensed by the Turkish government at Constantinople. From the Latin *currere,* to run.
(See also *Privateer.)*

Cot
A cot case

A cot (from the Hindi *khat,* bed) was a ship's bed made of canvas stretched on a wooden frame and slung like a hammock from the deck beams; it was about six feet long, two feet wide, and one foot deep, with a mattress in the bottom. It often had enclosing curtains and was used by officers before the introduction of permanent bunks and cabins. It must be remembered that, in the days of fighting sail, cabins were only temporary affairs, being divided from each other only by canvas screens or removable wooden bulkheads (the sailor's term for walls). In time of emergency, such as fire or battle, they could be quickly dismantled to provide space for movement, such as working the great guns.

Admiral Nelson's cot on HMS *Victory* was slung between two guns in the stern. Despite his many years at sea, he always experienced seasickness for the first few days on board ship; his recourse was to take to his cot until the illness wore off (because of the way in which these cots were slung from the deck beams above, they remained relatively stable even though the vessel might be rolling considerably).

Colloquially, a "cot case" is someone who is ill or exhausted or in some way quite incapacitated, and who must be confined to bed to recover. Such was the case with sailors who contracted scurvy, before the days of antiscorbutics. "She was a cot case after spending the whole day looking after her sister's twins."

Course

"The course of true love never did run smooth."
—William Shakespeare (1564–1616), *A Midsummer Night's Dream,* act 1, scene 1

The intended direction steered by a vessel. This may be a true, magnetic compass, or great circle course, according to the reference direction. The navigator "sets course" *(not* "sets a course") for the destination. From the French *cours* and the Latin *cursus,* run. Found in other nautical expressions, such as "fore-course" and "main-course" (sails on the ship). Used colloquially as in "She set herself a course that included the study of biogenics and human biology."

To be on a collision course

Collision is from the Latin *collidere,* to collide *(co,* with, and *laedere,* to hurt). The word is, of course, not nautical in origin, but the expression is. Two vessels are on a collision course if their courses, projected, converge. The metaphor carries a similar force: two people are on a collision course if their opinions, intentions, or behaviour are objectionable one to the other. "The radical notions of the trade union were on a collision course with the conservative views of the government."

To be on the right course

A course is the path or track that a vessel makes, or attempts to make, through the water. *To be on the right course* is to do

one's duty, to go straight or directly on the chosen path. The focus is on directness. *To get back on course* is similar in meaning. An expression with exactly the same meaning is *to be on the right heading.*
(See also *Tack; To be on the right [or wrong] tack.)*

To chart a safe course The meaning is clear. Where the mariner would literally plot or mark out on his chart the safest course for his vessel, so colloquially the wise person would plan ahead carefully so that her future actions would bring her safely to the desired goal; exactly as in *to steer a safe course.* Charting a safe course would result in plain sailing.
(See also *Sailing. It's all plain sailing.)*

To get back on course When a vessel is back on the original plotted track, after having been diverted for some reason (usually bad weather or some other emergency), she is said to be "back on course." The metaphorical use is obvious.
(See also *Course; To be on the right course.)*

To shape a course A course is the direction, given as a compass direction, toward which a vessel is sailing. To select or work out such a direction is *to shape a course;* also expressed as "to set a course." A course may be shaped to avoid some particular danger or obstacle. As a colloquialism, the phrase means simply to determine a path of action, a course of events to be followed to bring one to some desired objective or conclusion.

The lowest sails on each mast of a square-rigged ship are also called courses: forecourse, maincourse, and mizzen course (this last is rarely referred to as the mizzen course, but rather as the "crossjack," pronounced "crow-jak" and often written "crojack").

To steer a middle course Colloquially, to avoid extremes, to act moderately, to compromise. From the order given to the helmsman to steer through a series of hazards, leaving them approximately equidistant on each side of the vessel: "He decided to steer a middle course between the requirements of the department on the one hand, and the advice of the union on the other."

Cove Used in the Royal Navy, in the days of the Napoleonic Wars, as it is used in British and Australian speech, to mean an individual, one who stands out from his fellows in some way. The word is from the Romany or gypsy dialect *cova,* thing, *covo,* that man, *covi,* that woman, thence into sixteenth-century thieves' slang as *cofe,* hawker, itinerant

"There's a gentry cove here,
Is the top of the shire."

—Ben Jonson (1572–1637), English poet and dramatist, cited in the *Shorter Oxford English Dictionary* (1962)

seller of goods. Found in such metaphors as "a rum cove" and "a flash cove." "He was a bit of a strange cove; he preferred to live alone but he always attended the social get-togethers put on by his work-mates."

Cove meaning cell, recess, small bay, is a quite different word, from the Anglo-Saxon *cofa*.

Coxen See *Coxswain*.

Coxswain The petty officer who acted as helmsman of the ship's boat, and who was also in charge of its crew. He also had permanent responsibility for the condition of the ship's boat itself. Originally all boats carried on board were known as "cockboats" or "cocks"; hence the origin of the term.

"His captain steered the boat as cockswain."

—Drummond, *Travels through Germany, Italy, and Greece,* cited in the *Universal Dictionary of the English Language* (1897)

In modern usage this petty officer is the "coxswain" (from *cock* plus *swain),* and in the Royal Australian Navy this petty officer is often called the "swain" (from the Middle English *swein,* servant, and the Icelandic *sveinn,* boy). The word *cox* is used to describe the steersman of any boat, especially a rowing or racing shell, and the steersman of the large pulling boats used by surf life-saving crews on the Australian coast.

CQD The original radio distress call made by a ship requiring assistance; it was introduced early in 1904 (the form "SOS" became the international signal of distress in 1908). "CQ" was the call-sign for "all stations," and "D" stood for "distress"; the signal soon became popularised as "Come Quickly, Danger."
(See also *Mayday. SOS.)*

Crack
To crack on Nautically, to set all sail and proceed at top speed, usually to the limits of safety for those particular conditions; a bold move, especially in heavy weather. Colloquially, to pursue a course of action, especially in adverse conditions; to get going with all possible speed and determination: "The bush walkers decided to crack on until the light faded." Sometimes expressed as "to crack on regardless." Said to be an old mail-ship term, because mail contracts contained a penalty clause for late arrival.
(See also *Cracking; Get cracking.)*

Crackerjack A sea dish consisting of preserved meat or soup, mixed with broken ship's biscuit and other ingredients; other dishes well-known to the seafarer were "burgoo" (boiled oatmeal porridge seasoned with salt, sugar, and butter, and said to derive from the Vikings); "dandyfunk" (broken ship's biscuit and molasses); "lobscouse" (a stew consisting of salt meat, potatoes, broken ship's biscuit, onions, and available spices); and "sea pie" (a favourite, consisting of meat and vegetables layered between crusts of pastry).

The generic word for these odds and ends of food leftovers was *manavlins,* of unknown origin and variously spelled. From its earliest nautical meaning of tidbits of food, it came to mean small matters, extra fresh food belonging to whale-fishers, any small object, and the odd change remaining at the end of the day in the railway booking office (recorded in 1887). The word is used in its earliest sense by Rolf Boldrewood in his Australian classic *Robbery Under Arms* (1888).

The colloquial meaning has changed considerably. *Crackerjack* (sometimes written "crackajack") now refers to a person of marked ability, or something exceptionally fine, or to some event of note, as in "She was a crackerjack music teacher; everyone enjoyed her lessons."

Cracking
Get cracking

A colloquialism meaning "get busy," "hurry!," "start the job right away." From the days when mail-ships (or "packets," as they were usually called) had a penalty clause written into their contracts for late delivery of the mails. These vessels would crack on all possible sail to meet their contractual requirements; the expression comes from the fact that a mail-ship in a hurry would set all sail such that the canvas and rigging were taut and (nearly) cracking under the strain. "We'll have to get cracking if we want to catch that train." (See also *Crack; To crack on.)*

Craft

"Built for freight, and yet for speed, A beautiful and gallant craft. . . ."

—Henry Wadsworth Longfellow (1807–1882), American poet, *The Building of the Ship,* cited in the *Universal Dictionary of the English Language* (1897)

Not originally nautical, but with an interesting transition of sense. From the Anglo-Saxon *craeft,* small, cunning; found in the Teutonic languages, to mean skill, ingenuity, but without the degenerated sense of slyness. When applied to the idea of vessel (originally small vessels), the term was always accompanied by *small,* in such phrases as "vessels of small craft" (i.e., of small power, small activity). We still speak today of small craft, and of course the term *aircraft,* as with most of our vocabulary of the air, is modelled on the nautical usage.

Cranky

"In the case of the Austrian Empire the crank machinery of the double government would augment all the difficulties and enfeeble every effort of the State."

—*Times of London,* November 11, 1876

A vessel that is "crank" is one that lists (leans to one side or the other) easily, one that is not stable under canvas. The condition might be due to her construction, bad stowage of cargo or ballast, or a combination of any of these. Colloquially, *to be cranky* is to be ill-tempered, out of sorts, unsteady, out of order. Ultimately derived from Anglo-Saxon *cranc,* something bent (the modern term *crank handle* is from the nineteenth century).

Crew
A happy crew

Another basic term from seafaring. It is interesting to note that for centuries what we would call "the crew" was referred to by most commanders as "the people." The word is from the Latin *crescere,* to grow, through Old French *creue* and Middle English *crue,* to increase (probably related to the Modern English *accrue,* to grow, increase; and to *recruit).* Defined as a group of persons engaged upon a particular task; in this instance, the company of men who man a ship or boat.

"The king's own troupe came next, a chosen crew, Of all the campe the strength, the crowne, the flowre."
—Edward Fairfax (d. 1635), *Godfrey of Buloigne* (1600)

Sailors valued very highly—probably above all other considerations—the degree of harmony that they might or might not find in a vessel; they spoke openly of such-and-such a vessel as being "a happy ship." The reasons were many, but they centred about justice, discipline, the fairness of its officers, and the conditions of work, food, and accommodation, although it was rare for these last three to vary much from ship to ship. It was always his shipmates and their officers—the personal elements—who made or marred life afloat for the sailor. Used as in "The road gang became a happy crew under the new foreman."
(See also *People.)*

Crib

"In a cryb was he layde."
—*Towneley Mysteries,* cited in the *Universal Dictionary of the English Language* (1897)

The small, permanent sleeping berths once found in packet-boats, the vessels that carried mails and passengers between nearby ports on a regular basis. Such a vessel was originally known as a "post-bark" or "post-boat." Currently, any compact sleeping berth in a small vessel is known as a "crib." Also a stall, pen, or fodder rack for cattle; now widely used to describe a child's bed or cot, usually oval in shape and made of wickerwork. Various other meanings also attach to this word. From the Anglo-Saxon *cribb,* ox-stall.

Crimp
To crimp someone's style

A crimp is a person who shanghais or kidnaps seamen and delivers them aboard a vessel that is short-handed and about to sail. The word is related to the Danish *krympe,* to shrink, and refers to the coercion and swindling that was practised upon the unsuspecting seaman who was about to be shanghaied. The phrase *to crimp (or cramp) one's style* means to hinder or obstruct.
(See also *Shanghai.)*

"Coaxing and courting with intent to crimp him."
—Thomas Carlyle (1795–1881), English essayist, cited in the *Universal Dictionary of the English Language* (1897)

Cruel
To cruel it

A navy term, probably from the nineteenth century and later, meaning to spoil someone's chances of success, often by committing a foolish act. This is the seaman's adaptation

"Your brand-new hanky-panky system of drawing in sections cruelled their chances."
—*Truth* (Sydney newspaper), April 2, 1899

of the common London expression *to cruel the pitch,* earlier *to queer the pitch,* much used by thieves when some scheme of theirs has gone astray.

Cruise

From the Dutch *kruisen,* and influenced by the French *croisiere,* to cruise, to journey; ultimately from the Latin *crux,* cross, with the meanings related to the varying directions taken by the component parts of the cross.

Nautically, "to cruise" was a distinct task: a vessel would be detached from the main fleet to cruise independently in search of the enemy. She would then report back to her fleet if a strange sail (vessel) was sighted. Such a scouting vessel, called a "cruiser" (originally "cruizer"), had to be a fast and handy ship; hence most cruisers were frigates, three-masted full-rigged ships of fifth or sixth rate, with a single gundeck of up to 38 guns. Frigate captains often had great opportunities for taking prizes.

"Mid sands and rocks and storms to cruise for pleasure."
—Edward Young (1683–1765), English cleric and dramatist, *Night Thoughts* (1745)

Nowadays a cruise is simply an extended voyage made to a series of destinations; a pleasure trip. The phrase appears in nonnautical expressions, such as "the cruising speed of a motor vehicle or aeroplane," and there refers to something's ability to move along at a moderate speed. The essence of the original meaning is still retained: to move efficiently but at some leisure, without being unduly bound to a route or an itinerary.

Cuddy

An early nautical word from the French *cahute,* little hut, and influenced by the French *cabane,* cabin. A cuddy is a cabin in the forepart of a vessel, but originally it was located in the after part of a sailing ship under the poop deck, for the captain and his passengers. In larger ships, the cuddy was the compartment where the officers ate; it was also sailor's slang for the admiral's quarters. Now often found in colloquial speech, meaning small room, a hideaway. It is very similar to a "cubby," "cubbyhole," or "cubbyhouse," but the term *cubby* is from a very early English word *cub,* shed, partition, which is probably related to the German *kobe,* sty or cage.
(See also *Caboose.)*

Current
To swim against the current

An obvious allusion, more to the sport of swimming than to the seaman's world.
(See also *Stream; To go against the stream.* Entries under *Tide.)*

Currents
To be at cross-currents

Current comes from the Latin *currens,* running. It is a horizontal movement of water due not to tides but to the seasonal flow of surface winds, and to the effects of the earth's rotation. A countercurrent is a secondary current flowing alongside, but in an opposite direction to, the main current. A cross-current is a current moving across the main current, as a local stream set up by a bank or eddy and moving across or at an angle to the main stream or current. Such a cross-current could prove dangerous to the unwary seaman, and in fact many a vessel has been lost because of this phenomenon, particularly among certain island groups in the South Pacific.

"The current, that with gentle murmur glides. . . ."
—William Shakespeare (1564–1616), *Two Gentlemen of Verona,* act 2, scene 7

Metaphorically, a cross-current is a contrary sense or direction: a listener may detect cross-currents of opinion in an audience in response to some statement. The expression *to be at cross-purposes* implies a more active position: to be involved in a misunderstanding such that each person makes a wrong interpretation of the other's interests or intentions.

Cut

To cut along

To move quickly, with haste; to be off to one's task with expedition; to get going. Originally an expression from the days of fighting sail, especially the period spanning the Napoleonic Wars, 1800–1815, when the Royal Navy laid the groundwork for the tradition of duty and discipline that has been a feature of that service ever since: "Well, I'll have to leave you now and cut along to my meeting."
(See also *Run; To cut and run.)*

To cut in; cutting in

An old term from the days of whaling. The dead whale was cut up alongside the vessel by men working from the "cutting stage," a platform of planks slung outboard of the ship's rail. This job, also known as "flensing," was a very dangerous one, as the sea was usually alive with sharks attracted to the kill, and the vessel was at the mercy of the weather, making it liable to roll alarmingly during the process of cutting in. As a metaphor, *to cut in* means to interrupt: "Simon cut into the conversation with an interesting suggestion."
(See also *Try; To try, to try out.)*

To cut out

Originally a nautical term used to describe the action of deliberately singling out an enemy ship and by various means separating her from her companions, so as to engage her with gunfire and, ultimately, to board her. Used in everyday speech with essentially the same meaning: to oust, to remove, to separate, as in the operation of cutting the wethers out from a flock of sheep. An extended meaning is "to cut it out," stop, cease, bring to an end: "That's enough of that shouting! I told you to cut it out long ago."

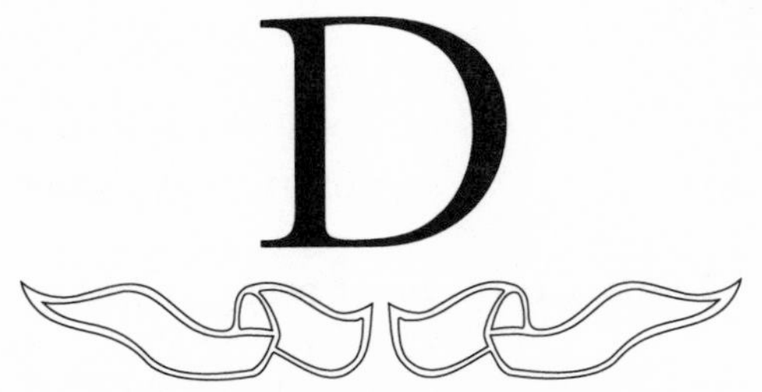

Dandyfunk A sea dish made of crushed ship's biscuit with fat, jam, or molasses added, and the whole baked in an oven.

Davit A nautical word of no metaphorical interest, but included here becuse of its interesting derivation. A davit is a small derrick or crane used for hoisting the flukes of the anchor to the top of the bow. Davits are also the pairs of curved pillars fitted to the deck close to a vessel's sides, from which lifeboats, the ship's launch, and the like are lowered and hoisted by means of two sets of tackles, known as "falls." The fifteenth-century term was *daviot,* from the Anglo-French and Old French *daviet, daviot,* both being a diminutive of the name "David" (interestingly, the German word for davit is *jutte,* from the name "Judith"). In the seventeenth century, the davit was referred to as the "david." The origin is almost certainly an allusion to the biblical story of David being let down from a window by his wife Michal to escape Saul's threat of execution.

Davy Jones In nautical mythology, Davy Jones is the spirit of the sea, usually cast in the form of a sea devil. Thus, the bottom of the sea is called "Davy Jones's Locker," the final resting place of sunken ships, of articles lost or thrown overboard, and of men buried at sea. It is the sailor's phrase for death, as in "He's gone to Davy Jones's Locker" when referring to anyone who has been drowned or buried at sea.

The reason for the choice of name is unknown; it is certainly reminiscent of the prophet Jonah (also known as Jonas), who brought misfortune upon the crew of the ship in which he was fleeing to Tarshish to escape God's wrath. Another suggestion is that Davy is a corruption of the West Indian word *duppy,* devil, or that Davy Jones was once a pirate. Hampshire, in *Just an Old Navy Custom* (1979), states that *Davy Jones* is from "Duffy" Jones, *duffy* being an Old English word for ghost; the phrase thus means "ghost of Jonah."

Dead on time Exactly on time; to arrive or happen exactly according to schedule. Said to derive from the lore of seamen, who believed that one died only when one's time was right: a sort of nautical kismet.

Deadwood The name given to the blocks of timber attached to the keel fore and aft, to form the upward extensions of the keel to the stemson and sternpost. Its primary function is to build up the ends of the keel so that other structural timbers may be securely located. The deadwood pieces in themselves add little, if any, strength to the hull; hence their name. In a similar sense, the term is used to describe anyone who is a nonproductive member of, say, a business firm or a sporting team, someone who isn't contributing to the overall success of the enterprise. *To get rid of the deadwood* would be the goal of a shakeup or a review of personal performance: "The general manager undertook a restructuring of the firm to get rid of the deadwood in the staff."

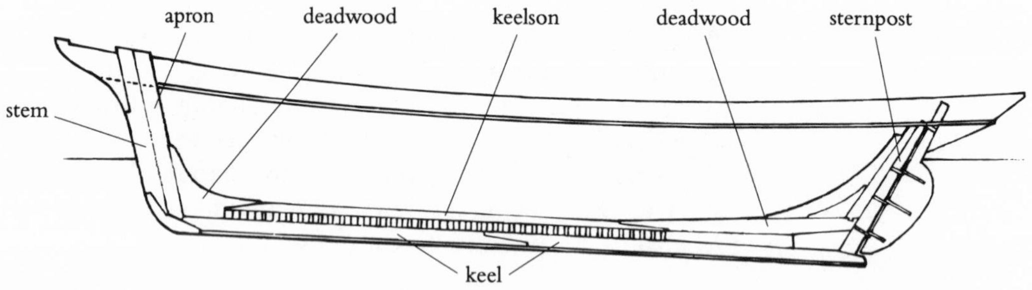

Debacle Surprisingly, of nautical origin; the word first referred to the breaking-up of ice on a river or navigable channel. From the French *debacle,* to clear, unbar; from *de,* away, from, plus *bacler,* bar, and ultimately from the Latin *baculus,* staff, crossbar. The word achieved widespread military use ("The enemy troops were crushed in a series of debacles from which they never recovered") as a result of the publication of Emile Zola's novel *La Débâcle* (1892). More generally, the term now means a breakup or rout, a sudden overthrow or collapse; overwhelming disaster.

"They could have been transported by no other force than that of a tremendous deluge or debacle of water."

—William Buckland (1784–1856), English religious scholar and geologist, *Reliquiae Diluvianae* (1823)

Decco Also "dekko." A slang word common in Australian speech up until the mid-twentieth century; it means to look at, to peer at, to take a "gander" (another colloquialism of the same era and meaning). Used as in "Looks like a fight over there—let's go and take a decco." From the Hindustani *dekho,* "look!," and into colloquial English by way of the British Army in India and the sailor's love of foreign idiom.

Deck

"Aeneas from his lofty deck holds forth
The perfect olive branch. . . ."
—William Cowper (1665–1723), English parliamentarian, *Translations from Virgil, Aenead,* book 8 (1791)

From the Dutch *dek,* covering, roof, and *decken,* to cover. The earliest English nautical sense is as a covering or roof rather than a floor. The word now, of course, means the floor (planked, steel, fiberglass, etc.) that runs the length of a ship, or part of it, connecting the sides and covering the various compartments and holds.

To be decked out

". . . or diamond drops
That sparkling deck'd the morning grass. . . ."
—William Wordsworth (1770–1850), English poet, *Excursions* (1814)

From *to deck out,* to array in fine clothing, ornaments, and such; nautically, to spread a full suit of sails. Figuratively, *to be decked out* is to be all dressed up in one's best, or to be attired in something unusual and noteworthy: "They both were decked out in their finery for the opening day of the Melbourne Cup."

To be on deck

Ship's crews generally worked a watch-on, watch-off system of duty, so that there was always a sufficient number of hands on deck available for duty, while the just-relieved watch was below resting or taking a meal. To be literally on deck, rather than below decks, signified that a sailor was on duty and was fit to do his work. The phrase has come to mean that a person has recovered from an illness or a setback of some kind and is once more able to carry on as before: "It was many months before he was on deck again following his attack of Ross River virus."

To clear the deck

To get everything out of the way, to sweep away everything that is unnecessary, including personnel. When a warship went into action, it was essential that the gundecks be immediately cleared so that the guns could be served by the gun crews, who had a great deal to do in the heat, smoke, and chaos of a gunnery duel. *To clear for action* carries a similar meaning. "The general secretary told each department to clear the deck for a thorough review of its performance."
(See also *Deck; To sweep the deck.)*

To hit the deck

A colloquialism that has apparent nautical overtones but little foundation in maritime parlance (compare with "shiver me timbers!"). The phrase is from stage and screen; the appropriate order to the crew would be "All hands on deck."

To hit the deck means two curiously opposite things. The first is to fall to the ground, generally as a precaution against being hit by flying missiles. The second means to rise from one's bed or some other place of rest and to stand up, feet firm to the ground; in short, to get ready, be prepared.
(See also other entries under *Deck. Timbers; Shiver me timbers!)*

To sweep the deck To carry off everything before one, as in winning all the main prizes in a contest or in some way clearing away all obstacles in one's pursuit of good fortune or reward of some kind. The expression derives from the heavy seas that would sometimes board a vessel in bad weather and literally sweep her deck from stem to stern, sometimes carrying away gear and men.

The colloquialism gains its force from the fact that heavily boarded vessels in a storm did occasionally have their decks literally swept clean of gear and superstructure, thereby offering no further resistance to overpowering seas. It is thus not the same as "clear the decks." "It was his intention to take over the firm and to sweep the decks with regard to personnel who weren't producing satisfactory results."

(See also *Deck; To clear the deck.)*

Deep An area of ocean of exceptional depth when compared to adjacent areas; depths of over 3,000 fathoms are given the generic name *deeps.* The word was originally used to refer to that part of the ocean as opposed to the shallows near the shore. It is found in a number of figures of speech: "That new treasurer is a deep one"; "to take a deep breath"; "to be in deep sorrow"; "deep in thought"; and so on. *To be in deep water* is an obvious nautical allusion, meaning to be in trouble or difficulties: "If you criticise her religious beliefs you will find yourself in very deep water indeed." From the Old English *deop,* deep.

"The goddess spoke: the rolling waves unclose:
Then down the deep she plung'd from whence she rose."
—Alexander Pope (1688–1744), English poet and essayist, Homer's *Iliad* (1720)

Deep six To *deep six* something is to heave it overboard, usually because it is no longer of any use. As a landsman's metaphor, it means to bury or get rid of someone or something (the traditional depth of a grave being six feet): "The washing machine finally gave up the ghost after 15 years of service, so we gave it the deep six at the dump last week."

The origin of the term is the leadsman's cry as he heaves his lead to determine the depth of water beneath his vessel. The hand lead line is marked in fathoms at certain intervals with bits of cloth, leather, duck (canvas), or cord; even at night the experienced leadsman can recognise each mark and call the correct depth (sounding) accordingly. The unmarked fathoms between the marks on the lead line are called "deeps"; if the lead is heaved and it comes to rest where there is no distinguishing mark on the line, the leadsman refers to the nearest mark that he can see above the water, and calls out to the officer of the watch "Deep—" followed by the observed mark above the water. (Readers will be familiar with the significance of "mark twain," the name of the two-fathom sounding adopted by Samuel Clemens, the American writer, as a memento of his days as a river pilot on the Mississippi.)

A cry of "Deep six!" would mean that the vessel was lying in between five and six fathoms of water; the pragmatic seaman, ever conscious of his own proximity to eternity, saw "deep six" in a far more personal light, hence the significance of the expression.

Defaulter's list
To be on the defaulter's list

The defaulter's list contained the names of seamen who had in that period (usually a week) defaulted in their adherence to regulations, duty, etc. The offence was usually a minor one, and was dealt with at defaulter's parade, at which the offending seaman, if found guilty, was summarily convicted by the captain and sentenced to a restriction of privileges. The expression is occasionally met with in everyday speech.

Dekko

See *Decco.*

Demure

Now meaning sedate, modest, decorous, as applied to a person's behaviour; but the word is of nautical origin, once used to describe the sea, to mean quiet, settled, untroubled. From the Anglo-French *demurer,* to stay.

Demurrage

"The ship was delayed at a demurrage of a hundred dollars a day."
—Edmund Burke (1729–1797), English jurist, essayist, and parliamentarian, *Against Warren Hastings* (1788)

As used today, the word refers to the detention of a railway car, or similar freighting conveyance, and the charge that is applied for that detention. Originally it referred to the detention of a vessel, and was the compensation payable to the shipowner when his ship was held up in port because the cargo had not been delivered on time by the consigning party. The word is from the Latin *demorari,* to linger. (See also *Lay day.)*

Depth
To be out of one's depth; to be over one's depth

The allusion is obvious: literally, to be in water too deep for one to touch bottom; thus to be in a potentially dangerous situation. Similarly, in a figurative sense, *to be out of one's depth* is to find oneself in a situation that calls for greater knowledge or experience than one has: "I felt quite out of my depth during the board's discussions on how to handle the economic downturn."

Derelict

"A government which is either unable or unwilling to redress such wrongs is derelict to its highest duties."
—James Buchanan (1791–1868), U.S. president, *Message to Congress,* December 19, 1859

From the Latin *derelictus,* that which is forsaken entirely; any vessel abandoned at sea, for whatever reason. However, if any live domestic animal, such as a cat or dog, is on board when the vessel is found, the owner is legally entitled to recover the ship within a year and a day if he is willing to pay salvage. The sense of abandonment, neglect, and dilapidation is preserved in the colloquial use of the term;

a derelict is a person who is completely down and out, on the skids, forsaken by society; usually occasioned by liquor.

Devil
Between the devil and the deep blue sea To have no real choice; to be placed between two alternatives, each of which is equally precarious or hazardous. To move toward either is to invite disaster.

The devil was the outermost seam on the deck, in the waterways against the vessel's side or bulwark; it was so called because it allowed almost no room for the seaman to hammer the caulking in to make the seam watertight. It is also the name of the garboard seam, the seam between the keel and the first plank (called the garboard strake). The garboard seam was also an extremely difficult one to caulk; it was very awkward to get to, and was usually too wet to caulk properly with oakum and hot pitch.

From the point of view of the sailor, all that lay between disaster and his present position was the thickness of the planking that stood between the devil on the deck and the sea alongside. He also had to rely on the integrity of the garboard seam, it being so difficult to maintain properly at any time. In both instances, the "deep blue sea" was the inevitable dire result if the sailor neglected to carry out the necessary and always difficult task of keeping the devils in good order. "Faced with the choice of going to prison or having to sell their house to pay their fines, the convicted accountant and his wife found themselves between the devil and the deep blue sea."

(See also *Devil; The devil to pay. Wind; Betwixt wind and water.)*

The devil to pay The term *to pay* means to caulk a seam; to force oakum into it and cover it with hot pitch. *To pay the devil* referred to the very awkward or difficult task of paying the outermost seam on the deck; it always generated trouble of one kind or another. Colloquially, the phrase means to be confronted with a situation so difficult that no means of solving it can easily be found. It also has an extended and related meaning, implying that if one persists in pursuing a particular course of action there will be trouble: "the devil to pay." "When your mother hears about this there will be the devil to pay."

(See also *Devil; Between the devil and the deep blue sea.)*

Dhobi Also "dhobie" and "dhobey." From the Hindi *dhobi,* washing, or a person who does the washing; adopted by seamen to mean the same thing. The word was taken up by British sailors and soldiers from the days of the British raj in India; it is still met with occasionally in everyday speech.

Dingbat Also "dingbats." A sailor's slang term for a mop made out of old rope-ends and used for swabbing the deck and other areas. The origin of the phrase is obscure; it is used today to describe a condition of being rather eccentric or uncontrolled in speech or actions, to be silly or dopey. In Australian slang, it is also a term for delirium tremens. The allusion is probably to the more or less uncontrollable teased-out fag-ends of rope being slapped around by the action of the mop. American usage is similar: the reference is to someone who is flighty and foolish, especially a woman. Used as in "If I have to listen to any more of your corny jokes I shall go dingbats."

"They ought to have put him away in Callan Park with the other dingbats."
—Sumner Locke Elliott (1917–1991), Australian novelist, playwright, and actor, *Water Under the Bridge* (1977)

It is revealing of our values that the English language contains a disproportionately large number of slang terms that describe the wit—or, rather, the lack of it—in our fellow man. American slang, for instance, employs more than 200 expressions for people who are supposedly a bit less sane than ourselves, from "airbrain" to "potatohead," "chucklehead" to "gump," and "goney" to "schlemiel," with "yo-yo," "zerk," and "zombie" bringing up the alphabetical rear.

Dip out To miss out on; not to receive one's expected share; to remain uninvolved, to avoid; to fail. Seaman's slang, but the origin is obscure; it may be connected with the "pusser's dip," the shipboard candle made by, or under the supervision of, the ship's purser ("pusser"). A common metaphor in Australian speech: "I was sure that I was going to dip out in my English examination."
(See also *Pusser's dip.*)

Discharge From the Old French *descharger,* to unload, and originally used in that sense to mean the act of unloading a ship's cargo; then used to describe the act of signing-off a member of the crew, thereby releasing him from the obligations he incurred when he signed on for a particular voyage or period of service. The expression is now more widely used to encompass the senses of letting go, to relieve of obligation, to fulfill or perform a duty to dismiss, and so on: "The principal commended her for the way in which she discharged her responsibilities as acting head of the math department."

"I will convey them by sea, in floats unto the place that thou shalt appoint me, and will cause them to be discharged there."
—1 Kings 5:9

Ditch The "ditch" is the sea; *to ditch* something is to throw it overboard. From the Anglo-Saxon *dic,* ditch, dike, and related to the German *teich,* ditch. As a metaphor, *to ditch* something or somebody is to get rid of, to get away from; also to crash-land an aeroplane, especially in the sea. "She ditched her boyfriend when it became clear that he was a petty criminal."

Ditty-bag See *Ditty box*.

Ditty box The ditty box, introduced in about 1870 as a small, strongly made chest with a lock and brass nameplate, was a small wooden box in which the seaman kept his personal valuables, such as letters from home, photographs, certificates, etc. His ditty-bag was a small canvas bag containing the gear that he needed when working on deck; it might hold a splicing fid, canvas gloves, sewing palm, and needle, etc. Both terms refer loosely to similarly small containers (usually portable) for storing items of a personal and sometimes valuable nature.

Now often used to apply to any small bag, sometimes carried on the person, in which is kept small personal necessaries and possessions. Probably the sailor's corruption of the Hindustani *dhoti,* loincloth, which is also found in the obsolete English word *dutty,* a coarse brown calico. It may also derive from the Old English *dite,* tidy.

Dock The area of water in a port or harbour totally enclosed by piers or wharves. The wharves themselves are commonly called docks, but in the strict meaning of the term the dock is the water in between.

To be in dock is a colloquialism meaning to be out of order, as a piece of equipment is taken out of service in order to be repaired; to be laid up, as a vessel is out of service temporarily while she is in dock: "I've been in dock ever since I broke my leg two months ago."

The word is related to the Low German *docke,* channel or runnel; and occurs in an early English dialect as *doke,* furrow. This sense of furrow is the earliest meaning of the word, and it referred to the furrow made in the sand when a vessel was beached. In the early fifteenth century, *dock* meant the bed made on the mud by the vessel when it was drawn up as far as possible at high tide. This area was then fenced off while repairs were in progress.

"I suggested that he might go to a dockyard, and work, as Peter the Great did."
—James Boswell (1740–1795), English jurist and man of letters, *Tour to the Hebrides* (1785)

To be put into dock To be out of order and being repaired (said of equipment), or to be ill or laid up (said of a person). From the dockside manoeuvre of putting a vessel alongside a berth, or into dry dock, for repairs, cleaning, or painting.

Dodge A fishing trawler was said to dodge when she hove to in heavy weather, still keeping some slow way on (i.e., still moving ahead very slowly), more or less head to sea. A

"Send humble treaties, dodge
And palter in the shifts of
lowness. . . ."
—William Shakespeare (1564–1616), *Antony and Cleopatra,* act 3, scene 2

dodger is a canvas screen laced to a ship's guardrails to provide shelter from wind or spray. Originally a dodger was a messdeck sweeper, one who cleaned up after the crew had eaten. Derived from the German *ducken,* to dodge or duck.

Dodo
Dead as a dodo

The dodo was a large, clumsy, flightless bird, about the size of a goose but with small, useless wings, that once inhabited the islands of Mauritius, Reunion, and Rodrigues, in the southwestern Indian Ocean. It was very easily captured by sailors and was used by them as food; the bird's complete lack of fear consequently led to its becoming extinct in the late seventeenth century. The word *dodo* is from the Portuguese *doudo,* silly. The phrase *dead as a dodo* means long since dead, forgotten, finished with, very much a thing of the past. In American usage, a dodo is a fool, a very stupid person.

"The dodo [is] a bird the Dutch call *walghvogel* or *dod Eersen;* her body is round and fat, which occasions her slow pace."
—T. Herbert, *Travels,* cited in the *Universal Dictionary of the English Language* (1897)

Dog house See *Doghouse.*

Dog watch See *Watch; To keep watch.*

Doghouse

A raised structure aft of the main cabin in a vessel; usually a short deckhouse or main hatchway that is raised above the level of the cabin top, or coachroof. Originally an American term referring to a small temporary structure built to accommodate extra people, as in a slaver ship. The phrase *to be in the doghouse* means to be in disfavour with someone; for example, during a matrimonial dispute: "He forgot his wife's birthday yesterday and has been in the doghouse ever since."

Dogsbody

A naval term meaning midshipman, who in the eighteenth and nineteenth centuries was of noncommissioned rank, next below that of sublieutenant. Generally they were young gentlemen who had gone to sea to learn how to become naval officers, and consequently were given a rigorous time of it during their training. They were at the beck and call of every officer and petty officer; hence their nickname "dogsbody," someone who had to fetch things, undertake the unpleasant duties, and so on, as an overworked drudge, someone who is constantly imposed upon. "The new boy in the office soon became everyone's dogsbody until the manager put a stop to it."

Doldrums
To be in the doldrums

To be in the doldrums is to be slack, depressed, in a state of lethargy or inactivity. The term probably derives from a combination of *dolorous,* sad, and *tantrums,* bad temper.

It is closely associated with the area of calm that lies just north and south of the equator, between the trade wind systems of the great oceans. These areas were of particular significance to the crews of sailing ships, as the men were almost always reduced to a state of severe depression and querulousness because of having to lie becalmed, often for weeks on end, in torrid heat and windless conditions, searching for the fitful gusts that occasionally reached out from rain squalls. *To be in the doldrums* is to experience physical and psychological torpor; for a sailor, the effect is quite pronounced, particularly when sailing single-handed. Used as in "She moped around the house, in the doldrums for days because he hadn't written to her."

Doll Originally a seaman's term for a woman of the ports, i.e., a prostitute, harlot, doxy, trollop, whore, hooker (curiously, the list of terms for women of loose morals is about twice as long as that for men). The word *doll* appears in sailors' ditties in the first half of the nineteenth century. The word is a diminutive of "Dorothy" in the same way that "marionnette" is a double diminutive of the French "Marie" (there is also a Scottish form *doroty,* doll, child's toy; the Dutch *dol* is a whipping-top). *Doll* was in common use to mean mistress, pet.

"They can scarcely rank higher than a painted doll."
—Vicesimus Knox (1752–1821), *Essays, Moral and Literary* (1778)

Now a colloquialism to mean an attractive woman, especially one who is young; the connotation of sexual looseness no longer applies. The once-popular song "Paper Doll" uses the word in its two current senses: the singer is going to buy a paper doll (toy) so that he can have a doll (girl) that he can call his own, one whom the other fellows cannot take away.

Dollar Not nautical in origin, but included here because of the importance of the dollar in the early romantic literature about pirates, buccaneers, and the like.

Dollar originates from the sixteenth century, when money was being coined from the silver mines in Bohemia. The location of the mint was in Joachimsthal (i.e., "Joachim's Valley," *thale* meaning valley or dale). The coins issued were called *Joachimsthaler,* and finally the word was shortened to *Thaler.* The later transition to "dollar" was simple.

Bank of England dollars were struck as bank tokens in 1797, and the United States first coined its dollars in 1794. The dollar sign $ is probably a modification of the figure 8 as it appeared on the old Spanish coins known as "pieces of eight," worth eight reals, and equivalent in value to the *Joachimsthaler.*

(See also *Doubloon. Pieces of eight.)*

Dooflicker Also "doohickie" (particularly in the United States, otherwise not commonly known elsewhere in the English-speaking world), "gilguy," "gadget," "doolackie" (once commonly used in Australian English), and "doodad." All are sailor's slang for labour-saving devices that enable the sailor to cut down on his work effort.
(See also *Gadget.)*

Doubloon Formerly a Spanish gold coin, one that figured largely in the literature of pirates and the Spanish Main. From the French *doublon* and the Spanish *doblon,* an intensive of *doble,* double.
(See also *Dollar. Pieces of eight.)*

"They had succeeded in obtaining from him a box of doubloons."
—Thomas Babington Macaulay (1800–1859), English essayist, *History of England* (1848)

Douse
To douse the light To extinguish the lamp, torch, or lantern immediately, for whatever reason; or to drench the source of light, such as a fire, with water so as to put it out.

From the sailor's term for striking or lowering a sail hastily, often in the face of some emergency; usually rendered in the early days of sail as "douse the top," or "douse topsail." Sailors still use the expression "douse the glim," meaning turn down or put out the lamp or light. From the Dutch *doesen.*

"Hee used to be dowssed in water luke warm."
—Philemon Holland (1552–1637), English scholar, *Suetonius* (1606)

Doxy Originally nineteenth-century sailor's slang for a prostitute. Now generally a mistress, a paramour, or a prostitute. From the Middle Flemish *docke,* doll, and the affectionate diminutive ending *-sy;* thence into the English language by way of maritime contact between the two nations.
(See also *Doll.)*

"Orthodoxy, my Lord, is my doxy—heterodoxy is another man's doxy."
—Ascribed to William Warburton (1698–1779), English literary critic and bishop of Gloucester, quoted in H. L. Mencken's *Dictionary of Quotations* (1942)

Drake's Drum A drum, said to have been in the possession of Sir Francis Drake and originally carried on board his ships to beat (summon) crews to quarters; it is supposed to have been played on his flagship when he sailed out from Plymouth Hoe to meet the Spanish Armada in July 1588. Legend has it that the drum will sound whenever England is threatened by invasion from the sea. Some doubts have been cast on its authenticity. Sir Henry Newbolt wrote the poem "Drake's Drum" in 1897, and the tune was played on board Allied ships off the coast of Normandy on the morning of D-Day in the Second World War (June 6, 1944). Many a schoolboy has learned by heart Newbolt's poem, one verse of which runs:

> Take my drum to England, hang et by the shore,
> Strike et when your powder's runnin' low,
> If the Dons sight Devon, I'll quit the port o' heaven,
> An' drum them up the channel as we drummed them
> long ago.

Dredge

"The oysters dredged in the Lyne find a ready acceptance."
—Thomas Carew (?1598–?1639), English poet, cited in the *Universal Dictionary of the English Language* (1897)

Found in the fifteenth-century *dreg-boat* (late Middle English); a vessel used for removing mud from harbours, slipways, etc. The maritime usage has given us the colloquialism *to dredge up,* meaning to find or stumble across, usually after a number of fumbling efforts: "He dredged up an argument as to why they shouldn't spend their inheritance on an overseas holiday."

Drift

"We know your drift. . . ."
—William Shakespeare (1564–1616), *Coriolanus,* act 3, scene 3

From *drive,* which comes to us from the Anglo-Saxon *drifan,* to convey the central sense of active movement. Nautically, it is the direction and distance that a ship is carried by a current at sea; figuratively, it refers to what one is aiming at, or driving at, in an argument or discussion: "She was so tired that she lost the drift of his argument long before he was finished."

Do you get my drift?

"Drift" is the distance a vessel makes to leeward as a result of the action of tide or wind, or both, on the hull and superstructure. It also describes the general movement of an ocean current that is under the influence of a more or less permanent wind system, such as that produced by the prevailing westerlies in southern latitudes.

The colloquial allusion is the direction that a person would seem to be taking when advancing an argument or explanation; one's "drift" is more by way of hint and ellipsis than by direct example or approach, as if to emulate the gradualness of a vessel's movement when drifting. Found in such metaphors as "Do you get my drift?" (Do you understand the aim of my argument?).

"In the mean time, against thou shalt awake,
Shall Romeo by my letters know our drift."
—William Shakespeare (1564–1616), *Romeo and Juliet,* act 4, scene 1

Drink
In the drink

Old navy slang for being in the sea, in the water. "Their dinghy tipped over in the surf and they all went into the drink."

Duck down

See *Duck up.*

Duck up

When the helmsman of a square-rigged vessel had his forward vision obstructed by the sails, the order "Duck up the clew lines" was given, and the lower corners (the clews or clues) of the mainsail and foresail were hauled up to their respective yards until the man at the wheel was able to see ahead properly. Colloquially, the phrase has variations: "duck up," "duck down," "duck over," etc. They all mean approximately the same thing: to go (or move) quickly, without fuss, to get something or improve matters: "Duck down to the store and get me some milk."

Dunnage Dunnage is baggage, personal effects. It is from the Dutch *dunnetje,* loosely together, and describes the loose material that is packed beneath or among items of cargo to prevent them from being chafed by excessive movement. We still use the term when we refer to our personal gear or baggage as dunnage, especially when it comes to stowing or loading it into some conveyance.

Dutch From the Middle Dutch *Dutsch,* and the German *Deutsch,* denoting the people of Germany, those of Teutonic stock; it also referred to the language spoken by them. The word derives from the Old High German *diot,* people, and is related to the Old Irish *tuath,* people. It is a word from the eighth century, but from about 1600 it tended to be restricted to describing the inhabitants of what is now called Holland or the Netherlands.

As a result of the Anglo-Dutch wars of the seventeenth century, fought almost entirely at sea, the English seaman coined a wide variety of phrases that depicted the Dutch in a less than flattering manner. Some such phrases are:

Double Dutch: Gibberish, jargon, as the Dutch tongue was to the English sailor.
Dutch bargain: A bargain settled over drinks.
Dutch comfort: Cold comfort; of almost no consolation at all.
Dutch defence: A sham defence.
Dutch nightingales: Frogs.
Dutch treat: To pay for oneself; "to go Dutch."
Dutch wife: A bolster used originally in the Dutch East Indies for resting the limbs in bed; a poor substitute for the real thing.
Dutch-built: Broad and bluff, without grace.
I'll be a Dutch Uncle: From the Dutch *baas,* originally uncle, now boss or master; an expression of great disbelief, the same as "I'll be a Dutchman."
I'll be a Dutchman: An expression of surprise and strong rejection; incredulity.
To be in Dutch: In trouble, out of favour.

The word *bumpkin* (a derivative of the nautical *boom* plus the addition of *kin,* a short boom) colloquially means awkward country yokel, fellow. Etymological research suggests that it was first applied to Dutchmen.
(See also *Dutch courage.* Entries under *Spanish.)*

Dutch courage The Dutch were, rightly or wrongly, considered to be heavy topers, and "Dutch courage" was the reinforcement that they were said to find in drink. One explanation for the origin of the term is that, during the seventeenth-century maritime wars between England and Holland, Dutch sea captains were said to have barrels of brandy placed on deck, from which the sailors helped themselves before going into battle.

"The Dutch their wine and all their brandy lose,
Disarmed of that from which their courage grows."
—Edmund Waller (1606–1687), English poet, *Instructions to a Painter* (1666)

Whether this is true or not, it is certainly a fact that liquor does tend to make men more aggressive. The phrase, once in wide use only among seamen, is now part of our language. The Hollanders have, wittingly or not, also lent their name to expressions such as "Dutch-built" (rotund), "double Dutch" (referring to the alleged unintelligibility of their speech), a "Dutch Uncle," the "Flying Dutchman," and so on.
(See also *Dutch.)*

Ears
To put one's ears back

An old naval term, meaning to eat to the full, to make a hearty meal of it. The allusion is to the need to have the whole face "streamlined," so to speak, in order to get into the food as easily as possible; to have no impediments to enjoying what lay ahead. Colloquially, it means to get stuck into something, to go at it with zeal and enthusiasm, to overdo it, to be overzealous. "When he began investigating his family tree, he really put his ears back and pestered everyone for information."

Ease
To ease off

See *Easy.*

Easy

An old nautical term, meaning to go or haul carefully, slowly, or less vigorously; to gently slacken; in general, to take the pressure off, as in easing the sheets to reduce the pressure of wind on the sail, in order to reduce the angle of heel. The metaphor, often expressed as "to ease off," carries much the same ground sense: to reduce severity, tension, or pressure so as to make something less painful or burdensome. "The football coach began to ease off the pressure of training two days before the Grand Final."

To take it easy

From the order *Easy!,* meaning to lessen the effort being put into a particular action; also, to take some care. Often used as an opposite of *handsomely,* which means with great care, slowly, to not lose the strain. The essential element of "easy" is to relax without actually abandoning one's duty or position. In the Royal Navy, a short break during working hours is called a "stand easy." "The lawyer told his client to take it easy, because the prosecution had only a circumstantial case."
(See also *Easy* and *Handsome.)*

Ebb
To be at a low ebb

Ebb is the receding tidal stream; the ebb of the tide follows high slack water, when the tide falls and flows out to sea, and is the opposite of *flood,* when the tide rises and flows shoreward. The word is from the Old English *ebba,* which is a replication of the Dutch and Old Frisian *ebbe, ebba,* return, change.

"The greatest age for poetry was that of Augustus Caesar, yet painting was then at its lowest ebb, and perhaps sculpture was also declining."
—John Dryden (1631–1700), English poet, dramatist, and essayist, *Dufresnoy,* cited in the *Universal Dictionary of the English Language* (1897)

Colloquially, one is said to be "at a low ebb" when one's spirits are down, when one is feeling low, depressed, mentally exhausted; as if one's life juices had been drained away: "By the time she sat for her final examinations in her nursing course, she was at a low ebb."

Interestingly, it was widely believed along the east coast of Britain that the ebbing tide was the time when those who were close to death finally died, as if the ebbing of their soul- or life-force were in some mysterious way connected to the back-and-forth flow of the forces of the sea.

Embargo

"Embargoes on merchandize was another engine of royal power."
—David Hume (1711–1776), English philosopher and man of letters, *History of Great Britain* (1761)

To embargo is to prohibit, to forbid; an embargo is also a temporary arrest or injunction. Especially applied to foreign ships to prevent them from entering or leaving port or to undertake any commercial transaction, particularly if war is, or is about to be, declared; such ships or goods may, in certain circumstances, be seized for the use of the state. Applied to describe any restriction imposed by law or union activity upon commercial activity. From the Spanish *embargar,* to hinder, impede, restrain.

Embark
To embark (on a course of action)

To begin a connected series of actions or words; entails the nautical use of *course,* the direction in which a ship travels. (See also *Embark; To embark [on a venture or enterprise].)*

To embark (on a venture or enterprise)

"He fraighted his ships and embarked his host."
—Goldyng, *Justine,* cited in the *Universal Dictionary of the English Language* (1897)

Originally, to put on board a vessel; from the French *ebarquer. Bark* (or *barque)* is the vessel, from the Latin *barca,* ship of burden. *To embark on an enterprise* is a metaphor meaning to initiate a business venture, to set out on a commercial undertaking, to invest money, and so on. *To embark* still retains the nautical meaning "to go on board a ship"; the usage generally now refers only to persons, whereas originally only goods were embarked.

End
A taste of the rope's end

Sailor's slang for a flogging; formerly a routine shipboard punishment for a wide variety of misdemeanors, administered with either a rope ("the rope's end") or the cat-o'-nine-tails.
(See also *Cat; No room to swing a cat.)*

Exonerate

From the Latin *ex-,* out, from, and *onus,* burden; hence, to unburden. Curiously, it was first applied in a literal sense to operations such as the unburdening of a ship, that is, the unloading of its cargo. This is a very early usage; it has now long since meant only to clear of blame, to relieve as from

"Vessels which afterwards all exonerate themselves into one common ductus."
—John Ray (1627–1705), English naturalist, *Wisdom of God Manifested in the Works of Creation* (1691)

an obligation, and it has quite lost its literal sense of a physical unburdening: "As a result of the enquiry into the accident, he was exonerated of all blame and responsibility for what had happened."
(See also *Discharge.*)

Eye
All my eye

The phrase in full is "All my eye and Betty Martin." It means nonsense, rubbish, without any foundation in fact. The colloquial usage is quite well known, but its origin is obscure. It is usually explained as a corruption of *O mihi, beate Martin* ("O [grant] me, blessed [St.] Martin"); originally a prayer or invocation offered by sailors of Catholic nations to St. Martin, usually in time of battle. The colloquialism is frequently shortened to "all my eye." "You reckon that Footscray will win the Grand Final? That's all my eye!"
(See also *Eye; Black's the white of my eye.*)

Black's the white of my eye

The sailor's indignant rebuttal of a charge of misdemeanour, to which he is pleading innocent. He is saying that the charge is as truthful in the same way that the white of his eye is black.
(See also *Eye; All my eye.*)

In the wind's eye

Nowadays more often expressed as "in the eye of the wind," or, more familiarly, "in the teeth of the wind"; to be opposed by powerful forces. The apportioning of bodily characteristics, such as teeth, eyes, back, etc., to natural phenomena and shipboard names is a well-known custom among sailors (see appendix 3). The phrase, or its variant, means "directly opposed to the wind"; in the days of square-rigged sailing ships, a contrary wind inevitably meant a protracted, tedious, and usually very uncomfortable passage.

Colloquially, it means to be opposed by forces such as public opinion, national sentiment, or the like. The eye of a tropical storm is that area in the centre where all is still and clear. The "eyes of a ship" (called by seamen "the eyes of her") is the extreme forward end of a vessel; the term derives from the very old Eastern and Mediterranean custom of painting an eye on each bow so that the vessel could see where she was going. This custom is still practised in various countries today.

To pipe one's eye

Sailor's slang meaning to snivel, to weep; a reference to the bosun's pipe or call or whistle; "to pipe one's eye" is to summon up tears, in the same way that the bosun's pipe summons the watch.

To turn a blind eye To pretend not to see or notice something; to overlook a small indiscretion. Said to originate from Lord Nelson's celebrated act of putting his telescope to his blind eye at the Battle of Copenhagen in 1801, when Admiral Parker signaled Nelson to break off action. Nelson disobeyed the order, saying at the time that because he had a sightless eye he had a right to be blind sometimes.

Horatio Nelson (1758–1805), first Viscount and British vice admiral, perhaps England's best-loved and certainly most famous seagoing commander, joined his uncle's ship HMS *Raisonnable* at the age of 12. After a variety of experiences at sea, including service in the West Indies, the East Indies, and the Arctic, Nelson was made lieutenant at 19. He fought in the American Revolution (1775–1782) and was made post captain at the astonishingly young age of 21.

In 1787, Nelson was put on half pay because of the greatly reduced needs of the peacetime navy; he endured this for five years, until the war with Napoleonic France began in 1793 and Nelson went back to sea, this time in command of HMS *Agamemnon*. It was during this period that he was blinded in the right eye, a wound that later gave rise to the famous incident at the Battle of Copenhagen.

While Nelson was attacking the Danish fleet, the commander of the British squadron, Admiral Sir Hyde Parker, signaled for Nelson to break off the action. Because his ships were in a dangerous situation in shoal waters, however, Nelson refused even to see the signal, and continued his attack. As a result of his actions in this engagement, and because of his adroit handling of the armistice terms with Denmark, Nelson was made commander-in-chief in Parker's place, who in turn was recalled to England.

Viscount Nelson became commander of the Mediterranean Fleet in 1803 as vice admiral of the Blue, with his flag on HMS *Victory*. (See *Red, white, and blue* for an explanation of these squadronal colours.) Two years later, on October 21, 1805, the great battle for which Nelson seemed to have been preparing himself all his life unfolded off Cape Trafalgar, on the southwestern coast of Spain, where he met and defeated the Franco-Spanish fleet under the command of Napoleon's admiral, Comte de Villeneuve (Pierre Charles Jean Silvestre, 1763–1806).

This engagement, known as the Battle of Trafalgar, in which Nelson himself was mortally wounded on the quarterdeck of the *Victory* by a French sharpshooter's bullet, annihilated the French forces and gave England almost total control not only of the English Channel but also of the

Mediterranean. This was also perhaps the last great fleet encounter of the classic days of sail.

It was during this momentous battle that Nelson hoisted the most famous signal in British maritime history. Lieutenant John Pasco was Nelson's signals officer on the *Victory* at the time. As the British fleet sailed into action, Nelson turned to Pasco and said, "Mr. Pasco, I wish to say to the fleet, 'England confides that every man will do his duty.' You must be quick, for I have one more signal to make, which is for close action." Pasco asked if he could use "expects" instead of "confides," because "expects" already had its own signal flag, whereas "confides" would have had to be spelled out with eight extra hoists. "That will do; make it directly," replied Nelson, and thus this famous signal was hoisted (quoted from Kemp's *The Oxford Companion to Ships and the Sea,* 1976).

F

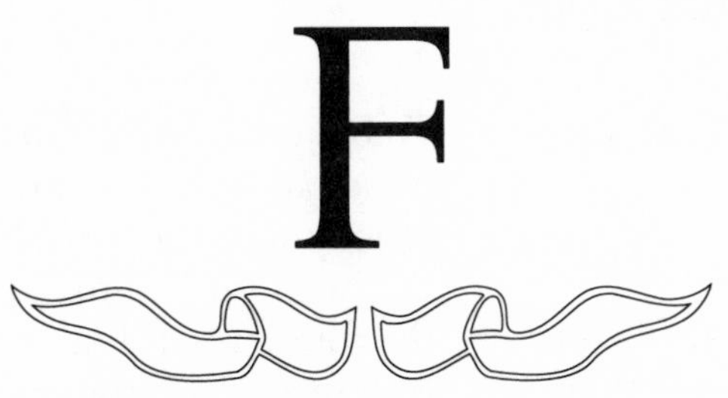

Fag
The fag end

See *Fagged; To be fagged out.*

Fagged
To be fagged out

A fag-end is the unwhipped end of a rope, which through constant use has become unlaid. *To fag out* indicates the tendency of the strands of a rope to fray out at the ends; also, *to fag* is to tease out these strands by hand. The origin of the word is the Greek *phakelos,* bundle, by way of the French *fagot* and the Italian *fagotto;* its first meaning in English had to do with sticks, loose bundles of wood. The word and its various forms are part of colloquial speech in most English-speaking countries, particularly Australia and Great Britain. *To be fagged out* is to be weary, exhausted, tired by labour, at the end of one's patience or strength.

"The kitchen and Gutters and other Offices of noise and drudgery are at the fag-end."
—James Howell (1594–1666), English writer, *Howell's Familiar Letters* (1619)

"From supper until nine o'clock three fags taken in order stood in the passages, and answered any praeposter who called 'Fag,' racing to the door, the last comer having to do the work. . . ."
—Thomas Hughes (1822–1896), English lawyer and writer, *Tom Brown's Schooldays* (1857)

A fag can be a number of things. In British public schools, a fag is a younger boy who is required to perform certain services for an older pupil, such as making his toast and cleaning his shoes. A fag is also a cigarette (seamen generally were inveterate smokers, and a diminished cigarette, at the end of its life, so to speak, is literally and colloquially a "fag-end"). The fag-end of anything is the last part, the final bit, especially a remnant, as of cloth. To arrive at the fag-end of a game or a party is to get there just as it is finishing; a place can be said to be at the far or fag-end of a road or lane; and so on.
(See also *Faggot. Swab.)*

Faggot

A man in the British Navy who, for a small fee—money, tobacco, spirits, or such—would answer to the names of those who were absent from a ship during muster (roll call) in port. In short, a faggot was a stand-in, a hireling. The term came to be used ashore with much the same meaning. Colloquially, a faggot is a person who will do one's bidding; in the United States, a faggot is a male homosexual.
(See also *Fagged; To be fagged out.)*

"There were several counterfeit books which were carved in wood, and served only to fill up the number like fagots [sic] in the muster of a regiment."
—Joseph Addison (1672–1719), English essayist, *The Spectator* No. 37

Fair and square

"My mother played my father fair. . . ."

—William Shakespeare (1564–1616), *Measure for Measure,* act 3, scene 1

To be just, openly honest, straightforward. From the nautical use of *fair,* which is to adjust and adapt something until it exactly suits the intended purpose; and *square,* as in "Square the main yard"—to adjust it so that it lies at right angles to the fore-and-aft line of the ship. *To square off* or *square away* is to make everything tidy, especially items of clothing; hence, to be just right, just so, all proper. "He was forced to admit that the policeman had caught him fair and square in the act of burglary."
(See also *Fair enough.)*

Fair enough

A phrase very common in shipbuilding and at sea. *To fair* means to shape or adjust something until it fits the whole properly, as in placing fairing stringers along the hull; *to fair in place* is to trim or adjust something without moving it from its place. *Fairing* means to correct a vessel's plans before building begins. A *fairlead* is any fixture used to lead a rope in a required direction. Fair weather is good, favourable weather that serves the purpose; and a fair wind is a wind that will set the vessel in the required direction.

Fair, to the seaman, means favourable, unobstructed, the reverse of foul; as in a "fairway," which is the navigable channel for ships entering or leaving harbour with all obstructions, if any, clearly marked by buoys and lights. "Fair enough" is an order—an imperative—for some manoeuvre to cease as it is, to hold or secure because that is its best position, as in setting a sail or catting the anchor.

As a colloquialism, it means acceptable, passable; a statement of agreement; all is well. A very common expression throughout most of the English-speaking world to signify agreement and approval: "The boss said that he would pay us overtime if we stayed to finish the job, and that is fair enough by me."

Fairway

In everyday usage, the part of a golf links between the tees and the putting greens; the driving ranges where the grass is kept short. From the original nautical usage, which referred to the navigable portion of a harbour or river, suitable for vessels entering or leaving.

Fall
To fall in with

"I fell in with a maist creditable elderly man."

—*The Steamboat,* cited in the *Universal Dictionary of the English Language* (1897)

At sea, *to fall in with* is to meet another vessel by chance. On land, as we have seen with so many nautical expressions, the sailor describes ordinary and everyday events ashore in the idiom of the sea, so that *to fall in* with someone is to meet him accidentally, by chance, or to agree with him in some matter. The phrase is now part of the landsman's idiom.

Fast
To hold fast, to make fast

Fast is from the Old English *faest,* related to the Icelandic *fastr,* fast, firm. *To make fast* is the sailor's term for securing, tying up (this latter a thoroughly lubberly expression to the ears of a seaman, who would never "tie up" a boat to anything); to attach or fix. The word is also the name of specific ropes or chains that secure a vessel to a dock or quay, such as "bow-fast," "stern-fast," and so on. In figurative language, *to hold fast* is to be firm, resolute, to stick to one's guns.
(See also *Guns; To stick to one's guns.)*

Fathom
To fathom something

"So grete trees, so huge of strengthe,
Of fourty, fifty fedme lengthe. . . ."
—Geoffrey Chaucer (1345–1400), English poet, *Book of the Duchess* (1369)

"The short reach of sense and natural reason is not always able to fathom the contrivance."
—Robert South (1634–1716), English cleric, *Sermons,* cited in the *Universal Dictionary of the English Language* (1897)

From Old English *faedm,* to embrace, deriving from the distance across the outstretched arms of a man of average size; this *faedm* (fathom) became the unit of measurement in most maritime countries for ocean depths and the length of rope and anchor cables.

Consequently, in the colloquial sense, *to fathom something* is to investigate it, plumb its depths, sound it out. To be unable to fathom something is to not understand it: "For the life of me, I cannot fathom why she agreed to marry him; he has no prospects whatsoever."
(See also *Sound; To sound somebody out.)*

Fend
To fend off

"Ye had aye a good roof ower your head to fend aff the weather."
—Sir Walter Scott (1771–1832), Scottish man of letters, *The Antiquary* (1816)

A back-formation from *defend,* which in turn is from the Latin *defendere,* to ward off, to offer resistance. All the associated metaphors contain this element of defence, for example "to fend off," "to fend for oneself."

"Fenders" are the seaman's method of protecting the sides of a vessel from being scraped or crushed by another vessel or a wharf due to the movement of the sea. They are usually portable and are taken in when the vessel is underway; used especially when coming alongside. They come in many shapes and sizes, but most commonly they are constructed from cork, coir matting, old rope, rubber tires, planks, and other shock-absorbing materials. *To fend a vessel off* is to push it off or keep it at a distance using a pole, spar, boathook, or the like, in the same way a rugby player uses his arm to fend off an attacking opponent.

Fetch

"Fetch me, I pray thee, a little water."
—1 Kings 17:10

From the Anglo-Saxon *fetian,* to go and bring; related to our modern word *foot.*

To be farfetched

Fetch (from the Anglo-Saxon *fetian, feccan,* from *foet,* a pace, a step) is the term that describes the distance of open water traversed by waves or wind; the longer the fetch, the higher the waves. A long fetch produces a long sea, where there is a greater distance between each wave than there is in a short

> "Like a shifted wind unto a sail
> It makes the course of thoughts
> to fetch about."
> —William Shakespeare (1564–1616),
> *King John,* act 4, scene 2

fetch. Similarly, fetch is also the distance a vessel must sail to reach open water. Colloquially, *to be farfetched* suggests that a tale or explanation is a long way from the truth or the facts: "His reason for being late for dinner sounded a bit farfetched to his wife."

To fetch up

To arrive at, to reach, to come to a destination; also to bring to a sudden stop; to reach a goal or final state: "You'll fetch up in prison if you don't change your ways."

> "We shall fetch to windward of
> the lighthouse this tack."
> —William Falconer (1732–1769),
> English poet, sailor, and lexicographer,
> *Universal Dictionary of the Marine* (1780)

Nautically, fetch is the area of sea surface over which the sea or swell is generated. The term embodies the concept of distance traveled before coming to a stop.
(See also *Fetch; To be farfetched.)*

Fiddle
To work a fiddle

To work a fiddle is to be dishonest, to cheat; as with the purser in the old sailing navy illegally selling the best of the ship's stores for his own gain, or a bosun stealing an item of gear, such as a new rope, taking it ashore secretly, and there selling it. The practices were many and devious; the losers in the long run were of course the crew, who inevitably found themselves on short rations or inferior victuals, using substandard gear (sometimes dangerously so), and so on. The expression is widely used ashore in exactly the same sense: "For many years the head cleaner was working a fiddle by selling some of his materials to a friend in the wholesale business."

The nautical usage probably derives from the "fiddle block," a pair of blocks fashioned together so that one (the larger) lies below, and joined to, the other. Perhaps the idea of movement and adjustment between the two blocks suggested the slang expression.

There is also "Fiddler's Green," the sailor's paradise, where all the accoutrements to a sailor's well-being are available in plenty: public houses, dance halls, and willing ladies. It existed as a sort of sailor's concept of heaven, but it is said that a number of places ashore were closely related to this ideal.

The "fiddler," of course, is the musician, found on many an old sailing ship, who provided the music (often on a simple fiddle and sometimes on a battered accordion) for the sea chanties that the seamen sang to the heave and haul of raising anchor, hoisting sail, and so on. The expression *to work a fiddle* might derive from the sailor's constant desire to frequent these palaces of delight, even if it was only a temporary respite provided by the sometimes impossible promises of his more graphic chanties.

The word is an old one, from the Anglo-Saxon *fithele,* fiddle, and bears some relationship to the Medieval Latin

vidula or *vitula* and to the Italian *viola;* hence our English name *fiddle* for that instrument.
(See also *Fiddler's Green.)*

Fiddler's Green The happy land that exists in the imagination of sailors, where there is perpetual mirth, with a fiddle that never stops playing for sailors who never tire of dancing, much grog, plenty of tobacco, and many amiable women: in short, a nautical nirvana. This seaman's paradise had an earthly equivalent in the delights to be found in such famous seaports as Wapping (in the east end of London), Portsmouth, San Francisco, Sydney, Shanghai, and others.
(See also *Fiddley.)*

Fiddley Now an idiom meaning difficult or exacting, such as a delicate task carried out with the hands. From a nautical term that referred to the iron grating to be found over an engine or stokehold on a steamship, so as to let the hot air and fumes escape.

Fiddle occurs in a number of nautical usages: the saloon table had "fiddles" (a rack or battern) on it to prevent crockery, cutlery, and such from sliding to the deck as the ship pitched and rolled; the "fiddle-head" is the carved scrollwork at the bow, similar to the scrolled end of a violin; and there was the "fiddler," who sat on a rail by the mainmast to play the shanty tunes to the men as they worked ship.

From the Anglo-Saxon *fithele,* the Medieval Latin *vidula* or *vitula,* and also the Italian *viola,* all associated with quick reduplicated movements of the hands.
(See also *Fiddler's Green.)*

Fiddly See *Fiddley.*

Field day This is another of those terms widely used ashore without its nautical origin ever being guessed at by landlubbers. It refers to the activity of cleaning up above and below deck, usually in readiness for an inspection, and might involve polishing, painting, or scrubbing any of the ship's gear.

"The field-day or the drill,
Seems less important now."
—Sir Walter Scott (1771–1832), Scottish man of letters, *Marmion* (1808)

It was part of the seaman's nature to be tidy and efficient in his daily work (his life and the lives of his shipmates depended wholly on his ability to work his ship properly and with due care), and he tended to be just as tidy and efficient in his personal habits. Seamen took inordinate pride in their ship, it being a matter of great honour to them never to permit another vessel to disgrace their own when it came to matters of appearance and conduct.

Field day has gone over into colloquial English to mean an enjoyable time or a successful event or outing. "She had

a field day in the shops when she went out to spend her year's clothing budget all at once."
(See also *Make; To make and mend. Tiddley.)*

Fights
To be in the fights

Fights were the wide strips of canvas that were rigged above the sides (the bulwarks) of a man-of-war before she went into action. The intention was to conceal the seamen working on the deck from the sharpshooters stationed in the masts and rigging of the enemy ships. These strips of canvas were also known as "waist-cloths," because the waist of the vessel was where the crew were assembled at their posts. The fights or waist-cloths were abandoned by the end of the sixteenth century because they were a serious fire hazard during battle.

"Who ever saw a noble sight,
That never viewed a brave sea-fight!
Hang up your bloody colours in the air,
Up with your fights and your nettings prepare."
—John Dryden (1631–1700), English poet, *Amboyna* (1673)

To be in the fights was to be in the thick of things, as the enemy's guns and marksmen poured their fire into the general deck area anyway. Colloquially, the expression carries the same meaning: to be at the centre of the action, to be closely involved in a quarrel or struggle, to be at battle (either literally or figuratively). "He looks as though he has been in the fights ever since he became chairman of the finance committee." Often also expressed, especially of children, as *to be in the wars.*
(See also *Close quarters; To be at close quarters.)*

Figurehead

A carved figure, usually human (but also very often animal), fixed on the stem high in the bows, just beneath the bowsprit; earlier and more accurately written as two words, "figure head." This was because shipping registry firms such as Lloyd's and Bureau Veritas used to describe vessels in terms of their rig, tonnage, dimensions, port of registry, and so on; their type of stern (round, square, counter, etc.); and the type of head the vessel had, that is, whether it was decorated with a figure of some kind and, if so, what sort.

Thus, a description of HMS *Brunswick* (late eighteenth century) would have noted that the vessel had a figurehead (the bow had a figure of some kind attached to it); in this instance, a carving of the Duke of Brunswick wearing a cocked hat and kilt. (When the cocked hat was shot away during an engagement in the battle known as the Glorious First of June in 1794, the crew expressed so much concern at the loss that the captain gave his own cocked hat for the carpenter to nail to the head of the hatless duke.)

The figurehead was intended as a decorative emblem that expressed some aspect of the ship's name or function. Its origin is probably both religious and personal, in a milieu where a ship was treated as a living thing. Perhaps the most famous of figureheads in the U.S. Navy was that of the USS *Constitution* (launched 1797, one of the six original frigates authorised by Congress in 1794), which in later years proudly carried at her bow a full figure of President Jackson.

Eyes were an important part of all figureheads, in the belief that the ship needed to be able to see her way across the waters. Many local fishing vessels in the Mediterranean paint a set of eyes on the bows of their vessels as an aid to seeking out shoals of fish. The religious element arose from the sailors' felt need to propitiate the deities of the sea. The forms figureheads took included lions, birds, horses, boars, warriors, swans, dragons, and saints.

Figureheads of females gradually became the most popular form of decoration, which is a rather interesting development because women were considered by seamen to be very unlucky to have on board ship. Nevertheless, a naked woman—or at least the naked upper half of a woman—was supposed to be able to calm a storm at sea, presumably because the gods of the sea were invariably thought of as being male, and therefore could be somewhat charmed and mollified by the sight of a beautiful woman.

Figureheads as a decorative maritime art have almost disappeared in the twentieth century; only a few vessels—predominantly one or two Scandinavian lines—carry a figurehead of the traditional style. Perhaps the best known figurehead in recent English maritime literature is that of the *Cutty Sark,* the famous tea-clipper built in 1869. This vessel survives, fully restored, in dry dock on the Thames. Its figurehead is Nannie the witch, in flowing garments, reaching forward with outstretched arms. The story is told in the poem "Tam O'shanter" by Robert Burns (1759–1796).

Tam O'shanter, a young Scottish farmer, had late one Halloween night come upon the young and beautiful witch Nannie and her companions dancing in a clearing in the forest. He edged nearer in order to see them better, knowing full well that, according to Celtic legend, it would be a serious matter if he were discovered spying on the cavorting figures. Nannie, however, caught sight of Tam and in a fearful rage lunged toward him; the young man, frightened almost out of his wits, leapt onto Meg, his terrified horse, and galloped for his life with Nannie in hot pursuit. Fast as Meg was, she was almost not fast enough; Nannie's outstretched hands managed to grasp the end of Meg's tail and pull it off; horse and rider then bolted for freedom through the midnight forest.

One moral that can be drawn from this story is that we may "pay too dear for our whistle," a reference to a story told by Benjamin Franklin (1706–1790), an American

author, inventor, printer, publisher, scientist, and diplomat, often called "the first civilised American." Franklin told the tale of his nephew who, desperate to acquire an ordinary tin whistle, bought one from another boy for four times its value. In the same way, Tam O'shanter—through his hairbreadth escape and the loss of his horse's tail—paid dearly for his pleasure in spying on Nannie and her companions. Burns gives us these lines of poetry:

> Think, ye may buy the joys owre dear—
> Remember Tam O'shanter's mare.

Captain Jock Willis had the *Cutty Sark* built in 1869 as a challenge to the British clipper *Thermopylae;* he intended to enter the tea trade with the China coast and it was his ambition to beat the *Thermopylae,* probably the fastest sailing clipper ever built. Captain Willis also owned the *Tweed,* another very fine and fast clipper, whose lines Willis used as the basis for the *Cutty Sark.* Willis was an ardent admirer of Burns, and for the figurehead of the *Tweed* he installed a bust of Tam O'shanter, the young Scottish farmer.

It seemed logical, then, for Willis to name his new vessel the *Cutty Sark,* both for the sure, revengeful swiftness that Nannie had shown in her midnight chase and to symbolise the proud literary connection between his two vessels (you will not be surprised to learn that Captain Willis also owned the *Halloween).* He had the figurehead of Nannie mounted on the cutwater, immediately under the bowsprit; it then became customary for seamen to put a piece of frayed rope in her hands, as a symbol of the fact that the ship would overtake every other rival.

It is not widely known that Captain Willis's *Cutty Sark* was not the first sailing ship to bear that name. Just before he built his famous vessel in 1869, there was another *Cutty Sark* trading on the Australian coast between Melbourne and Darwin; not much is known about her except that she disappeared in 1867, probably in one of the cyclones that occasionally ravage these northern coasts during the summer months, between November and February.

The name *Cutty Sark* refers to the short shift or shirt worn by Nannie on that occasion:

> Her cutty sark, o' Paisley harn
> That while a lassie she had worn
> In longitude tho' sorely scanty
> It was her best, and she was vauntie.

Loosely translated, this reads: "Her shift was made from very coarse Paisley linen and she had worn it since she was a very young girl; it was rather short in length, but it was her best garment and she was somewhat vain about it."

Metaphorically, a figurehead is a person who is nominally the head of a society or community; an apparent leader, but one who in fact plays no real part in leading; without real authority or responsibility, but nevertheless a person whose social, academic, or other position inspires confidence. From the fact that the shipboard figurehead was visible, out front, at the head of things, attracting attention and perhaps admiration, while the real business of conducting the ship across the waters went on elsewhere: "He was installed as managing director of the firm, but it was well known that he was merely a figurehead: the real authority lay with the company secretary."
(See also *Superstitions.)*

Filibuster

Filibuster is from the Dutch *vrijbuiter* and the Spanish *filibustero,* freebooter, which in 1790 came into English by way of the French form *flibustier,* and later in 1850 as *filibuster;* it is the old name by which buccaneers or pirates were originally known in Britain. Literally, it meant one who obtained his plunder or booty free.

> "The gold-diggers and the Mormons, the slaves and the slaveholders, and the flibustiers. . . ."
> —Henry David Thoreau (1817–1862), American poet and philosopher, letter in the *Atlantic Monthly,* vol. 72 (1893)

In the nineteenth century, the term described the bands of raiders who operated out of the United States in their efforts to invade and revolutionise certain Spanish-American territories in the Caribbean. At about the same time, the phrase came into use in the United States to mean the use of obstructive tactics in the legislature, as a derivation from the original idea of raiding and blockading. "His favourite tactic was to filibuster the opposition with a five-hour tirade in which he vigorously supported the values of free speech in a democracy."
(See also *Booty. Pirate.)*

Finger
Get your finger out

A time-honoured, if vulgar, colloquialism, much used in English speech. It means to hurry, to get on with it, to look alive, don't be so stand-offish. The expression is, more immediately, a warning to be less stuck up; don't be so absorbed in oneself (less delicately rendered by "pull your finger out"); take note of what is going on: "The boss told the delivery van driver that if he didn't pull his finger out he would find himself without a job."

The expression dates from the days of muzzle-loading cannon on board ship. When the powder and shot were being wadded home into the breech, one of the gunners would hold his thumb over the vent hole so that oxygen from the outside air could not enter the chamber and ignite the hot gases from previous firings. When all was ready, he was ordered to "get his finger out"; any slowness at this point would probably mean getting his fingers burnt from the slow-match that was applied to the vent hole to ignite the gunpowder.

The indelicacy of the expression springs from the fact that a stand-offish person is said to be interested only in himself, as if he has his finger inserted in his own vent hole.

Fire
To hang fire To delay, to be irresolute, to be slow in taking action, to hold back. From gunnery, when for whatever reason the gun is slow in firing the charge. (Other metaphors from the era of powder firearms include "a flash in the pan" and "lock, stock, and barrel," although of course these are not nautical in origin.) "Because of the uncertain economic times, our plans for expansion will have to hang fire for a while."

Fishy A bit suspicious, improbable, of questionable character. Of obvious derivation: from the telltale odour of fish that are going bad, thus giving rise to suspicions as to a thing's freshness or authenticity: "His wild enthusiasm for that particular brand of computer sounds a bit fishy to me; his wife works for the company that makes them."

From the language of fishermen; other idioms include "a big fish (in a small pond)," "drink like a fish," "to fish in troubled waters," "to have other fish to fry," "like a fish out of water," "a queer fish," "there are plenty more fish in the sea," and "a pretty kettle of fish."

Fitting-out The general preparation needed to make a ship in all respects ready for sea; installing masts, rigging, anchors, cables, boats, and other gear so as to make her seaworthy. In the case of a vessel that has been out of service or laid up for a considerable period, a major refit may be necessary.

The term has long been adopted by the language to apply to other areas of endeavour, and curiously the word-order has usually been inverted, as in "gentleman's outfitters," "a camping outfit," and so on. (In the United States, of course, an *outfit* can be anything from a pocket knife to a railway company.) "His fishing boat was fitted out with the latest echo-sounding equipment."

Fix
To be in a fix

A fix is the determination of a ship's position at sea by referring to any visible landmarks; by using electronic methods, such as radio or radar; or by taking sights of various heavenly bodies, such as the sun or the moon, and using tables to work out a position. A good or reliable fix was one where a number of position lines met in a small triangular space known as a "cocked hat"; the smaller the cocked hat, the more reliable the fix.

In the sense that a small cocked hat limited the possibilities for a ship to be other than in that triangular space on the chart, so colloquially *to be in a fix* is to be limited in one's ability to manoeuvre, to be in difficulties. "He realised that he was in a fix when his bank insisted on repayment of the loan that he had foolishly squandered at the race track."

Flag

"Their drowsy, slow,
and flagging wings
Clip dead men's graves. . . ."
—William Shakespeare (1564–1616), *Henry VI, Part 2,* act 4, scene 1

The word *flag* is of uncertain origin; it may be related to "flap" as an imitative sound, which in turn might derive from the Dutch *flappen,* to clap, imitating the typical sound of cloth slapping in a breeze.

Flags have been associated with sailing ships since the earliest times, and many nautical expressions to do with flags have evolved over the years. Some of those that have entered the language as colloquialisms are: "flag of convenience," "flag of distress," "to have the flags out," "to hoist the flag," "to keep the flag flying," "to show the flag," "to strike the flag," among others. Some of these are discussed in the following entries.

A flag of convenience

This refers to the twentieth-century practice of registering ships in certain small countries (such as Liberia or Panama) for the sole purpose of avoiding the taxes levied in the shipowner's country. It frequently happens that the lifesaving equipment and crew's conditions are markedly inferior on such vessels, compared with those registered with the traditional maritime nations: "The Australian brewing company registered their head office in the Cook Islands solely as a flag of convenience, to escape federal income tax charges."

A flag of distress

When a ship's ensign is flown upside down, it is an internationally recognised signal of distress. An interesting story involving this practice is told by A. Cecil Hampshire (see bibliography) concerning an incident in a treaty port in China in pre–World War II days.

A British navy gunboat had arrived in the harbour, to find a British merchant ship at anchor with no ensign flying. As the gunboat anchored, the merchantman hoisted her Red Ensign, but it was upside down. The gunboat captain sent off a motorboat to investigate, with armed sailors concealed below decks.

When the gunboat came alongside the merchant ship, the British sailors quickly boarded the ship and rounded up several Chinese seamen, many of whom were armed. All of them proved to be pirates. The chief engineer of the merchant ship, a British seaman, then explained that he had persuaded his Chinese captors to let him hoist the ship's ensign because the gunboat's captain would become suspicious if there were no flag on the merchantman. He had banked on the pirates' not knowing the significance of a flag's being flown upside down.

Nowadays, yachters and boaters sometimes inadvertently set off search and rescue operations when, in ignorance, they fly their flags the wrong way up.

To fly the flag at half mast It was long the custom for vessels to indicate mourning for a death on board, or for the death of a national figure, by flying the flag at half the height of its usual hoist—i.e., at half mast. This is also known as "flying the flag at the dip"; *to dip a flag* is to haul it down to the half-mast position and then rehoist it. This is the usual salute between ships at sea.

It is now a well-established custom ashore to fly the flag at half mast to signal mourning for the death of a well-known figure; this is done by governmental, semigovernmental, and commercial bodies, and often by private individuals who own a flag and flagpole. The nautical reason for flying a flag of mourning at half mast is to leave room above for the (invisible) flag of Death: "He was a figure of fun to his friends because he always wore trousers that were so short they seemed to be at half mast."

To lower one's flag To yield, to surrender, to confess oneself defeated or in the wrong; to eat humble pie; sometimes expressed as "to haul down one's flag."
(See also *Flag; To strike the flag.)*

To nail one's flag to the mast Flags are particularly important as a means of recognising the nationality of ships at sea. The earliest record of flags being used as a system of communication at sea is in 1653, when a small number of different flags were used according to an agreed scheme. *To nail one's flag to the mast* was clearly and firmly to display a ship's nationality and intentions as she was sailed into battle by a determined commander.

Similarly, as a figure of speech one *nails one's flag to the mast* when one makes it clear that a certain plan of action has been decided upon and that, come what may, one is going to do one's utmost to carry it out: "She nailed her flag to the mast in the dispute by advertising her intentions in the local paper."
(See also *Colours; To come in with flying colours.)*

To show the white flag Originally, the white flag was used when prisoners were being exchanged, especially by vessels that carried out the exchange between the opposing sides. These vessels—called "cartel ships"—displayed a white flag, and this became internationally recognised as the sign of a temporary truce, or cessation of hostilities. Gradually it also came to include the intention to surrender, so that *to show the white flag* now means that one party to the dispute wishes to lay down its arms and surrender.

To show the flag means to make one's presence known. In the days of empire, it was common for British warships to visit foreign ports to remind the relevant authorities that England still exercised considerable world power. The colloquial usage follows much the same intent: "We feel that since all the other insurance companies will be represented at the conference, someone from this firm should go along to show the flag."
(See also *Cartel.)*

To strike the flag To lower one's flag completely, as a token of surrender.
(See also *Colours; To lower one's colours. Flag; To nail one's flag to the mast. Sail; To strike sail/to strike the colours.)*

Flake
To flake out; to be flaked out

To flake down a rope is to coil it on deck in a figure-of-eight so that it will run out without twisting or kinking; often used for preparing the anchor rope or a halliard for immediate use. *To flake out* in the colloquial sense is to lie down for a rest, usually after physical exertion of some kind. The allusion is to the limpness of the body, likened to that of the loosely coiled rope (the sometimes-used alternative, "to fake-down a line," is generally unknown at sea). "I rush about so much during the day that I simply flake out as soon as I get home in the evening."

American usage suggests someone who fails to do a job quite properly, either as a deliberate ploy or because of an inability to understand; such a person is regarded as being flighty, unreliable, or, in the vernacular, a "flake." Someone who is "flaky" is a bit eccentric, unconventional, perhaps even haywire.

Flannel

"Of all his gains by verse he could not save
Enough to purchase flannel and a grave."

—John Oldham (1653–1683), English satirist, *Satire against Virtue* (1681)

Sailor's slang, meaning nonsense or rubbish; often applied to a long-winded or meaningless speech. *To flannel through* is to talk or bluff one's way out of an awkward situation. Flannel is also an ingratiating manner, an insincere speech or pep talk, the equivalent of "soft soaping" someone. The slang term probably derives from the introduction of flannel material as cold-weather clothing for seamen; the comfort of the warm fabric was likened to the intended comfort or reassurance of the flattering speech: "The political candidate's address to the pensioners was a load of old flannel." Charles II decreed that, as a means of promoting the wool trade in Britain, all coffins should be lined with flannel.

Flat

In the British Commonwealth countries, a suite of rooms forming a complete residence; often rented, and usually found on one floor only. From the name given to the open spaces between decks, such as the "tiller flat," "sick-bay flat," and so on. A Scottish contribution to English from the Anglo-Saxon *flett,* floor, dwelling: "They rented a flat in the city to escape the attentions of the press." Americans would normally use *apartment,* a word equally understood and used in this sense elsewhere in the English-speaking world.

Flaw (of wind)

"And he watched how the veering flaw did blow."

—Henry Wadsworth Longfellow (1807–1882), American poet, *The Wreck of the Hesperus* (1841)

Found in the Scandinavian languages; for example, the Norwegian *flaga,* gust of wind or rain. Commonly used by seamen, especially in reference to wind; in particular, the sudden, vicious gusts of wind that hurtle down from the mountains in the Straits of Magellan were known by the early explorers as *flaws.*
(See also *Flurry.)*

Fleet

A company of vessels sailing together; a national fleet (such as Germany's "High Seas Fleet" of World War I), or a portion of it (for example, Russia's "Black Sea Fleet"). From the Old English *fleotan,* to float. The word can also encompass all the vessels owned by a shipping company, fishing vessels operating out of one port, those owned by one company, and so on. The word has been adopted in everyday usage to mean a number of aeroplanes, buses, cars, trucks, etc., moving or operating in company: "The taxi company has equipped its whole fleet with 'No Smoking' signs."

"Within sextene dayes hys fleet whas assemblede."

—*Mort d'Arthur,* cited in the *Universal Dictionary of the English Language* (1897)

From the Anglo-Saxon *fleot,* a bay of the sea; literally, a place where ships float.

Flensing To strip blubber from a dead whale. Also "flench" and "flinch," as well as "flense"; from the Danish *flense,* to strip.
(See also *Cut; To cut in.)*

Flimsy Originally a certificate of conduct issued in the Royal Navy by the ship's captain to an officer on the termination of his appointment and his subsequent transfer to another appointment. The report or certificate was written on thin paper, and the name *flimsy* derives from the word *film.* A *flimsy* today usually refers to any very thin paper, particularly the kind used by journalists when they prepare their copy for the press. A flimsy excuse is a story that one has great difficulty in believing: "His account of the reason for his defeat in the election contest seems very flimsy to me."

"Those flimsy webs, that break as soon as wrought, Attain not to the dignity of thought."
—William Cowper (1731–1800), English poet, *Retirement* (1782)

Flip A drink once greatly favoured among seamen, introduced in the late seventeenth century. It is a mixture of beer, spirits, and sugar, the whole brew being heated with a red-hot iron, as is mulled wine. The more modern refreshment *eggflip* derives from the nautical drink; it is made from milk containing a raw whipped egg, sugar, and sometimes flavouring to taste.

Float
To float a loan Of apparent nautical parentage, although it is unlikely to have had much, if any, nautical usage. *To float a loan* is to set about getting or acquiring a sum of money as a loan; the force of *to float* lies in the idea of the loan being launched, set afloat, ready to be used: "We finally managed to float a loan with the state bank for our water-purifying plant."

Flog A slang word derived from the Latin *flagellare,* to beat. Flogging is one of the oldest forms of punishment for serious crimes in the sailing navy; it was not uncommon for seamen to be flogged for quite petty offences. *Flogging round the fleet* consisted of rowing the victim alongside every ship lying in harbour, where he was given 12 strokes of the cat-o'-nine-tails by the bosun's mate on each vessel.

In the Royal Navy, the law fixed a limit on the maximum number of strokes a man could receive, but some captains—known universally as "master under God"—exceeded these limits and made reputations for themselves as vicious disciplinarians. It was not unheard of for a seaman to be awarded 500 lashes, sometimes at once, sometimes in instalments. The victims usually died of bodily shock or massive infection, from the fact that the cat with its nine knotted thongs was always encrusted with the gore of its work, so that sepsis was inevitable. Flogging became less frequent after the mutiny of the *Nore* in 1797, and was made an illegal punishment early in the nineteenth century.

"How he was flogged or had the luck to escape. . . ."
—William Cowper (1731–1800), English poet, *Tirocinium,* cited in the *Universal Dictionary of the English Language* (1897)

Colloquially, *to flog* is to sell or attempt to sell; also to steal, often with the purpose of selling the stolen item. Found also in expressions to do with speed, haste, or urgency: "The decrepit old Land Rover came flogging across the paddock in fine style." The connection with the nautical usage is that the metaphors preserve the sense of earnest application, of a single-minded carrying-out of a task, that was necessarily once a gruesome part of flogging on board ship.
(See also *Horse; To flog a dead horse.)*

Flotilla From the Spanish *flota,* fleet, thence the diminutive *flotilla,* little fleet, a squadron of small ships, generally under the collective command of a captain; *squadron* has now replaced the term *flotilla.* We sometimes speak colloquially of a flotilla of ducks or swans on the water.

Flotsam Originally strictly nautical, and today still closely associated with the sea. *Flotsam* (from the Old French *floter,* to float) refers to goods accidentally lost overboard, or articles of cargo or wreckage that may float up from the hull of a wrecked vessel. The term *jetsam* (from the French *jeter,* to throw out) describes any goods or gear deliberately thrown overboard for the purpose of lightening ship in an emergency. Both terms described goods and wreckage found at sea; they now apply more widely to wreckage cast up on shore.

"Flotsam is where goods continue swimming on the surface of the waves."
—Sir William Blackstone (1723–1780), English jurist, *Commentaries on the Laws of England* (1765–1769)

In a general sense, *flotsam and jetsam* refers to the aftermath of some event, such as the litter from a party or picnic, where a sense of wreckage is implied: "The immigrants who arrived on the shores of Australia throughout the 1950s were the flotsam and jetsam of the war in Europe."

It is noteworthy that one of the earliest meanings of *swim,* from the Anglo-Saxon *swimman,* was to float, to be borne up by the water. The term is used in this manner in Shakespeare's *As You Like It:* ". . . or I will scarce think you have swam in a gondola." Even as late as Nelson's time (1758–1805), it was very common for seamen to speak of the way a vessel *swims.*
(See also *Jettison.)*

Fluky Describes a wind that is light and variable in direction, one that has not settled down to blow steadily from any one particular direction. Derived from an English dialect's *fluke,* a guess, but not related to the whale fluke nor to the flukes of an anchor. We use the expression to describe something obtained by chance rather than by skill; what we call a *fluke.* From the Anglo-Saxon *floc,* a flatfish; in the early 1800s, *flat* was a slang word for someone easily taken in, gulled, hoodwinked. By extension, the element of chance became attached to *fluke:* "It was by a mere fluke that she won the spelling competition."

Flurry

"The boat was overset by a sudden flurry from the north."
—Jonathan Swift (1667–1745), English cleric and man of letters, *Gulliver's Travels* (1726)

Originally, in nautical usage, a sudden squall; connected with an obsolete Old English word *flurr,* to scatter. Also used by seamen to describe the death-struggle of the whale when it has been lanced, following the initial harpooning. Now used to mean a rush of emotion or excitement, confusion or nervous hurry, as well as a light gust of wind, snow, leaves, etc.: "Her boss's unexpected arrival at mealtime put her into a nervous flurry in the kitchen."
(See also *Flaw [of wind].)*

Fly
To let fly

From the Anglo-Saxon *fleogan,* common in the Teutonic languages, and related to the Latin *pluma;* not cognate with the English *flee.* The phrase *to let fly* is nautical in origin, and it means to let go instantly, without hesitation; usually with reference to the sheets of a sailing vessel, and always in an emergency. Figuratively, *to let fly* is to throw something suddenly or sharply; or to strike a blow with the fist, without warning, usually in anger and under provocation; or to give vent to a sudden burst of temper, usually as a result of provocation of some kind: "When she accused him of being unfaithful to her, he let fly with a torrent of abuse."

Fly-by-night

A "fly-by-night" was an extra sail, set in the manner of a studding sail (pronounced "stuns'l"), but in a more temporary arrangement, rather than permanently. Sometimes a spare jib was used, being sheeted from the masthead to an upper yardarm. Fly-by-nights were used in the eighteenth and early nineteenth centuries. The one-horse hackney-carriage, known also as a "fly-by-night" (or "fly," for short), did not come into use until 1809, thus long postdating the seaman's use of the term.

Colloquially, a secret departure for parts unknown; also the name given to a very dubious character, one who is irresponsible and unreliable. The connection between the nautical usage and the metaphor is probably that the temporary fly-by-night sail was used when it was desired that the ship be kept moving; for example, in light airs, or—even more appropriately—in time of danger, as when threatened by an enemy vessel, a lee shore, and so on: "You should always be cautious about doing business with fly-by-night companies."

Flying Dutchman One of the most famous legends of the sea. The story goes that a Dutch captain on a voyage home from Batavia persisted in trying to round the Cape of Good Hope in the face of a howling gale. His refusal to acknowledge God's wrath (manifested in the form of the gale) condemned him to go on sailing for all eternity in his attempt to reach Table Bay. A strong superstition among sailors is that anyone who sets eyes on the vessel will die by shipwreck. Occasionally said of the reappearance ashore of some person or thing that had long since been thought dead and gone; usually in a jocular rather than serious manner.
(See also *Mary Celeste.*)

Footloose Colloquially, to be *footloose* is to be free of all responsibilities and all ties, and to be able to travel about at will; a degree of irresponsibility is implied by the term, but this is not a necessary characteristic.

The expression derives from the loose-footed sail that was common in certain fore-and-aft-rigged craft, where the sail was set without a boom (such as in the mainsail of a barge). A loose-footed sail could also be set on a boom but with only the tack and the clew secured.

A loose-footed sail could sometimes be very difficult to control, especially if it was not attached to a boom at the tack and clew; hence the force of the expression *to be footloose:* "Jack Kerouac won for himself a reputation as a writer through his vivid descriptions of his footloose life on the road across America in the immediate postwar years."

Forecastle Always pronounced, and often written, "fo'c'sle" or "foc'sle" (pronounced "foke-s'l"), but never as "fo'castle." The foreward part of the upper deck, extending from the beakhead (or bowsprit) to the foremast or to just aft of the foremast.

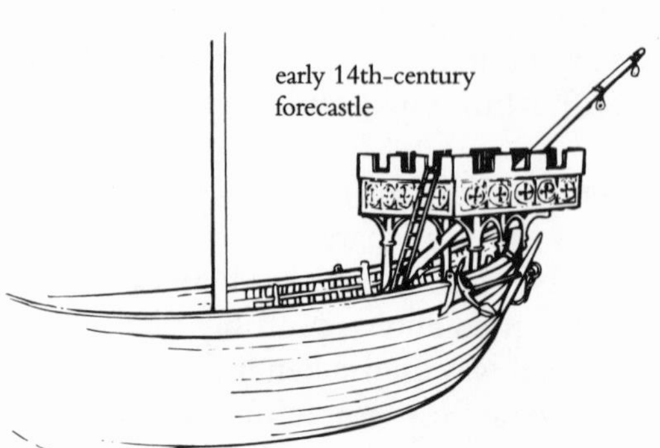

In navy and merchant vessels, the forecastle was for hundreds of years the seamen's quarters; officers and petty officers were quartered in the aft sections of the vessel. The word became synonymous with seamen in general (crew other than officers). Included here because the forecastle was the breeding ground for so much of the colourful nautical language that has, over the centuries, been adopted into our everyday speech.

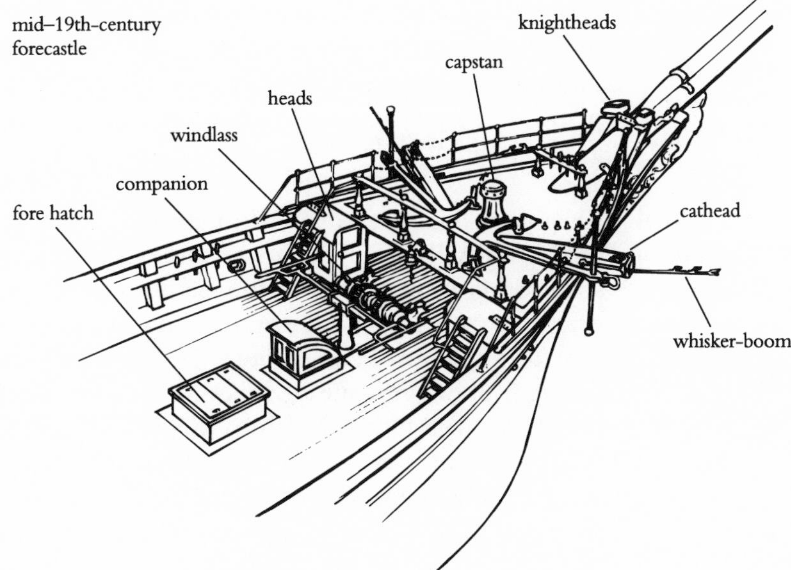

The origin of the word *forecastle* lies in the fact that, in the oldest ships, a wooden castle was built up over the bows. Archers were stationed in this fortified area to attack the crews of enemy vessels and to prevent boarders from entering the waist of their own vessel. The forecastle disappeared with the changing art of warfare at sea, in particular with the advent of shipborne cannon.

"The superstitions of the forecastle. . . ."
—Thomas Babington Macaulay (1800–1859), English essayist and historian, *History of England* (1848)

To be up in the forecastle is to be angry or annoyed about something, and seemingly charging ahead into an argument like a ship ploughing into stormy seas.

Foreign devil The common epithet earlier given by the Chinese to all foreigners of Anglo-Saxon stock, as opposed to their own celestial ancestry. The expression is a mistranslation of *yang-kiwei,* ocean ghost, a name given to the Dutch seamen who first ventured to the shores of China; their fair hair and pale faces appeared ghostly to the Chinese. Under the present Chinese government's cautious embrace of Western capitalist economic measures, it is unlikely that any politically aware Chinese citizen would today refer to a foreign guest as a "foreign devil"—certainly not within the hearing of any party official, anyway. The expression is still sometimes encountered in literature; certainly the author of this book was known as a foreign devil during his sojourn in Singapore and Penang in the 1960s.

Forge
To forge ahead; to forge over

A vessel was said "to forge ahead" when she was moving rapidly under a full press of canvas. She "forged over" when she was forced to sail over a shoal or bar that momentarily checked her progress. *Forge* is from the sailor's earlier pronunciation of "force." Colloquially, *to forge ahead* is to

"To forge over is to force a ship violently over a shoal by the effort of a great quantity of sail."
—William Falconer (1732–1769), English seaman and lexicographer, *An Universal Dictionary of the Marine* (1780)

carry on with one's purpose and direction, often with renewed vigour; *to forge over* is to press on regardless of hindrances. "Despite the many setbacks to her day-to-day plans, she forged ahead with her intention to build a career as an architect."

Foul
To fall foul of

"If they be any ways offended they fall foul."
—Robert Burton (1577–1640), *The Anatomy of Melancholy* (1621)

Originally a nautical expression, meaning to become entangled with, as an anchor becomes fouled by a wreck or some other obstruction on the sea bottom. Used in everyday speech as an idiom meaning to collide with, crash into, to quarrel or be in dispute with: "He has a knack of falling foul of everyone he meets." From the Anglo-Saxon *ful* and derived ultimately from the Sanskrit *pu,* to stink.

A "foul bottom" is the condition experienced by virtually all vessels, when seaweed and barnacles grow so profusely as to seriously impede the ship's way through the water. For example, the sailing ship *Daylight* reached Philadelphia early this century after a five-month voyage, and she was put into dry dock to have 40 tons of barnacles scraped from her bottom.

Found
To be well-found

"The present consul, and last general
In our well-found successes. . . ."
—William Shakespeare (1564–1616), *Coriolanus,* act 5, scene 2

To be well-found is for a vessel to be well equipped and well supplied with food, stores, spare sails, and all other necessities for efficient operation. In a similar sense, an argument, opinion, or attitude is *well-found* if it is based on careful forethought, planning, and preparation. From the Latin *fundus,* bottom. "His suspicion that she detested Indian music proved to be well-founded when she refused to attend the concert with him."

Founder

A vessel founders when it fills with water and sinks as a result of damage or flooding; colloquially, an enterprise founders when it fails or goes bankrupt; the idea of wreck is common to both usages. From the Old French *enfondrir,* to engulf, sink: "The old firm foundered because the board of management failed to use modern business methods."

"The ship no longer foundering by the lee,
Bears on her side th' invasion of the sea."
—William Falconer (1732–1769), English seaman and lexicographer, *The Shipwreck* (1762)

One of the most famous founderings in history was that of the *Mary Rose,* built for Henry VIII early in the sixteenth century. In 1545, she sailed out from Portsmouth to engage the French, was immediately swamped through her lower deck gunports, and quickly sank, with the loss of nearly all her complement of 400. Her hull was discovered by divers in 1968.

Frank

One of the earliest meanings of *frank* had to do with sailors' description of a wind that was steady and free

"Thou hast it won; for it is of frank gift
And he will care for all the rest to shift."

—Edmund Spenser (?1552–1599), English poet, *Mother Hubberd's Tale,* cited in the *Universal Dictionary of the English Language* (1897)

(a *free wind* was one that allowed the vessel to sail its course under an easy press of sail, without steering difficulties). The word is of Latin origin, *francus,* meaning free, descriptive of the Frankish (Germanic) tribes of early Europe, known for their independent, if also warlike, spirit and love of freedom (it was these people who conquered Gaul in the sixth century A.D. and gave their name to France). The name passed into Arabic as *ferenghi,* foreigner, "of the Franks."

Fraught
To be fraught with danger

"A vessel of our country, richly fraught. . . ."

—William Shakespeare (1564–1616), *The Merchant of Venice,* act 2, scene 8

Fraught is from *freight,* which in turn is from the Old German *vracht,* freight money, earnings. Whereas freight is the cargo or merchandise carried for pay, *fraught* describes the condition of being so loaded or burdened (i.e., to be "freighted with"). In the early days of commerce by sea, ships were said to be "fraught with precious wares." To be fraught with danger, horror, or the like describes a situation or event that is attended (burdened) with that danger.

Free and easy

"Clubs of all ranks, from those which have lined Pall Mall and St. James's Street with their palaces, down to the free-and-easy which meets in the shabby parlour of a village inn."

—Thomas Babington Macaulay, (1800–1859), English essayist and historian; *History of England* (1848)

A rope or fall (a fall is the part of the rope that is to be pulled on) is "free" when it is unobstructed, unencumbered, clear for running. A sailing ship is said to be "free" when she is sailing with the wind abaft (astern of) the beam, i.e., blowing over the stern quarters. Consequently, her sheets (the ropes and tackle controlling the sails) will be eased so as to present a squarer aspect of the sails to the wind, without undue restraint from her working gear (as opposed to tacking close-hauled into the wind, often called "flogging" because of the strain imposed on the standing and running rigging and sails).

Hence the colloquialism *to be free and easy,* to be informal, casual, without restraint or hindrance; in a relaxed manner. "He had little regard for the social niceties; instead, he preferred to be perfectly free and easy with everyone he met."

Free on board

When goods are to be delivered on board ship at the seller's expense, they are said to be sold "free on board" or "FOB." These goods become the property of the buyer as soon as they arrive on board; thus, the buyer is responsible for insurance and freight charges. This system of consigning freight has undergone many changes since the earliest days of venturing cargoes abroad, but it is still widely used in the world of commerce.

Freebooter

See *Filibuster.*

Friday sail, Friday fail The seaman's belief of old that it was very unlucky to set out on a voyage on a Friday; probably from the fact of Christ's crucifixion on that day. The belief is still prevalent among sailors today.
(See also *Superstitions.)*

Gadget A small device or mechanical aid or fitting on board ship used to help get things done. Often called by the seaman a "gilguy" or "gillickie." Adopted in the round by the landsman to describe things of a similar nature. Probably from *gadge,* an early Scottish form of "gauge." (See also *Dooflicker.)*

Gaff As a spar, the upper boom of a gaff-rigged vessel. The gaff originally had a forked end so as to fit itself against the mast; other methods of attachment are also used. A gaff is also a fishing spear or pole with a hook at one end, used for securing fish. From the French *gaffe,* hook, and related to the Anglo-Saxon *gafol,* fork.

To blow out one's gaff To eat so much that one is bloated, the stomach being distended and uncomfortable. From the fact that when the peak halliard is eased, the gaff peak drops and the sail bellies out to leeward, like a balloon. The metaphor's allusion is obvious.

Gam Also "gamm." A nautical term from the nineteenth century, mainly to do with the whaling ships of that period; it means to talk, to gossip, to have a social meeting or visit between two or more sailing ships at sea *(gam* was also the whaler's word for a group or pod of whales). Once a common colloquialism in American speech and recorded in Professor Robert L. Chapman's *Thesaurus of American Slang* (New York: Harper & Row, 1989); probably due to the intense interest that Americans took in whaling in the last century. (More common synonyms today in American usage would be "bull session," "chinfest," "gabfest," "pow-wow," and "tongue-wag," to list but a few examples; all of these would be understood in much of the rest of the English-speaking world.) From the Old English *gamen,* pleasure, glee. "The two old men sat on the bench and gammed together for hours."

Gamm See *Gam.*

Gang

The word has an early nautical use in the sense of "crew," from the related Anglo-Saxon *genge,* a troop of people. The notions of direction (going), and companions (crew) are, of course, central to seafaring. *Gang* is also the old name used to describe the full set of standing rigging used to set up a mast in a square-rigged sailing vessel; even here the ground-sense of support (togetherness) is apparent.

"We works in gangs from three to five men."
—Henry Mayhew (1812–1887), English man of letters, *London Labour and the London Poor* (1862)

The common use of the word today, to mean a band or group usually working or operating together, preserves one of the earliest nautical senses, that of crew. "It was his custom to join his gang of friends at the pub every Friday evening."
(See also *Crew.)*

To gang up

From the original usage of *gang* for crew, and also related to the meaning of a ship's full set of rigging. *To gang up,* colloquially, is to combine against, to associate together for some common purpose; to form a gang. The earliest sense of grouping together for a common purpose is still found in the fisherman's "ganghooks," on which a number of hooks are arranged in a group for more efficient striking. "The players ganged up on their coach to force him to give them a day off from training."

Gangway
To make gangway

A gangway was originally the boarded way or bridge (sometimes called the "gangboard") in the old galleys, which allowed the rowers to pass from one end of the vessel to the other, as required. *Gang* is from the Old English *gang,* alley, and is related to our Modern English *go* and to the German *gehen.*

"I had hardly got into the boat, before I was told they had stolen one of the ancient stanchions from the opposite gangway, and were making off with it."
—Captain James Cook (1728–1779), navigator and explorer, *A Voyage Towards the South Pole and Round the World in 1772–1775* (1777)

In later sailing ships, the gangway came to be the platform that connected the after-deck to the fore-deck, thus allowing quick access fore and aft without the need to descend to the ship's waist. By extension, it has come to mean the movable bridge or passageway by which passengers and crew can enter or leave a ship when she is alongside a wharf or pier. The phrase is widely used as an exclamation meaning to make way, to clear a path. "The ambulance driver yelled angrily for the spectators to make gangway so that he could get to the injured cyclist."

Garland
Wedding garland

"Call him noble that was now your hate,
Him vile that was your garland."
—William Shakespeare (1564–1616), *Coriolanus,* act 1, scene 1

A custom still practised in the Royal Navy. In the eighteenth and nineteenth centuries, British warships would hoist a garland of evergreens in the rigging to indicate that shipboard discipline had been relaxed and consequently women would be allowed on board. The garland was also hoisted on the day any member of the crew was married, and this custom exists to the present time. From the Old French *garlande,* and ultimately from the Middle High German *wieren,* to adorn.

Gash Sailor's slang for meal leftovers; leavings and pickings. (A much earlier term used by seamen in the early days of sail was *manavalins,* from *manarvel,* to pilfer small stores; origin unknown.) Loosely, *gash* also means "free."

Gasket An original nautical word; it refers to the short rope used to secure a furled sail to its yard. When not in use, it is kept coiled, lying in front of the sail. Somehow this word was taken over by the machine age, to refer to the fibrous material used to make the joints and mating surfaces of engines tight against leakage (as in a head gasket of an automobile). The connection between the earlier nautical usage and the modern-day machine application is puzzling, but certainly the word was in widespread use at sea in the early 1600s.

The word is from the French *garcette,* rope's end; the modern-day meaning, as a joint packing, may derive from the early use of rope and asbestos fibre in making engine stuffing-boxes and propellor-shaft stern-glands steamtight and watertight. *To blow a gasket* is a colloquialism meaning to lose one's temper, usually in a sudden eruption of feeling, as a gasoline engine may blow its cylinder head gasket without warning: "When the telephone account came in, he blew a gasket over the extraordinary number of calls his son had made."
(See also *Grommet.)*

Gauntlet
To run the gauntlet

Originally this was a Swedish form of punishment; from the Swedish *gat,* gate, and *lopp,* run, gate run, a lane, a passageway. In English it first became *gantlope* or *gauntlope,* the space or passageway between two files of sailors or soldiers. The expression became established in English during the Thirty Years' War, in about 1640, when *gantlope* was soon replaced by *gauntlet,* a word more familiar to English speakers.

"Some said he ought to be tied neck and heels, others, that he deserved to run the gantelope."
—Henry Fielding (1707–1754), English novelist and playwright, *Tom Jones* (1749)

Running the gauntlet (pronounced "gantlet" by the British and "gontlet" by the Americans) was a form of punishment that involved the whole ship's crew. The victim, usually a sailor accused of stealing from his shipmates, was made to run between two rows of seamen while they, in turn, lashed him as hard as they wished with a short knotted rope or "nettle." This punishment was known as running the gantlope or gauntlet.

Metaphorically, *to run the gauntlet* is to be attacked on all sides, to be severely criticised: "When she married the disgraced priest, she had to run the gauntlet of her neighbours' disapproval."

Get cracking! See *Cracking; Get cracking.*

Gingerbread
To take the gilt off the gingerbread

"An' I had but one penny in the world, thou should'st have it to buy gingerbread."
—William Shakespeare (1564–1616), *Love's Labours Lost,* act 5, scene 1

Gingerbread cakes were small cakes made with treacle and flavoured with ginger, often made up into toy shapes such as gingerbread men, and gilded with Dutch gold (imitation gold leaf). These cakes were sold at fairs from medieval times until the middle of the nineteenth century.

Gingerbread-work is the term given to the artificial and sometimes tawdry attractiveness of fanciful shapes, ornate carvings, and such used to decorate furniture, buildings, and the bow and stern sections of warships of the fifteenth to eighteenth centuries. *To knock the gilt off the gingerbread* originally alluded to incurring the captain's wrath by damaging the gilt work or gingerbread on his vessel; it is now a colloquialism meaning to destroy the illusion, to rob something of its attraction by removing the charm, advantage, sheen, etc., and leaving behind only the dull base; to spoil the best part of a story in the telling: "The fact that I have to complete this book during my annual holiday takes the gilt off the gingerbread."

Glad rags A term used to describe the shoregoing sailor of the 1860s, when he was given liberty to have a "run ashore," and for which he always dressed in his best and brightest clothes. Seamen, by virtue of their occupation, were extremely skillful in needlework and decoration, and they usually took great pride in their appearance when given leave to go ashore. The expression now refers to one's best clothes, worn for special occasions: "Don't worry, I'll have my glad rags on for Helen's party."

Godown In Southeast Asia, and particularly in the Malay Archipelago, a godown is a warehouse, nearly always situated on the waterfront, since virtually all trade is ultimately by means of the highways of the sea.

From the Malay *gadong* or *godong,* deriving from the South Indian tongues Tamil and Telugu. The English word is probably a corruption of the native *godong,* as these storehouses were often partly below ground level, and one had to "go down" to enter them. Included here because of their importance in the great days of the Spice Islands trade of the fifteenth and sixteenth centuries.

Grabbies Another slang term for soldier, from the fact that they have so little sense of balance when at sea that they are always grabbing at something to steady them.
(See also *Bullocks. Jollies. Pongo. Turkeys.)*

Grapple
To grapple with

"The gallies were grappled to the Centurion in this manner."
—Richard Hakluyt (?1552–1616), English cleric and maritime historian, *Principall Navigations, Voiages, and Discoveries of the English Nation* (1589)

"In the grapple I boarded them."
—William Shakespeare (1564–1616), *Hamlet,* act 4, scene 6

Originally nautical. The word is a corruption of "grapnel" (from the Old French *grappe,* hook), usually called a "boarding grapnel," a small, four-pronged anchor often used in small boats. A boarding grapnel was heaved at an enemy vessel's rigging so that she could be held close for the purpose of boarding. Grapnels are still used today for dragging the bottom for gear lost overboard, or for the bodies of drowned persons. *To grapple with* is to seize, to hold or fasten to, as in wrestling; or to attempt to understand, as in "He grappled with the concept of differential calculus in mathematics."

Greek fire A highly flammable mixture consisting mainly of naphtha and other combustibles, and discharged by mortars as an offensive weapon against other ships. The liquid mass was especially effective against masts and sails and, of course, against the galley-rowers who were chained to their benches. It derives its name from the fact that it was developed by the Byzantine Greeks in the seventh century, and used with great success against the Arab fleet that attacked Constantinople in 678. The introduction of naval guns in the fourteenth century hastened the demise of what was an effective but essentially very primitive weapon of war.
(See also *Wildfire.)*

Griff Sailor's slang for information. The word is used in New Zealand in the form of *griffin,* meaning genuine information, the facts, what Australians would call "the good oil." The origin is quite obscure, but it might be related to the Anglo-Indian word *griffin,* meaning a new arrival in India, a green hand. It was probably adopted by seamen as a corruption of some native word.
(See also *Blighty.)*

Gripe A vessel is said to "gripe" when she carries excessive weather helm and shows a strong inclination to round up into the wind. A gripe is also a lashing or fitting by which a ship's boat is secured on the deck, or on the davits, of a ship. From Old English *gripan,* to grip or seize, and related to our modern *grip* and *grope.*

Colloquially, *to gripe* is to complain constantly, to grumble about the prevailing order of things. The figure gains its force from the inherent notion of contrariness, as in the original nautical usage: "He was always griping about the Taxation Department's disallowing his travel expenses."

Grog Spirits, alcohol, liquor, booze. Originally *grog* was the name given to rum that had been diluted with water. Neat rum replaced brandy as the sailor's daily ration in the late seventeenth century, and in 1740 Admiral Vernon, commander of the British fleet in the Caribbean at the time, ordered that the rum be diluted with water in an effort to combat the drunkenness that was then prevalent among his sailors.

"Deceased had been accustomed to drink a vile mixture procured at spirit stores known as grog, and compounded of drippings from wine, spirit, and beer casks."
—*The Standard* (English newspaper), February 20, 1884

Vernon was already known by the nickname of "Old Grogram," from the coarse cloth from which his seagoing cloak was made *(grogram* is from the French *gros-grain,* coarse, rough). His seamen speedily transferred the name *grog* to the watered-down rum. The word *groggy* derives obviously from this source. It wasn't until 1970 that the formal issue of a tot of rum to seamen was discontinued in the British navy; and the word *tot* still survives from the days when rum was issued daily.

Grommet Another nautical word that has undergone some interesting evolutions. The word is related to the very early English *groom,* which in the 1200s was a boy, or young male child. The Old French origin was *gromet,* lad; this went into early English as *gromet* or *grummet,* a ship's boy, common in French and English vessels from the thirteenth to the eighteenth centuries. A ship's boy was the menial who did all the dirty work on board ship; usually referred to as a servant but in fact treated more as a slave.

In the early 1600s, the word came also to mean the rings or metal eyelets that accepted the gaskets on the yards. Curiously, the original sense-meaning is still retained in this usage, since these eyelets or rings (which we call *grommets* or *grummets* to this day) are held captive, as it were, by the ropes or lines attached to or threaded through them.

Interestingly, the word *grommet* is used today as a colloquialism in the Australian surfing scene to mean a young surfer, a beginner, usually in his or her early teens; a meaning that preserves the sense of the early Middle English word from the thirteenth century.

Ground
To break new ground To weigh the anchor and lift it from the sea bed; the "ground" will be broken where the flukes of the anchor have embedded themselves. The metaphor means to commence a new project, to venture into a new area of activity; the reference is to the turning of the sod, as a new

settler might do, echoing the anchor's breaking of the ground as the vessel makes ready to set off on a new stage of its voyage: "She broke new ground by becoming the first female engineer ever employed by that company."

Growl Sailor's slang for conversation in the forecastle, the seamen's quarters in the bow of the ship. Probably from the fact that much of the verbal exchanges between seamen would have been grumbles and complaints, real or imagined, concerning their food and their treatment by the ship's officers. From the Middle English *groll, groule,* to rumble in the bowels; from the eighteenth century onward, the word took on its current meaning of angry complaint.
(See also *Growl; Growl you may, but go you must.)*

"Growled defiance in such angry sort. . . ."
—William Cowper (1731–1800), English essayist and man of letters, *The Task* (1784)

Growl you may, but go you must Early nineteenth-century British merchant sailor's advice to anyone complaining about conditions of duty or the destination of the vessel. Having signed the "Ship's Articles," every crew member was legally bound to the ship and to his stated duties for the duration of that voyage.

The Articles, which applied (with some variations in detail) to both British and Australian merchant ships, spelled out the rates of pay, the duties to be carried out, the scale of victuals, daily hours of work, and so on; they constituted a contract between the ship's owner and the crew, and were signed by the ship's master as well as by each crew member, making it a binding agreement on both sides. Shipboard discipline was also based on the contents of these Articles, and the captain was duly authorised to punish anyone who transgressed them.

In the U.S. Navy, the terms of agreement between the naval authorities and seamen were colloquially known as "Rock and Shoals," a wry allusion on the part of the crew to the fact that danger lurked in every paragraph of the "Ship's Articles" for the sailor who was unwary enough to ignore the provisions.
(See also *Articles; Ship's Articles.)*

Gudgeon Also "gudgeon pin." Originally a nautical word, meaning the metal clamp bolted to the sternpost, with a hole to accept the pintle on the rudder, so that the rudder then hinges on the sternpost. The word now embraces the ring portion of any hinge that fits onto and thus turns on a pin or a hook. The pervasive influence of matters maritime has reached even into the bowels of the modern petrol or diesel engine, where the gudgeon pin is the pin that connects the piston to the little (or upper) end of the connecting rod (also called the "wrist pin"). From the Middle English *gudyon* and the French *gouge,* wench, prostitute: the allusion is clear, though perhaps indelicate.

Guernsey The close-fitting knitted jumper, much worn by seamen, footballers, and the like. This piece of clothing takes its name from the fact that it was first manufactured on the Isle of Guernsey; it was introduced into the Royal Navy as an item of clothing during the Napoleonic Wars in the early nineteenth century. Admiral Horatio Nelson was wholly in favour of the guernsey as a protection against cold weather aboard ship. The word came into ordinary language through the garment's popularity with British and Australian seamen.

Guess
By guess and by God Originally a form of dead reckoning (from "deduced" reckoning) whereby a vessel's position was more or less arrived at by a combination of the navigator's day-to-day reckoning, experience, and—finally—guesswork. When the ship's master had done all that was possible to ensure his vessel's safe arrival at its destination, it was hoped by all on board that God would then exercise His divine powers to bring the voyage to a satisfactory conclusion.

By extension, the phrase refers to the act of trying to carry out a task or enterprise of some kind without the benefit of knowledge about all the factors that could materially aid one; to finally trust to luck: "When he estimated the distance to the next water hole in the desert, it was a case of by guess and by God."

Guff An old seafaring colloquialism meaning empty or foolish talk, humbug, nonsense; still used in everyday speech to mean exactly the same thing. Possibly a form of *guffaw:* "His story about catching snapper at the blowholes is a bunch of guff."

Guinea The gold coin, first minted in 1663 from Guinea gold (West Africa), for the purposes of "the Guinea trade" (i.e., the slave trade). Introduced into English by English sailors on the "Guineamen," the slave ships that made the triangular voyage from England to Guinea with trade goods, thence to the West Indies and South America with slaves (the "middle passage"), and finally to England with produce from the New World (notably rum and sugar) purchased with the proceeds from selling the cargoes of slaves.

"The guinea, so called from the Guinea gold out of which it was first struck, was proclaimed in 1663."

—Pinkerton, *On Medals,* cited in the *Universal Dictionary of the English Language* (1897)

Gun From the Middle English words *gunne, gonne,* which in turn are related to the Icelandic *Gunna, Gunnhildr,* a woman's name: *gunnr* is Icelandic for war, *hildr* means battle. *Gunnar* is also a common Scandinavian name for a man.

Son of a gun Formerly a term of contempt among sailors, but now widely used in a friendly and jocular manner in Britain, Australia, Canada, New Zealand, and the United States, in all of which countries it can also do duty as an expression of surprise or astonishment—i.e., a mild expletive. It stems from the days when women—a few of whom were sailors' wives—were allowed to live on board and, occasionally, at sea. Because the working space on the gun decks always had to be kept clear and ready for action, women in labour had only the spaces between the guns in which to give birth.

A male child was inevitably entered into the ship's log as a "son of a gun," often because the child's paternity was uncertain. Such a birth gave rise to the saying: "Begotten in the galley and born under a gun. Every hair a rope yarn, every tooth a marlin spike, every finger a fishhook, and his blood right good Stockholm tar." This particular expression died out at the turn of the eighteenth century.
(See also *Garland; Wedding garland.)*

To be a big gun Colloquially, to be an important person; to be regarded by others as such: "The community regarded her as the big gun in the local repertory company." Almost identical in meaning with *to be a great gun,* except that "great gun" implies a degree of respect and liking, whereas to be a "big gun" denotes respect only.
(See also *Gun; To be a great gun.)*

To be a great gun Used colloquially in expressions such as "He's a great gun"—a man of note, of consequence; the opposite of *no great guns.*
(See also *Gun; To be a big gun. Guns; No great guns.)*

Guns
Great guns! An exclamation of surprise and wonderment at some incident; likening that event to the clamour and smoke that accompanied the firing of a ship's guns. The expression implies astonishment rather than fear.

No great guns To be a person of no note or consequence; similarly, for an event, a washout or failure: "He's no great guns as a singer."
(See also *Gun; To be a great gun.)*

To blow great guns To be very rough, boisterous, and windy, making a noise or a tumult such as that made by a ship's cannon. These weapons were always referred to in fighting sail as the "great guns," never just "guns," and gunnery practice was termed "exercising the great guns." When something is performing well, it is said "to be going great guns." "He told his boss that the new sales team was going great guns in their drive for increased market share."

To bring one's guns to bear When men-o'-war (sailing ships of the navy) engaged the enemy, they turned broadside-on so that all the guns down one side of the vessel could be brought to bear on the opposing ship, pointed and aimed for the most telling effect. The firing of all the guns on one side was called a "broadside."

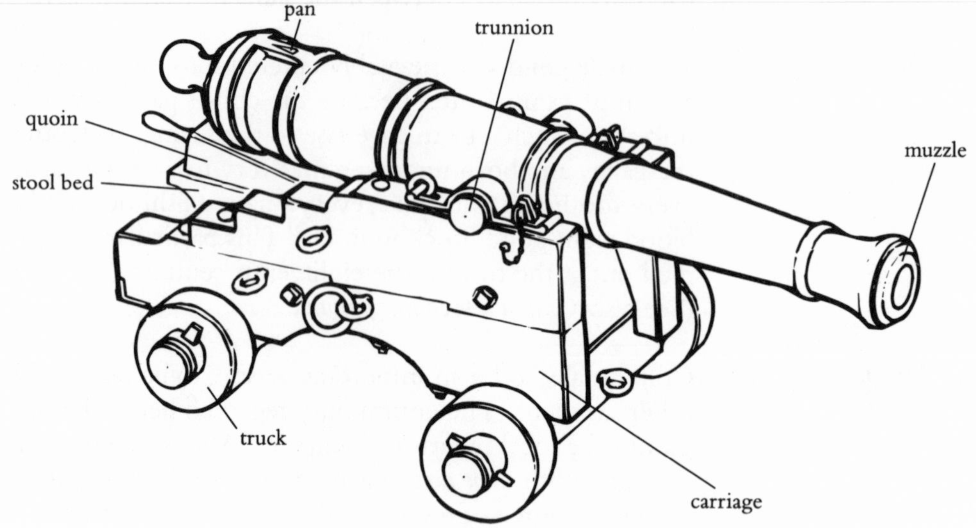

Guns are first recorded as being used on board ships during an attack on Antwerp in 1336. These early guns were cast in bronze or made of wrought iron. Cast iron later came to be the preferred medium, because of the high cost of bronze in large-scale manufacture.

Guns were made in a great many sizes and types. The largest, called the "whole cannon," threw a ball of more than 70 pounds (some 35 kilograms); the smallest fired a ball of about 1 pound or less (about 1/2 kilogram). These large guns or cannon were called the "great guns." Many other types of cannon were also introduced (such as the "culverin," "saker," "minion," and so on), but during the seventeenth century these medieval names were abandoned and naval guns were identified simply by the weight of the shot they fired.

To bring one's guns to bear is a widely used metaphor meaning to concentrate one's forces—for example, the telling points of one's argument—so as to demoralise and overcome the opposition: "The Shadow Minister for Finance brought his guns to bear on the government's budget proposals for health and welfare."
(See also *Broadside. Guns; To blow great guns.)*

To go great guns To be eminently successful, to be doing well, to be moving steadily toward one's goal. "The basketball team was going great guns against its opponents from Interstate."
(See also *Guns; To blow great guns.)*

To stick to one's guns From the days of fighting sail, when close engagement of the enemy meant a horrific din of ship's guns, great palls of acrid smoke, and the manic screams of excited and often terrified men. Coupled inevitably with a broadside duel with the enemy was the appalling butchery on both sides, when round shot, grape shot, bar shot, and flying splinters of wood wreaked such carnage on board that the decks often literally ran streams of blood out through the scuppers into the sea. To this end, the gun decks were generally painted red, to lessen the visual impact of the slaughter on the crew. The toll of dead and wounded was known informally as "the butcher's bill" and, more officially, as "the price of Admiralty."

To stick to one's guns, then, under these conditions, was something of an achievement (a gun crew worked a gun on one side of the vessel and a gun on the other, depending on which side the captain chose to engage his adversary). Colloquially, the phrase means to maintain one's position in spite of intense opposition: "No one believed her story, but she stuck to her guns and firmly maintained that she was right."

Guy Originally nautical, as in a "guy-rope," or some object used to steady something that is being raised, lowered, or set into place; to secure. Guy-ropes are commonly found ashore in tents, circus tops, derricks, and so on. From the Middle English *gyen,* to guide, and found in most European languages.

Guzzle To drink (or sometimes eat) frequently and greedily. Originally, *guzzle* or *guz* was the slang name in the British navy for Devonport, where it was traditional for sailors returning from a long voyage to gorge themselves on copious quantities of Devonshire cream, butter, cakes, etc. The word was in use in the sixteenth century, and it may be connected with the French *gosier,* throat. "The children at the birthday party guzzled themselves sick on ice cream and chocolate cake."

"They fell to lapping and guzzling, till they burst themselves."

—Roger L'Estrange (1616–1704), English journalist and pamphleteer, cited in the *Universal Dictionary of the English Language* (1897)

H

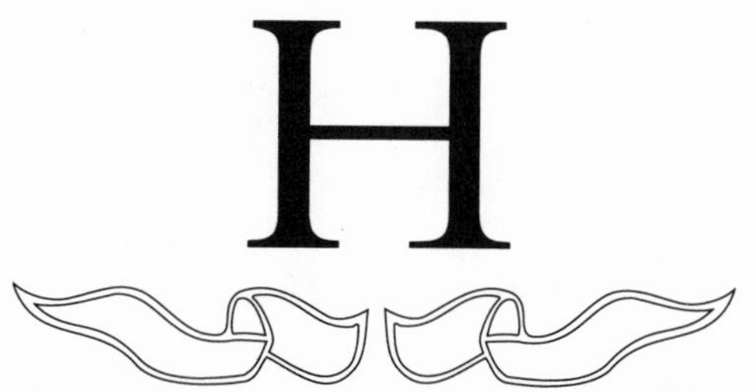

Hail
To hail from

"But ere he came, like one that hails a ship, / Cried out with a big voice, 'What, is he dead?'"
—Alfred, Lord Tennyson (1809–1892), English poet, *Geraint and Enid,* cited in the *Universal Dictionary of the English Language* (1897)

Hail, an exclamation of welcome; from the Icelandic *heill,* hale and healthy (not related to *hail* meaning frozen rain). By extension, *to hail from* is to belong to or come from a particular place by reason of birth or residence. Mariners customarily hailed a passing vessel to ascertain her ports of departure and destination and, of course, to exchange navigational and weather information.

Halcyon
Halcyon days

"If Anna's happy reign you praise, Pray, not a word of halcyon days."
—Jonanthan Swift (1667–1745), English cleric and man of letters, *Apollo's Edict,* cited in the *Universal Dictionary of the English Language* (1897)

Colloquially, times of happiness and prosperity. *Halcyon* is from the Latin *halcyon,* and the Greek *halkuon,* kingfisher; it means "to brood on the sea." In ancient times, seafarers believed that the kingfisher laid its eggs in seaweed on the surface of the sea in mid-December, just before the coming of winter, and that because of the two-week period of incubation the waves were calm and unruffled; William Cowper used the term in this sense in *Table Talk* (1782) when he writes, "Thus lovely halcyons dive into the main."

Hence the seaman's respect for and welcoming of the kingfisher's season of breeding, because it heralded the onset of good weather: "The month we spent on the island consisted of long, halcyon days of swimming and sunbathing and forgetting about the rest of the workaday world."

Half and half

Another term from the fisheries. It reflected the principle of the owner having one half of a fishing vessel's profits and the crew the other half. Used colloquially in exactly the same way: "They agreed to share the cost of the rental car half and half."

Half pay

The practice of putting officers on half their normal rate of pay. This originated in the British navy as an economy measure during peacetime, when many a ship was laid up and her officers taken off the active list. Also known as "kicking upstairs," when senior captains in the British navy of the mid-nineteenth century were reduced in number by being promoted to flag rank, and thus being relegated to half pay.

Half shot See *Shot; To be half shot.*

Hamburger The well-known American dish of fried or broiled minced or ground beef, sometimes with onion, egg, and other seasonings added, made into a flat cake and usually sandwiched between two layers of bread or bun. Not, of course, a nautical term as such, but introduced in the nineteenth century to America by sailors from the Baltic region, where this form of meal had originated hundreds of years earlier, particularly in the German port of Hamburg.
(See also *Tango.)*

Hammock
To sling your hammock To go, to pack up, usually for good. *Hammock* is from *hamorca,* a Carib word for the native bed that is suspended between two poles or trees. Columbus first recorded the word when he explored the Caribbean seas in the late fifteenth century (note that the word *cannibal* comes from the Spanish *Caribal,* a description of the Carib Indian).

"A great many Indians came for the purpose of bartering their cotton and hamacas or nets in which they sleep."
—Christopher Columbus (?1445–1506), Genoese navigator and explorer, cited in the *Universal Dictionary of the English Language* (1897)

The seaman slung his hammock from hooks in the deck beams. When not in use, the hammock was rolled and lashed into a tight bundle and stowed around the perimeter of the upper deck, to act as extra protection from flying wood splinters and sniper fire during battle. When properly lashed, the hammock was also an excellent lifebuoy.

Hammocks were first officially issued in the Royal Navy in 1597. When a seaman died at sea or was killed in action, his body was sewn up in his hammock, with a round shot placed at both head and foot. The sailmaker completed the job by running the last stitch through the dead man's nose, to ensure that the man really was dead and not in, say, a state of catalepsy; anyone who didn't respond to a large sailmaking needle through the fleshy part of the nose was confidently assumed to be quite dead.

It is typical of the way in which nautical usage sometimes becomes inverted that we use the metaphor to mean to leave, to strike camp and go elsewhere, whereas literally the phrase means to stay, to set up for a while, to settle in one particular spot: "He decided to sling his hammock and go to the city in search of work."

Hand A member of the ship's crew. From the Anglo-Saxon *hand,* and found in most other Teutonic languages; for example,

"A dictionary containing a natural history requires too many hands as well as too much time."
—John Locke (1632–1704), English philosopher, cited in the *Universal Dictionary of the English Language* (1897).

Dutch and German *hand,* Old Norse *hond,* and the Gothic *handus.* Widely used in nautical expressions because of the obvious importance of having "hands" to work the ship's gear; most of these phrases have found their way into everyday usage.
(See also other entries under *Hand.)*

A dab hand A "dab-dab" is a seaman, whose duties include a great deal of painting ship. Naturally, after a lot of experience he becomes something of an expert: a "dab hand." A "fair dab" is a good sailor. Probably a derivation of the Latin *adeptus,* adept, skilled; and influenced by *daub,* from the French *dauber,* as in "wattle and daub" (wattle twigs and branches plastered with mud or clay, and used as a building material). "Your new employee is certainly a dab hand at carpentry."

A green hand Originally an inexperienced sailor, a greenhorn (no reference to Cape Horn). *Hand* is the traditional term for a seaman, although in Elizabethan and pre-Elizabethan ships the crew were frequently referred to as "the people." Colloquially, a green hand is anyone who is a novice, new to the job and consequently inexperienced.

Green means young, fresh, immature in age and judgment, usually easy to impose upon (a period of life often called one's "salad days"; Shakespeare's Cleopatra speaks of her ". . . salad days, when I was green in judgment").

Do you want a hand? A very common expression that includes a widely used nautical term. Captain Frank Bullen, in his classic account of whaling, *The Cruise of the Cachalot* (1910), joins the crew of an American whaler by asking the captain, "Do you want a hand?" It means literally what it says: "Do you need another crew member?" Colloquially, the expression means "Do you need any help?"

Hand over fist Also rendered nautically by the phrase *hand over hand.* Colloquially, *hand over fist* indicates large quantities, as in "to make money hand over fist." From the fact that a competent and experienced seaman could swarm up a ship's rigging with great dexterity; the metaphor thus imparts the sense of an obstacle being overcome with ease, or a "large amount" (of rigging) being "subdued" as it passes through the sailor's hands quickly and efficiently. "He was making money hand over fist until the auditors caught up with him."
(See also *Hand; Hand over hand.)*

Hand over hand To do something with ease, to carry out a task efficiently, often to arouse admiration in others for one's skill. The emphasis is upon orderly control and manipulation. The phrase derives from the order to seamen to haul on a rope in a continuous and rapid motion, by alternating one hand in front of the other along the rope. The movement is best illustrated in climbing a ladder, or swarming up the ratlines in the shrouds. Sailors work best when under the influence of rhythm; hence the well-known capstan shanties or chants sung when weighing anchor.
(See also *Hand; Hand over fist. Overhaul.)*

To be a poor hand To be unskillful, to be able to do only a poor job.
(See also other entries under *Hand.)*

To be an old hand One who is experienced at something, well versed in a particular occupation or skill; from the common word for a seaman or a crew member. An "old hand" was, of course, a sailor of vast experience, one who knew his duty, known in the language of the day as a "prime seaman." "Let me help: I'm an old hand at chopping wood."
(See also other entries under *Hand. Ropes; To know the ropes, to learn the ropes.)*

To be short-handed To have insufficient help for the job. The allusion comes directly from shipboard life, when a vessel might be undermanned through illness, injury, or desertion. Sailors were commonly called "hands"; when a vessel was "short-handed," it usually meant that the available crew had to do double watches so that the ship could be worked safely. Workers on farms are often called "farm-hands," "station-hands," or "hired hands." "When the shearing team found itself short-handed because of the flu epidemic, the boss and his family had to pitch in and help."

To come to hand Colloquially, to come within one's reach or grasp; to be received, remembered, recalled; usually without much effort, in the same way that a seaman had to be able to identify correctly every rope and piece of rigging on board without having to peer at it or its location. "If you give me a moment, the client's name will come to hand."
(See also *Ropes; To know the ropes, to learn the ropes.)*

Hand-me-downs See *Reach-me-downs.*

Hands
All hands on deck! *Hands* is the nautical term for a ship's crew; *"All hands on deck!"* is the familiar cry in an emergency, when the watch below is called to assist the watch on deck, usually done as a

matter of some urgency. The colloquial usage is in a similar vein; the call is given when all available help is needed to deal with a situation, which may range from the serious to the light-hearted. "When the storm blew the roof off the living room, it was all hands on deck to rescue the furniture." (See also *Pumps; All hands to the pumps.)*

Hands off!

It has been claimed that the origin of this expression lay in the pirates' practice of cutting off the hand (or hands) of any seaman found guilty of stealing or of drawing a knife on his shipmates.

This, of course, is a preposterous speculation. For one thing, the literature of the sea does not support the claim; for another, any seaman with one or both hands taken off is a useless article on board any ship. No captain, piratical or otherwise, would willingly feed and clothe from ship's stores a man who was unable to add his labour to the working of the ship. The idea is absurd.

It is true, however, that in the early Elizabethan navy the drawing of a weapon with the intention of striking the captain or of "causing tumult" (in the phrase of the day) was punished by the loss of the man's right hand; if he escaped hanging for mutiny, he would then be thrown ashore at the first available opportunity.

The two most common punishments on board ship were hanging (for murder, mutiny, sodomy, and some other serious crimes) and the lash, known as the "cat-o'-nine-tails," awarded in a variety of ways for a vast range of offences. Other, less serious punishments involved disrating and having one's pay stopped for a period, both still practised in today's navies.
(See also *Cat-o'-nine-tails. Gauntlet; To run the gauntlet.)*

Handsome

"A light foot-man's shield he takes with him, and a Spanish blade by his side, more handsome to fight short and close."

—Philemon Holland (1552–1637), English classical scholar, *Livy* (1600)

"His garments are rich, but he wears them not handsomely."

—William Shakespeare (1564–1616), *The Winter's Tale,* act 4, scene 3

Connected with the seaman's usage of the word *hand.* The term *handsome* now means of fine or admirable appearance; to be dexterous, graceful. Originally, though, it meant easy to handle.

Handsomely means to handle something with great care, slowly, easefully, as in lowering a ship's boat, handling ropes that are under strain, or passing an injured person over the ship's side. The words *generous* and *graceful* also suit the metaphor, as in "It was very handsome of you to lend me your car."
(See also entries under *Hand. Handy.)*

Handy

On board a sailing ship, *to hand* means the act of furling the sails. A "hand" was, and still is, a member of the ship's crew, commonly expressed in such orders as "All hands on deck" and "All hands to the pumps." A vessel was "handy" if it was easy to handle or manoeuvre; one of the most useful tackles on board was called a "handy billy," a simple rope-and-pulley arrangement used for shifting heavy weights, especially in the ship's cargo hold. By extension, anything that comes to hand easily and that quickly and efficiently serves the purpose is said to be "handy." "Because she was so well-read, she was a handy person to have on the quiz team."

Happy hour

A brief period of relaxation for the crew of a ship, or for as many as possible, consistent with the need for the ship to remain alert and efficient; said by John Rogers (see bibliography) to be a navy term from World War I (presumably Rogers refers to the U.S. Navy; it is inconceivable that the Royal Navy of that period would have permitted frivolity of any kind on board His Majesty's vessels).

Today the happy hour is almost religiously celebrated ashore by some groups of people, gathered together in a common cause (such as office workers, school teachers, and so on), who hail the end of the working week and the advent of the weekend by letting down their hair and having a few social drinks with each other.

Many bars and taverns host a daily happy hour, usually in the late afternoon or early evening, when drinks are customarily reduced in price. The yachting fraternity, especially those hardy types who cruise the Caribbean, have stoically insisted on refusing to allow this naval tradition of the happy hour to die out.

Harbour
To harbour a grudge

"The harbour is safe and commodious."
—Captain James Cook (1728–1779), English navigator and explorer, *Voyages,* cited in the *Universal Dictionary of the English Language* (1897)

Harbour is from the Anglo-Saxon *herebeorg,* shelter (originally for the army, but the nautical sense of the term appears early in Middle English); also related to *harbinger,* a preparer, one who goes before to make things ready (as used in Modern English). The word is made up from *here,* army, and *beorg,* refuge; the name of Hereward the Wake, the English chieftain, reflects the primary sense of army, together with *ward,* protector.

For the seaman, a harbour is a sheltered area of calm water providing ships with a safe anchorage protected from wind and heavy sea. *To harbour* implies containment; hence the metaphor *to harbour a grudge* is to entertain in the mind—to indulge in—unfavourable feelings or attitudes; to hold hard to, to encircle and protect, these thoughts. *To bear a grudge* carries the same meaning. "For a long time he harboured a grudge against the water board for imposing a levy on his own well system."

Hard
Hard and fast

A "hard-and-fast rule" is one that is inflexible, to be obeyed at all times. The term derives from the condition that a ship was said to be in when she had run aground (*fast* is an old nautical term meaning fixed, tied, immovable). The term *fast,* as in "fast asleep," comes from the same source as *to hold fast.* "There are few hard-and-fast rules about the use of hyphens in English."
(See also *High; High and dry. Stranded; To be stranded.)*

Hard up

To be broke, short of money. When heavy weather conditions forced a vessel to bear off or turn away from the wind, the helm (tiller or wheel) was put "hard up" to windward to bring about the desired alteration of course to leeward (pronounced "loo-ard"). Thus, when a person is "hard up," she has to weather her personal financial storm as best she may. "Many a businessman found himself hard up and short of funds because of the stock market crash of 1987."
(See also *Beam; To be on one's beam ends. Poles; Under bare poles. Stocks; To be on the stocks.)*

Hard tack

See *Tack; Hard tack.*

Hardcase

Also "hard case." Any person who has proved to be difficult to deal with and who is resistant to reform of any kind. The expression is often used with grudging admiration of someone whose stubbornness is not entirely foolhardy. "Some of the criminals in this prison are very hard cases indeed."

Nautically, a hardcase is a very tough character. Some of the most noteworthy hardcases in maritime literature were the masters and mates who drove the American clippers around the Horn on the San Francisco route from the East Coast, during the heyday of the California goldstrikes in the late 1840s and 1850s. A "hard-caser" in the merchant service is any vessel, usually a tramp steamer, in which the conditions of service are uniformly bad.
(See also *Bucko.)*

Harden
To harden up

Originally rendered *to harden in,* the operation of hauling in the sheets of a sailing vessel so as to present the sails at a more acute angle to the wind. *To harden up* is the same operation, so called because at a more acute angle the sail cloth and sheets become harder set or stiffer from the apparent increase in wind velocity over the curvature of the sail. Colloquially, the phrase means to become firm in one's resolve; to be obdurate or unpitying; to be unrelenting.

Harness cask From the Old French *harnas,* armour. Recall the remark of Shakespeare's Macbeth as he prepares to meet his deadly foe, Macduff:

> Blow, wind! come, wrack!
> At least we'll die with harness on our back.

The harness cask was a large cask usually kept on the deck of a sailing vessel; it contained the salted provisions that had been brought up from below for immediate use. The meat—salt pork and salt beef—was usually known as "salt horse" because the meat was so hard and unpalatable; another name for this was "salt junk."

The barrel was called the "harness cask" because, the seamen said, it was where the horse without its harness was stabled; some even claimed to have found bits of leather and horseshoes in their provisions. Be that as it may, salt beef was enormously tough; Dampier once used a piece of it to stop a leak in the side of his ship, the *Roebuck.* Horsemeat is quite palatable when treated properly, but ships' galleys were not set up for interesting cuisine, and ships' cooks were generally an uninspired lot.

Harriet Lane The seaman's name for all tinned meat; the phrase was especially prevalent among Australian merchant seamen. Harriet Lane was said to have been a girl or young woman who was murdered and then chopped up into little pieces, early in the twentieth century; the name is the merchant service counterpart of "Sffggweet Fanny Adams." (See also *Sweet Fanny Adams.)*

Harry Freeman Sailors' slang term for free of charge, a gift, or something obtained for nothing. The original Harry Freeman is believed to have kept a bar at Freeman's Quay on the Thames in the eighteenth century. It is said that he provided free beer to the porters who worked for him.

Harry Tate's Navy A rather rare example of a nautical expression being coined from the name of a person living in the twentieth century (Mae West is another that springs to mind).

Harry Tate was an English music-hall artist whose specialty was a riotous motoring sketch. With Harry Tate's stage car, nothing worked properly, everything was slipshod and out of place. This act was soon picked up by sailors, who loved music-hall entertainment, and the performer's name was applied to any naval situation where discipline was slack, the ship was slovenly, and the gear always malfunctioned. Furthermore, *Harry Tate's Navy* was applied to any irregular naval formation, such as trawlers used for minesweeping and manned by ordinary fishermen, and the flotilla of private craft that evacuated the British Expeditionary Force from Dunkirk in 1940.

Hash

"The dishes were trifling, hashed and condited [seasoned] after their way."
—John Evelyn (1620–1706), English man of letters, *Memoirs* (1818)

Hash is sailor's slang for food; specifically, a dish of recooked meat, potatoes, and anything else available, all mixed up together; from the French *hachis,* to chop, and related to the English word *hatchet.* A hash is therefore a mess, a muddle, a mix-up: "He made a dreadful hash of repairing my radio; it's never worked properly since." It appears in expressions such as "hash marks" (service or good-conduct badges worn on the sleeve of a sailor's jacket in the U.S. Navy); "hash slinger" (a steward in the dining room of a passenger liner, or more generally a waiter); and "to hash over" or "to hash out" (to discuss, talk over, to arrive at a solution to a problem, a usage primarily from American English). "The author and the publisher met in the lawyer's office and hashed out their differences concerning the contract."

To make a hash of

See *Hash; To settle one's hash.*

To settle one's hash

To settle one's hash is to spoil or end someone's plans, to cook someone's goose; probably from the ground meaning of *hash* as a muddle or mixture. To settle someone's hash, then, is to sort that person out, to put matters right, to make him see what's what: "He thinks that he's going to marry my daughter, but I'll soon settle his hash!"

Hat
To take one's hat off to someone

A very common figure of speech, and used as a mark of praise or admiration; often rendered as "I take my hat off to you," or "Hats off to . . . " with the person's name following. Until Queen Victoria came to the throne, the only form of personal salute in the Royal Navy was that given by doffing the headgear. The naval seaman always removed his hat to an officer, and of course junior officers removed theirs to their seniors. The Queen put a stop to this because, she said, it looked ridiculous for uniformed men to be standing about bare-headed.

To take one's hat off to another person was, literally, to salute him or her, to show respect: "I take my hat off to him for the professional finish he achieved on that paving job." The expression was used by Admiral of the Fleet Sir John Jellicoe when he paid a tribute to the men of the Harwich Striking Force in World War I: "The officers and men serving out of Harwich earn and deserve all the leave they receive, and what is more, whenever I meet them I'll

take off my hat and I won't expect to receive a salute in return."
(See also *Bowing and scraping. Naval salutes.)*

Hatch
Down the hatch

"In at the window, or else o'er the hatch."
—William Shakespeare (1564–1616), *King John,* act 1, scene 1

Strictly speaking, a hatch is the covering over the hatchway (from the Old English *haec,* a gate); more loosely, the term refers to the deck opening as well as to the hatch covering. *Down the hatch* is a colloquialism for drinking heartily, with the enthusiastically open mouth and gullet being, of course, the "hatch." "'Down the hatch!' cried the captain, and his team raised their glasses to salute their hard-won victory." (See also *Hatches; Batten down the hatches.)*

Hatches
Batten down the hatches

In a figurative sense, to make oneself secure, to shut out the weather, to shelter from the onslaught of wind, rain, or other more metaphoric onslaughts such as trouble, a quarrel, or the like. From the practice of securing the hatches of a ship while underway at sea, to protect the cargo from the weather. "I've just seen the boss and she looks furious, so we'd all better batten down the hatches."

To be under hatches

To be under hatches is, literally, to be below deck. Used as a metaphor, it means to be down in the mouth, depressed, not up to the mark, or even dead.

Haul

"I immediately hauled up for it, and found it to be an island."
—Captain James Cook (1728–1779), English navigator and explorer, *First Voyage* (1771)

From the French *haler,* to pull or haul (found also in the Dutch *halen). Haul* is the common rendering today, although *hale* still exists in such expressions as "He was haled off to court." *Haul* is used colloquially in "to haul over the coals" (to rebuke or scold); "to haul up" (to have someone brought up for a reprimand, to call to account); "to haul off" (to draw the arm back in readiness to strike a blow); and "a haul" (the taking or gaining of anything, as in a robbery).

The word has widespread nautical usage: "to haul away" (to pull on a rope); "to haul off" (to sail with the wind before the beam); "to haul the wind" (when a vessel hauls its wind, it turns closer to the direction from which the wind is blowing); and others. Inherent in the term is the idea of determined, forceful movement.

To haul off

To haul off has two meanings. Nautically, it is to alter course to bring the wind ahead of the beam of the vessel. Figuratively, *to haul off* is to move one's body in such a way as to be in a good position to deliver a blow; more specifically, it means to draw the arm back preparatory to striking the blow. The original nautical sense of planned, deliberate movement is evident in the metaphor. "Without

a second's hesitation, he hauled off and struck the thief full in the face."
(See also *Haul.)*

Hawse
To freshen the hawse

The seaman's expression to describe the action of officers who would take a few nips of spirits to revive themselves a little after a long spell on deck in stormy weather. The hawse is the entry point in the ship's bows through which the anchor cables pass; colloquially, it is the seaman's throat. *Hawse* is from the Anglo-Saxon *heals,* neck, the forepart or prow of a ship; still found in the English dialect *halse,* to embrace, to neck, to cuddle with someone.
(See also *Mainbrace; To splice the mainbrace.)*

Haze

"Light haze along the river shores. . . ."
—Alfred, Lord Tennyson (1809–1892), English poet, *The Gardener's Daughter,* cited in the *Universal Dictionary of the English Language* (1897)

A mist, usually of minute, suspended droplets of water vapour, but often also composed of dust and other particles. The word is a back-formation of *hazy,* a nautical term of the late sixteenth century to describe these conditions. By extension, *to be hazy* is to be vague, confused in the mind, or unclear; as in "a hazy proposition" (an uncertain plan or proposal). Of obscure origin; said to be derived from the German *hase,* hare, but not immediately related to the verb *haze.*
(See also *Haze; To haze someone.)*

To haze someone

To bully, to inflict unnecessary hardship directed against novices or during initiation ceremonies. The term derives from the practice of some captains and mates of the big square-riggers, particularly in the nineteenth century, of making life on board ship as uncomfortable as possible for the crew by keeping them hard at work at all hours of the day and night, often to the extent of inventing work for the occasion. It was a method of asserting authority over the crew.

The "bucko mate" was one who hazed unmercifully with tongue and fist, and by his brutality made life a hell for the crew. The practice arose mostly in American square-riggers, because of the competition among ships to service the East Coast–to–California run, especially in the era of the gold strikes in California and Alaska. Success depended upon speed, and speed in turn often depended upon driving the crew to exhaustion, especially during the rough and dangerous rounding of Cape Horn, when sails had to be worked frequently. Many an exhausted seaman, hazed and driven aloft by fists or a rope's end, missed his footing on the yards or in the rigging and fell to his death.

"Away with you! go forward every one of you! I'll haze you! I'll work you up! You don't have enough to do! If you ain't careful I'll make a hell of the ship! . . ."
—Richard Henry Dana (1815–1882), American author and lawyer, *Two Years Before the Mast* (1840)

From the Middle French haser, to irritate, annoy. The common slang form *to hassle* may be a derivative of this old

French verb: "The playground bully hazed the new boy so unmercifully that the other children told their teachers about it."
(See also *Shanghai.)*

Head
To head up

The head of a vessel is the front or fore part, including the bows on each side. The figurehead is also often called the head; a head sea is a sea meeting the vessel head-on. The phrase *to head up* means to steer the ship so that she swings to meet an oncoming sea (the seaman's term for a larger-than-usual wave or series of waves, or a storm-tossed sea surface in general), or so that she swings closer to the wind—that is, she is steered to be close-hauled. Note that a helmsman might be ordered to "keep his head (or the head) up"; this of course refers to the vessel's head, not his own head.

Colloquially, *to head up* is to change to a new (given) direction: "If we are to find the road before nightfall, we had better head up toward the break in the skyline."

Head money

A reward paid for each person captured or brought in. Originally it was the bounty paid to British naval vessels that were engaged in suppressing the slave trade in the 1860s. Each ship was paid a bounty for the slaves it released (£60 for a male, £30 for a female, and £10 for a child). The money was shared out among the officers and crew of the patrol vessel; it was, naturally enough, a ready incentive to engage with the slavers.

"Head money" (sometimes known as "prize bounty") was also an inducement paid by the Admiralty for the capture or destruction of enemy ships of war; this bounty was reckoned as so much per head of the crew of the enemy vessel (merchant ships excluded). Now simply a tax or charge of so much per head or person, as in a cover charge or surcharge levied in a nightclub. The controversial poll tax introduced in Britain in the early 1990s by the Thatcher government was, literally, a head tax *(poll* is from the Dutch *pol* and the Low German *polle,* crown of the head).

Heading
To be on the right heading

A heading in sailor's language is a bearing, a navigational direction, the direction in which a ship points at any instant. *To be on the right heading,* then, is to be headed or moving in the right direction, as in a police investigation, or in any endeavour involving detection and analysis.
(See also *Bearings; to find one's bearnings, to lose one's bearings, to take one's bearings.)*

Heads

The "heads" are the vessel's lavatory, corresponding exactly to the domestic toilet. The name dates from the days of sail, and refers to a section forward of the forecastle that was provided with gratings and served as the sailor's privy (what Dr. Johnson in his *Dictionary* calls "the place of retirement"). It derives from the fact that early sailing ships had a small deck built over the stem (the foremost structural timber of the vessel), which in turn had evolved from a similar, very strong pointed projection known in the ancient warships as a "beak" or "beak-head," so named from its shape. This beak can still be traced in the clipper bow designs of the nineteenth and twentieth centuries.

Heads was always used in the plural to indicate both sides at once, seamen being expected to use the lee (down-weather) side so that all waste should fall clear into the sea. The decking in fact was usually a grating so that the sea could assist in keeping the area clean. The name is still in use by seamen today, even though all vessels of any size now carry the modern flush-bowl toilet as a matter of course. It has found some vogue in colloquial speech ashore, especially among weekend sailors in the clubhouse.

Heads or tails

The invitation to guess (and in Kalgoorlie, Western Australia, to legally gamble on) whether a coin or coins spun up into the air will both come down with head-side uppermost. The word *tail* is simply a folk etymology to provide an opposite to the "head" of a coin (usually an impression of a sovereign's head). Included here not because it is a nautical term—it isn't—but because the Romans used to say "heads or ships"; their coins had the emperor's head on one side and the image of a ship on the other. The expression is an indication of the enormous importance to the Roman Empire of the ships that fed Rome from the granaries of Egypt.

Headway
To make headway

Similar to making leeway, except that the term *headway* implies a more positive outcome, perhaps due to a more determined and better-informed effort. Headway is the forward movement of the vessel through the water, and is a contraction of *ahead-way,* that is, progress forward. As a figure of speech, *to make headway* is to advance, to be successful in one's efforts. "The climbers made considerable headway in their determination to reach the summit before midafternoon."
(See also *Leeway; To make leeway.)*

Health
A clean bill of health

Said of a vessel when all the ship's company are in good health. A bill of health was a document, signed by the authorities in the port of departure, stating that no contagious diseases existed in that port, and that none of the crew was infected with any notifiable diseases at the time of sailing. A clean bill of health was thus of great importance to any vessel wishing to enter harbour.

The term has come to enjoy a wide figurative usage, as to say that something is quite acceptable, that it has passed scrutiny, or has passed muster. "The mechanic closely examined my son's used car, and when he finished he gave it a clean bill of health."
(See also *Muster; To pass muster.*)

Heave
To heave in sight

Nautically and figuratively, to become visible to an observer. From the fact that at sea a distant object such as a landmark or another vessel rises into view from below the horizon, frequently in an up-and-down manner because of the natural scend or heave of the sea itself. *Heave* is the sailor's word for move, hoist, lift, throw, etc.: "We expected the riders to heave in sight sometime in the forenoon, but the dust storm prevented our sighting them until after lunch."

To heave; to heave to

Found in figures of speech such as "to heave a sigh," "to heave in sight," and so on. From the Anglo-Saxon *hebban,* to lift with effort. The word has many uses in the seaman's vocabulary, among which are "to heave inboard" (as a ship's boat); "to heave overboard" (as an anchor); "to heave a vessel to" (i.e., to heave-to, to slow her down or stop her); and "to heave a line" (throw it vigorously).

As a figure of speech, *to heave-to* (used with the subject included, as in "to heave [someone] to"), means to stop that person in his tracks, to put a stopper on his argument or behaviour.
(See also *Bring; To bring-to. Stopper.)*

Heave-ho!

"Yo, heave ho! Heave and pawl! Heave hearty ho!"
—Richard Henry Dana (1815–1882), American author and lawyer, *Two Years Before the Mast* (1840)

An expression used by sailors when hauling up a heavy object, such as a mainyard or the anchor. It was used in the older days of sail, but doesn't appear frequently in maritime literature of the past 200 years or so. *Heave* is a word common in the seaman's vocabulary, as in "heave astern," "heave away" (this one is found in a number of capstan chanties), "to heave in sight," and many others. The expression is a common colloquialism to mean dismissal, rejection, to get the sack: "I'm upset because my boss gave me the old heave-ho yesterday and now I'm out of a job."

Helm
To be at the helm

To be in control, to be at the nerve-centre of things, to be responsible for the safe bringing-about of an enterprise. The "helm" of a vessel is the tiller or steering wheel, the means by which the rudder is turned as desired. *Helm* is from the

"I then sat at the helm of the commonwealth."

—Charles Robert Maturin (1782–1824), English novelist, *Melmoth the Wanderer* (1820)

Old English *helm,* deriving from the Dutch and German *helm* and the Old Norse *hjalmer,* meaning cover, protector *(helmet* is from the same source). The sense of care, protection, and guidance is quite clear (note the popularity of the English name *William,* from the German *Wille Helm,* resolute, protector). "With the chairman out of retirement and back at the helm of the family business, it wasn't long before the balance sheet began showing a profit."

To take the helm To take charge of, to take over control, as a helmsman assumes control of a vessel when he takes over the wheel. (In sailing ships, both the tiller and, later, the wheel are always referred to as the "helm.") "The board appointed a woman to take the helm of the computer company."

High

High and dry Said of a ship that has run aground so that the tide, falling away, gradually exposes the keel; to go aground at high water is a sorry predicament, because there will be no higher tide by which the vessel can be floated free. This is the origin of the familiar phrase that refers to someone being left stranded, helpless, in a difficult position, unable to continue normally: "Her husband left her high and dry without any money."

(See also *Hard; Hard and fast. Stranded; To be stranded.)*

Himself

Every man for himself The order given to the crew when it is clear that nothing more can be done to save the ship; it releases each man from waiting for further instructions. It would have been the last order given, for example, to the seamen and soldiers on board HMS *Birkenhead,* as it sank off the coast of South Africa in 1852 (see *"Remember the Birkenhead").* "When the government released the land to the homesteaders, it was every man for himself as they and their families scrambled and fought for the choicest locations."

Hitch

A hitch in one's plans An obstruction, a delay; to be caught up in things, in the sense that a nautical hitch "catches" a rope. "There was a

hitch in the proceedings when the chairman revealed that three of the votes were forgeries."
(See also *Hitched; To get hitched.*)

To go without a hitch

To go without a hitch is for a project or task to be brought to a successful conclusion, without interruption of any kind. The force of the metaphor derives from the fact that a hitch, in the nautical sense, is a stopper, preventer, or interrupter. "The dedication ceremony for the new chapel went without a hitch."
(See also *Hitched; To get hitched.*)

Hitched
To get hitched

Nautically, a hitch (from the Middle English *hitch, hotch,* to raise with a jerk, and the twelfth-century French *hocher,* to lift) is a series of knots by which one rope is joined to another, or made fast to some other object, such as a spar, buoy, or part of the vessel's gear. The allusion, meaning to get married, is obvious, and it is a well-known expression ashore: "They got along so well together that it was no surprise to learn that they had become hitched during a trip to the city."

Hogwash

Sailor's slang for nonsense, rubbish, a tale with no truth in it; any worthless stuff: "His claim that he is an experienced motor mechanic is all hogwash."

Hoist

A nautical word found in most European languages. In fifteenth-century Middle English, the form was *hysse,* from the Dutch *hijschen,* to lift. The ultimate source is obscure; it may be Low German. Nautically, the term *to hoist* means to draw up a weight by means of tackles; it is also the word for the part of a sail that is bent (secured) to a yard or stay.

"Hoising up the sailes for to get the ship acoast in some safer place. . . ."
—Richard Hakluyt (?1552–1616), English cleric and historian, *Principall Navigations, Voiages, and Discoveries of the English Nation* (1589)

A string of flags raised as a signal is also called a "hoist." Generally, though, the word is used in connection with things that have to be lifted. (An exception is a yard of a square-rigged ship; it is "swayed" up, never hoisted.) *Hoist* has a secure place in our everyday speech; we hoist our hands, our trousers, our socks; we are, on occasion, hoist by our own petard, i.e., made the victim of, or ruined by, the very trick with which we intended to ruin or harm someone else. The most famous reference is found in Shakespeare's *Hamlet,* act 3, scene 4, where the Prince of Denmark slyly remarks:

> . . . For 'tis the sport to have the enginer
> hoist with his own petard, an't shall go hard
> but I will delve one yard below their mines
> And blow them at the moon.

A petard in Shakespeare's time was an iron container that could be filled with gunpowder and then set off as a mine.

Hold
To hold off; to hold on

"Hold off your hands. . . ."
—William Shakespeare (1564–1616), *Hamlet,* act 1, scene 4

"The trade held on for many years after the bishops became protestants."
—Jonathan Swift (1667–1745), English cleric and man of letters, cited in the *Universal Dictionary of the English Language* (1897)

To hold on is to keep a vessel to her course, without deviating; similarly, *to hold off* means to bear away, to keep clear of some point or obstacle. The sense of *hold* here is to maintain—or to vary in some way—a particular direction. The ground-sense derives from the helmsman's need to hold the wheel firmly so as not to allow the vessel to deviate from the given course; in certain conditions of weather this was a very trying task. From the Anglo-Saxon *healden* and the German *halten,* and common to all the northern languages. The *hold* of a ship is from a different source.

Colloquially, *to hold on* means to persist, to continue, to wait: "If you can hold on a minute I'll ask her to come to the telephone." *To hold off* is to keep aloof, remain at a distance, refrain from action: "You should hold off buying those shares until the market reports are in."

Holiday
A negro's holiday

An old name for Sunday at sea, because, despite the fact that Sunday was meant to be a day of rest, the work of the ship had to be carried out regardless of what day it was. The term derives from the fact that negro slaves on the American plantations were made to work on Sundays as well as weekdays. If such a "holiday" could be celebrated on a plantation by a full day's work, so also could it be celebrated at sea; such was the thinking of the navy, at any rate. Nevertheless, many captains did try to give at least a half-day's holiday, conditions permitting.
(See also *Make; To make and mend.)*

Holystone
To holystone the deck

A "holystone" is a piece of sandstone used for scrubbing decks on board ship; large holystones were known as "bibles" and smaller ones as "prayer books."

The name *holystone* derives from various sources. Sunday mornings were traditionally given over to intensive cleaning of the ship; the blocks of sandstone used for scrubbing the deck were often taken from headstones in churchyards; and to get the best result seamen had to use the holystone while on their hands and knees (while in an apparent attitude of prayer). Whatever the case, a wooden deck well scoured with a holystone soon takes on a smooth, white appearance.

Hoop
To put through the hoop

This expression does not, as is often thought, come from the circus act of training tigers, lions, etc., to jump through a hoop (usually one wreathed in flames). Instead, the reference is to the old custom on Royal Navy ships of checking the tightness of rolled-up hammocks with a cane hoop.

When in use, hammocks were slung below decks from hooks in the deck beams; in the morning they were tightly rolled, with the blankets inside them, and lashed up with nine turns of a rope. The seaman then took his hammock topside, where its firmness of roll and lashing was checked by one of the bosun's mates, who passed his cane hoop over the rolled hammock.

If the hammocks passed this inspection, they were placed in the nettings on the ship's rail, where they helped protect the crew from shell-splinters and sniper fire during battle. (These rolled hammocks could also float free if the ship were sunk; thus was born, in fact, the first ship's lifebuoy.) If the hoop could not pass over the hammock without obstruction, the seaman was made to do the job again, and (naturally) was awarded a punishment for his initial sloppiness.

The "hoop" was also an old form of naval punishment meted out to men guilty of fighting below decks. They were stripped to the waist, their left hands bound to a wooden hoop, and knotted cords or rope placed in their right hands. They had to lash each other until one of them gave in. The loser would also be given a few strokes with the cat-o'-nine-tails, which was a means of ensuring that each man laid on with a will while undergoing the punishment of the hoop.

The word *hoop* is from the Anglo-Saxon *hop* and the Dutch *hoep,* ring. Colloquially, the expression means to put a person through an unreasonable test or series of trials, often in order to find fault: "The television interviewer put the political candidate through the hoop in an effort to discover the weak points in his party's election policy."

Hoosegow Also "hoosgow." Seaman's slang for a prison ashore; also once a common colloquialism in American speech for gaol (jail). From the Spanish *juzgado,* court of justice, gaol.

Hoosgow See *Hoosegow.*

Hornpipe A wooden pipe, now obsolete, with a reed mouthpiece at one end and horn at the other. The dance of this name, once particularly associated with seamen, was originally accompanied by this old Celtic instrument. Originally it was a solo dance that gained wide popularity with mariners at about the beginning of the eighteenth century.

"Before them yode a lusty tabrere, / That to the many a hornpipe played."
—Edmund Spenser (?1552–1599), English poet, *The Shepheards Calendar* (1579)

Horse
A right hard horse

Sailor's slang for a tough nut, a hard-headed fellow, a stern disciplinarian, such as the ship's bosun was usually expected (and found) to be. The expression probably arose from the fact that sailors' meat provisions were made up of salt beef and salt pork. This meat was often so old, so bad, and so hard that it was known as "salt horse." The meat barrel was known as the "harness cask," and sailors of the old sailing navy swore that occasionally they found horseshoes in their salt junk.

The expression is still met with in everyday speech. "The athletics coach was a right hard horse when it came to expressing a bit of sympathy for my unhappy love affair." (See also *Harness cask.)*

To flog a dead horse

To try to revive interest in a worn-out topic; to resurrect a matter that has, by general consent, long since been settled. It is still a widely used colloquialism taken from the language of the sea, and has an interesting background.

The dead horse is the term used by seamen to describe the period of work on board ship for which they have been paid in advance when signing on—usually a month's wages, but sometimes two. There was a custom in merchant ships where the seamen celebrated having "worked off the dead horse" (i.e., having completed the duties covered by their pay advance) by parading a stuffed straw horse around the decks, hanging it from the yardarm, and then heaving it overboard.

To flog a dead horse, then, is to expect—vainly—to get extra work out of a ship's crew while they are still engaged in working off the "dead horse." Hence the colloquial allusion to the lack of interest that is implicit in the phrase: "Doesn't he know he's flogging a dead horse trying to interest us in his daylight saving scheme?" "The Dead Horse" is said to be the only sea shanty composed and sung for pleasure; all other shanties were sung to accompany various kinds of work.

Horse latitudes

A semitechnical sailing term with no colloquial application but an interesting history.

The horse latitudes is a region of calms straddling an area of the Atlantic Ocean some 30° north and south of the equator. A narrower band along the equator is known as the "doldrums." The winds in the horse latitudes were well known for their unreliability and their frequently baffling nature. The area was greatly disliked by sailors because of the heat and calms that often unduly prolonged a voyage, sometimes causing vessels to run dangerously short of food and water.

There are some ingenious theories as to how the region acquired its name. One is that the name is adapted from the Spanish *Golfo de las Yeguas,* the gulf of mares, because of the fickle and quite unpredictable nature of the winds in the area. Another is that it was so named because of the contrast it offered with the stretch of ocean to the west, the *Golfo de las Damas,* the gulf of ladies, reflecting the smoother and more favourable winds to be found in this area between the Canaries and the West Indies—a poetic compliment, no doubt, to Spanish womanhood of the period.

Closer to the truth is the fact that sailing ships carrying horses across the Atlantic to the Spanish colonies in the New World were frequently becalmed in these seas, and were forced to jettison their cargo to lighten the vessel so as to take advantage of whatever breeze was offering. In fact, horses often did have to be tossed overboard in this part of the ocean, for the simple reason that the vessel could not carry sufficient water for both crew and animals while drifting for weeks, making little headway toward the West Indies. It was a pragmatic solution—not always successful—to a problem that has beset sailing ships since man first put to sea.

One modern authority on geographic place names makes the intriguing suggestion that horses aboard sailing ships often had to be lifted overboard into the sea to relieve their thirst, which naturally enough in these latitudes of unreliable wind, great heat, and little rain was severe. The idea of horses thus slaking their thirst in salt water is fascinating, but almost downright ludicrous.

Another explanation is that in the older days of sail, ships out of England took about two months to win clear of these particular latitudes, by which time the crew had worked off the advance of pay given to them at signing on. The crew celebrated this event by parading a straw horse around the deck, flogging it, and then throwing it overboard; hence the name given to this general area. There may indeed be some basis to this version.
(See also *Doldrums. Horse; To flog a dead horse.)*

Hover To wait near at hand; to linger or waver; originally purely a nautical usage, to describe a vessel that stood on and off the coast. Derived from *to hove,* to appear in sight. From the Middle English *hoven,* to hover, but its ultimate origin is uncertain.
(See also *Off and on.)*

Hulk The "hulks" were old, dismasted men-of-war vessels anchored in the Thames and off Portsmouth and used as

"A huge black hulk that was magnified
by its own reflection
in the tide. . . ."
—Henry Wadsworth Longfellow (1807–1882), American poet, *The Landlord's Tale,* cited in the *Universal Dictionary of the English Language* (1897)

prison ships. Originally, a hulk was a large ship employed mainly in the Mediterranean as a transport or cargo vessel. At one time, *hulk* was the name given by seamen to the hull of any ship, but this usage had disappeared by the end of the eighteenth century. The word is from the Greek *holkas,* trading vessel, and the modern usage of *hulking* (bulky, heavy, and clumsy) stems from this original reference to a heavy, unwieldy vessel.

I

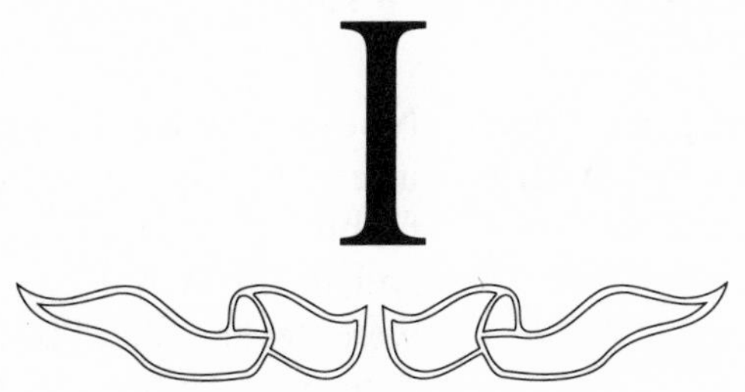

Ice
To break the ice

An ice-breaker is a specially designed and strengthened vessel, built for the purpose of forcing a path through pack ice in extreme latitudes.

Such a vessel is frequently employed to prepare the way for other vessels that need to reach some distant, ice-bound objective (as in opening a lane in an ice-bound port such as Vladivostok).

Colloquially, an ice-breaker is anything that breaks down reserve or reticence, such as in one's first meeting with a stranger, or in preparing the scene so that unpleasant or unwelcome news can be imparted. Note that the phrase "It cuts no ice with me" comes from an expression of the Iroquois Indians, a tribe from the Great Lakes area of North America: *Katno aiss vizmi*—"I am unmoved, unimpressed." Not nautical in origin, of course, but introduced into English by the Americans during the War of Independence in the 1780s. "Let's break the ice by inviting our new neighbours over for a meal."

Idler

An "idler" was originally a class of worker on board ship; specifically, a member of the crew who worked during the day but did not stand the usual night watches. The carpenter, cook, sailmaker, boatswain (bosun), and painter were the usual members of the roundhouse mess where idlers were accommodated. These men had duties that took up most of their daylight hours; hence, they were off watch at night, except of course in an emergency. They were also sometimes called "day workers" or "daymen," and were much envied by the rest of the crew.

The term expressed little or no critical attitude on the part of the crew, as idlers worked just as hard as others during their hours of duty. However, the word is now one of denigration; colloquially, an idler is a person who idles, a slacker, someone who is work-shy, habitually avoiding duty. From the Anglo-Saxon *idel,* empty, useless.
(See also *Waister.)*

"In" a ship or "on" a ship Not in itself a colloquial expression of nautical origin, but inserted here to instruct the neophyte and to remind the faithful. One enters or serves *in* a vessel, never *on* it—always; and, in the Royal Navy at least, the vessels one served in were never called "boats" unless they were submarines or destroyers. In the U.S. Navy, however, destroyers are ships, while submarines remain boats.

Submarines were originally described as "submarine boats," designs for which date back to 1578. A number of semi-submersible prototypes were being built by the middle of the nineteenth century. Perhaps the most successful of these was the *David,* the Confederate States Navy submarine, which, on February 7, 1864, attacked and sank the federal ship *Housatonic* during the American Civil War (1861–1865). Submarines are known today in the Royal Navy as *the Trade.*

Destroyers took their name from the fact that they were specifically designed to chase and destroy the fast torpedoboats that navies of the late nineteenth century were building. They were originally known as "torpedoboat destroyers," a rather clumsy name that was quickly foreshortened to "destroyer."

A British warship is always referred to with the prefix HMS *or* the definite article "the," so that one serves "in HMS *Warspite"* or "in the *Warspite."* Reference to a warship's name without either of the two prefixes *HMS* or *the* traditionally indicates only her captain; this is a long-standing tradition, and is intended to save time in the transmission of signals. Thus, *"Warspite* will report to the Admiral at 1400" means that the captain of the *Warspite* will attend the admiral in person.

Invest Referred to here in the sense of money, not the military sense of envelopment or siege. This financial usage goes back to fourteenth-century Italy, and its first occurrence in English came via the great East India Company of England (known as the Honourable East India Company), which was founded in the late sixteenth century for the purpose of exploiting maritime trade in India, the East Indies, and the Far East. For a long time the company held a monopoly; indeed, it was directly responsible for the gradual subjugation of the whole of the Indian subcontinent. As a result of this, the British government found itself obliged to assume political, financial, and military control of India. When the company was set up in 1600, it had a share capital of some £72,000 subscribed by 125 shareholders. By 1813 the company's monopoly over trade with India had been removed by the government, and individuals were then free to trade and invest on their own, private behalf. In 1833 the monopoly over the China trade was similarly broken, and investment in the Far East was open to private individuals.

Irons
In irons

Irons is an old term for fetters or shackles. A vessel is said to be in irons—"prevented"—when she cannot complete her tack and lies head-to-wind, unable to pay off either way. In this condition she is temporarily unmanageable.
A vessel that fails to pay off onto the other tack is also said to be "in stays," the same as being in irons. Colloquially, *to be in irons* is to be restricted in movement. Sailors often complained of being in irons when they were short of money.
(See also *Beam; To be on one's beam ends. Broke.)*

To clap in irons

The old nautical term for securing a seaman in leg irons and handcuffs. Now a colloquialism for imprisonment: "If they catch you with that stuff, you'll be clapped in irons forever!" From the Middle English *clappen,* a sudden stroke or blow.

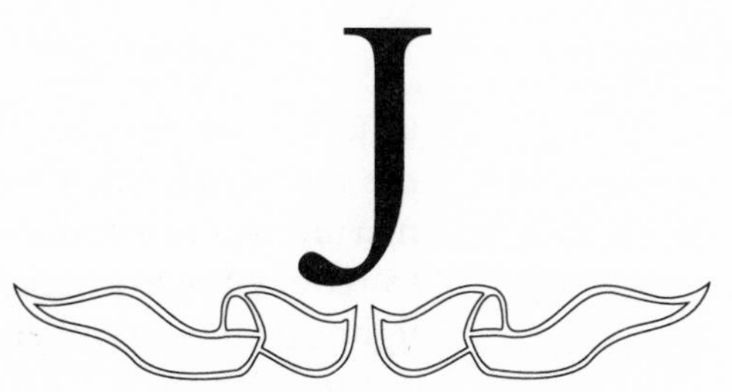

J

Jack
Every man jack of them All, without exception; the whole lot; everyone. *Jack* was originally the name applied to the seamen who worked the masts and yards of square-rigged ships, as distinct from the ship's boys, but gradually it came to refer to all British naval seamen. The name is found in such colloquialisms as "Pull up the ladder, Jack, I'm inboard" ("I'm all right, Jack"), the Australian saying relating to the *Jack system,* which is the pursuit of one's self-interest.
(See also *Jack Tar.)*

I'm all right, Jack From the phrase "Pull up the ladder, Jack, I'm inboard," denoting the pursuit of self-interest and complete disregard for the comfort and interests of others. Widely known as the "Jack system"; sometimes expressed as "Up you, Jack, I'm OK."

Jack Tar An old nickname for a sailor. Said to derive from the tarred canvas that seamen used to wear in bad weather; also from the fact that sailors were constantly engaged in the task of applying tar and tallow to the rigging and cordage of the vessel. The term is a contraction of *tarpaulin;* only after about 1750 was tarred canvas (tarpaulin) used for purposes other than clothing. *Tarry Breeks* is another term for a sailor, from the North Country of England. It is worth noting that the earlier British seaman used to dress his pigtail with tar.
(See also *Jack; Every man jack of them.)*

Jackknife A knife with a blade that folds into the handle. It is tempting to suggest that such a knife was named after the British sailor, who himself was universally known as a "jack," but such is not the case. The term is an American usage, but the word itself is derived from the Scottish *jockteleg,* a large clasp knife, which in turn came from the name of a French cutler, one Jacques de Liege, who apparently invented this type of knife.

The seaman serving in sail needed a knife that was instantly available for severing seizings and other lines in times of emergency. It was carried at the small of his back, usually with the point broken off. One of the first things the mates did when signing on a new crew in the merchant marine was to break off the points of the men's knives, so as to reduce the possibility of dangerous wounds among fighting crew members. It was also a precaution in case any of the crew should later think of turning against the captain and officers.

The size of the jackknife varies; in most navies, it fits more or less within the closed fist when the blade is folded, but larger types are also in common use.

Jam Used widely in everyday speech, meaning to press or squeeze tightly so that motion or withdrawal is made difficult or impossible; to fill or block up by crowding; to cause to be wedged. Colloquially used as in "He jammed his finger in the door"; "We were caught in a traffic jam." American usage (which in a pragmatic sense also means extended usage elsewhere in the English-speaking world, because of American dominance in the entertainment industry) also includes *jam* as meaning to have a good time, as in a group of jazz or rock musicians getting together for some inspired improvisations. It can also refer to the need to get away quickly from somewhere: "Let's jam," i.e., "let's go." Harassment by police officers can be called a "jam." It is likely that all these colloquialisms share the same origin.

"The ship stuck fast, jamm'd in between two Rocks."
—Daniel Defoe (1659–1731), English novelist and pamphleteer, *Robinson Crusoe* (1719)

Of nautical origin and with the same meaning; for example, running rigging can get jammed in a block (the seaman's word for a system of pulleys); a vessel can be jammed on a lee shore when the wind or tide (or worse, both acting together) make it difficult and perhaps impossible for her to fight her way off (nautically, *to claw off).* From *jamb* (door siding), which is the French *jambe,* leg, the word that the French formerly used for the jamb of a door *(jambage,* what we today still call the doorjamb), from the notion of a door frame being two legs passing down either side of the opening.

Jamboree Now usually associated with the Boy Scouts and referring to a rally or large gathering of Scouts, national or international. The word was in use by seamen in the 1840s, however, thus predating the Scouts by some 70 years.

Originally a jamboree was a carousal, a noisy merrymaking, a spree involving singing and dancing and—when possible—alcohol of some kind. Perhaps derived from combining the English *jabber* and the French *soiree,* a social gathering, with the *m* added from the dialect word *jam,* crowd. There may also be a connection with the French *burree* or *bourree,* dance.

Jaunty
To be jaunty

The nickname in the Royal Navy for a Chief Petty Officer of the Regulating Branch, i.e., the Master-at-Arms, responsible for discipline and other police functions within the service. It is perhaps a corruption of the French *gendarme;* it might also derive from the French *gentil,* noble, genteel. The ordinary seaman often regarded the master-at-arms with some suspicion and fear, and the expression *to be jaunty* probably derives from the airs that the master-at-arms was said to assume as a result of his position of authority. It is these airs, this attitude of sprightliness and self-assuredness, to which the colloquial usage of *jaunty* refers. "We wondered why she was looking so confident and self-satisfied these past few days, but the news of her recent engagement immediately explained her jaunty attitude."

"I felt a certain stiffness in my limbs, which entirely destroyed that jauntyness of air I was once master of."
—Joseph Addison (1672–1719), English essayist, *Spectator* No. 530 (1713)

Jaw

Sailor's slang for insolent backchat to a superior officer; now an everyday colloquialism for talkativeness, continual chatter, gossip. "The boys were always jawing about their weekend exploits."

Jerked beef

Meat, especially beef, that is preserved by being cut into strips and cured by drying in the sun. The term was brought into English and the other maritime languages by sailors who roamed the Caribbean in the heyday of the Spanish Main. The phrase is from the South American Spanish *charquear,* from *echarqui,* meat dried in long strips, a word borrowed from the Quechua Indians of Peru. Jerked beef—called "jerky" at the time—played an important part in the provisioning of the early explorers and pioneer settlers of the whole North American continent. The Jamaican dish known as "jerk chicken" or "jerk pork" (meat done in a spiced stew or sauce) is quite likely the same word, but it seems finally to have lost the connotation of the flesh being dried, at least in this particular instance.

Jerry-built

That which is flimsy or insubstantial. Possibly the word is connected with Jericho, the walls of which, we are told, came tumbling down at the sound of trumpets. However, this derivation seems unlikely; the walls of ancient cities were of necessity built far more strongly than the story would suppose. It is more probable that the term is a corruption of *jury-built,* meaning makeshift, temporary, as for an emergency, as in "jury-mast," "jury-leg," "jury-rigged," "jury-meal," and so forth.

It may also derive from a contemptuous abbreviation of *Jeremiah,* when the Puritans were the butt of so much ridicule after the Restoration (1660); Old Testament names were commonly used among them.

"Two lumps of plaster fall from the roof of the jerry-built palace; then the curse begins to work."
—*Pall Mall Gazette* (London), February 15, 1884

The term *jerry-built* occurs in the early nineteenth century in connection with substandard building in the northern suburbs of Liverpool, a major seaport where the housing shortage was acute in the post-Waterloo years, shortly after the passing of the Beerhouse Act in 1830. This makes it far more likely that the word is of nautical origin. Etymologically, *jury* is from the old French *ajurie,* relief, help, and the Latin *adjutare,* help. "We had always thought the beach shack to be a jerry-built affair, but it stood up to the hurricane surprisingly well."
(See also *Jury; Jury rig.)*

Jetsam See *Flotsam.*

Jettison Ultimately from the Old French *geter,* to throw. *To jettison* is to throw cargo and ship's gear overboard, to lighten a vessel that is in danger of foundering because of heavy seas or some other emergency. The verb is used figuratively to mean to abandon unwanted or surplus goods or parts, as when a motor vehicle is being lightened to get it through a sandy track. "The pilot was forced to jettison his spare fuel before attempting the emergency landing."

"Jetsam is where goods are cast into the sea, and there sink and remain under water."
—Sir William Blackstone (1723–1780), English jurist, *Commentaries on the Laws of England* (1769)

Jib The triangular foresail or headsail on a sailing vessel. Of uncertain origin, but perhaps derived from *gibbet,* the gallows (Middle English *gibet,* from the Old French *gibe,*

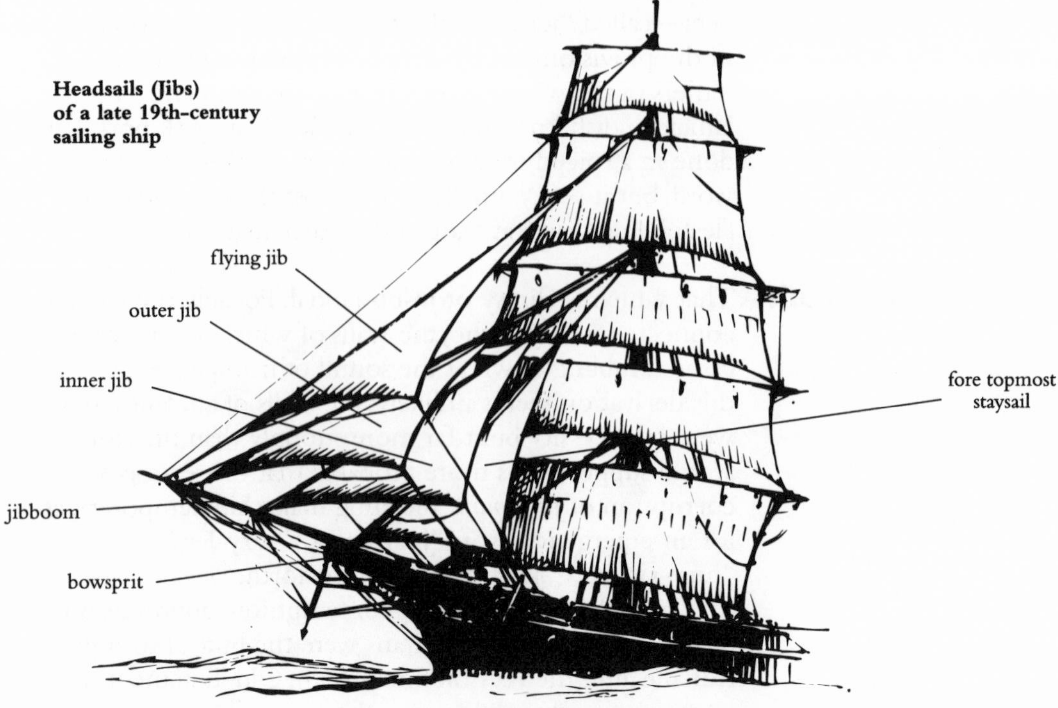

Headsails (Jibs) of a late 19th-century sailing ship

staff). The connection is not clear. However, the word may simply be a corruption of *gybe,* from the Dutch *gijpen,* to swing from side to side.

The cut of his jib

The characteristic way a person looks or acts; the art of recognising a person by, originally, the shape of his (or her) nose because of the close resemblance between the outline of the jib on a sailing ship and the silhouette of the human nose.

Sailors could recognise the nationality of other warships at sea by the variations in the shape of this triangular foresail (the jib) long before the ship's flag of nationality could be determined. For instance, Spanish ships had either a very small jib or none at all; French ships often had two jibs in a period when other ships flew only one. Other differences lay in the ways in which jibs were actually cut: French jibs had a more acute angle at the clew, thereby making it readily distinguishable from the jibs of other sailing navies.
"I don't like the cut of his jib; he spends far too much time finding fault with the management."

"There must have been something very innocent and confiding in the cut of our jib."
—Lord Dufferin, *Letters from High Latitudes* (1857), cited in the *Universal Dictionary of the English Language* (1897)

To bouse his jib

A sailor's way of saying that someone has been drinking until his face is flushed and swollen. The word *jib* was sailor's slang for a person's nose, and later the face, i.e., the foremost part, as it is the foremost sail in a ship. *Bouse* is an old nautical word meaning to hoist, also to make tight ("to bouse down the halliards," for example, is to haul on them in successive pulls until all slackness has been taken out of them). The expression *to bouse one's jib* is simply a pun: to get "tight" by drinking too much, the effects of which are easily observable in the face.
(See also *Booze. Jib; The cut of his jib.)*

"Then bouses drumly German water,
To mak himself look fair and fatter."
—Robert Burns (1759–1796), Scottish poet, "The Twa Dogs" (1785)

To jib at something

To express alarm at something; to back out of some standpoint or enterprise; to have second thoughts. Often applied to a horse, which is said to *jib* when it is startled by something. The essential element is surprise at some unexpected development or event.

The phrase derives from the term for a nautical manoeuvre, *to gybe,* often spelled *jibe,* which means to allow the wind to blow from astern over the same side that the mainsail is set, in a fore-and-aft rigged vessel. This causes the boom and sail to swing with considerable violence to the other side, often with serious results to standing rigging or an unwary crew member. A controlled gybe is a deliberate and prepared-for evolution; it is the accidental gybe that takes the helmsman by surprise. The word comes from the Dutch *gijpen,* to swing from side to side.

Jiffy A very short period of time; in a moment, a brace of shakes. The origin of the word is unknown, but it was in use in the eighteenth century, and is part of the sailor's idiom. The word is also part of the trademark name used by Australia Post for its "jiffy bags," the strong, padded paper bags used for sending objects through the mail. "Tell the taxi to wait: I'll be down in a jiffy."

Jigger Colloquially, a jigger is a "thingamy," a "gadget," a "what-do-you-call-it," a "thingummybob," a "thingummyjig"; more exactly, an indefinite name for a thing or person that the speaker cannot define or designate more clearly. The word is from *jig,* a dance, from the French *gigue,* dance, and the Old French *gigue,* a fiddle, and finally applied to a wide variety of small mechanical devices.

Nautically, a jigger was originally a light tackle used for many small purposes on board ship, usually associated with holding or helping to haul on moving parts, such as ropes, anchors, and booms. The essence is that it was a gadget with many applications. The word was also used to name the jigger-mast, a small mast set right aft in some sailing vessels; the mizzenmast of a yawl is sometimes called the jigger-mast, and the fourth mast in a schooner of four or more masts is also named the jigger-mast.

The expression *I'll be jiggered!,* a mild oath of astonishment, probably derives from the *chigre,* known also as the "jigger" or "chigger" (French *chique,* Spanish *chico,* small), the flea-like insect in the West Indies that burrows into the skin of the feet and breeds there unless quickly removed. It is a source of great annoyance to the victim. (See also *Gadget.)*

Jingo Probably a Basque word, *Jinko* or *Jainko,* meaning God. Basques were among the earliest organised whalers in Europe, and as harpooners their expressions would have carried some weight with other seafarers. The word came into the English language in the late seventeenth century, and a hundred years later it had acquired a political overtone, to mean aggressive patriotism, equivalent to the term *chauvinism.* "If they dare to come onto this property, then, by jingo, we'll show them who's in charge!"

"In the days when Jingoism had to be combated and overcome. . . ."
—*Pall Mall Gazette* (London), June 12, 1884

In the late nineteenth century, there arose in England a group of politicians who loudly advocated the cause of the Turks in the Turko-Russian War of 1877–1878; they were identified with the sentiments of a music-hall song that was popular at the time, the first lines of which were: "We don't want to fight, but by Jingo if we do, We've got the ships, we've got the men, we've got the money too." Naturally enough, they became known as "jingoists," descriptive of one who clamours for war and advocates a firm and spirited foreign policy.

Jollies Another name for the Royal Marines. Originally all soldiers carried on board a British warship were known as "jollies," with a "tame jolly" being a militiaman and a "royal jolly" a marine.
(See also *Bullocks. Grabbies. Pongo. Turkeys.*)

Jolly Roger The much-feared flag of the old-time pirates and mutineers, on which was depicted a skull with crossed thigh bones beneath. There is no evidence that such a flag was ever flown by pirate ships as a whole; the generally recognised pirate symbol was a plain black flag, which some pirate ships were occasionally reported to have flown from their main masthead.

However, a number of particularly fierce (and therefore well-known) pirate captains did fly flags adorned with skulls, bones, and similar morbid devices, and there is no doubt that these flags captured the public's attention and served to identify all pirates with such flags.

The early eighteenth-century French pirate Emanual Wynn, for example, favoured a skull placed on crossed bones, with an hourglass below to advise his victims that time was running out; Henry Every preferred a skull in profile, adorned with headband and earrings, and crossed bones beneath. Blackbeard (who began life as Edward Teach or Thatch or Tash or even Drummond, the last according to Daniel Defoe, an early chronicler of pirate history), the man who best fitted the public's image of what a real pirate should be like, flew a flag that sported a horned devil-skeleton with an hourglass in one hand and a spear in the other. Whatever the pirate captain's fancy in flags, it was certain to convey the appropriate chilling message to his victims.

The origin of the name *Jolly Roger* is obscure. Some say it is a corruption of *joli rouge,* a French expression meaning "pretty red," a reference to the red flag often flown by privateers. Another possible explanation, however, is that *Jolly Roger* arose from the fact that from the sixteenth to the eighteenth centuries, the word *roger* in English meant to have sexual intercourse, usually of a vigorous kind, and often in the nature of rape. One of the earliest names for this flag was *Old Roger,* recorded in 1723, and even before then *roger* was a slang term for penis. It is known from the literature of the period that pirates generally treated women in a less than gallant fashion: in short, they were often bound and

"rogered at the rail" by all and sundry, and then frequently thrown overboard to fend for themselves.
(See also *Pirate. Privateer. Skull and crossbones.)*

Jollyboat A nautical term with no application in colloquial language, but included here because of its interesting origin. The word is a corruption of the Middle English *jolywat,* which itself is a corruption of *gellywat* or *gellywatte,* a small ship's boat. The etymology points to the East Indian *galivat* and the Portuguese *galeota,* a diminutive of *galley.* The term *jollyboat* today refers to a ship's work boat, only moderate in size, and hoisted at the stern of a sailing vessel for handy use.

Jonah
To be a Jonah Also "Jonas." A person whose presence is said to foretell the visitation of bad luck upon his companions. The origin of this belief lies in the Old Testament story of Jonah, who fled by sea to Tarshish (in southeastern Spain) to escape from the Lord. His presence on board ship brought great misfortune to the sailors, in the form of wild and unrelenting storms. His companions threw him overboard as punishment, whereupon he was swallowed by a whale and regurgitated three days later. However, a number of authorities dispute the truth of this story on the grounds that a whale's gullet is of too small a size to admit the body of a man.

Jonah's name has spread far beyond maritime circles as a description of a person who brings ill fortune to all with whom he comes into contact: "For heaven's sake don't bring Bill on the trip—he's a Jonah when it comes to the rest of us catching fish."

Jonnick *Jonnick* is sailor's slang for honest, fair, correct, true; sometimes spelled "jonick" or "junnick." The word is from an English dialect *jannock,* meaning fair, straightforward. It was once part of Australian metaphorical speech, but in the decades following World War II it has gradually disappeared from use.

Jumper An outer garment, a pullover or sweater, usually made of wool, for covering the upper part of the body. More particularly, a jumper was a loose outer jacket worn by sailors; it was the nautical elaboration of *jump* or *jump coat,* a short coat worn in the seventeenth century. The word is from the French *jupe, jupon,* skirt, jacket, originally Arabic *jubbah,* mantle. *Jumper* also appears in other nautical expressions, such as "jumper stay," "jumper strut," and "jumper wire," but this is a different word from the one discussed here.

Junk In the seaman's world, junk is, strictly speaking, old or useless rope or cordage. The word derives from the Latin *juncus,* a reed or rush once used in the making of cordage. The word was also applied to the salt meat that made up the sailor's staple diet, through its alleged similarity to the ends of old rope. It is interesting to note that salt pork continued to be issued in the British fleet as late as 1926. The colloquial meaning applies to anything that is fit only to be condemned; the emphasis is upon uselessness: "We went to the garage sale that had been widely advertised in the local paper, and found there was nothing but a lot of old junk for sale."

The Chinese vessel known to the Western world as the "junk" is so named because its sails were commonly made of reeds or rushes *(juncus).* The Portuguese gave it the name *junco,* which later went into English as the familiar word *junk.*

(See also *Fagged; To be fagged out.*)

Jury
Jury rig Anything that is "jury-rigged" on board a vessel is a temporary affair to replace a permanent structure that has been carried away, as in a "jury mast," "jury rudder," and so forth. The term *jury leg* is sometimes applied to a person's wooden leg. The colloquial application ashore is obvious, as in to have some jury chairs and tables—i.e., temporary or makeshift furniture.

(See also *Jerry-built.*)

K

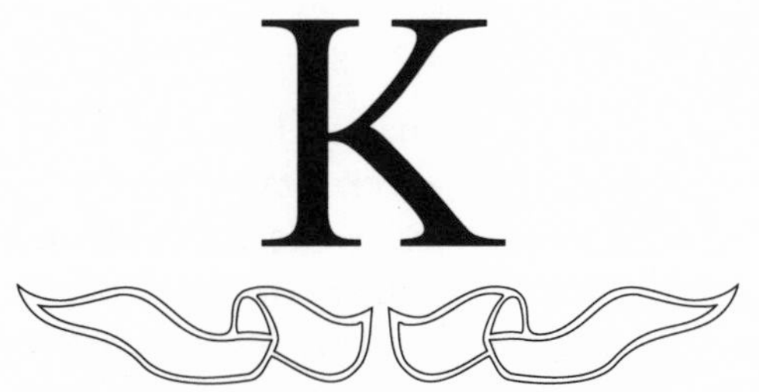

Kedgeree Originally a vegetable curry, popular with seamen, and now a well-known dish ashore; it consists usually of rice and fish. From the Hindi *khichri, khicari,* and the Sanskrit *k'rsara,* a meal of rice and sesamum.

Keel
To be on an even keel

Figuratively, to be stable, in a state of balance, as in a person who is said to have both feet on the ground, as distinguished from someone who, in contrast, has his head in the clouds. Nautically, a vessel is said to be "on an even keel" when she floats exactly upright in the water without any list to either side.

"He had come along with three young fellows of his acquaintance who worked in the keels."
—Tobias Smollett (1721–1771), English novelist, *Roderick Random* (1748)

There are two origins of the word, and interestingly enough they are not related. One is the Old Norse *kjol-r,* corresponding to the modern meaning of *keel;* the other is from early Dutch *kiel,* which originally meant "ship." After the sixteenth century, the word took on the now-common meaning of evenness and stability: "He kept his business on an even keel despite the many problems imposed by the recession."

To keel over *To keel over* figuratively means to lose one's balance or stability, generally as a result of a shock or unexpected event. The metaphor gains its force from the fact that a vessel resting only on its keel is in a state of potential and violent instability. "She seemed to be perfectly well before dinner, then she just keeled over halfway through the meal." Although the expression draws on nautical words, it is not a seaman's phrase; it might have become popular by means of the stage.
(See also *Keel; To be on an even keel.)*

Keelhaul An old naval and merchant service punishment, which involved tying ropes to the hands and feet of the offending seaman and dragging him under the vessel's keel from one side to the other. (In extreme cases, the victim would be dragged from stem to stern—i.e., from the front of the ship to the back; such instances were rare and would have been used when there was no intention of giving the wretched man a chance of surviving.) The result was naturally often fatal, if not from drowning, then from laceration by barnacles, loss of blood, or the infection that inevitably followed.

A far less severe method was to pass a line beneath the vessel from one side to the other, with one end secured to the victim; tie a deep-sea lead to his feet; drop him overboard; and haul him under the ship and up the other side. The lead weight would keep him free of the barnacles on the hull (one could only hope that the operation was carried out in the sailors' usual efficient manner).

"The unfortunate Smallbones was to be keelhauled."
—Frederick Marryat (1792–1848), British naval officer and novelist, *The Dog Fiend or Snarleyow* (1837)

The punishment (which in the Royal Navy was not a standard form of dealing with malefactors, nor was it ever awarded by any naval court-martial) was said to have been introduced by the Dutch, who were still using it in 1813; it was certainly common in other navies between the fifteenth and seventeenth centuries. From the Dutch *kielhalen, kiel,* keel, and *halen,* haul.

Metaphorically, the phrase carries a note of dire threat of reprisal; to haul someone over the coals unless matters are quickly put right; to reprimand severely: "It was perfectly clear that the superintendent intended to keelhaul the young police officer for his insensitive handling of the incident."
(See also *Keel; To be on an even keel.)*

Kick
To kick upstairs

Originally a nautical idiom; it means much the same today as it did 200 years ago in Britain's Royal Navy. Colloquially, it is to get rid of, to have someone out of the way, by promoting him or her to a position where that person's influence is less likely to be felt. "The board kicked him upstairs, from the position of line superintendent to that of personnel manager, to minimise the effect of his incompetence."
(See also *Half pay.)*

Kickback

Any sum of money paid for favours received or hoped for; usually a corrupt practice. A nautical expression from the days when seagoing captains sought to augment their already meagre salaries by entering into a fraudulent agreement with, for example, a ship's chandler, whereby the captain would return or "kick back" a proportion of the ballast, ship's stores, or such into the merchant's stock. The value of goods thus returned would be divided between the captain and the merchant; the ship's owners, of course, unwittingly paid for the full amount as entered on the ship's papers.

The practice is widespread in many areas of politics and commerce. "The property developer was widely suspected

of providing kickbacks to government ministers who gave him preferential treatment."
(See also *Slush fund.)*

Kidnap

"He had long been a wanderer and an exile, in constant peril of being kidnapped."
—Thomas Babington Macaulay (1800–1859), English historian, *History of England* (1848)

The term *kidnapping* originated in the seventeenth century, when it referred to the "nabbing" of a "kid" or child for sale to sea captains, who then transported that unfortunate person to the plantations in the American colonies. Its origins were essentially maritime; nowadays the phrase embraces the capturing of persons of any age for the purpose of holding them for ransom. Another term of identical meaning is *barbadose,* which additionally meant to transport convicts to the Barbados Islands in the Caribbean in the time of Cromwell.
(See also *Spirit; To spirit away.)*

Kite
To fly a kite

Kite was the general name given to the light-weather square sails that could be spread at the masthead to make the most of light following winds. Included would be the moon-rakers and skyscrapers of the late nineteenth- and early twentieth-century grain ships and nitrate ships that marked the end of the great age of sail.

To fly a kite—to hoist such a sail—meant literally to see what would happen, to see whether any improvement could be made in the vessel's speed; hence the idiom, to do something tentatively (in word or deed) to test the reactions to an idea or a plan: "His proposal to shift the time of the meeting to early morning was simply kite-flying." From the Anglo-Saxon *cyta* and related to the German *kauz,* a kind of owl.

Knock
To knock down

When a cask was dismantled into its component parts—the staves and hoops—it was said to be "knocked down." Sailing ships of any size carried a cooper on board, whose duty was to maintain and repair the casks so that they were in good enough condition to carry the crew's food and drinking water. For many hundreds of years there was no other way of successfully storing the ship's provisions for a voyage of any length; hence the importance of casks as part of the vessel's equipment.

This sense of disassembly is echoed in everyday figures of speech, such as to "knock down" a vehicle or a machine; that is, to take it apart or to reduce it to its parts, usually to facilitate its handling or despatch. "It is common for some motor manufacturers to export their farm vehicles in a CKD condition—i.e., Completely Knocked Down."
(See also *Stave; To stave in.)*

To knock off This expression means to stop work, to stop whatever one is doing. It also carries the additional meanings of to steal; to kill; to quickly compose something such as music or a poem; to deduct an amount of money from the total; and so on, but in this context it refers to that hallowed time of day when the world's workers may lawfully cease their labours and go home.

But where did the phrase come from? *To knock off* makes as much linguistic sense as *It cuts no ice with me.* In fact, there is a logical explanation for the term and it comes from the sea. It traces back more than 2,000 years to the time of the ancient Romans, when slaves spent their days (all of them) chained to the oars of the galley, busily heaving the ship from one end of the Mediterranean to the other, conveying armies or important functionaries on official business. Frequently they were also required to row the vessel into battle (and, if they were lucky, out of it; otherwise they went down with their ship).

The only way for the rowers to keep the vessel moving efficiently was to work the oars to a definite rhythm, and the easiest way for them to keep a rhythm was to have a person at the stern beating a drum or slotted or hollow block of wood with mallets to the required cadence. From time to time the rowers would have to rest from their labours, and the signal for this was a blow or a knock on a separate drum or wooden block that gave out a quite different note. This was the signal for the galley slaves to stop rowing; instead of "leaning on" their oars (still a term in rowing and boat-pulling today), they could "lean off" at the sound of the special knock or beat. It was "knock-off" time.

Knots

At a rate of knots No sailor would ever use the expression *at a rate of knots;* the word *knot* (from the Anglo-Saxon *enotta)* already expresses the idea of rate. It is therefore rather puzzling that Captain Frederick Marryat (1792–1848), an experienced and distinguished captain in the Royal Navy, should write in one of his popular novels, *Mr. Midshipman Easy* (1836), that a vessel was "running about three knots an hour." To use the expression in this way is a tautology.

A knot is the nautical measure of speed, and is defined as a speed (or rate) of one nautical mile per hour. A nautical mile in practice is almost exactly 6,080 feet; in theory, it is one minute of arc measured on a meridian (the meridian chosen for the standard is at latitude 48°N), with the apex of the arc at the earth's centre. As a measure of speed, the expression is always just so many knots, never knots per hour; a ship may be doing seven knots, but never seven knots per hour.

The term *knot* is a direct descendant of the old chip-log (sometimes called a "Dutch log") used for centuries on sailing ships to measure the speed of their progress through the water. The log (or chip) was a flat timber about the size of a dinner plate, with a long line attached to it. This line had knots tied into it at certain intervals, which were arrived at as follows. Experience told seamen the total length of line that could be heaved and retrieved by hand, given the likely best speeds of various types of sailing vessel. It was found that the sandglass best suited for timing the operation was the 28-second glass; a glass of greater duration (say 30 seconds or more) would give a slightly more accurate result, but the much greater length of log-line running over the stern in that time would be a considerable burden to haul inboard. Thus, the proportion of 28 seconds to one hour gave the proportion of 47.25 to 6,080 feet:

$$\frac{28}{3600} = \frac{47.25}{6080}$$

The log-line was then knotted at intervals of 47 feet 3 inches.

When the log (or chip) was heaved into the sea astern of the vessel, one seaman would let the line on the reel run out through his fingers until he felt the "start knot," which was placed so that the chip would be far enough astern to be clear of the ship's wake. He would shout "Turn!" and another seaman would immediately upend the 28-second glass. The log-line operator then kept count of the number of knots that passed through his fingers as the log-line unwound itself from the reel.

As soon as the 28-second glass was emptied, its tender would yell "Nip!" The number of knots that had run out through the first man's fingers in that period gave the speed of the ship in nautical miles per hour, otherwise simply expressed as knots. For even greater accuracy, the speed was sometimes expressed as knots and fathoms, indicating more exactly how much line had gone overboard during the timed interval of 28 seconds.

Many of the tea and wool clippers of the late nineteenth century logged occasional bursts of 15 knots or more, and some recorded 19 knots and even higher speeds. To handle a vessel at those speeds would be a hair-raising and hazardous experience indeed. The average speed for everyday pleasure sailing craft varies between four and eight knots, while offshore racing yachts consistently maintain double figures, depending on hull type and weather conditions.

Kye The British, Australian, and New Zealand seaman's name for cocoa made from solid slabs and served hot on watch (sometimes called "ki"). The slab is put into boiling water, and condensed milk is then added. Cocoa is now an official victual issue in the British navy. Various nautical references state that the origin of the term is unknown or, at best, obscure; but it is quite probable that it derives from the Melanesian pidgin *kaikai,* food, from the days in the nineteenth century when the British flag was to be found throughout the Western Pacific.

L

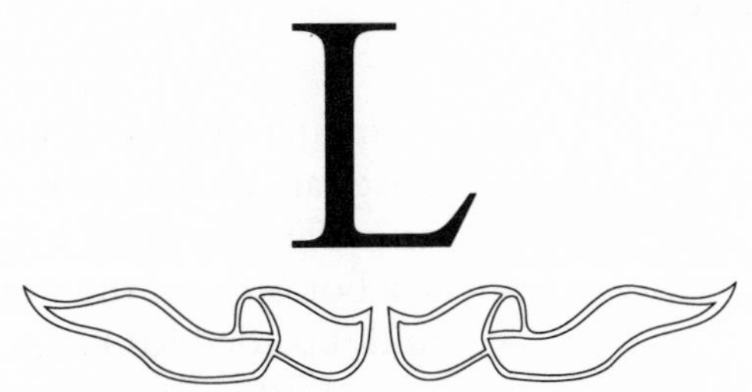

Laid
To be laid up

"Lay up these my words in your heart. . . ."
—Deuteronomy 11:18

To lay up is to store away, or to take a ship out of service. (In another usage, *to lay up* is to twist the strands of a rope together.) *To be laid up,* then, is to be out of action, out of commission; a person temporarily incapacitated through injury or illness is said to be "laid up," especially if confined to bed: "I've been laid up all week with influenza."

Land

The word *land,* of course, is not nautical, but *to land* is to bring to or put on land or shore. From this we have a number of nautical metaphors:

"Thus, royal sir, to see you landed here,
Was cause enough of triumph for a year."
—John Dryden (1631–1700), English poet, *To His Sacred Majesty,* cited in the *Universal Dictionary of the English Language* (1897)

Landfall: Land first sighted or approached when coming in from the sea.
Landsman (earlier *landman):* Someone who is not a seaman; a landlubber.
To make the land: To come within sight of land.

From the Anglo-Saxon *land,* with similar forms in the Teutonic languages, and related to the Welsh *llann-,* enclosure, church.
(See also *Land; To see how the land lies.)*

No-man's land

The space amidships of a vessel, between the after part of the forecastle and (generally) the foremast. In this space were stored the blocks, rope, and other tackle that might be needed when working the forecastle. It derives its name from being neither on the starboard nor the port side, and neither in the waist nor on the forecastle.

The term later came to be applied to the area of land between hostile lines of entrenchments, or to any space contested by both sides and belonging to neither. More freely, it is a wilderness, a place to be avoided as dangerous: "His book deals with the uneasy no-man's-land that lies between sociology and politics."

To see how the land lies

Colloquially, to see whether things are promising or not; to see what sort of conditions one might be facing, often rendered as "the lie of the land"; to investigate a situation or

a circumstance. From the days when sailing ships without adequate charts often had to work slowly in to an unfamiliar coast to navigate safely; the condition of the sea bottom and the nearby coastal terrain would be noted and recorded for future reference. "I can't say what I'll do until I listen to their grievances—I shall just have to see how the land lies."
(See also *Land.)*

Land shark Sailor's slang for lawyer, considered very unlucky to have aboard for any purpose whatsoever; probably akin to Shylock's "land-rats and water-rats" in Shakespeare's *The Merchant of Venice.*

The seaman's distrust of lawyers may stem from the fact that naval crew and officers could not be pursued or prosecuted for debt once they were safely aboard their vessel; conversely, though, once ashore they were fair game for the tipstaff and bailiff, who were constantly on the lookout for seafarers known to owe money. Times have changed; a *land shark* is nowadays a person who makes excessive profits from speculating in land.

Landmark A conspicuous object, whether natural or artificial (such as a lighthouse, beacon, or unusual contour of the land), which is visible from seaward and can serve as an aid to navigation when closing the land or locating a harbour. Such landmarks are usually clearly shown on charts.

"Now, the earth has no landmarks on it to indicate degrees."
—Sir William Herschel (1738–1822), British astronomer, *Astronomy* (1858)

Metaphorically, a landmark is an event or decision by which subsequent events are measured: "The Eureka rebellion in 1854 was a landmark in Australian political history"; "The jury's verdict in the fraud trial was a landmark decision in the history of contract law."

Lash To bind, to secure objects in place or together, with cord or other small stuff. From the Old French *lachier, lacier,* to lace together. *To lace* is an even earlier nautical usage, meaning to beat or whip, usually with a rope *(to lace into someone* is to attack with vigor). Also *to lash* as with a whip; hence *to lash out,* meaning both to hit wildly at someone and to spend money in large quantities: "For our anniversary we decided to lash out and have a big party."

A "lash up" is sailor's slang for a temporary or badly performed job; *to have a lash at* is an Australian colloquialism meaning to attempt, to have a go at something. "I've never played soccer before, but I'll have a lash at it." There are a few other metaphors on *lash,* all of which retain the central meaning of effort, of bringing together.
(See also *Lash; To lash out.)*

To lash out To strike out vigorously, usually in anger and with vehemence; often as a result of provocation: "Their repeated tauntings about his small size caused him to lash out in rage at the nearest boy."
(See also *Lash.)*

Lashings
To have lashings of something

Once a common colloquialism among the English, the Irish, and the Australians. It meant to have plenty of, a surfeit, as in food or drink; probably derives from the Anglo-Irish *lashing,* meaning abundance, floods of. To the seaman, *lash* also means to secure with a rope or cord, but the term is best remembered for its association with the cat-o'-nine-tails and the lashes or strokes administered therewith. For the erring seaman, there was always an excess of lashings: "The camp cook kept the boys happy with lashings of meat and potatoes."
(See also *Cat; No room to swing a cat.)*

Lassie In itself, *Lassie* is not a nautical term, but the name of this famous collie has an interesting connection with maritime history.

The first British battleship to be torpedoed by a German submarine was HMS *Formidable,* sunk just off Portland Bill in the English Channel in 1915. A few hours after the sinking, some fishermen found the body of a seaman that had been washed ashore in Lyme Bay; they carried it to West Bay and laid it out on the floor of the Pilot Boat Inn, and out of decency covered it with a tarpaulin.

However, the dog belonging to the landlord of the inn kept pulling aside the tarpaulin and licking the face of the dead seaman. Despite every discouragement, the dog persisted until the landlord was forced to see for himself what the dog had apparently known all along: that the seaman was not yet dead. The man was revived, and that is the end of his part in this story. Eventually, though, the incident inspired the famous film featuring the collie who won the hearts of millions of children the world over for her bravery, loyalty, and intelligence.

The point of this anecdote is that the dog was named after the survivor of the sinking of HMS *Formidable,* John Lassie.

Latitude
To give some latitude

Latitude is the angular distance of a place on the earth's surface measured north or south of the equator; the word is from the Latin *latitudo,* breadth. Mariners in the northern hemisphere have always been able to determine their latitude, even if only approximately, by observing the altitude of the Pole Star; but for many hundreds of years the calculation of longitude was a serious problem.

"I took this kind of verse, which allows more latitude than any other."

—John Dryden (1631–1700), English poet, *Second Miscellany,* cited in the *Universal Dictionary of the English Language* (1897)

In the colloquial sense, *latitude* means space or freedom; *to give someone some latitude* is to permit a certain degree of freedom of action or opinion. "Because the football coach consistently achieved outstanding results from his team, the committee was prepared to give him a wide degree of latitude in his training expenses account."
(See also *Leeway; To make leeway.)*

Launch The name given today to a variety of boats driven by oar, sail, or motor, usually for pleasure trips or passenger sightseeing. In the earlier days of sail, a launch was a rather lengthy, flat-bottomed craft used mainly as a gunboat, albeit an unwieldy one. A ship's boat (the largest were equipped with mast and sails) was also called a "launch," as was the ship's pulling boat; it was also often the largest boat carried by a warship for harbour duties. The word is from the Portuguese *lancha,* not to be confused with the verb *to launch.*
(See also *Launch; To launch [something], to launch into.)*

To launch (something); to launch into Deriving from the Old French *lancier,* to pierce, probably from the obvious idea that a newly built vessel, when slid or heaved down to the water's edge, then "pierces" the surface of the water so as to float.

The naming of the vessel takes place at the moment of launching, when a bottle of wine or champagne is broken on the vessel's bow. This is a remnant of an ancient custom of pouring wine over the vessel and the nearby sea as a libation or offering to the sea-gods, to appease them during the launching, that is, to placate them for the rude piercing of their domain when the vessel entered the water. The Vikings used to tie slaves onto the launching skids, so the blood from their crushed bodies spattered the hull and thereby became an offering to these sea-gods.

"Their cables loose, and launch into the main. . . ."

—Alexander Pope (1688–1744), English man of letters, Homer's *Odyssey* (1726)

As a metaphor, the phrase is used in "to launch a scheme," "to launch into something," and so on; the controlling idea is to cause to move, to set going: "He launched himself into the task of running the finance department as efficiently as possible."

Lay day Traditionally the days permitted to a charter party for loading and unloading a vessel. From earlier times, when a certain number of days were allowed a merchant ship for the loading or discharging of cargo while lying in port. At the end of this period of *lay days,* the vessel was obliged to pay demurrage. The term is possibly from *delay day.* Widely used to indicate days in which there will be an interruption in work or activity, as in yacht racing or international

athletic meets: "*Australia II,* the America's Cup challenger from Perth, claimed a lay day so that her crew could work on repairing the yacht's rigging."
(See also *Demurrage.)*

Lazarette Also "lazaretto." A storeroom for ship's provisions, usually in the after-most section of the ship, so that it could be under the direct eye and control of the master. It was also a room used to quarantine any person with a contagious or infectious disease. From Lazarus of the Bible, who was laid daily at the rich man's gate, and originally derived from the Hebrew *Eleazar,* one helped by God. The word was early connected with leprosy.

Lazaretto See *Lazarette.*

Lead
A lead-swinger; to swing the lead

A very common expression, meaning to avoid duty by feigning illness or injury; to malinger. Its origin is interesting.

The term as used today is a corruption by twentieth-century military of an earlier nautical expression, *to swing the leg,* which referred to a dog's habit of running sometimes on only three legs either to rest the fourth or to elicit sympathy from an onlooker. Soldiers confused this phrase with the sailor's technical term *heaving the lead,* meaning to take soundings with the hand lead line to roughly determine a vessel's position when offshore. (Note that it is never *swinging* the lead when taking soundings—it is always *heaving* the lead.)

It was assumed by soldiers that this seaman's duty was an easy one, allowing of loafing and slacking, but in fact it is a task requiring considerable skill, effort, and experience on the part of the leadsman. The lead weight was necessarily quite heavy, about 14 pounds for the deepsea (pronounced "dip-see") lead line, which itself was 100 fathoms (600 feet) in length. Furthermore, the lead line had to be retrieved by hand, often at night and frequently in stormy conditions, during moments of considerable stress and anxiety when the vessel had no other means of immediately fixing its position. The task was anything but a sinecure for the leadsman, who couldn't have shirked his duty even had he wanted to, as the officer of the watch, and perhaps the captain and pilot as well, were often watching him closely so they could plot his shouted depths as quickly as possible.

An extension of the colloquialism means to spin a yarn, to tell a tall tale; the connection lies in the fact that the storyteller is exaggerating the facts of his yarn to elicit admiration, sympathy, or such. *Swinging the lead* is a verbal device for neglecting one's work, inventing excuses to hide the fact of one's own mistakes or inefficiency: "Most of the people working on this project are very keen to see it succeed, but the remainder are swinging the lead."

League The seaman's old measure of distance, now obsolete. A *league* was 3.18 nautical miles (the equivalent of four Roman miles), but in practice the fraction was ignored; on land, the distance varied greatly from country to country. From the Late Latin *leuca* or *leuga,* and the Spanish *legua,* Italian *lega,* and French *lieue;* apparently still used in Scandinavian countries. Not related to *league* as in an alliance, which is from the Latin *ligare,* to bind.

"A league from Epidamnum had we sailed. . . ."
—William Shakespeare (1564–1616), *The Comedy of Errors,* act 1, scene 1

Leak
To spring a leak When a seam opens up in a ship and admits water, it is said to *spring a leak.* When the butt end of one of the planks in a wooden vessel breaks loose of its fastenings and, because of hull curvature, springs outward to project beyond the side of the ship, the plank is said to be "sprung." The phrase *to spring a leak* now applies to any break or hole in a ship's hull, regardless of how it occurs, that allows water to come in.

The phrase is widely used ashore, both literally and metaphorically: "It was well known that the government select committee on corruption had sprung a serious leak, and that the press was about to be handed the story of a scandal of breathtaking proportions."

Leatherneck See *Bootneck.*

Lee From the Anglo-Saxon *hleo,* shelter, warmth. Nautically, the side of the vessel that is sheltered from the wind (as distinct from the weather side of a ship); also the direction toward which the wind blows.

Some related phrases are:

lee board: Boards hung on the lee side of a vessel to prevent it making too much leeway.
lee shore: The shore or coast that lies downwind from a vessel; usually a very dangerous situation.
lee side: The sheltered side of a vessel.
lee tide: A tide running in the same direction as the wind is blowing.
leeward (pronounced "loo-ard"): In or toward the lee; the opposite direction is *windward,* or the weather side.
under the lee of a ship: To be sheltered from wind and sea by the bulk of a vessel lying immediately to windward of one's own vessel.
under the lee of the land: To be sheltered by land from wind and wave.

"For now in front her trembling inmates see
The hills of Greece emerging on the lee."
—William Falconer (1732–1769), English sailor and lexicographer, *The Shipwreck* (1762)

Lee has exactly the same meaning ashore: "We sheltered from the rain in the lee of the shearing shed"; "Because he was always such a wonderful father to their children, she gave him considerable leeway whenever he wanted to have an occasional night out with his teammates."
(See also *Weather.)*

A lee shore

"What made it more appalling was that we were on a lee shore."
—Captain Frederick Marryat, R.N. (1792–1848), English naval captain and novelist, *Peter Simple* (1834)

The coastline onto which the wind blows directly; it is thus downwind from any ship in the offing (a ship that is within sight of the coast), and can be dangerous because the wind tends to force a vessel onto it. Called the "lee shore" because it is under the lee of any vessel in the vicinity.

Colloquially, a "lee shore" is any situation that could threaten disaster if approached too nearly.

To be taken by the lee

To be brought up short. "He found himself suddenly taken by the lee when his wife innocently asked if she could go with him to the sales convention in Singapore."
(See also *Lee; To bring by the lee. Turn; To bring up with a round turn.)*

To bring by the lee

Said of a vessel which, when running with the wind, experiences a sudden wind change from one quarter across the stern to the other quarter. Not a safe point of sailing, for it could lead to broaching and capsizing.

Colloquially, *to bring someone by the lee* is to bring her up sharp, to cause her to be taken aback; to be very surprised and disconcerted: "When the fisheries inspector insisted on examining the haul of rock lobster, the diver was clearly brought by the lee."
(See also *Lee; To be taken by the lee. Turn; To bring up with a round turn.)*

Leeway

Leeway is the distance a vessel is set down to leeward (pronounced "loo-ard") of her course by the action of wind or tide or a heavy seaway. The term describes the amount of offset between the vessel's charted course and the course actually sailed over the ground, the difference between the two being the result of the action of weather and sea on the hull and superstructure of the vessel. *Lee* is from the Old English *helo* and *hleow,* covering or shelter.

To make leeway

To make leeway is to get on or to struggle effectively against odds of some kind, as, for example, in an argument or in some task requiring sustained effort. Often expressed as "Are you making any leeway?"

To have leeway means to have room to manoeuvre, especially to have space or time in which to overcome some problem. In this sense the phrase also means to have fallen behind in something, to have widened the gap between performance and objective: "He has a lot of leeway to catch up before he can claim to have completed the project." *To give leeway* is used in the same sense: "Her client gave her a lot of leeway in deciding when to begin the job."

"There are plenty of difficulties in the road, and there is a great deal of leeway to be made up."
—*Pall Mall Gazette* (London), November 25, 1884

To make up leeway is to make up or recover the ground or distance lost by the action of leeway caused by wind or tide. As a metaphor, the expression also applies to the effort exerted in trying to make up distance or advantage lost (as in the distance in a footrace, or a student's classwork after an absence).

Leg
Shake a leg

A common expression on board, meaning "come on! hurry up! get going!," and understood in these senses wherever English is spoken. The allusion is obvious: "If you want to catch the next train, you're going to have to shake a leg." (See also *Leg; Show a leg.)*

Show a leg

A nautical expression meaning "Jump out of bed and be sharp about it!" In general, a cry of encouragement to urge someone into activity of some kind; to get on with the job. Used ashore in exactly the same way as it was (and still is) used at sea: "Come on you lot! Show a leg! It's six o'clock and the fish are biting!" From the traditional call used to rouse or turn out the crew in a sailing warship.

In the old days (until about 1840), naval seamen were refused shore leave for fear that they would desert; as some sort of recompense, women—ostensibly wives—were allowed to live on board while the ship remained in harbour. Naturally, they had to sleep somewhere, so they joined the men in their hammocks at night.

When the crew was called to turn-to in the morning, the boatswain (pronounced "boe-sun") would check a hammock that was still occupied by requiring the sleeper to show a leg over the hammock's edge. If it was hairy, it was probably a male; if less so, probably female. By this means the bosun felt able to detect any malingering seaman. (See also *Leg; Shake a leg.)*

Lie
To lie-to

To cease doing something, to take a break. From the manoeuvre at sea of preventing a vessel from making progress through the water. This was done by reducing sail—generally by brailing up the courses—and counterbracing the fore yards so that the wind struck the forward face of the foresails, thereby retarding the vessel's forward motion. Hence the metaphorical usage ashore: "The yardman decided that he would lie-to and keep out of

"We now ran plump into a fog, and lay to."
—Lord Dufferin, *Letters from High Latitudes,* cited in the *Universal Dictionary of the English Language* (1897)

sight for a while, until the boss recovered his usual good temper."
(See also *Aback; To be taken aback. Laid; To be laid up.)*

Lifebuoy A lifebuoy, or lifebelt, is a buoy designed to support the human body in the ocean. The most common shape is circular, generally cork covered with painted canvas. At one time, a Royal Navy lifebuoy (pronounced "boo-ee" in American English but "boy" elsewhere) had a pocket in it for holding a bottle of brandy, to be used by any seaman who found himself adrift in cold waters—but the authorities quickly discovered that men were falling overboard *after* drinking the contents rather than before.

It is recorded that Captain James Cook's ship *Resolution* carried a life-saving device that could be both seen and heard, it being brightly painted and fitted with a bell; apparently at least one life was saved by it. The account of this incident contains the first use of the word *lifebuoy.* The story is told by John Ledyard, one of Cook's midshipmen, in his *Journal of Captain Cook's Last Voyage.*

The *Resolution* (the name has a very old history in the British navy) that Cook commanded was launched in 1770 at Whitby, on the east coast of England, as the *Marquis of Granby;* four months later she was acquired by the Admiralty and renamed the *Drake.* Within a year or so she was named yet again, this time as the *Resolution.* Between 1771 and 1779 HMS *Resolution* took part in Cook's second and third voyages of discovery; she was captured by a French force in 1781 while serving as an armed transport.

Lifeline A rope or wire stretched along the decks of a vessel in rough weather, so that men can hang on to it as a safety measure when they are working on deck. Colloquially, any device or means by which a situation, project, or other circumstance can be saved: "My daughter proved to be my lifeline when my manuscript had to be typed up much earlier than I had expected."

Light
According to his lights As he sees it; according to his opinion or argument. From the fact that ships carried lanterns at night for the purposes of identification, navigation, and safety, especially when sailing in company. An astute commander could often determine another vessel's nationality by the lights it carried. Also, ships could signal at night using various combinations of lantern colours, and it is this fact that probably most directly contributes to the expression: "According to his lights, he was a good father, but his children thought he was terribly strict."

To be a leading light A leading light is a light fixed atop a mark such as a pole, spit, or tall building ashore. Such marks are placed so that ships can line them up (according to local sailing instructions) and thereby avoid danger, such as a reef, shoal, or wreck, when entering or leaving harbour. Lights are of crucial importance to vessels when closing the coast at night, as witness the terrible successes of the wreckers on the southern coasts of England in the days of sail.

Colloquially, a leading light is a person who is outstanding in a particular sphere, such as a competent actor in a local repertory club, or the president of a very successful dust abatement committee: "She is one of the leading lights of the new movement in education."

Limey

"They would not go on a limejuicer, they said, for anything."
—*Pall Mall Gazette* (London), August 25, 1884

An American and Australian slang term for a British sailor, a British ship or—in more recent decades—a Briton himself. The name derives from the practice of issuing lime juice to British crews to combat scurvy. Vessels that did so were widely known, especially among American sailors, as "lime-juicers."

It is interesting to note that although the cure for scurvy was discovered by Dr. James Lind (d. 1794) in 1735, another 40 years elapsed before lemon juice was made a compulsory victualing issue in the Royal Navy. Lime juice has in fact only half the scorbutic value of lemon juice, and it wasn't until 1912 that vitamins were discovered and the true cause of scurvy established.
(See also *Scurvy*.)

Line
To cross the line

A well-known and long-established custom at sea: *to cross the Line* is to cross the equator. When this happens, all those on board are summoned to "King Neptune's court" and are dealt with in a number of (sometimes rough-and-ready) ways designed to initiate the first-timer into the mysteries of the sea. These celebrations were a popular diversion from shipboard routine, and afforded a harmless, albeit vigorous, means of letting off steam for all concerned.

A number of King Neptune's attendants in the ceremony are designated as "nymphs" and, oddly enough, "bears," who ensure that the novices are soundly ducked in a bath after having been attended to by the ship's surgeon and barber. A certificate is then awarded, which exempts the first-timers from a repetition of this treatment on any future crossing of the Line that they may undertake.

The ceremony owes its origin to ancient pagan rites connected with the propitiation of the sea-god Poseidon or Neptune. With the spread of Christianity, many of the vows and offerings made to the heathen gods were transferred to the saints of the church. It is worth noting that the belfry, which once contained the ship's bell, was probably the site of a very early shipboard shrine; this may explain the well-established tradition of saluting as one enters the ship.

To cross the line has an additional meaning in American slang. A person who acts irresponsibly, in a way that exposes him or her to serious criticism or even danger, is said to have "crossed the line." This is a colloquial development of the original usage. To cross the line in the social sense is likened to the crossing of the equator: once done, it cannot be undone.

This notion is also expressed in the saying *to cross the Rubicon,* a reference to the river of that name which separated ancient Italy from Gaul; any army commander who crossed the Rubicon was deemed by the Roman Senate to have declared war on Rome. When Caesar crossed this stream in 49 B.C., he was taking the irrevocable step of precipitating war with Pompey and the Senate; there was no turning back.

Liner A vessel belonging to a shipping company that carries passengers on scheduled routes. The term is from the days of sailing warships and described a "ship of the line," i.e., a vessel of a rate that permitted it to join the line of battle. Nowadays liners tend to be vessels that cruise certain routes, catering mostly to tourist and holiday traffic.
(See also entries under *Rate.)*

Lines
Hard lines A nautical witticism built on the term *hard tack,* which is ship's biscuit. Taking *tack* in its original sense of rope or line, we have *hard lines:* initially the tough, double-baked, and usually weevil-infested ship's biscuit, obtained from navy victuallers ashore; and then anything that was uncomfortable, dirty, or contrary to expectations.

The colloquialism refers to bad luck, unfair treatment, and the like: "It was hard lines for him—he applied for a posting in a coastal town, and instead was sent to the Goldfields."
(See also *Tack; Hard tack.)*

On (along) these lines From shipbuilding. A ship's lines are the designer's drawings of the vessel, usually consisting of three plans: the sheer plan, which shows the hull cut vertically down the centre line and viewed from the side; the body plan, which shows vertical cross-sections when viewed looking aft or looking forward; and the half-breadth plan, which shows views of the vessel from above as it is sliced horizontally at different levels.

It was only late in the sixteenth century that ships began to be drawn up on paper; until then, ships had been built "by eye," with the shipwright's own know-how and the rule-of-thumb methods passed down from father to son. With the introduction of sets of drawings for a proposed vessel, it was possible to anticipate problems and modify designs in the light of previous experience. To build a vessel "along these lines" was, of course, to construct her according to the plans as laid down.

Colloquially, the phrase means "in this manner," "in this fashion," "similar to the way I've shown you." "Now that we've discussed the problem, why don't you go to the manager and put your argument along these lines?"

List From the Anglo-Saxon *lystan,* to please, which in turn derives from the Anglo-Saxon *lust,* pleasure, delight, enjoyment; found in most other Teutonic languages as well.

"Those Irish lords made their list the law to such whom they could overpower."
—Thomas Fuller (1608–1661), English cleric and writer, *The Worthies of England* (1662)

The current sense of *lust,* meaning passionate or overmastering desire, is peculiar to English. *List* gradually changed its shades of meaning through "if you list" (if you please) to the sense of inclination or leaning, as a physical quality; hence the nautical meaning, the tilt of a vessel to one side or another. The only other usage is found in *listless,* which is for the earlier *lustless; list* as in to listen is from a different source.

This nautical application of *list* is an interesting, and rare, instance of a word's meaning moving toward, and ultimately lodging with, the sailor's vocabulary, while at the same time the value of its coinage diminishes and finally disappears from the everyday speech of landsmen. Usually, the opposite happens, as with the expressions *to rummage, to the bitter end,* and *to keep aloof.*

To be on the sick list Sailing men-o'-war carried a surgeon as part of their complement of men. (It ought to be remembered, though, that surgeons in those days were held in very low esteem, and for good reason. Many of them were mere blood-letters, from the days when barbers carried out this function; yet there were also undoubtedly many surgeons who were highly capable men in that field.)

When a seaman reported sick, he was examined by the surgeon or his assistant and, if necessary, accommodated in the sick bay. His name was then placed on the list of men considered unfit for shipboard duty; he was literally "on the sick list." The expression has become part of our colloquial language; *to be on the sick list* is to be ill, not well, and to be known to be so. "He can't play in the tennis tournament this week—he's been on the sick list for some days now." (See also *Loblolly.)*

Listless

"Hence an unfurnished and a listless mind,
Though busy, trifling; empty, though refined."
—William Cowper (1731–1800), English man of letters, *The Progress of Error* (1782)

Originally a seaman's word to mean that there was no wind and therefore the vessel had no list on her; *listless* is a replacement for the earlier *lustless,* without pleasure. Today we use the word to mean rather the same sort of thing, as when someone feels no inclination toward, or interest in, doing anything at all; to be in a listless mood, to be bored, full of ennui: "I suspected something was wrong with my daughter when she became unusually listless during the day."
(See also *List.)*

Lloyd's of London

Lloyd's of London is the well-known international insurance market situated in the city of London; it is also the world centre of maritime intelligence of the daily movements of merchant ships, marine casualties, and the like. Its history of marine underwriting dates from 1601, when Edward Lloyd's Coffee House in Lombard Street became the gathering place for marine insurance underwriters. Insurance is accepted at Lloyd's by individual underwriters representing different firms, not by Lloyd's, which simply provides the premises and information-gathering facilities.
(See also *A1. Lutine Bell.)*

Loaded

Seamen's slang meaning to be drunk. The reference was to the load marks on the side of the vessel, cited by Rogers (see bibliography) as eighteenth century, but certainly not in connection with any loading or lading marks on sailing ships. These marks were not introduced until the passing of the Merchant Shipping Act in 1876, as a result of the efforts of Samuel Plimsoll, M.P., who fought in Parliament for better conditions for seamen.
(See also *Bender. Tight.)*

Loblolly
Loblolly boy

"I was known by the name of loblolly-boy. . . ."
—Tobias George Smollett (1721–1771), English naval surgeon and novelist, *The Adventures of Roderick Random* (1748)

Loblolly is the mariner's term for food that requires a spoon to eat it with, as gruel, pap, etc. It was also the usual name for the rations prescribed by the surgeon for the sick. A "loblolly boy" was a lad rated as a surgeon's mate, sometimes a ship's steward; so called because he was said to be young enough to be not yet weaned from spooned food.
(See also *List; To be on the sick list.)*

Lobscouse

"That savoury composition known by the name of lobs-course. . . ."
—Tobias George Smollett (1721–1771), English naval surgeon and novelist, *Peregrine Pickle* (1751)

A sea dish consisting of minced salt beef stewed with vegetables and ship's biscuit; potatoes and onions were added if available, along with seasoning. The dish was particularly well-known in Liverpool; hence the term *scouse* for someone from that city (a Liverpudlian).

Lodestone
One's lodestone

Magnetic oxide of iron, known to the ancients as "lodestone," a variation of "load," from the Anglo-Saxon *lad,* way, course, direction (originally a ditch that channelled or guided runoff water into a river). Connected with the verb *to lead.* Much later, the goods that were taken along on a journey themselves became known as the "load."

Lodestone was the stone of ancient times that responded to the earth's magnetic force, and which, when discovered and utilised by seamen, helped unlock the oceans for navigators around the world. Curiously enough, the magnetic qualities of the lodestone were once thought to be counteracted by garlic or onion; thus sailors were often forbidden to eat these vegetables while at sea, in case their breath should demagnetise the compass needles.

"Your eyes are lodestars. . . ."
—William Shakespeare (1564–1616), *A Midsummer Night's Dream,* act 1, scene 1

Lodestar is the name given by mariners to the North Star or Pole Star (Latin *Polaris),* because of the fact that for all practical purposes this star remains fixed above the North Pole, and is thus a true north-bearing heavenly body from all points in the northern hemisphere.

The metaphor alludes to any person, event, authority, or the like that is regarded as the exemplar or model to be copied for behaviour, attitudes, and so on; the pattern by which one can safely and profitably regulate one's own life: "The pop singer, who for many years had been the lodestar for a whole generation of school children, fell into disgrace when he was convicted on a drug charge."
(See also *Pilot.)*

Log

A log was originally a speed-measuring device for ships at sea. Whenever the vessel's speed was measured, each log of the watch was recorded in a journal kept for that purpose. Gradually this journal became known as the "log book," and was also used to record the general proceedings of shipboard life and navigational matters. Misdemeanours and more serious offences were also entered into the ship's log, and a person so reported was said to be "logged."

To log or *log-in* means to record oneself as being present or having attended. Users of computer networks must usually "log themselves in" before they can operate the system.

Loggerheads
To be at loggerheads

To be squabbling, arguing, exchanging blows; to be in a state of disagreement over something. A loggerhead was a tool used in the caulking and sealing of seams on board ship. It consisted of a long rod with a ball of iron attached to one end (sometimes the rod would have a ball at each end); the balls were heated in a fire to red heat and then plunged into a bucket of tar or pitch to soften the pitch.

A loggerhead was also a bar-shot, i.e., a bar with a cannonball attached one at each end, and generally fired at the rigging of an enemy vessel in an attempt to cut it down. It was—along with "chain shot," "grape shot," and "langrel" (bits and pieces of iron fired in a canister)—a very effective antipersonnel device: it killed men in great numbers. The loggerhead was also a sturdy wooden bitt or stanchion in the stern of a whaling boat, with which the harpoon line could be controlled after the whale had been struck with the harpoon.

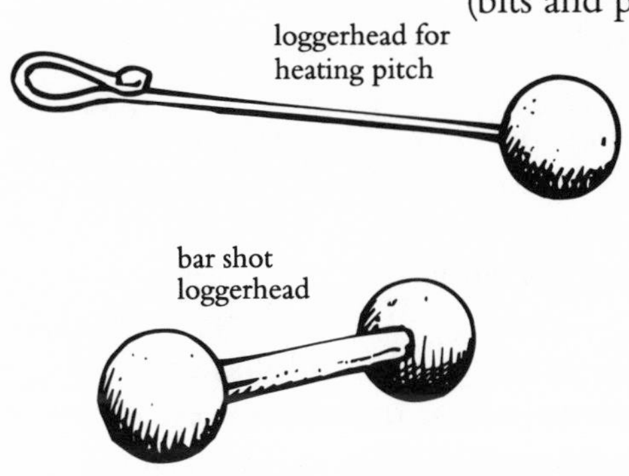

Because of the shape of this caulking tool, the iron spheres at opposite ends of the bar could never come together; the tool could also be an effective weapon in a fight between seamen. Hence the metaphor, to be on bad terms with someone, with little chance of reconciliation: "Unfortunately we have been at loggerheads with our neighbours for years concerning the boundaries of our properties."

Longshoreman An American term for a waterside worker, what Australians would call a "wharfie" or "lumper." From the combination of *alongshore* (at or by the shore) and *man*. Note that the British sailor of the eighteenth and early nineteenth centuries referred to his shoregoing clothes as "long clothes," which was an abbreviation for "longshore clothes."
(See also *Lumper.)*

Look
To look out for From the member of a vessel's crew responsible for keeping visual watch and for reporting anything unusual. *To look out for* is to do a favour for someone, to keep an eye out for a friend, to do his duty as a willing substitute, to take watchful care of someone. "Don't worry, I'll look out for Simon while he's with me on the boat."
(See also *Lookout; To be on the lookout.)*

Look alive! An old naval and merchant service term, meaning to hurry, get going; now firmly embedded in everyday speech. "She told the group of children to look alive or they'd miss their bus to the fairgrounds."

Lookout The person who kept watch from the bow or some elevated place, such as up the mast in the crow's nest. Used also as an intensive, as in "Look out! You'll get hurt if you stand there!" In the days when navigation lights were run on oil, the lookout on duty would cry, on the hour, "Lights burning bright and all's well."

Widely adopted into the language, to mean to be on guard, to take watchful care, to take care for oneself: "If you do go to Europe, you'll need to be on the lookout for con men and other tricksters."

(See also other entries under *Lookout.)*

Not my lookout; that's his lookout That's not my problem; not my affair. "He insisted on buying that old car, so it's his lookout if it keeps breaking down."

(See also other entries under *Lookout.)*

To be on the lookout The "lookout" (from Old English *locian,* to look) is the member of a vessel's crew whose duty is to keep visual watch and report anything unusual. Lookouts are generally stationed as high and as forward in the ship as possible.

The figurative meaning is a borrowing from maritime usage: to look forth, to be on guard, to take watchful care, as in "to look out for oneself." There is also a secondary meaning of to keep an eye open for the best advantage. Rendered also as "to keep a sharp lookout." "You'll need to be on the lookout if you're not to miss the turnoff into the homestead."

(See also *Look; To look out for.)*

Loom
To loom, to loom large

"The giant Apennines of Sabina loom afar off."

—Dennis, *Cities and Cemeteries of Etruria,* cited in the *Universal Dictionary of the English Language* (1897)

Originally a nautical usage (early 1600s) to describe an indistinct atmospheric effect. It is from the Anglo-Saxon *leoma,* ray of light. The word is often used in the sense of some distant object appearing large through mist, dust, heat, haze, etc., or appearing indistinctly at a distance; this is still the modern meaning. As a metaphor, *to loom* or *to loom large* is to appear, indistinctly at first but quite irrevocably, as in "Disaster loomed large as the directors surveyed their bankrupt financial empire."

Loose
To let loose

"Now I stand / loose of my vow. . . ."

—Joseph Addison (1672–1719), English poet, dramatist, and essayist, *Cato* (1713)

To release, to set free; to speak one's mind openly, without being fettered. From the act of setting loose the ropes that held the guns immobile, in preparation for firing them.

Lord
Drunk as a lord

See *Bender. Booze. Pickled. Tight.*

Lubber
Landlubber; lubberly

A lubber is a clumsy sailor, a landsman who knows very little about sailing; from the Old French *lober,* to deceive, sponge upon. The term, as still used by seamen, is explicitly contemptuous.

"I came yonder at Eton to marry mistress Anne Page, and she's a great lubberly boy."
—William Shakespeare (1564–1616), *The Merry Wives of Windsor,* act 5, scene 5

"If you will measure your lubber's length again, tarry, but away."
—William Shakespeare (1564–1616), *King Lear,* act 1, scene 4

Experienced sailors scorned the timidity of the greenhorn, and held that the "lubber's hole"—the opening in the floor of the top of a lower mast, which gave access from below to the tops above—was for those who were too frightened to go by way of the futtock shrouds (that is, over the outside edges of the top, the platform at the base of the upper masts). For example, Marryat writes in *Peter Simple* (1834), "He proposed that I should go through the lubber's hole." By extension, *lubberly* was associated with all attempts at evading or wriggling through difficulties.

Related to this is the "lubber's line" (never the "lubber line") on the compass; so called because such a line, inscribed in a fore-and-aft direction on the compass bowl, made steering easier for the inexperienced helmsman; the seasoned sailor makes use of the imagined centre-line of his vessel. "He gave a lubberly display of incompetence when he was called upon to respond to the speech by the father of the bride."

(See also *Hand; A green hand.)*

Lump sum

The sum of money paid to a "lumper," or waterside worker, when he had finished a particular job of loading or unloading a ship. The phrase today carries much the same meaning: to accept one's payment, entitlements, or such as a final payout rather than in installments: "The federal government caused a great deal of concern with its new law concerning taxation levels on superannuation lump-sum payments."

(See also *Lumper.)*

Lumper

"He was going to bring the lumpers upon us. . . ."
—Richard Doddridge Blackmore (1825–1900), English poet, *Lorna Doone* (1869)

Lumper is a colloquial term once widely used in Britain and Australia to describe a wharf labourer, someone whose job is to load and unload vessels. In North America, he is known as a "longshoreman" or "stevedore," from the Spanish *estivador,* to pack, to stow. The lumper got his name from the fact that he was paid a lump sum for his services in unloading a ship.

(See also *Longshoreman. Lump sum. Stevedore.)*

Lurch

A nautical word that means suddenly to lean, roll, or stagger about; said of a ship or a stumbling person. The word was taken into landsmen's use and, surprisingly, has retained its original meanings exactly. Not to be confused with "to

"The crew laboured violently amid the lurching."
—John Tyndall (1820–1893), natural philosopher, *Fragments of Science,* cited in the *Universal Dictionairy of the English Language* (1897)

leave in the lurch," which is from an old French game called *lourche;* this latter sense is still prevalent in cribbage, where in certain circumstances one player can leave the other "in the lurch." The nautical word is probably from the French *lacher,* to let go.

Lutine Bell The bell that is rung whenever an important announcement is to be made at Lloyd's of London, the famous international insurance market and world centre of shipping information.

The bell is from HMS *Lutine,* which sank in a gale off the Dutch coast in 1799 with the immediate loss of everyone on board except one person, who died shortly after being rescued. A great deal of coin and bullion was lost in the wreck (some £500,000 at contemporary values), and during salvage operations in 1858 the ship's bell and rudder were recovered, along with about £50,000 of the bullion. The bell was presented to Lloyd's, who had insured the ship and her cargo, and the rudder was made into a chair and desk for Lloyd's chairman and secretary.

The Lutine Bell is rung once whenever a total wreck is reported, and twice for an overdue ship. It was also rung in 1963 to signal the death of President John F. Kennedy, and in 1965 for that of Sir Winston Churchill.

(See also *A1. Lloyd's of London.)*

Made
To be made; to have it made Originally, *to be made* was for a midshipman in the Royal navy to pass his lieutenant examinations and then, when a vacancy occurred, to be given his first command. This would be at the rank of captain of a small vessel; after sufficient experience, he would be posted into a rated ship with the rank of post-captain.

Until a midshipman made his lieutenancy and thence his captaincy, there was very little future for him in the navy. His prospect of a commission rested almost entirely on whether his country was at war with another maritime power. Paradoxically, the onset of peace meant hard times for these men, for they usually found themselves ashore, thoroughly skilled as seamen but totally unsuited to the occupations of city and village.

The phrase has found its way into everyday speech; *to have it made* is a colloquialism meaning to be assured of success: "If he backs that horse in the fifth race he's got it made."

Maelstrom Not essentially a nautical word, but included here because it is a place name once in wide usage among early seafarers. The term generally means a whirlpool, but in fact it originally referred to a strong current that rips past the southern end of the island of Moskenaes (Moskoe) off the west coast of Norway. It appears in Mercator's *Atlas* of 1595. The word is taken from the Dutch *maalstroom,* whirlpool, millstream, from *malen,* to grind, and *stroom,* stream.

The word has found its way into the literature of English and the Scandinavian languages. Colloquially, in English a maelstrom is a restless confusion of ideas, an unsteady state of affairs: "The farmers were in a maelstrom of discontent following the government's ruling on wheat marketing."

Maiden voyage The initial voyage of a ship; its first trip. *Maiden,* in the sense of untested or untried, is ultimately from the pre-Teutonic *moghus,* boy, virgin.

Main
In the main

The "main" is the old term for the ocean, the high seas, often used specifically to refer to the Spanish Main, an area of sea in the Caribbean stretching from the Isthmus of Panama to the Orinoco River on the north coast of South America. It is also an even older word for the coast of the mainland; this was in fact the original meaning of *Spanish Main,* i.e., the mainland coast that bounded most of the Caribbean sea.

Colloquially, *in the main* means broadly speaking, on the whole; reflecting the wide-sweeping emphasis in the nautical usage of the phrase. "In the main, girls have greater reserves of stamina than boys do."

Main is derived from the Old Norse *meginn* or *megn,* strong; *mainland* is rendered by the Old Norse *megenland.*

The Spanish Main

See *Main; In the main.*

Mainbrace
To splice the mainbrace

A naval expression denoting an extra issue of rum or grog to the ship's crew, to celebrate something by indulging in strong drink. The mainbrace itself is the purchase (rope or chain) attached to each end of the lowest yard on the mainmast of a square-rigged ship, used to brace or swing the yard and its sail round to the wind. Because this sail (the mainsail) was the largest on board (as was its yard), it was necessarily the most difficult to haul round. The effort required to brace this sail was often very taxing, especially in bad weather. The exertions of the crew on these occasions were very infrequently rewarded with a tot of rum, more as a pick-me-up than a reference to any actual splicing or joining together of the parts of the mainbrace, an operation that would have been very rare indeed. (Note: The mainbrace should not be confused with the mainstay.)

Harland (see bibliography) cites a source in which, he says, there is an account of the actual practice of splicing the mainbrace. However, it is clear, firstly, that the splice would have to be a long splice for it to reeve through the braceblock; and secondly, that a spliced mainbrace would have to be replaced at the earliest opportunity, because the splice would have lessened the strength of the brace itself. One wonders if in fact it would not have simply been quicker and more seamanlike to rove a fresh mainbrace immediately, rather than trying to splice the old one.

We suggest that this old naval custom is a simple recognition of the fact that the seaman's mouth, throat, and gullet constitute a type of mainbrace—one that was of extraordinary importance to the seaman himself, fed as he was on generally substandard food. Being given a special

rum issue constituted a very obvious, and equally very welcome, "splicing" of these parts.
(See also *Hawse; To freshen the hawse. Tot; A tot of rum.)*

Mainstay
To be one's mainstay

A "stay" is a part of the standing rigging that supports a mast in the fore-and-aft direction; forestays prevent a mast from collapsing aftward, and backstays prevent a mast from collapsing forward (stays that prevent sideways movement are called shrouds, not stays). Stays take their name from the masts they support; thus, the mainstay supports the mainmast, being secured at or near the base of the next mast forward (i.e., the foremast).

"The laws which the Irish parliament of 1703 conceived to be the mainstay of the Protestant interest. . . ."
—*The Edinburgh Review* (Scottish periodical), July 1857

The mainmast is so named because it carries the largest and most important sails. The loss of such a mast, in battle or exceptional weather, often rendered the vessel unmanageable. Such an event was likely if the mast's mainstay (together with perhaps the helper or preventer stay) was shot away; if the wind was then accidentally permitted to get round onto the forward side of the sails, the mast was certain to be brought down, because the wind pressure on the sails would not be counteracted by the forward pull of the mainstay.

Colloquially, one's mainstay is a person or object that continually proves to be of great help in one's work or life. "His extraordinary patience was the mainstay that enabled him to persevere in the task of winning over the suspicious committee members."

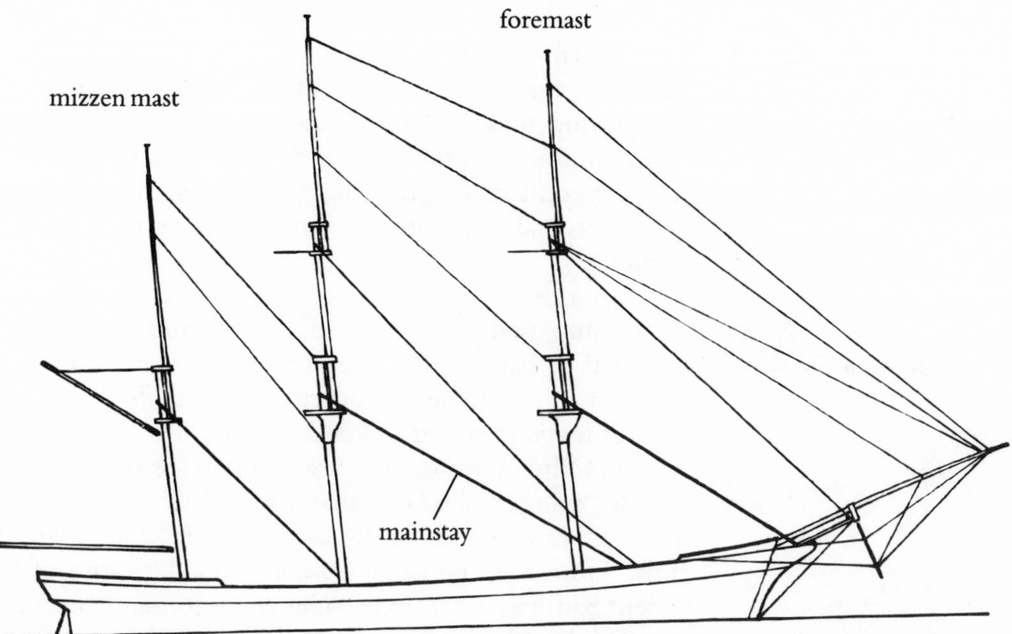

Mainstream
To be in the mainstream

Colloquially, to be the dominant trend, the chief tendency, as in a stage of development; for example, in the realm of fashion. From the nautical use of *stream,* which is a steady current in a river or ocean (such as the Gulf Stream). It is also the main body of water in the tide as it ebbs or flows. A vessel might or might not wish to find itself in the mainstream, according to its port of destination, weather conditions, any local hazards, and so on: "She worked hard at her job in order to keep in touch with the mainstream of political thought."
(See also *Vogue.)*

Make
On the make

When a vessel is able to keep to a desired course when tacking, it is said to be "on the make." The phrase is also sailor's slang for feathering one's nest. The everyday colloquialism carries much the same meaning: to be on the lookout for oneself, to look after Number One, to be keen to get ahead: "The young lawyer was forever on the make in his efforts to improve his position in the large firm."

To make and mend

For a long time this has been, in the Royal navy, an afternoon free of routine work, when seamen were encouraged to mend their clothing and other essential personal items. Sailors have traditionally been expert at making their own clothing, especially in the days when they had to supply their own needs, or purchase—at considerable cost—necessary gear from the slops chest. The metaphor is sometimes applied to a break from work that is periodically given in other labour-intensive organisations.

To make up

An old term from the fisheries; it means to conclude a fishing voyage and settle wage and expense accounts. The ground-sense is that of settlement, and we find this in the common expression *to make up* with somebody, i.e., to become reconciled after a disagreement: "She was anxious to make up with her boyfriend after their bitter quarrel."

Man
To man the boats

Commonly used in everyday speech, meaning to furnish with staff or hands: "man the pumps," "man the ropes," or whatever it is that needs concerted human effort. From the nautical usage meaning to stand by at a particular part of the rigging. Other common nautical expressions of this kind include "man overboard," "man the ropes," "man ship," "man the capstan," "man the cat-haul taut," and "man the yards." From the Old English *mann* and a derivative of the ancient Sanskrit *manu,* man. "Get ready to man your cash registers: the sale begins in two minutes!"

Manned A vessel is "manned" when she has her full complement of crew aboard; the expression *to man ship* means to perform a ceremonial salute by having her men line the yards and standing rigging and delivering three cheers to the personage being saluted. We speak today, for example, of a fire engine being "manned" by volunteers, or a school stall being "manned" by some of the students' mothers. "The children manned the oars and happily rowed themselves across the pond."

Mare
To ride the Spanish mare

An old nautical punishment. The seaman to be chastised was bound to a boom, which was hoisted over the side with the controlling lines slackened off; the victim was thus repeatedly dipped into the sea as the vessel rolled from side to side. In anything of a seaway, this would be a hazardous position for the malefactor and at best one of great discomfort.

Marine
A dead marine

A marine (from the Latin *marinus,* of the sea) is a seagoing soldier. Marines have been an established and recognised force in the Royal navy since 1755, and were familiarly known—especially to sailors—as "jollies" or "leathernecks." Most naval nations have a marine corps, but in very few cases, except in Britain and the United States, do they actually serve at sea. The marines of both countries have won an enviable reputation for courage, discipline, and fighting skill.

Sailors also used to refer to empty bottles as "marines" because, in their view, both were useless. Legend has it that the Duke of Clarence (York, in another version) was dining in the mess on board one of his ships. When he ordered the steward to remove the "dead marines," one of the officers present protested, to which the Duke replied that, like the marines, the bottle had done its duty nobly and was ready to do so again.

Lind (see bibliography) suggests that the expression originated from the alleged custom in French ships of carrying the bodies of their dead back to port for burial. If the ship was sunk or wrecked on the voyage home, the bodies often floated to the surface. This explanation seems unlikely for two reasons. First, why would the dead bodies of *French* seamen give rise to the expression? The term *marine,* with reference to seagoing soldiers, is British in origin (1664). Second, very few French nautical words and phrases have been adopted by the English; virtually all English seafaring expressions of foreign origin are from the Dutch, Scandinavian, and Germanic languages, in that order.

Empty bottles, especially beer bottles, are today still frequently called "dead marines," and in Australia and England people who are licensed to collect bottles for reuse are called "marine dealers" or "marine collectors." In America an empty liquor bottle is often called a "dead soldier." The difference between British and American usages may be due to the fact that in the American armed services, the marines enjoy a particularly proud and honourable reputation, of which they are fiercely jealous. It may be that American sailors (and American marines in particular) are reluctant to entertain the notion of a dead marine.

To *tell it to the marines* is to express disbelief, to indicate that the story one has just heard is an extremely unlikely one; as to say that the marines themselves, notwithstanding their discipline and obedience, would never believe such a tale. However, it is equally valid to say that because the marines have served their country in every part of the world, and have vast experience, then if they will believe an otherwise unlikely story, it must be true.

Marines
Horse marines

Commonly a derisory comment, as in "Tell that to the marines!" or "Tell that to the horse marines!" The implication is that the story or yarn must be unbelievable, as the notion of there being a body of "horse marines" is thought to be a logical absurdity. But history records that in 1861 the Royal Marines provided a mounted detachment to fight in Mexico, and later in the Sudan and in Egypt they formed a special Camel Regiment.

"Tell that to the marines—the sailors won't believe it."
—Sir Walter Scott (1771–1832), Scottish man of letters, *Redgauntlet* (1824)

One authority has it that Samuel Pepys, in 1673 the First Secretary to the Admiralty, mentioned flying fish to Charles II. The court was skeptical, but an officer of the Maritime Regiment of Foot claimed that he himself had seen them. The king thereupon accepted his evidence and said, "From the very nature of their calling no class of our subjects can have so wide a knowledge of seas and lands as the officers and men of Our Loyal Maritime Regiment. Henceforth ere we ever cast doubts upon a tale that lacks likelihood we will first tell it to the Marines" (quoted from Brewer; see bibliography). This anecdote has some credence because of Pepys's fame as a diarist.

Rudyard Kipling in *Soldier and Sailor Too* (1892) illustrates the cheerful contempt with which the ordinary sailor regarded the seagoing soldiers known as marines:

> 'E isn't one o' the reg'lar line, nor 'e isn't one o' the crew;
> 'E's a kind of a giddy harumfrodite-soldier and sailor too.

(See also *Marine; A dead marine.)*

Maroon
To be marooned

To maroon is to put a person ashore in an isolated place with no facilities for escape. Perhaps the best known case of a marooned seaman was that of Alexander Selkirk, whose experiences formed the basis of Defoe's *Robinson Crusoe* (1719). Selkirk was marooned on Juan Fernandez Island in the South Pacific in 1705, and there he stayed, living on the fruit and vegetables planted by the original Spanish discoverers, until he was taken off by an English ship in 1709.

"A marooning party . . . is a party made up to pass several days on the shore or in the country."
—Bartlett, *Americanisms,* cited in the *Universal Dictionary of the English Language* (1897)

As a metaphor, *to maroon* is to isolate someone, usually socially (as in "to boycott" or "to send to Coventry") or physically, as in to leave someone stranded without help or transport. The word is from the French *marron,* which is a rendition of the Spanish *cimarron,* wild. This itself is the American word *cimarron* for Rocky Mountain sheep; also Spanish for a runaway slave. "His extreme views on political economy left him marooned among the rest of his colleagues."

Mary Celeste

Often wrongly spelled "Marie"; perhaps the most famous mystery of the sea. The *Mary Celeste* was a hermaphrodite brig (two-masted, square-rigged on the foremast, fore-and-aft rigged on the mainmast, with a square sail above the gaff mainsail). In 1872 she was found abandoned in the Atlantic by the crew of the *Dei Gratia.* Most of her gear was in good working order, although there were signs of a hasty departure by the crew, which consisted of the captain, his wife, their two-year-old daughter, and a complement of seven hands. None of them was ever seen again. The *Mary Celeste* was sailed to Gibraltar by a salvage crew, but despite a searching and sometimes heated marine enquiry, no satisfactory explanation has ever been put forward that accounted for all the facts of the matter.

The ship's name is now sometimes used as a sobriquet for some event that defies explanation.
(See also *Flying Dutchman.)*

Mast
To sell before the mast

To auction off a dead man's possessions. His messmates usually bought the clothing, implements, etc., at somewhat inflated prices so that his dependents could be better provided for. The money so raised did not then have the stigma of charity attached to it. After the sale, the dead man was rarely, if ever, referred to again by his friends, it being regarded as bad luck to talk about one's dead messmates.

The phrase derives from the fact that for hundreds of years the accommodation for crew other than officers was in the forecastle (usually written "fo'c'sle" and pronounced "foke-s'l"), which is the crew's living space (including bunks and mess) built into the bows forward of the foremast. No other seagoing term so forcefully demonstrates the difference between officers and crew.

The common seaman was expected to somehow make a life of sorts in the dark, dingy, crowded, and always damp (if not outright wet) confines of the living space allocated to him up in the bows, where the two sides of the ship meet. It was for the most part a brutal existence presided over by officers and captains who, in many cases, exercised their own particular kind of brutality in the form of harsh discipline and, frequently, beatings and floggings. It is this writer's view that throughout history, no other class of worker has been so systematically and heartlessly exploited than the common seaman, who served his country either in a man-o'-war or as a servant of the forces of commerce and trade.

The phrase *before the mast* became indelibly embedded in the English language as a result of Richard Henry Dana's account of his experiences at sea, which he wrote about in his book titled, appropriately enough, *Two Years Before the Mast* (1840). Dana went to sea as an ordinary seaman and spent two years in the California hide and tallow trade; his subsequent description of what life was like for the seaman helped bring about much-needed changes in their conditions of employment.

Colloquially, *to be sold before the mast* is to be dealt with, to be dismissed roundly, often to be treated badly: "The young farmhand felt that he had been sold before the mast by the unscrupulous employment agency in the city."

Mate

"It seemed, like me,
to want a mate,
But was not half
so desolate. . . ."

—George Gordon Byron (1788–1824), English poet, "Prisoner of Chillon" (1816)

The officer immediately in rank below the master of a vessel; technically known as the First Mate, but generally called simply the Mate. This rank of "mate" is divided into first mate, second mate, third mate, etc., to indicate seniority on board. The word is ultimately connected with the Old English variant of *gemetta,* sharer of food. The British and Australian use of *mate* as comrade, friend, associate, workmate, is deeply entrenched in the language, and derives ultimately from the old nautical usage. "The old tramp regarded his dog as the best mate that he had ever had."

Maul
To be mauled; to maul

"A man that beareth false witness against his neighbour is a maul, and a sword, and a sharp arrow."

—Proverbs 25:18

A maul is a heavy wooden or iron hammer used in the operation of caulking. The caulking iron, a type of wide, blunt chisel, is driven into the seams between the planks by the maul, and the oakum in the seam is thereby tightly secured. Also, *to maul a ship* was to engage it in battle and rake it repeatedly with broadside after broadside. The ground sense is to handle roughly, to injure through rough treatment; the idea of force is present in both usages.

Mayday Under international radio regulations, *Mayday* is the radio-telephonic distress signal used by ships or aircraft. It is primarily a voice signal, as distinct from "SOS" and "CQD," which are telegraphic or Morse signals. The phrase is the English phoneticisation of the French *m'aidez,* help me. (See also *CQD. SOS.)*

Mayonnaise A sauce made with pepper, salt, oil, vinegar, egg yolk, and sometimes other seasonings, beaten up together into a thick paste. Not a nautical word, but certainly nautical in origin. When the Duc de Richelieu captured Port Mahon, Minorja, in 1756, he came ashore and demanded to be fed. There being no prepared meal, he took whatever he could find and beat it up together; hence the original form *mahonnaise,* which in English became the modern *mayonnaise.*

John Byng, the English admiral in charge of relieving the British garrison that the French had put under siege on Minorca, was court-martialled for failing to do his utmost to recapture the island. He was found guilty and sentenced to death, and finally was shot on the quarterdeck of HMS *Monarch* in 1757. His execution inspired Voltaire's famous remark that in England it was sometimes necessary to shoot an admiral *pour encourager les autres,* "to encourage the others."

Mess
To lose the number of his mess Seamen in the days of fighting sail had their hammocks numbered in sequential order; this was also their mess number, the number of the group with which each man habitually ate his meals. This was one method of keeping track of a ship's complement and was certainly a convenient way of organising meals, watches, and the like. When a seaman died, his numbered hammock would be unoccupied for a time, and his death meant that he had lost (ceased to have title to) his hammock and mess number.
(See also *Number; Your number is up. Painter; Cutting his painter.)*

To mess about; to mess around From *mess,* the group of four at a meal; *to be messing with* is to be allocated a mess, an eating area on board ship (from Latin *missum* to Italian *messa,* a course of a meal). In the Inns of Court, London, a mess also consists of four persons.

Seamen of all backgrounds and natures ate together in dimly lit, badly aired spaces below decks, to the accompaniment of shouted conversation, drunken fighting, belching, and farting, which was the generally raucous behaviour to be expected of men who were often the dregs of society and who were, for the most part, treated as such by their officers. Life afloat, particularly aboard a vessel in the older days of the sailing navy, was usually much harder than the hardest life ashore.

"He took and sent messes unto them . . . but Benjamin's mess was five times so much as any of theirs."
—Genesis 43:34

"There is nothing—absolutely nothing half so much worth doing as simply messing about in boats."
—Kenneth Grahame (1859–1932), British writer, *The Wind in the Willows* (1908)

To mess about and *to mess around* are colloquialisms meaning to busy oneself in an untidy or confused way; to waste time or to play the fool. American usage favours *to mess around,* which can also carry the additional meaning of being unfaithful in one's sexual responsibilities. "He enrolled in law at the university, but he was always messing about with radical groups and consequently he failed his final examinations."

To mess together; to make a mess of things; to get into a mess

Originally the term *mess* referred to a portion of food; then it came to mean food that had been mixed together; and ultimately a jumble or confusion. A parallel meaning developed that stood for a group of people, usually four, who sat together and ate from the same dishes. Hence the "mess" found in the armed forces, the place where meals are served and eaten *en masse.* Colloquially, the word derives from the crowded and often noisy and confusing nature of the mess, or mess-hall. "Things in the stockroom are in a terrible mess."

For hundreds of years, British seamen messed under what was known as the "standard messing system." In this arrangement, the items of staple diet in the sailor's daily ration, such as meat, potatoes, bread, flour, peas, jam, tea, sugar, and so on (when available) were issued in bulk to each individual mess. The food was then prepared by each mess cook, and taken to the galley for heating and cooking. It wasn't until the twentieth century that "general" messing was introduced and accepted, whereby all meals were cooked by the catering branch in a centralised system of galleys.

Mind your p's and q's

Be careful and exact in your behavior; be circumspect. Said to derive from the bosun's warning to seamen going ashore on leave: "mind your p's and q's," that is, "mind your pints and quarts"; don't get drunk, or you'll be in trouble when you come aboard. This origin was offered in a newspaper article on nautical expressions, but an extensive reading of the literature of the sea does not support the notion of a bosun solicitous for the welfare of his men to the point of cautioning them in this fashion.

The origin of the expression is doubtful. It may indeed be connected with drink: it is said that alehouses would mark up "p" for pint and "q" for quart in keeping customers' accounts, and of course a drinker then needed to mind his p's and q's when the reckoning came. It seems even more likely that the expression stems from the warning to children who are learning the alphabet, to be careful to distinguish between the forms of these two letters; and equally likely, to printers' apprentices in handling and sorting type. Whichever the case, the phrase is not nautical in origin.

Misfire Said of any weapon when it fails to fire, or fires at the wrong time; a very common problem in the early days of guns, the first of which were the large cannon mounted on board sailing ships. Damp or poor-quality gunpowder was the usual cause of a misfire. The expression is widely used as a metaphor, meaning to fail to have the desired effect; to be unsuccessful, as when a plan goes awry or a practical joke goes the wrong way and rebounds on the perpetrator: "He intended to impress his beautiful new neighbor with his charm, but his plans misfired when he was transferred without warning to the country for a month."

Mizzen
Mizzen mast; mizzen sail

The mizzen mast (also sometimes spelled "mizen" in earlier writings) is the third aftermost mast of a sailing ship. It is also the small aftermast of a two-masted ketch, yawl, brig, brigantine, and the like. The sail on this mast also takes the name *mizzen,* as in "mizzen sail," but more commonly as just "mizzen."

It is a word of interesting origin. Some authorities derive *mizzen* or *mizen* from the Italian *messano,* middle, which in turn is from the Latin *medianus,* middle. This places the word as being closely related to *mezzanine,* a floor, storey, or gallery located between two other levels of greater height.

"The ship was laid to under a balance mizen, tumbling about dreadfully."
—William Hickey (1749–1830), writer and voyager, *Memoirs* (1913–1925)

"The mizen is a large sail of an oblong figure extended upon the mizen-mast."
—William Falconer (1732–1769), Scottish poet and lexicographer, *Shipwreck* (1762)

In other words, the mizzen (originally only a sail, now both sail and mast) appears to be a Mediterranean invention, but the Italian *mezzana* and the French *misaine* are the names for the foremast, so a curious change must have taken place when the word was adopted by the English. If English *mizzen* owes its origin to the Latin for "middle," then it is puzzling to see in just what way this sail was a "middle" sail, because the English, French, and Italians between them have placed it at one end or the other of the ship, but not in any sense in the middle.

The more likely explanation for *mizzen* is that the word comes from the Arabic *mizan,* balance; the mizzen has always been used as a balancing sail, and the reef in a mizzen is still called the "balance reef." The lateen sail, which is the immediate forerunner to the mizzen sail, was the common rig of the Mediterranean, and even after square sails were introduced from the northern countries, the lateen on the aftermost mast was still retained as an efficient balancing sail, as it still is today in the modified form of a gaff sail.

Monkey
Freeze the balls of/off a brass monkey

A coarse expression from the days of sail, which now means extremely cold, sufficiently cold to produce the interesting effect alluded to in the expression.

In fact, the phrase derives from the brass cannon called a "monkey" in the seventeenth century. In very cold temperatures, the iron cannonballs and the brass cannon would contract at markedly different rates, so much so that the gun would be unusable. Sailors referred to this phenomenon as "freezing the balls of a brass monkey," the key word being *of,* not *off,* and hence the expression was literally true at the time.

Monkey-jacket

A "monkey-jacket" was the short coat worn by seamen, so called because it had no tail or skirt to it (in the same way that a monkey—more strictly, an ape—has no tail). It was also called a "jackanapes coat," from its imagined likeness to the jacket worn by the monkey belonging to the organ grinder of those days. It was generally close-fitting and made of thick material such as serge, and was worn for watch-keeping duties in cold or stormy weather; its shortness kept the legs free for climbing aloft. The closeness of cut and fit led to the modern formal dinner jacket being named after the original naval garment.

Moonlighting

"The prisoners, with two other men, were arrested on a charge of moonlighting [nighttime raids] in county Clare."
—*The Daily Chronicle* (English newspaper), January 17, 1888

The carrying on of activities, especially illegal ones, by moonlight. Originally nautical, referring to smugglers who landed their contraband goods at night. The expression now means that one is holding two jobs, working at the second after finishing one's regular, full-time employment for the day (or night, as the case may be): "He worked as a carpenter's assistant by day and moonlighted as a waiter at night."

Moorings
To lose one's moorings

A mooring is a permanent position to which vessels can secure without having to use their own anchors; the attachment is usually quite sufficient for most vagaries of

"There is much want of room for the safe and convenient mooring of vessels."
—Edmund Burke (1729–1797), English jurist and parliamentarian, *Letters on a Regicide Peace* (1795–1797)

weather. Figuratively, *to lose one's moorings* is to become confused, dazed, lost, unsure. "He seems to have quite lost his moorings since his fiancee broke off their engagement."
(See also *Adrift; To come adrift.)*

Morse Code

A method of signalling invented by Samuel Morse (d. 1872). It utilised a system of dots and dashes and had certain specified periods of time governing the transmission of a radio signal for each letter and numeral of the language, with similar rules governing the time lapse between letters and between succeeding words. The first telegraphic transmission of Morse Code took place in 1844 in America; until then Morse himself had nearly starved to death trying to arouse official interest in, and support for, his invention.

The code can be worked easily in radio, sound, light, and by handheld signal flags. Perhaps the most famous of signals in the Morse Code is "SOS," the internationally agreed distress call. It does not stand for any phrase, such as "save our ship" or "save our souls," as is commonly thought; the phrase was chosen simply because the letters were easy to read and make: three dots, three dashes, three dots.

Mother Carey's chickens

See *Petrel; Stormy petrel.*

Muster
To muster up a crowd

"Our present musters grow
upon the file
To five and twenty
thousand men."
—William Shakespeare (1564–1616), *Henry IV, Part 2,* act 1, scene 3

Muster is from the Latin *monstrare,* to show. In nautical usage, *to muster* was to gather the entire ship's company for a roll call of names. This was used as a check against fictitious names being recorded for a double issue of food rations (victuals), grog, or pay. The word is now widely used in such expressions as "to muster up all one's courage," "to pass muster," to "muster" a herd of cattle, and so on: "He was ordered to muster his men on the parade ground for an inspection by the visiting dignitary."
(See also *Muster; To pass muster.)*

To pass muster

Colloquially, to pass inspection, to get by, to be allowed to pass; from the nautical usage. "His French was not good enough to allow him to pass muster as an interpreter."
(See also *Muster; To muster up a crowd.)*

Mutiny

A revolt or rebellion by soldiers or seamen against their officers, against constituted authority. From the obsolete verb *to mutine,* from the Old French *mute,* rebellion, which in turn derives from the Latin *movere,* to move.

From the strictly legal point of view, *mutiny* implies the use of force, but historically the refusal to obey the legal order of a superior officer is considered to be mutiny. In the days of fighting sail, the penalty for mutiny in all navies was hanging at the yardarm. One of the best known of all naval mutinies was that on board HMS *Bounty* in 1789, when part of the crew, under the leadership of Fletcher Christian, mutinied against their captain, William Bligh, while in the South Pacific.

"On the 14th April, 1797, Lord Bridport, the admiral, unsuspicious of the mutiny, making a signal to prepare for sea, the seamen of his own ship, instead of weighing anchor, ran up the shrouds, and gave three cheers."

—Belsham, *Great Britain,* cited in the *Universal Dictionary of the English Language* (1897)

Bligh and 18 followers were cast adrift in an open boat, and eventually they reached Timor after a voyage of 3,600 miles—perhaps the greatest feat of seamanship and navigation in maritime history.

Another famous mutiny was that in Germany's High Seas Fleet in 1918, which helped bring about Germany's defeat in World War I. The trouble arose because of a mixture of boredom, left-wing propaganda, poor food, and insensitive handling of the men.

The 1797 British naval mutiny at Spithead, the important naval anchorage in the East Solent, off the naval base of Portsmouth, resulted from growing discontent and resentment against bad food, low pay, and the wretched conditions of the service. The mutiny at The Nore, off the mouth of the Thames, followed in the same year for the same reasons. Twenty-five mutineers were hanged, including Richard Parker, the leader of the mutiny on HMS *Sandwich.*

Nevertheless, the mutiny won for seamen an increase in pay, better conditions of provisioning, and greater access to shore leave, deficiencies in which had led to their dissatisfaction in the first place. It is worth noting, for example, that the able seamen's pay remained at 24 shillings a month from 1653 to 1797 (the time of the mutiny); thus for nearly 150 years the British seaman had no increase in pay despite the enormous upheavals in the social conditions of Britain at that time.

N

Nausea That feeling in the stomach familiar to persons who are susceptible to motion sickness: a sensation of impending vomiting; also a feeling of extreme disgust. From the Greek *nausia,* seasickness. When nausea is combined with a drunken headache, the resulting condition is nicely expressed by the word *crapulous.*
(See also *Nautical. Navy.)*

"He let go his hold and turned from her, as if he were nauseated."
—Jonathan Swift (1667–1745), English cleric and satirist, *Gulliver's Travels* (1726)

Nautical From the Greek *nautikos,* pertaining to ships or sailors, which in turn is from the Greek *naus,* ship.
(See also *Nausea. Navy.)*

Naval salutes From the Latin *salutare,* to hail, to wish health to.

For a long time, the only form of personal salute in the navy was by doffing the headgear. Naval ratings always removed their hats when approaching or being approached by any officer, and junior officers removed theirs to all senior officers. Queen Victoria put an end to this practice because she did not like the idea of seeing her fighting men in uniform standing about bareheaded. However, in the modern navy, hats are still removed under certain circumstances.

The origin of the present form of the hand salute is lost to us. Some authorities state that it dates from the days when an inferior always uncovered his head in the presence of his superior. The hand movement is explained as the first part of the motion needed to remove the headdress. Another school of thought maintains that the salute is a holdover from the days of armour; when two warriors raised their visors to each other with opened hands, they were exchanging tokens of trust, as each was laying himself open to attack from the other. Yet a third theory suggests that the hand salute is a corruption of the oriental custom of shading the eyes when in the presence of an exalted personage.

All officers and men must salute whenever they set foot on the quarterdeck and when they cross the gangway on boarding. There is a strong suggestion that this custom derives from the fact that ships used to carry a religious shrine in the after part of the ship, and that the salute was a mark of obeisance to the crucifix. However, it is difficult to see how this custom could have survived the religious controversies and upheavals that marked postmedieval England. It may simply be that the salute is a mark of respect to the sovereign whose authority is represented by the ship's colours, which are displayed at the stern.

Until 1923, all hand salutes in the British navy were given with the left hand; this was altered to the right hand because of the fact that a salute given by the left hand was considered a gross insult by Indian and African servicemen, who at that time were present in large numbers in the British armed forces.

Gun salutes were always fired bows-on to the ship being saluted, because a broadside of shotted guns (necessary to make a satisfactory noise) could be construed as a hostile act if fired toward the other ship; a vessel firing bow-on could not possibly hit the ship being saluted. Unarmed vessels saluted another ship by striking (lowering) their topsails.

When sail was displaced by steam, a new means of saluting by an unarmed vessel had to be devised. The custom that evolved required that the ensign be dipped—that is, lowered halfway and not rehoisted until the ship being saluted had acknowledged the salute. Merchant ships today dip their ensigns to warships of all nations on the high seas. (See also *Hat; To take one's hat off to someone.)*

Navigation

"Tho' the yesty waves confound and swallow navigation up. . . ."
—William Shakespeare (1564–1616), *Macbeth,* act 4, scene 1

The art of conducting a vessel from place to place in safety; now more broadly applied to the direction and management of any mode of travel, whether ship, aircraft, spacecraft, motor vehicle, or other form. The term does not apply to vehicles that ride on rails, such as trains.

Originally a navigator was one who "drove" a ship; from the Latin *navis,* ship, and *agere,* to drive. In the eighteenth century, the labourers engaged on the construction of canals were known as "navigators"; hence the corrupted form *navvy* for any labourer working on roads, railways, or the like. (See also *Navvy.)*

Navvy

"It was proved that one English navvy would do as much work as two French labourers."
—Fawcett, *Manual of Political Economy,* cited in the *Universal Dictionary of the English Language* (1897)

Once widely used in Britain as a descriptive term for road-menders, ditch-diggers, and others employed in heavy work, such as excavating and trenching. Not in fact a nautical term, but it derives from a word widely associated with the maritime profession: *navvy* is from *navigator,* the name given to workers engaged in the construction of canals, which in turn were called "navigations." (See also *Navigation. Navy.)*

Navy

"None but wood ships were built, either for the war navies or the merchant navies of the world."

—*British Quarterly Review,* 1873

Taken from the Old French *navie,* fleet, which in turn is from the Latin *navis,* ship. Remembering that the Romans did not use the letter *u* (neither were *j* and *w* to be found in their alphabet), we see that the Latin *navis* is from the Greek *naus,* both meaning ship. The "nave" of a church is so named from its fancied likeness to the shape of a ship. (See also *Nausea. Nautical.)*

Navy blue

Dark blue, a colour long associated with the Royal Navy; hence its name.

Edward the Confessor (d. 1066) set up a fleet of ships chartered from the barons of the Cinque Ports and crewed by "shipmen" (the then-common term for a seaman, and used by Chaucer in his *Canterbury Tales* in the late fourteenth century), who wore a type of uniform made of coarse woollen cloth dyed blue. This was a form of camouflage, and in fact the Romans a thousand years earlier had used clothing and sails of a similar dark blue colour when they patrolled the coasts of Britain to keep watch for the approach of enemy vessels. In the sixteenth century, British seamen in search of the famed but elusive Northwest Passage wore clothing of "watchet," a sky-coloured material made in the town of Watchet, Somerset.

However, it was many years before blue was adopted as the standard colour for navy dress. Because of the temporary nature of a ship's commission, the men who manned them wore pretty much what they liked. Then, in the early 1600s, the slop system was established. In 1663, the Duke of York detailed the type of clothing seamen had to wear; included were blue shirts and blue neckcloths, all to be drawn by the men from the slops chest against their pay. For many years, red and white cloth also figured in the dress that seamen were beginning to wear in a more or less organised fashion. By the end of the eighteenth century, the predominant colour was blue (jackets, breeches, and waistcoats) and at about this time long trousers began to appear. The term *bluejacket,* the name by which British seamen have long been known, came into being at the beginning of the 1800s, when they adopted a blue jacket as an essential part of their dress.

Early in 1857, the Admiralty recommended that sailors in the British navy wear a "regulated" form of dress: jacket, trousers, frock, peajacket, all of blue serge or "jean," together with hat, tapes, silk handerchief, etc. The "navy blue" uniform was officially adopted by the Admiralty toward the end of that year, and promulgated by appropriate regulations. The term has long since been

absorbed into the language as a description of a particular colour.
(See also *Slops.)*

Nelson's Blood Since the Battle of Trafalgar in 1805, rum, which is a reddish colour, has been called "Nelson's Blood" by seamen. It was widely believed that Admiral Horatio Nelson's body had been conveyed back to England inside a barrel of neat rum, so as to preserve it.

In fact, the legend is based on myth and not on fact; Nelson's body was placed in a leaguer, the largest cask on board ship, and the cask was then filled with brandy. The spirit was renewed a number of times before the body reached England. This method of transfer was used because the *Victory* carried no lead sheeting on board for the making of a coffin.
(See also *Pickled.)*

Nicknames Our word *nickname* is from the Middle English *nekename,* thence "an eke-name," where *eke* means also, additional. Surnames were not common in England before the thirteenth century, and the eke-name was a useful aid to identification, to brand people by their occupation or by some aspect of their appearance, as in Baker, Farmer, Smith, Long, Brown, Bull, etc. The phrase *an eke-name* quickly became corrupted to *nickname.*

A nickname is a means of maintaining friendly familiarity and social intimacy, while still permitting the natural dignity of one's own name. Shipboard life has always demanded that the individual sacrifice a significant proportion of his personal living space, his *lebensraum,* and his need for occasional solitude; these are luxuries in any navy, particularly so in the days of sail when men ate together, worked together, and slept *en masse* in their regulation 14 inches of individual hammock space. A nickname is a kind of barrier or defence, behind which the individual can maintain his personal sense of dignity and identity, and yet which at the same time confers on him the approval and acceptance of his fellows.

Some common nicknames still in use afloat, and frequently met with ashore, are: Dinger Bell, Daisy Bell, Nigger Black, Nobby Clark, Bandy Evans, Harry Freeman, Jimmy Green, Dodger Long, Pincher Martin, Dusty Miller, Spud Murphy, Nosey Parker, Spike Sullivan, Sharkey Ward, and Slinger Woods, among many others. Most of these nicknames derive from a person of that name who distinguished himself in some way, usually by a habit or personal mannerism (such as Nobby Ewart). Others are references to popular songs or actors of the day

(for example, Bill Bailey and Nellie Dean), and still others from their progenitors' physical characteristics or obvious allusions (Dicky Bird, Bob Tanner, Happy Day, Lofty, and Tich). "The Andrew" is perhaps the best known nickname in the British navy.
(See also *Andrew.*)

Nip

"Young Eyre took a full nip of whiskey."
—William Black (1841–1898), *A Princess of Thule* (1873)

A small drink, a sip; more specifically, a small (legal) measure of spirits as served in a bar or tavern. From the Dutch *nipperkin,* a small measure, and into the English language via the extensive maritime trade that existed for centuries between England and the Low Countries.

Nipper

Slang for a small boy; still in widespread use in England and Australia. From the fact that when an anchor was heaved-in, the large hemp anchor cable was frequently too heavy to be brought round the capstan. A smaller endless cable, called a "messenger," was passed with a few turns around the capstan and led forward so that it would run close alongside the anchor cable; it thence returned to the capstan.

As the capstan was turned, the anchor cable was quickly temporarily bound to the messenger by short lengths of rope called "nippers." Several nippers were required in this operation, and they were worked by young boys or men who had to be nimble and alert as they bent to their tasks.

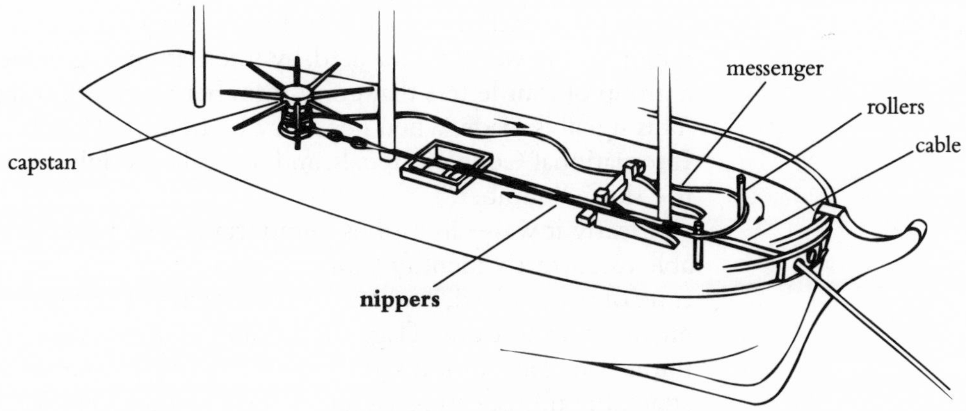

Colloquially, *nipper* still refers to a small boy who is generally always full of energy and mischief: "He quickly bustled his wife and their two nippers into the railway carriage."

Noggin

A noggin is a small cup or mug; it can also refer to a small quantity of liquor, usually a quarter of a pint. "Nog" was a kind of strong beer brewed in East Anglia. *Noggin* was also

"His worship gave noggins of ale. . . ."
—Lloyds; "Song" in *The Capricious Lovers,* cited in the *Universal Dictionary of the English Language* (1897)

the sailor's word for a tub fashioned from a cut-down cask or keg; the origin of the word is obscure.

As a slang expression, *noggin* commonly refers to one's head, one's loaf. "He used his noggin for once and bought the shares that were being offered to him at a greatly reduced price."
(See also *Nous.)*

Nous

"Because a man nous seems to lack. . . ."
—Richard Harris Barham (1788–1845), English clergyman, *The Ingoldsby Legends* (1840)

Pronounced to rhyme with "house"; from the Greek *nous,* mind. The word is in widespread use in current British and Australian idiomatic speech to mean brains, common sense; it occurs frequently in maritime literature such as Captain Frank Bullen's *The Cruise of the Cachalot* (1910).

It is suggested here that the term came into the language via the Mediterranean, the cradle of maritime history; and thence into Australian colloquial speech through the close cultural links that existed between Britain and her Australian colonies: "I wouldn't put him in charge of organising the picnic: he hasn't much nous."

Number

A soft number

Sailor's slang for an easy job or duty; a sinecure; the same as a soft option: "That radio officer's job on Cocos Island sounds like a bit of a soft number to me." Often rendered as "a cushy number."

I've got your number

You don't fool me; I can see through your game; I twig. The emphasis is upon recognition, and the usage derives from the fact that each merchant vessel from every maritime nation in the world is allocated, by international agreement, a group of four letters that constitutes her recognition signal. This signal is made, when necessary, by hoisting flags in the International Code of Signals, and it is called, oddly enough, the ship's "number."

Clearly, it was—and still is—important for a vessel to be able to correctly identify another vessel on the high seas in time of war; indeed, it was a favourite tactic of certain enemy ships to camouflage their outlines, hoist a false number or recognition signal when challenged, and then to attack the unsuspecting victim. *To have someone's number* under these circumstances would be to see through the deception, and to take whatever action was appropriate.

Opposite number

One's shipboard "opposite number" was the man having the same seagoing station or duties as oneself, but in the other watch; for example, the opposite number of a man in the port watch is the man in the starboard watch who carries out the same duties.

Similarly, one's opposite number in civilian life is the person who does the same job as oneself during another shift of work, or in some other similar occupation: "Our sales manager is having discussions with his opposite number in the other firm."

To make her number When the International Code of Signals was adopted by the world's maritime nations, a system was devised whereby each maritime authority got the use of blocks of distinguishing letters. Four of these letters were assigned to a vessel as her identification, known as the ship's "number." When she hoisted her signal flags showing her identification number to a shore station or some other vessel, for subsequent reporting to the owners and to Lloyd's, this was called "making her number."

The colloquialism is much the same: to identify another, to recognise: "He was pleased that he had made her number before she introduced herself to him."
(See also *Number; I've got your number.)*

Your number is up From the days of fighting sail, when ships belonging to a fleet were allotted a number for the purposes of quick and easy signalling during the heat of battle. Often the admiral would call a conference of his captains aboard his flagship, and would signal his intentions by flying the number of the ships whose captains he wished to confer with (in fact, a ship's number was a block of four letters, not digits). As each distinguishing number or identifying code was hoisted on the admiral's ship, so it was said to be "up."

It not infrequently happened that a captain would be summoned for a less-than-cordial conference with the admiral, during which the erring officer might be roundly castigated by his superior officer for some lapse in conduct. Hence, when a captain saw his ship's number flown by the admiral as a recall signal, he could never be certain of his reception on board the flagship.

The colloquial usage means "You are caught," "All is up with you," "You are in serious trouble." It also carries the additional meaning of "You are about to die"; usually expressed by the seaman as "to lose the number of his mess." "When the police arrived, the thieves knew that their number was up."

O

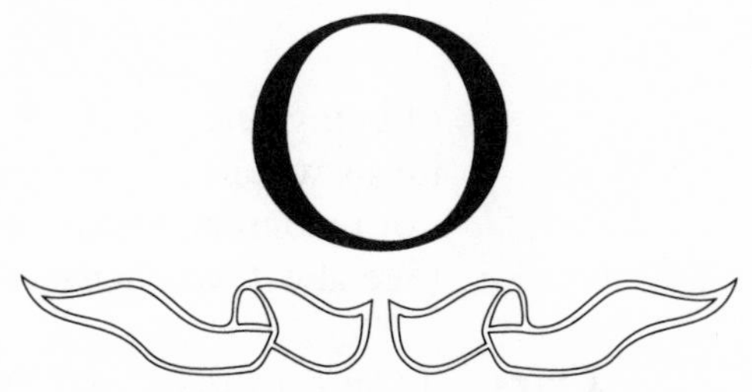

Oak Much valued by shipwrights as the very best timber available for building enormously strong and durable vessels. About 3,500 full-grown oaks (up to 900 acres of oak forest) were needed to provide the timber for a large, three-decker line-of-battle ship.

Hence, in tribute to the sturdy qualities of the English oak emerged the famous English patriotic battle song "Heart of Oak," written by the actor David Garrick (1717–1779), which begins: "Come cheer up my lads, 'tis to glory we steer, To add something more to this wonderful year." "This wonderful year" is a reference to the military and naval victories won by England during the Seven Years' War (1756–1763), including the capture of Quebec in 1759. "Heart of Oak" became the tune played in the British fleet as it sailed into battle, and the same drumbeat sent officers and men to their appointed action stations whenever the ship beat to quarters.
(See also *Quarters.*)

Oakum
To pick oakum

"They make their oakum, wherewith they calk the seams of the ships, of old seer and weather-beaten ropes."
—Sir Walter Raleigh (?1552–1618), *History of the World* (1614)

Oakum is old rope that has been picked and unravelled; it is used for caulking the seams of wooden ships, being driven in tightly so as to render the planking watertight. "Picking oakum" is an appallingly tedious task, and was the employment given to prisoners and inmates of the workhouses. Usually they had to pick a pound of oakum per day. The word is from the Anglo-Saxon *acumbe,* off-combings; originally it was the coarse leftovers of flax. As a colloquialism, *to pick oakum* means to be set to do some tedious and disagreeable task, usually highly repetitive by nature.

Oar

"Spread all your canvas, all your oars employ."
—Alexander Pope (1688–1744), English man of letters, Homer's *Iliad* (1720)

From the Anglo-Saxon *ar,* a Viking word taken from the Old Norse tongue. Legend has it that when Odysseus wanted to retire from the sea, he was told to journey inland carrying an oar over his shoulder, stopping only when people asked him what it was he carried. When that happened, he would know that he could build his house right there, safe in the knowledge that he was in no danger

of being lured back to sea by nautical tales, as none of the locals would be familiar with things of the sea if they could not recognize a ship's oar.
(See also *Oars; To rest on one's oars.)*

Oars
To put/shove/stick in one's oar

To interrupt, to interfere, to break into a conversation to say one's piece; to add one's bit; as when one applies one's oar to help pull a boat through the water. From an older expression, "to have an oar in another man's boat," meaning to have an interest in someone else's affairs. The widespread use of this once purely nautical term is a measure of how thoroughly maritime terminology has permeated everyday speech: "We are quite capable of coming to an agreement—there's no need for you to stick your oar in."

To rest on one's oars

The oar is one of the best-known adjuncts of life at sea. It is, in its oldest form, a wooden pole flattened at one end, which, when used as a lever, pulls a boat through the water. It has three parts: the blade, the shaft, and the loom (the inboard end on which the rower pulls).

Rowing—pulling on the oars—is a very strenuous activity; colloquially, then, to rest on one's oars is to take a spell, a breather, after a period of hard work or intense physical effort. The original phrase was "to lie upon one's oars." "After the hard work of the last few weeks, I think that I am entitled to rest on my oars for a day or two."

Odds and sods

Extras; hands aboard the ship other than the regular crew. "Idlers" and "waisters" might be regarded as odds and sods, as they took no part in the daily running of the ship. The term expresses a measure of the sailor's contempt for anyone who is not a real seaman.
(See also *Idler. Waister.)*

Off and on

Also "on and off." Colloquially, this phrase has the force of "now and then," or "sometimes it is, sometimes it isn't," "occasionally": "I see him off and on at the club." Originally it referred to a vessel's deliberate tactic of alternately sailing toward the land (on) and then away from it (off). This was done (most often at night) when she was waiting for her pilot, or when entering an unfamiliar harbour. The emphasis was upon the deliberate back-and-forth movement of the vessel.
(See also *Stand-offish.)*

Offing
In the offing

The offing is that vaguely defined part of the sea lying between the horizon and the harbour entrance or coastal waters; it is the expanse of ocean that can be seen from any particular point on shore. To *keep an offing* is to keep a distance away from land because of navigational hazards, bad weather, or the like; to keep clear of all danger. Ships visible at sea from land are said to be "in the offing," that is, they are often about to approach port or some nearby anchorage. The term has come to mean "about to happen"; if a storm, wedding, election, or other event is likely to occur, then it is said to be "in the offing." "He has a new job in the offing, but I don't think he will be able to handle it."

"The discrepancy in the estimate of the vessel's offing. . . ."
—*The Daily News* (English newspaper), September 30, 1881

Oil
To pour oil on troubled waters

To soothe ruffled tempers; to use tact and gentle words to restore peace after an argument: "He is always getting into strife with people, and his wife spends a lot of time pouring oil on troubled waters." From the well-known fact that oil floats on water, and that when poured onto the surface of a stormy sea it very markedly decreases the violence of the waves. In a storm, the usual method was to hang an oil bag over the side of the vessel and allow the oil to drip into the sea. An oil slick would form, thus preventing the waves from breaking.

Oldster

An old navy term, from the days of fighting sail, for a midshipman who had more than four years' seniority to his credit. He occupied the cockpit of the ship with the master's mates, who were also known as "oldsters." Junior midshipmen of less than four years' seniority messed in the gunroom, under the supervision of the gunner. The term is well-known in colloquial speech; it refers to an older person, as in "Go and ask him about the procedure—he's one of the oldsters in this place."
(See also *Time; To serve one's time. Youngster.)*

"Leave all us oldsters to bore one another to death."
—Henry Kingsley (1830–1876), English novelist, *Ravenshoe* (1862)

Ordinary

To be laid up in ordinary is an old naval term indicating that a ship is laid up in harbour or in the dockyard. Such vessels usually had their masts, rigging, guns, etc., removed and stored ashore. The term *ordinary* originally referred to the men, the reserve staff, who remained in charge—usually the warrant officers and their servants. *Ordinary* has a deprecatory sense attached to it, as in "ordinary seaman" (abbreviated to "O.D."), one who is not an able seaman. It is found also in the French *vin ordinaire.* This is the sense of the word in common use today: that which is commonly met with, of the usual kind, average (and sometimes inferior in quality to the average). *To be in ordinary* is to be in regular service, as is a physician-in-ordinary to a king. From the Latin *ordinarius,* of the usual order.

Outboard Strictly, the outside of a vessel's hull; in a direction away from the central fore-and-aft line. Also said of anything attached to or projecting outward from the vessel's side. The word is also a shortened form of *outboard motor,* a gasoline-powered engine (usually two-stroke) with propellor and tiller, and mounted by clamping it to the stern of a boat.

Outpoint Nautically, to sail closer to the wind than another vessel (i.e., to be able to point one's vessel a little more directly into the direction from which the wind is blowing). *To point* is a verb widely used in the seafaring lexicon. Metaphorically, *to outpoint* is to excel in a number of characteristics, to outdo or to outclass: "He is only a math teacher, but he outpointed his debating opponent with considerable skill."
(See also *Sail; To sail close to the wind.)*

Outrigger An original nautical word, altered from the fifteenth-century English *outligger,* which is almost certainly from the Dutch *uitlegger,* outlyer. The immediate reference is to the framework that extends outboard from the sides of certain boats, such as South Pacific canoes; the framework supports a float that provides considerable stability for the vessel. The meaning of the word has been extended to include the bracket that supports the rowlock on a racing shell; various projecting frames or parts on an aeroplane; and, in the building trades, a beam that projects from a building to support certain kinds of scaffolding.

"Carried into action on an outrigger stretching ahead of a ship."
—*British Quarterly Review,* 1873

Overbear Originally a nautical term to describe a wind that overwhelms a ship. *To overbear* is to bear over or bear down by weight or force; to overcome; to domineer.
(See also *Overbearing.)*

Overbearing To be domineering or dictatorial; arrogant or haughty, generally rude. From a combination of *to bear up* (to bring a vessel even closer to the wind) and *to bear down upon* (to approach another vessel from the windward side and thus be in a position of great advantage). The common element is one that suggests intimidation, as is reflected in the figurative use of the expression: "He was a very efficient manager, but many of his workers found him to be insufferably overbearing in his attitude toward them."
(See also *Overbear.)*

Overboard
To go overboard about something

"All of us sacrifice our sins, cast them overboard. . . ."
—Brinsley, *A Groan for Israel,* cited in the *Universal Dictionary of the English Language* (1897)

Board is from the Old English *bord,* meaning board, plank, table. *To board* meant to enter a ship by force; *aboard* describes the state of being in—never "on"—a ship. *To go overboard* meant that something had fallen over the side; in the case of a member of the crew going over the side, the cry is "Man overboard!" When a mast or some other substantial piece of gear was carried away by storm or battle, it was said *to go by the board, board* being the general term for the ship's deck.

Used figuratively, the phrase means to harbour an excess of feeling about something, to lose one's emotional footing, as it were, and plunge into a wave of unbridled enthusiasm: "She has gone overboard about her new boyfriend, mostly because he plays in a rock band."

To throw overboard

The meaning is clear: *to throw something overboard* is to heave it over the sides of a vessel into the water, as would be done when lightening a ship that was aground on a sandbar or reef. The intention is to get rid of articles of gear that are judged to be no longer useful, given the present circumstances. Similarly, *to throw someone overboard* is suddenly to abandon or desert that person without regard to his or her feelings or immediate future: "When she saw him dancing with the new secretary, she threw him overboard and had nothing more to do with him." (See also *Jettison.)*

Overhaul

"The 20-ton cutter *Irene* is getting a complete overhaul."
—*Field Magazine,* April 4, 1885

The phrase nowadays means to inspect, test, and repair machinery or the like, but originally it meant to increase the distance between two sets of blocks in a tackle system, by running the rope back through the sheaves; i.e., to separate the two sets of blocks still further. To bring them so close together as to prevent further relative movement between the blocks is to cause them to be "block and block." *To overhaul* also means to gain steadily upon some other vessel, vehicle, runner, or such, so as eventually to pass it. (See also *Chock-a-block.)*

Overpressed

Nautically, to carry too much sail for the prevailing conditions; to be over-canvassed; to be in danger of foundering. As an idiom, the expression is used to describe the condition of someone whose creditiors are insisting on payment, or someone who is getting the worst of an argument: "The middle period spanning the 1980s and 1990s saw a great many entrepreneurs being overpressed for money by their bankers."

Over-rated

The rank held by a naval seaman is known as a "rate," and the man himself as a "rating" (one who fills that rate or position). Each seaman held a rate according to his ability. If he entered the ship as a boy, he became an ordinary seaman (the first rating) at age 18, and—other things being equal—he was rated an "able-bodied" seaman (an "A.B.," which properly means one who could "hand, reef, and steer") at about age 21.

From there he could be promoted successively to Leading Seaman, Petty Officer (from the French *petit,* small), and so on. In the early days of sail—for example, in the Royal Navy at the time of the French Revolutionary Wars and the Napoleonic Wars (1792–1814)—the avenues of promotion were a little more flexibly organised, but at the same time a seaman had fewer promotional positions for which he could strive.

"Overrate their happiness. . . ."
—Thomas Babington Macaulay (1800–1859), English historian, *History of England* (1848)

Captains could rate their own men; indeed, they had to after any battle that took its usually high toll of casualties. It often happened that, in the nature of things, a man was rated to a position for which he was unsuitable either by skill or temperament or both. In time he would be found to be "over-rated," in which case the captain could, if he wished, derate the seaman to a lower rating. Derating was also a common means of punishment, as a disciplinary measure against, for example, frequent drunkenness or insolence to an officer. In a similar fashion, a man might be found to be "under-rated," deserving of promotion to a rate that he was better fitted for.

Hence the metaphors that have been derived from this nautical practice: *to be over-rated* is to be overestimated, overvalued; and *to be under-rated* is the reverse, to be held at too low a value. "She is said to be a good singer, but I listened to her last night and I think that she is far over-rated."
(See also *Broke; To be broke.)*

Overwhelm

"Humming water must o'erwhelm thy corpse. . . ."
—William Shakespeare (1564–1616), *Pericles,* act 3, scene 1

Nautically, to be buried by an onrushing and breaking sea, as in broaching; to be unable to resist the combined forces of the prevailing weather conditions. As a figure of speech, the phrase means to be overcome completely in mind or feeling; to be defeated by force of numbers: "He was overwhelmed by her offer to stand bail for him"; "The visiting players overwhelmed the home team without any difficulty at all."

Over is from the Old English *ofer,* which in turn derives from the Sanskrit *upari,* above in place or position. *Whelm,* which itself is the archaic word for to submerge, to engulf ("sorrow whelmed her"), is a combining of the Old English *gehwelfan,* bend over, and *helmian,* cover.
(See also *Broach.)*

P

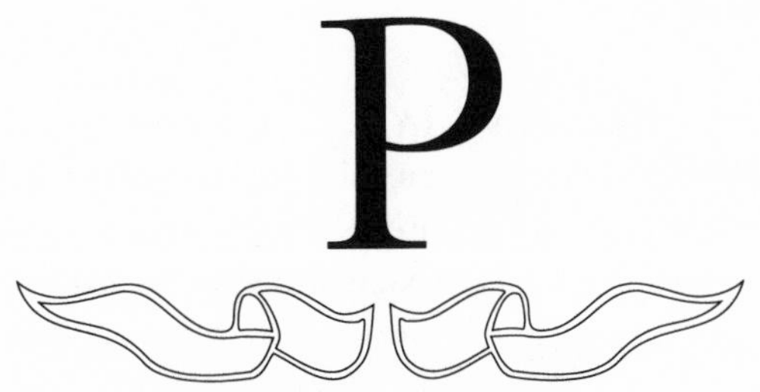

Paid
To be paid off

See *Pay; To pay off.*

Painter
Cutting his painter

A painter is the rope secured to the bow of a boat for the purpose of making her fast to a quay, jetty, or buoy, or to another vessel; a very old word of obscure origin. In the fifteenth century, a "shank-painter" was a rope or chain that held the shank and flukes of the anchor fast to the ship's side.

"The hemp is so poor that it breaks like the painter of a boat."
—G. Macdonald, *Seaboard Paris,* cited in the *Universal Dictionary of the English Language* (1897)

In seaman's language, *to cut one's painter* is to depart this life, as in the silent and clandestine cutting of a boat's painter, which allows it to slip away unnoticed; it is as if the sailor's personal lifeline has been severed. *To lose the number of his mess* is another naval equivalent of this phrase.

Parcel

To parcel is to wrap fabric, such as hessian or canvas, around the end of a rope that has been "wormed"—prepared for parcelling—to ready it for serving, so that the rope end will be protected from the rot that constant wetting will otherwise induce. Usually the fabric used for parcelling was tarred canvas. *To worm* a rope is to lay a thin line in the grooves or lays of the larger rope; *to serve* (originally, "sarve") is to wind spun yarn tightly and closely over the parcelling, so that the completed work is firmly bound together and is virtually waterproof. The old rule for this complete operation is: "Worm and parcel with the lay, Turn and serve the other way." The word *parcel* was certainly in use some 300 years before the parcel post was established in England in 1883, but it is not clear whether the nautical usage preceded general usage.

Pass
To pass for

To be accepted as or recognised as what one purports to be. The phrase is from the old naval form; when a midshipman had served the requisite number of years afloat (generally, six years), he took an examination for the rank of lieutenant. If he was successful, he was said "to pass for" lieutenant. The phrase is peculiarly nautical: in all other fields of endeavour and examination we "pass the test" rather than pass "for" the objective.

Passage
To work one's passage

To pay for one's fare on a sea voyage by working as a member of the crew. This means of cheap travel was once more widely available than it is now; the growth of the maritime unions, and the demise of the small shipping companies, have together made it all but impossible to sign on in this manner.

The expression has come to be applied to any instance in which a person joins an enterprise as a latecomer, so to speak, on the understanding that he will contribute his labour, skills, and knowledge in return for the privilege of participating in the group's rewards or goals; for example, a hitchhiker could work his passage by helping with the driving, repairing flat tires, and so on.

Passenger

"Apelles, when he had finished any work, exposed it to the sight of all passengers, and concealed himself to hear the censure of his faults."

—John Dryden (1631–1700), English man of letters, *Dufresnoy,* cited in the *Universal Dictionary of the English Language* (1897)

Another word of nautical origin, referring to the earliest travellers or wayfarers taking passage on board ship. From the Middle English and the French *passager,* and ultimately the Latin *passare,* to take passage (aboard ship), with the intrusive *n* following the pattern of "messenger" and "scavenger." Nowadays a passenger is any person travelling on virtually any type of conveyance, be it by land, sea, or air.

Passport

An official document granting permission to a specified person to visit foreign countries; it authenticates the bearer's identity and citizenship and right to protection while abroad. Such documents are sometimes issued to neutral vessels in time of war, so that they may enter certain waters without fear of molestation.

"Let him depart; his passport shall be made,
And crowns for convoy put into his purse."

—William Shakespeare (1564–1616), *Henry V,* act 4, scene 3

Passports required for travel to the continent were in common use during the reign of Elizabeth I, and an early record (1554) tells of one Patrick Colghon being committed to Marshalsea Prison in London for altering the details on his passport. The term *passport* shows quite clearly that its original use had to do with travel by sea. From the French *passeport,* to enter or pass through a port or harbour.

Pay
To pay off

Originally, *to pay off* was to close the accounts of a naval ship when she reached the end of a commission; all the ship's company were then given the balance of monies due to them. Merchant seamen were paid off at the end of a voyage. Many a naval vessel in the seventeenth century was sent straight back to sea after having come in to port to be paid off, for want of cash on the part of the Navy Board. It was not uncommon for seamen—and thus their wives and families—to be denied their regular wages for years on end. How seamen's dependents lived ashore under these conditions, in the hard times of that century, defies the imagination.

In the colloquial sense, *to pay someone off* is to get even, to exact retribution, to pay off an old score; from the earlier sense of closing the accounts: "The foreman had been unnecessarily harsh with us on the assembly line, but we paid him off by sabotaging the production machinery." Rendered also by the expression *to pay someone out*—i.e., "I'll be a match for him, I'll get even."
(See also *Pay; To pay out. Tick; To get something on tick.)*

To pay out

"It was marvellous to me how the boatman could see . . . to pay out the line."
—*Field Magazine,* December 17, 1885, cited in the *Universal Dictionary of the English Language* (1897)

From the Latin *pacare,* to pacify. Colloquially, it means to hand out money, as in wages; also to retaliate for an injury, to punish in revenge. The phrase derives from the nautical usage, which refers to the act of slackening a cable or rope so that it can run out freely by a desired amount.
(See also *Pay; To pay off.)*

Peepers

Sailor's slang for eyes; the expression was in common use in ships at the beginning of the 1800s. The word has long since passed into common use, and is enshrined in at least one 1938 song of music-hall fame, the first line of which runs: "Jeepers Creepers, where'd you get those peepers?"

Peg
To take one down a peg

"The brilliant young athlete wanted taking down a peg."
—*Literary World,* February 3, 1882, cited in the *Universal Dictionary of the English Language* (1897)

To deflate a conceited person; to puncture his pretension, to damage his self-esteem. From the manner in which signals and flags (the ship's colours) were attached to the halyard by which they were hoisted. They were secured to the halyard by toggles, a simple peg-and-loop arrangement similar to the fastenings on duffel coats. The higher a ship's colours were raised, the greater the honour, and to cause them to be taken down a peg would be to diminish the honour. Used as in "He thought that he was a very clever chess player, but he was taken down a peg when he was beaten in a tournament by a 10-year-old."

People

Not originally a nautical term, but curiously this was the word used for many hundreds of years to describe a crew. Admiral George Anson (1697–1762), in the account of his circumnavigation of 1740–1743 (written by his ship's chaplain), refers constantly to his seamen as "the people." Hakluyt, that remarkable compendium of early voyages, abounds with this particular and peculiar usage (Richard Hakluyt, clergyman and translator [1551–1616], *The Principal Navigations, Voiages, Traffiques and Discoveries of the English Nation* [1589]).
(See also *Crew.)*

Perks

From *perquisites* (Latin *perquisitum,* that which is sought for), a fringe benefit or bonus as part of a particular post or position; an allowance in cash or kind appertaining to a particular employment: "One of the perks that he enjoyed as groundsman at Lord's was being given tickets for every cricket match played there."

One of the most notorious sources of perks in the old British navy related to the office of purser, who was the official responsible for issuing provisions and clothing. He was paid partly by salary and partly by a commission on the daily issue of food. Provisions were drawn from the ship's stores at 16 ounces to the pound, and reissued by the purser at 14 ounces. The purser pocketed (or sold) the balance of 2 ounces, often to become a rich man in the process.
(See also *Slops. Slush fund.)*

Petrel
Stormy petrel

The name used by British sailors to refer to small seabirds, the presence of which near a ship was supposed to indicate the approach of a storm.

The petrel is traditionally so named from the Italian *Petrello,* little Peter, because during storms these birds seem to be able to fly by patting the water with each foot alternately, as if walking on it, reminiscent of St. Peter, who walked on the water in biblical times. A common name given to these birds by sailors is "Mother Carey's chickens"; the birds were said to belong to "our Lady, Mater Cara" (thus "Mother Carey"), meaning "Mother Dear," a reference to the Virgin Mary.

In figurative speech, a stormy petrel is a person whose coming is supposed to portend trouble. This is from the fact that the bird was usually seen only when a storm was imminent; in times of calm they were never in evidence. "We were all a bit worried when the new shop steward took up his duties in the factory—he was said to be something of a stormy petrel concerning relations with management."

Pickled

To be very drunk. One contemporary authority (Lind; see bibliography) suggests that this expression refers particularly to the pickling of Lord Nelson's body in a cask of brandy for transit back to England after the Battle of Trafalgar in 1805. This origin may be correct, but it seems just as likely that, by popular analogy, the consumption of large quantities of alcohol would also pickle one from the inside, so to speak.

However, the manner of returning Nelson's body to England did give rise to a widespread (albeit erroneous) belief among British seamen not only that rum was used for the task, but also that the sentries tapped (siphoned off) some of this rum while they were guarding the cask. Both stories are, of course, untrue: brandy, not rum, was used, and the cask was so charged with the gasses of putrefaction from the body's organs that the head of the cask began to lift, causing great alarm to the sentries and necessitating the replenishment of the brandy a number of times. It is highly unlikely that any seaman or soldier would have broached Nelson's coffin-cask in these circumstances.

It has also been suggested that the expression *drunk as a lord* owes its origin to the same set of incidents. This, too, seems unlikely, although it is obvious why seamen would have regarded Nelson as being thoroughly drunk, steeped in brandy as he was. The expression would certainly have been in common usage before Nelson's time; excessive drinking was common among the nobility of the eighteenth and nineteenth centuries, and many a man of fashion and title prided himself on the number of bottles of wine he could consume at a sitting.
(See also *Nelson's Blood.)*

Pidgin

"The grammar of pigeon [sic] English is not English but Chinese."

—Sayce, *Comparative Philosophy,* cited in the *Universal Dictionary of the English Language* (1897)

Originally pidgin was a jargon used on the China coast, from the seventeenth century onward, as a consequence of contact between English sea traders and local Chinese merchants, using English words and Chinese syntax. It was—and still is in many other areas, such as West Africa—the *lingua franca* of the East. *Pidgin* (sometimes erroneously spelled "pigeon") is the Chinese modification of the English word *business.* The development went from *business* to *bisin* to *pisin* to *pidgin.*

Pidgin proper is a simplified language made up of elements from two or more tongues, so that traders who speak different languages can still do business with each other. Missionaries in developing countries such as Papua New Guinea typically conduct their affairs with the local people in pidgin English.

Pidgin is not the mother tongue of any particular speech community, but when it does attain the status of a language it is known as a "creole," from the Portuguese *crioulo,* meaning a person of European descent born and brought up in a colonial territory. The term *creole* gradually came to be applied to the language these people spoke.

The common expression *That's not my pigeon* flows from the word *pidgin,* the spelling having been altered in the process. It means, quite literally, "This is not my business, not my affair." "I'm not involved in the financial side of the company I work for—that's my partner's pigeon"; "We made contact with some villagers on the Sepik River who could speak a local version of pidgin."

Pieces of eight

Along with doubloons, pieces of eight figure largely in the tales of piracy on the Spanish Main; hence the inclusion of the term in this collection. A piece of eight was the old Spanish dollar or *peso,* worth eight *reals* (itself a Spanish silver coin, meaning "royal," from the Latin *regalis,* regal).
(See also *Doubloon.)*

Pile up

Nautically, to run a vessel ashore or aground on a shoal or rock; colloquially, to crash, to come to grief: "His lack of attention to the weather conditions caused him to pile up his new car on the freeway."

Pillage

"They were suffered to pillage wherever they went."
—Thomas Babington Macaulay (1800–1859), English historian, *History of England* (1848)

First used as a noun (fourteenth century); from the French *piller,* to plunder, and earlier from the Low Latin *piliare,* to pill (obsolete for "to peel").

By ancient law of the sea, the captors of a ship had the right to seize any goods that were strewn on the upper deck; what often happened was that the holds were broken open and their contents scattered on the deck, to be immediately picked up a moment later and claimed as pillage. Nowadays the term means to strip of money or goods by open violence, on land as well as on sea; to take as booty; to rob and plunder.

Pilot

"Passengers in a ship always submit to their pilot's discretion."
—Robert South (1634–1716), English preacher, *Sermons,* cited in the *Universal Dictionary of the English Language* (1897)

From the Italian *pilota* and *piedota,* probably connected with the Greek *pedon,* rudder; also related to the Dutch *peillood,* a sounding lead. A pilot is a qualified coastal navigator taken on board a ship at a particular place for the purpose of conducting that vessel to some landfall or port.

The modern aircraft pilot's title derives directly from this ancient usage, as do the terms *pilot balloon, pilot engine, pilot fish, pilot scheme,* and so forth. *Pilotage* (the act of piloting a vessel, and the fees and charges thereby payable) is originally a nautical term. The earlier term for pilot was *lodesman* or *lodeman,* from the Anglo-Saxon *ladmann.*

Pinch
At a pinch; in a pinch

"Hang therefore on this promise of God, who is an helper at a pinch."
—John Foxe (1516–1587), English cleric, *Book of Martyrs* (1563)

To pinch-up is to sail a vessel so close to the wind that her sails shiver and consequently her speed is reduced. Sometimes it is possible to just fetch, or round, a desired mark by deliberately pinching the vessel up to the wind, even though considerable way may be lost. Similarly, when something can be done "at a pinch," a sacrifice—or a threat of a sacrifice—of some kind may be necessary; one may then just scrape through. "At a pinch we could run that engine on kerosene if the fuel oil isn't delivered on time"; "If it comes to the pinch, I'll play the piano for you, but I'm not very good."

Pipe

To pipe down

From the call made by the boatswain (bosun) on a naval vessel, generally made last thing at night. The call is done with the bosun's pipe or whistle, and is the order for lights out and all hands to turn in (to go to their bunks); for silence generally. The phrase is in wide use, meaning to verbally restrain someone from being too noisy or aggressive, or making a nuisance of herself: "Will you pipe down for a minute? I want to listen to the news."

"The skipper he stood beside the helm,
His pipe was in his mouth. . . ."
—Henry Wadsworth Longfellow (1807–1882), American poet, *The Wreck of the Hesperus* (1841)

From the Anglo-Saxon *pipe* and the Latin *pipare,* to pipe or cheep, like a young bird.

To pipe the side

When high-ranking officers or officials board a naval vessel, their arrival (and departure) is saluted by "piping the side," which is a particular call or series of calls on the bosun's pipe or whistle. The custom, still observed in today's navies, originates from the days when visitors were hoisted aboard on a bosun's chair on a yardarm tackle manned by a group of seamen detailed for the purpose. The bosun stood where he could see the hoist, and controlled the operation by calls on the pipe so that the seamen knew when to lift or lower.

If a group of officers or high-ranking civilians was embarking or disembarking, the most senior person present would be the first to enter the ship and the last to leave it, so as to prevent his exalted personage from being unduly exposed to the wind and spray that generally accompanied these transfers.

"As fine a ship's company as ever was piped aloft. . . ."
—Captain Frederick Marryat (1792–1848), English naval captain and novelist, *Peter Simple* (1834)

The pipe, or whistle, goes back many hundreds of years, to the days when the galley slaves of ancient Rome and Greece kept stroke by the sounding of a flute or whistle. The bosun's pipe, as a means of communicating orders, has always been honoured as a badge of rank, even as far back as 1485, when it was worn as the emblem of rank by the Lord High Admiral of England.

The English navy had as many as 22 different calls on the bosun's pipe, each with a different meaning; today there are but 8 such calls. In 1833, the French navy had an astonishing list of 118 orders that could be given by the bosun's pipe.

To pipe up

Probably formed in the language as the antithesis of *to pipe down.* Its origin is likely not nautical, because *to pipe up* means to call—on the bosun's pipe—the watch from below to their duties on deck. As the off-duty watch is nearly always turned in and asleep, a bosun's pipe would be unlikely to be heard. Instead, the bosun's mates invariably called the seamen in person.

The expression means to begin to talk, especially unexpectedly; to make oneself heard; to speak up and assert

oneself. "The child in the corner piped up that she wanted milk instead." All these senses are opposite to those of "pipe down." The expression is used nautically, though, to describe a wind that is beginning to pick up, to increase noticeably in strength.
(See also *Pipe; To pipe down.)*

Piping hot Food that is hot, freshly cooked, straight from the ovens; a familiar domestic expression. It originates from the days when seamen were piped to their meals with the bosun's pipe or call; when the men heard the mess-call on the pipe, they knew that the food was hot and ready for serving: "Be careful, the soup is piping hot!"
(See also *Pipe; To pipe the side.)*

Pirate One who robs or commits illegal violence at sea or on the shores of the sea; a plunderer.

To pirate something Piracy is the act of taking a ship on the high seas from the possession or control of those lawfully entitled to it. Pirates have infested the world's maritime routes since the dawn of man's first venturing forth on the waters. For some hundreds of years, piracy was organised on a national scale along the northern coast of Africa, with Tunis and Algiers as the main centres (Captain Joshua Slocum, the world's first single-handed circumnavigator, was chased by pirates a few days out from Gibraltar in the late 1890s).

"Property captured from pirates is liable to condemnation as droits [rights] of the Admiralty, to be restored, if private property, to the rightful owners, on payment of one-eighth of the value as salvage; while fitting rewards are assigned for services against pirates."
—Sir William Blackstone (1723–1780), English jurist, *Commentaries on the Laws of England* (1769)

"The pirated edition, a copy of which I have seen, grossly misrepresents my drawings both in style and colouring."
—*Scribner's Magazine,* September 1877

Pirates flourished in the West Indies and the Gulf of Mexico following the discovery of America in 1492. In English waters, the seamen of Devon and Kent were notorious for their acts of piracy in the English Channel. Piracy is still prevalent in the seas of southeast Asia, particularly in the approaches to Singapore Harbour, where many a large vessel has been boarded and robbed by gangs of pirates operating from small, high-powered craft. They can also be met with in Philippine waters.

The modern-day sense of the word includes the appropriation of the literary, artistic, or other work or invention of some person and reproducing it for one's own profit, as in the pirate radio stations that operated in Europe for some time in the 1960s and 1970s. The computer and video home movie industries of the 1980s have also spawned a vast and profitable racket in pirated copies of copyrighted material.

The word is from the Latin *pirata,* which derives in turn from the Greek *peirates.*
(See also *Filibuster.)*

Piss
Poor as piss and twice as nasty

Sailor's slang for anything that is really bad; the expression needs little by way of explanation. *Piss* is from the French *pisser,* from the Latin *pissare,* probably imitative in origin of the act of urinating. It is interesting that the Teutonic languages borrowed the word originally as a euphemism.

The expression has found great favour among the cognoscenti of the various brands of beer available in Australia. For those whose interest is now aroused, *pisco* was a potent liquor brewed in Peru and on the Chilean coast (from a Spanish word, which in turn is also from the Latin source *pissare).* The name was shortened in English to "pis" or "piss," and applied to any cheap drink of dubious origin and quality.

Pitch
To pitch and pay

"The word is Pitch and pay:
Trust none."
—William Shakespeare (1564–1616), *Henry V,* act 2, scene 3

To pay up at once; from the fact that vessels had their seams sealed with pitch, that is, "payed." The task could be done properly only when the pitch to be applied was hot. The original sense of *pay*—to pour hot pitch into a seam caulked with oakum—was not connected with *pay* in the sense of money or debt. The one became linked with the other because of the idea of immediacy or requirement necessarily attached to both.

Pitch in

To deal with something, to sort some matter out, to encourage others to help in a common cause: "If we all pitch in we can get this ground dug up before lunchtime." From the notion of cooperation required when seamen were paying pitch into the seams of a vessel.
(See also *Pitch; To pitch and pay.)*

Pitch black

See *Pitch dark.*

Pitch dark

Not, of course, a nautical phrase; but pitch no doubt was first discovered and applied by seamen thousands of years ago. Pitch is the dark-coloured, viscous liquid obtained from the distillation of coal tar (coal-tar pitch) or wood tar (wood-tar pitch), sometimes known as bitumen or asphalt. Its earliest widespread use was almost certainly for coating the seams of primitive vessels, as in canoes, hide-boats of the coracle type, and of course planked vessels that required waterproofing at the joins of the planks. Pitch was known to the Romans, and the word comes to us through the Anglo-Saxon *pic,* from the Latin *pix.*

Plank
Walk the plank

As a metaphor, to be put to the acid test, to be put on trial for one's life; also, to be about to die. Literally, a popular means of disposing of prisoners at sea, whereby a plank or

"I got my back up at that and they walked the plank."
—*Scribner's Magazine,* November 1878

gangway was run out from the ship's side and unwanted prisoners were prodded to and beyond the end of the plank. Their arms were usually bound behind them to hinder their chances of survival. "The jailer grinned sardonically and told the prisoner that he had been condemned by the court to walk the plank."

Plimsoll line The mark painted on the side of a merchant vessel, fixing the maximum load line according to the season (winter or summer), and the nature of water being traversed (fresh or salt). It takes its name from Samuel Plimsoll (1824–1898), Member of Parliament for Derby, who campaigned vigorously against the gross and unsafe overloading of cargo shipping widely practised at that time.

Plimsoll mark See *Plimsoll line.*

Plot
To plot a course of action

"Here's the plot on't. . . ."
—Ben Jonson (1572–1637), English dramatist and poet, *The Alchemist* (1610)

From the Anglo-Saxon *plot,* patch of ground. The word gradually developed a number of meanings, all deriving from the basic idea of an area or patch of earth, and thence to plan and design. Thus, "to plot a course" is to mark on a chart the intended direction of the vessel; to determine such a course. By extension, the figurative usage is clear: to plan a course of action that will lead toward some desired objective. "We will have to plot a new course of action if we are to save the firm from bankruptcy."
(See also *Shape; To shape up.)*

Plug Originally a nautical word from the Dutch and found in the German *pflock,* a peg or plug, as in a bung or stopper. The stopper fitted in the bottom of a ship's boat, which enables it to be drained when hoisted aboard or onto the beach, is called the "plug." A "plug" of tobacco is named for its plug-like shape. *To plug on*—to work hard—is from rowing.

Plum duff A kind of flour pudding containing raisins or currants, cooked by steaming or boiling in a cloth; once a very popular part of Christmas celebrations in Australia in the early days. Originally the seaman's name for plum pudding, a much-favoured but rarely seen delicacy on board ship.

Ply
To ply back and forth

"We plyed all the floods to the windewardes."
—Richard Hakluyt (?1552–1616), English cleric and maritime historian, *Principall Navigations, Voiages, and Discoveries of the English Nation* (1589)

Descriptive of a vessel as it makes regular voyages between certain ports, often scheduled, but not always; to ply for trade; to seek cargoes by sailing or steaming from one port to another as opportunity offers, as did tramp steamers earlier in this century. The word is a variation of the Middle English *aplye,* to apply. The word found its first application in this sense by seamen, in particular the Thames watermen.

It is now used generally to mean to carry on, to practise, to pursue.

Point blank From the French *point blanc,* white point or centre, the white disk that marks the bull's-eye of a target. When a ship's gun is fired "point blank," it is fired at a distance (usually quite short) such that if the line of sight to the target is parallel with the axis of the barrel (i.e., as if one were sighting at the enemy target by peering down the bore of the barrel instead of along it), then the projectile will travel direct, without curve or deviation, to hit the object at the point of aim. At point blank range, the gun is close enough to hit the bull's-eye without having to allow for the curve of trajectory.

"Point-blank over against the mouth of the piece."
—Brewer, *Lingua,* cited in the *Universal Dictionary of the English Language* (1897)

Hence the colloquialism: to be direct, to the point, without beating about the bush; straightforward. "She accused him point blank of embezzling funds."

Poles
Under bare poles

To be *under bare poles* means to have no sails set, because of bad weather. The vessel invariably still makes headway, being driven by the force of the wind on the masts and spars. Figuratively, the phrase applies to a person who is driven to his last extremity; to be broke, down on one's luck.
(See also *Beam; To be on one's beam ends. Hard; Hard up.)*

Pompey Sailor's slang name for Portsmouth, the British naval base on the English Channel. The origin of this curious nickname is quite unknown.

Pongo The sailor's name for a soldier (also called a "grabbie"). The word may have come from Africa, where it is used to indicate a gorilla *(mpongi),* or any other great ape, by the Kongo people, a tribe of Bantu who live on the lower Congo. The slang term is more common in New Zealand than in Australia. Seamen probably adapted it as a satirical description of the awkwardness of soldiers on board ship.

Poodle faking Sailor's slang meaning going ashore to meet young ladies. The origin of this figure of speech is obscure, but it might derive from the tried-and-true manoeuvre of buttering up to a girl by fondly admiring her dog as the lady walks it for exercise.

Poop
To be pooped

The poop deck is the highest deck at the stern of a sailing vessel, raised (where fitted) above the quarterdeck. From the Latin *puppis,* stern. A ship is "pooped" when a heavy sea breaks over her stern while she is running before the wind

"A press of canvas that may have saved her from being pooped."
—*The Daily Telegraph* (English newspaper), November 12, 1885

in a gale—a very dangerous situation, because the vessel's speed in this circumstance is approximately the same as that of the following sea. She therefore loses steerage way and becomes uncontrollable, with the likelihood of broaching-to and foundering. *To be pooped* metaphorically is to be exhausted, finished, at one's last resort: "By the time we had scrambled to the top of Mount Claire, we were all thoroughly pooped."

Port
Any port in a storm

The allusion is obvious. Mariners caught in storms at sea would wish to be safely in port—any port—rather than battle what might prove to be dangerous conditions in stormy waters. On the other hand, if the port or harbour offers only an exposed anchorage, most ships will put to sea to have greater sea-room in which to endure the onslaught of a severe storm.

"The king has the prerogative of appointing ports and havens, or such places only for persons or merchandise to pass into and out of the realm, as he in his wisdom sees proper."
—Sir William Blackstone (1723–1780), English jurist, *Commentaries on the Laws of England* (1769)

The word *port* comes from the Latin *portus,* haven; *Portugal* also derives from this word. *Port side* or *port,* meaning the left-hand side of a vessel as seen when facing forward, comes from *portus* as well. The usage came to mean this side because of the presence of the (original) steering-board on the right-hand or starboard side of the vessel. The steering-board or steering-oar prevented the ship from presenting its starboard side to the dock or wharf.

More generally, the phrase refers to the tendency to retreat from some unexpectedly threatening situation, such as an argument or a lack of some otherwise desirable article or set of conditions, and seeking refuge in a rearrangement of matters such that some safety or relief is obtained. Often it is the act of compromise, of having to accept the nearest solution to some difficulty: "With three young children to care for, she decided that remarrying was preferable to remaining a widow; she was ready to seek any port in a storm."
(See also *Starboard, larboard* in appendix 2.)

Posh

There are two explanations for the origin of this word, which means stylish, high-class, upper-class, as in "a posh hotel," "posh clothes," "a posh accent."

The most commonly accepted story is that it comes from the heyday of the British Empire, when travel from Britain to India, Australia, and the Far East was by P&O steamship through the Suez Canal (the Peninsula and Oriental Steam Navigation Company carried mails and passengers between England and India in the period 1842–1970).

The passage down the Red Sea and across the Indian Ocean north of the equator was, at the best of times, an unbearably hot one. It is said that passengers booking the return journey from Britain to the colonies would try to secure a cabin for the outward-bound journey on the port side of the vessel—i.e., on the left-hand side. Because the ship was approaching the equator from the north and west, the sun was always on the right-hand or starboard side in the afternoon, the hottest part of the day. Choosing a cabin on the port side would put the passenger on the side of the ship that was presumably a little cooler in the evening. Similarly, the voyage home would be booked for the starboard side, as this part of the vessel would be away from the direct glare of the afternoon sun.

"He has not got the posh [money] yet."
—*Sessions Paper Old Bailey* (1824–1833), cited in the *Oxford English Dictionary Supplement* (1982)

This story insists that the P&O booking clerk would endorse the ticket "POSH," their acronym for "Port Out, Starboard Home." Naturally, because of the demand for these better-located berths, the steamship company would charge a premium on the fare. Consequently, the acronym POSH became associated with travellers who could afford the higher fare, and they themselves became known as "posh," people who belonged to a better or higher class.

However, there is one major obstacle to this story, despite its widespread acceptance—there appears to be no evidence to support it. Officials of the P&O Steamship Company have asserted that there is no record at all of tickets ever being endorsed in the manner just detailed.

In 1937, Mr. Boyd Cable published *A Hundred Year History of the P&O,* in which he described the story behind "posh" as a "tale"; and in 1962 the librarian of the P&O reported that he could find no evidence that the initials POSH were ever stamped on the company's tickets or documents of any kind.

"Practically every posh family in the country has called him in at one time or another."
—P. G. Wodehouse (1881–1975), *The Inimitable Jeeves* (1924)

Indeed, one must ask the obvious question: Why would a P&O booking clerk need to stamp a ticket in any particular way at all? The clerks would be perfectly familiar with the arrangement of the cabins on the company's ships, and if a passenger wanted a berth on the cooler port side on the voyage to India, it would have been a simple matter for the booking clerk to give him or her the appropriately numbered ticket. It may well be, of course, that people who were familiar with travel in this region might have themselves devised the POSH acronym as a means of passing on advice to others making the trip for the first time, but it is certainly not the case that the P&O Company used it in their booking arrangements.

The second (and less colourful) story is the more likely of the two. The word almost certainly derives from the Romany slang word *posh,* meaning both "dandy" and "money." *(Romany* is the name preferred by so-called gypsy peoples.) In this slang, anyone who had a bit of money was a "dandy," a "swell," or what in America would be called a "swank" person, and who was therefore said to be "posh." In time, *posh* came to be associated with the comfort and convenience that money could buy, as well as with anyone who was stylish or who affected high-class manners.

Posh, to mean stylish, swank, is no longer as current as it used to be, although it is still understood in the English-speaking world. It enjoyed a heyday at the turn of the century, and was to be found in the novels of P. G. Wodehouse, the British writer. Today it would be used as a description of a person or a place, as in "We stayed at the poshest hotel we could find in Singapore"; "When Gloria came back from her working holiday in England, she had acquired a very posh accent."

Post
To be posted

"Whispers were afloat, which came to the ears of the Admiralty, and prevented him from being posted."
—Captain Frederick Marryat (1792–1848), English naval captain and novelist, *Peter Simple* (1834)

In the Royal Navy there were two grades of captain. Lieutenants who were promoted to captain were given the command of a small ship other than a rated vessel; after sufficient experience in command of such a ship, they were then "posted" (given command of) a rated ship, where they took the rank of post-captain.

The phrase is commonly used nowadays as in *to be posted* to the country, interstate, overseas, etc., or to be given a post in a firm. It is also found in expressions such as "trading post" and the "last post" (a military bugle call). The word is from the Italian *posto* and the Latin *positus,* placed, put.

Powder
Not worth powder and shot

Not worth the trouble; the thing aimed at is not worth the cost of the ammunition. The nautical reference is obvious. Metaphorically, not worth the effort; save your breath: "It wouldn't be worth the powder and shot to repair that old car—you ought to get rid of it."

Powder monkey

"Ellangowan had him placed as cabin-boy, or powder-monkey, on board an armed sloop."
—Sir Walter Scott (1771–1832), Scottish man of letters, *Guy Mannering* (1815)

Originally a ship's boy in a sailing warship, whose duty during battle was to carry powder from the magazine (which was situated below the waterline) up to the gundecks. The powder was weighed out into silk bags in the form of cartridges for the guns. Nowadays a "powder monkey" is the person in charge of explosives, wherever they might be in use, particularly in a stone quarry, or an open-cut mine, such as are found in countries that produce iron ore.

So named from the fact that ship's boys had to be fleet of foot and very agile as they rushed from the powder magazine deep down in the ship up to the gundecks above. They had to time their arrival at the guns more or less exactly: to be too early exposed everyone to the risk of the cartridge being ignited by the heat and flame of battle; to be late meant that a gun could not be served and fired as quickly as circumstances required.

Press From the Latin *pressare,* to press, and *praestare,* to warrant, vouch for, to perform. Not to be confused with the term *prest,* from the Old French *preter,* to land.

Press gang; to press The British press gang was, for the most part, made up of seamen or ex-seamen, who, under the command of a naval lieutenant, went ashore to scour the seaports (and often the towns further inland) to seize men for enforced service at sea. Pressed men were paid for their services, but at a lower rate than enlisted men or volunteers.

In the eighteenth century, the Royal Navy established an Impress Service (to which Nelson himself once belonged), and the system lasted until the mid-1800s, when conditions of service improved sufficiently to attract volunteers in suitable numbers. The system was detested by all, not least the men who were caught in its net.

The word is not from the French *presser* and the Latin *pressare,* to squeeze, as we might otherwise have expected, but instead is from the Old French *prêt,* loan, *prêter,* to lend, Latin *praestare,* to warrant; in this case, a sum of money given to a recruit. This was known as "prest money"; it was a shilling, and the man who accepted it was deemed thereby to have entered into a legal contract to serve the king (hence the origin of the military phrase *to take the king's shilling).*

"I have misused the king's press."
—William Shakespeare (1564–1616), *Henry IV, Part 1,* act 4, scene 2

Confusion with the word *press* arose because, as far back as the 1200s, the king had the power to compel certain seaports to provide ships and crews for his interminable wars with the French (the most permanent collection of ships and men belonged to Dover, Hastings, Sandwich, Hythe, and Romney; this was the origin of what are known today as the Cinque Ports). The king could thus "arrest," or detain for his own use, those ships and seamen.

The term in use at the time was the Old French *empresser,* to commandeer, arrest; but it quickly became confused with *imprest* (sometimes *emprest),* money lent in advance, or "prest money." The man who accepted it—knowingly or not—was thenceforth a "pressed man," from "prest man." Etymologically the two words—*prest* and *pressed*—are completely unrelated.

No matter what the landsman's occupation, whether he were businessman, in a profession, or a mere labourer, married or single, father or no, he was knocked on the head if he showed fight, and carried aboard ship, to remain there until eventually the ship was paid off or the war ended. In addition, he had no leave and no pay until the end of the ship's commission, no matter how many years this might last.

It was not unknown for a bridegroom and half the male congregation to be carried off at the church door by the very efficient net of the Impress Service. Tattooed and bowlegged men were especially vulnerable, as these were deemed to be physical peculiarities of the seafaring man; thus many a tailor found himself, willy nilly, in the king's service instead of in his own shop making clothes. The practice was so widespread, albeit detested, that children in the eighteenth and early nineteenth centuries played their own games of "press gangs."

"They heard that the press-gangs were out."
—Captain Frederick Marryat (1792–1848), English naval captain and novelist, *Peter Simple* (1834)

The phrase has long been colloquially used to refer to any system of force or coercion that is set up to provide workers or members for a task, project, or activity that would otherwise be difficult to staff. "There was such a crowd at the function in the hotel dining room that even the managerial staff had to be press-ganged into helping the waiters."
(See also *Andrew. Crimp.)*

To press on To push on or carry on with all speed, vigor, and power, so as to get the task completed; not to be delayed or waylaid by trifles: "If we press on we'll reach the wharf just in time to catch the ferry." The phrase is from the sailor's habit of crowding on as much canvas as conditions would allow to complete the passage as swiftly as possible. Such a vessel might occasionally be "hard pressed," and in any case, if she is setting as much canvas as possible, she is said to be under a "press of sail." From the fact that the square-rigged ship was at her best when sailing before the wind.
(See also *Sail; To crowd on sail. Pressed; To be hard-pressed.)*

Pressed
To be hard-pressed To be closely pursued, in both the literal and metaphorical senses. "The businessman was hard-pressed by his creditors." The land usage follows the sailor's phrase for describing a ship under a press of canvas; that is, when all working sails are set and are drawing well. The colloquial allusion is to the constant and sometimes overpowering pressure exerted by one's pursuers.

Priddied
To be priddied to the nines The sailor's version of "dressed up to the nines"; to be very smartly dressed, in the height of fashion; very fetching and elegant. The origin of *priddied* is unknown; it may be a derivation from "pride" or "prided," or—quite likely—a corruption of "prettied." *To the nines* is a corruption of the Early English *to then eyen,* to the eyes, an allusion to the fact

that someone has gone to some trouble to be well dressed from top to toe.

Prime To fill up, as in "to prime the ship's pump." From the Anglo-Saxon *prim* and the Latin *prima.* The earliest sense of the word referred to the loading of a ship; hence the nautical word *primage,* which is a percentage addition to freight charges. A "prime seaman" is one who is fully trained and experienced; one who can hand, reef, and steer. The "prime meridian" is longitude 0°, and is now internationally agreed to be the meridian of longitude that passes through Greenwich, England. It is from Greenwich that longitudes are measured east or west. *To prime,* in ordinary usage, is to prepare or make ready for a particular purpose: "The committee primed the candidate for his maiden speech in Parliament."

Privateer A privateer was a privately owned vessel given a licence by the state to wage war on enemy shipping. This licence was known as a "letter of marque" and was in effect a commission. The name *privateer* subsequently applied to both the ship and the men who sailed in her. The first official privateer was an English vessel, commissioned by a letter of marque issued in 1293.

"The granting of letters of marque has long been disused, the conference which met at Paris in 1856, after the close of the war with Russia, having recommended the entire abolition of privateering."
—Sir William Blackstone (1723–1780), English jurist, *Commentaries on the Laws of England* (1769)

Privateering was abolished by the declaration of Paris in 1856, and it finally became obsolete as a result of the Hague Convention of 1903. Sometimes used colloquially to describe a modern-day businessperson who engages in a takeover bid or some other daring and risky move of commercial appropriation.

Prize From the French *prendre,* to take, *prise,* a taking; not related to *prize* meaning reward. A prize court was a British court of law set up in time of war to examine the validity of capture of ships and goods made at sea by the navy. Such a vessel lawfully captured was then said to be "condemned in prize." Prize money is the net proceeds of the sale of enemy shipping and property captured at sea.

"The court of Admiralty has, in time of war, the authority of a prize-court."
—Sir William Blackstone (1723–1780), English jurist, *Commentaries on the Laws of England* (1769)

Until 1692, all prize captured at sea was forfeit to the Crown; after that date the proceeds of the sale of prize were granted to the captors on a sliding scale according to rank. This made service in the British navy somewhat more popular than it had been, and acted as a considerable incentive to recruitment.

There were some instances of enormous fortunes being made through the distribution of prize. For example, the capture in 1762 of the Spanish treasure ship *Hermione* yielded the two captains involved £65,000 each (possibly

£500,000 in today's money values), down to £485 for every seaman.

Proof spirit

The system of labelling spiritous liquors today as over-proof or under-proof derives from the early method of treating Jamaica rum in the navy victualling yards before issuing it to naval ships.

The rum arrived in England at 140 degrees over-proof; it was then reduced to 95.5 degrees under-proof by having water added to it in certain proportions. This was done by pouring a small amount of the alcohol-and-water mixture over some grains of gunpowder and igniting it, usually with a magnifying glass. If the burning alcohol then just managed to ignite the gunpowder, the mixture was said to be "proof"; if it exploded, it was "over-proof"; and if the gunpowder failed to ignite at all it was, of course, "under-proof." Proof spirit today is legally defined as that which has a specific gravity of 12/13 (92.3 percent) at 51°F.

Pull
A long pull

"His boat was lowered down and getting in with his men, he pulled to another vessel."
—Captain Frederick Marryat (1792–1848), English naval captain and novelist, *Peter Simple* (1834)

A difficult time, a long wait, an arduous experience. From the pulling boat manned by a crew with oars (what landlubbers would call a "rowboat"). Pulling a ship's boat through anything of a sea for some distance is a very exhausting task. "When John caught pneumonia, it was a long pull before he was fit enough for work again."

To pull together

To pull, in most navies, is to row a boat with oars. Naval tradition defines the activity as "pulling," not "rowing." The oars are pivoted in small yokes called "rowlocks" (pronounced "roll-ocks"). If the pulling boat is to be moved from one place to another smartly and efficiently (as in transferring the captain to shore, or abandoning a vessel that has a fire near its powder magazine), then the seamen must pull together, in time and with a will.

Similarly, in a figurative sense, people who have a common goal must work together and cooperate as a team, as in a sports match or other endeavour: "If we all pull together we can get this car out of the sand before the tide comes in."

Pumps
All hands to the pumps

Nautically, this is the call for assistance from everybody available when the vessel is in danger of sinking from being holed or boarded by a large sea. *All hands* means literally everyone, including the cook, his helpers, and other members of the crew who normally would not be engaged in working ship on a watch basis. Thus, the order "all hands" emphasised the gravity of the situation.

Colloquially, the expression carries the same force: everyone is needed to help out in a desperate situation: "It's a case of all hands to the pumps; typists and messengers, as well as administrative staff, must contribute significantly if our trading position is to be rescued from bankruptcy."

Man the pumps *Man* is an ancient word, and comes directly into English from the Anglo-Saxon *manu*. *Pump* is from the French *pompe,* Dutch *pomp,* and German *pumpe;* the word was first used in reference to the pump on board ship. *To man the pumps* is to call all available hands to pump ship because of excess water in the holds. It is generally regarded as a cry or order of considerable urgency.

We find the word *pump* in a number of colloquialisms:

To prime the pump: To give financial aid to an enterprise in the hope that it will become self-supporting.
To pump ship: Sailor's slang for urinating.
To pump someone: To extract information by asking many questions; to draw from someone all he or she knows, as one draws water from a well by gradual pumping.
To pump someone's hand: To shake his or her hand vigorously, up and down.

(See also *Pumps; All hands to the pumps.)*

Purser See *Pusser's dip.*

Pusser's dip

Seaman's term for a candle, once called a "dip-candle." The title *purser* comes from a fifteenth-century word, from the Anglo-Saxon *purs* and the Late Latin *bursa,* hide, leather; whence the small draw-bag made from leather, a purse (and, incidentally, the origin of the word *budget).* The purser was responsible for issuing all food, clothing, and implements according to the scale of rations laid down by the Admiralty.

"In those days . . . the commanders of the vessels were also the pursers."
—Captain Frederick Marryat (1792–1848), English naval captain and novelist, *Snarleyyow* (1837)

The purser (always pronounced "pusser" by seamen) made candles by dipping the wick into tallow, or into the greasy slush that came from the galley. Repeated dipping enabled the candles to be built up to a serviceable size. An early nickname for the purser was naturally "dips"; his candles were also often referred to as "purser's glims." Selling these dips to the crew was one of the purser's perks.

Purser, or *pusser,* is found in other expressions:

Purser's name: A false name given to the purser of a passenger ship by someone who wishes to travel incognito.
Pusser built: Built to navy specifications.
Pusser's dirk: A seaman's name for his knife.
Pusser's leaf: Tobacco leaf issued to sailors.
Pusser's loaf: Ship's bread.
Pusser's medal: A food stain on clothing.
Pusser's tricks: A term reflecting the general disdain that seamen once held, quite rightly, for pursers, many of whom were dishonest in the extreme.

Perhaps it was inevitable that pursers were tempted to dishonesty; the state did not usually pay them a salary—the purser had to remunerate himself, usually by way of taking a commission of two ounces in the pound (12½ percent) of all provisions issued by him to the crew, and by other means. Furthermore, the purser had to buy his pursery, so he had a good deal of leeway to make up.

In addition, in the early 1800s he had to provide a bond or surety against the ship's business bills that he was permitted to run up. For a first-rate ship, the bond was £1,200, a very large sum of money indeed in those days. His personal income depended therefore on how much coal, lanterns, provisions, and such he contrived *not* to issue.

The purser was a businessman, a capitalist pure and simple, and given his peculiar status in the ship's company it is not surprising that he committed many a fraud, nearly always at the expense of the seaman's general health and welfare. It wasn't until the 1840s that the purser was rated, and salaried, as paymaster, and hence was delivered—after

some hundreds of years—from the impossible temptations of his anomalous situation.
(See also *Slops. Slush fund.*)

Put
To put in for A vessel is said "to put in for" a particular harbour or port when she enters it, or intends to enter it; especially when turning aside from her regular course to seek shelter, repairs, provisions, and the like. Colloquially, the expression means to make application, to make a bid, as in applying for a position: "He put in for the job of recreation director."

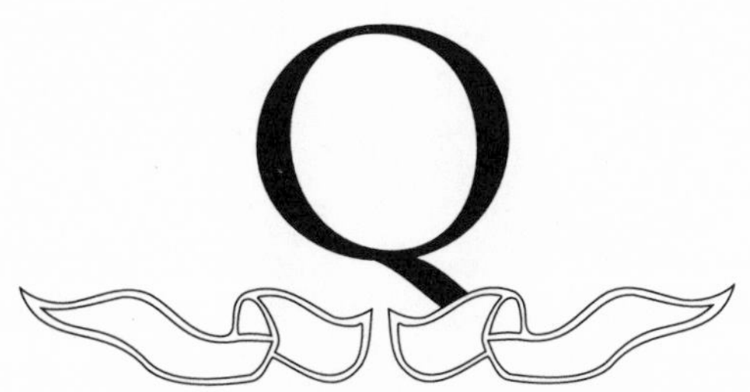

Quarter
To blow from another quarter

When the wind shifts, it is said to blow from another quarter. As a metaphor, the expression describes the situation when a person being argued with is attacked—verbally—by another person or from a different point of view. "When I mentioned the cost of an overseas holiday, she changed tack and went at me from another quarter."

Quarterdeck
A quarterdeck manner

The quarterdeck is the raised part of the upper deck that runs from near the mainmast to the stern. It was, in sailing ships, the sole preserve of the captain and his officers, to be approached by other seamen only when detailed for special duties in that area. It was the part of the ship from which the whole vessel was commanded; hence the colloquialism "to behave as though he were on his own quarterdeck," to act as though he owned the place; to be overbearing and domineering, as a ship's captain or officer might well be.

Quarters

From the French *quartier* and the Latin *quartarius,* fourth part, a measure.

"His praise, ye winds! that from four quarters blow, Breathe soft or loud."
—John Milton (1608–1674), English poet, *Paradise Lost* (1667)

The word has very early specialised nautical applications. Sailors speak of the wind as blowing from a particular quarter. The quarterdeck is that part of the upper deck of a ship aft of the mainmast. In medieval British warships, the religious shrine was set up on the quarterdeck, and was saluted by every man's taking off his hat or cap as he passed it; British warships still maintain the tradition of saluting the quarterdeck when entering it.

The quartermaster was a petty officer of the fifteenth century, who assisted in maintaining the ship's working gear but who now is associated with steering duties and upkeep of the navigational equipment. The quarterbill is a list of officers and men in a warship showing the action station for every man on board when the ship went into battle. When this happened, the order "Beat to quarters" was given and the ship's drummers would beat out a particular rhythm. (See also *Quarterdeck; A quarterdeck manner.)*

R

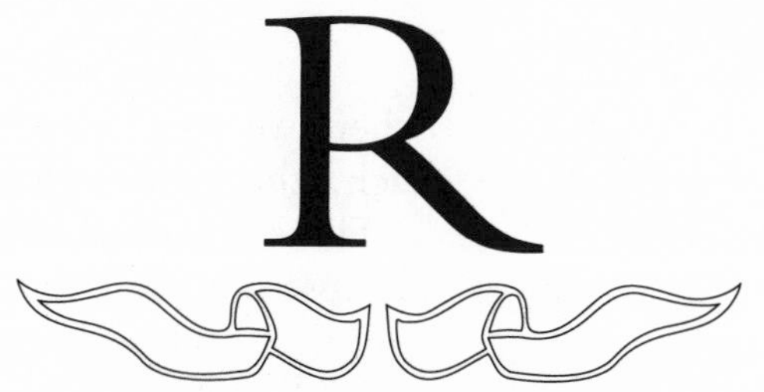

Rack and ruin *Rack* here is a variant spelling of "wrack," which is itself another version of "wreck"; but *wrack* and *wreck* have now become differentiated in sense. *Wreck* is from the Anglo-Saxon *wraec,* exile, misery; whereas *wrack* is from the Middle English *wrac,* originally seaweed. *Wrack* later came to mean anything driven ashore by the waves. *Rack and ruin* is a direct outgrowth of *wrack;* as a colloquialism, it means destruction, wreckage, disrepair, collapse (especially that brought about by neglect). "The miners' old cottages have gone to rack and ruin now that the caretaker has left."

Rag
Don't get your rag out Don't get angry, don't be upset. A colloquialism much in use in the postwar years, but now, like most slang, very dated and, in this particular case, probably almost obsolete.

The expression dates from an early practice in the Royal Navy, when seamen wore their hair in a queue, a fashion that began with officers of the mid-eighteenth century and was then quickly taken up by "the people." The seaman who wished to be more "tiddly" than his messmates (i.e., to be known as a snappy dresser) would embellish his queue with an eelskin as its heart or core, together with rope yarns woven in to increase its size and length. Such a queue took a good deal of time and trouble to prepare, and it became common for close friends to do this for each other; from this practice, they came to be known as "tiemates."

But all fashions change in time, and the queue had almost disappeared in the navy by the mid-nineteenth century, when warships were beginning to be built of iron instead of wood and the navy itself was being thoroughly reorganised and brought up to date. Tiemates then became *raggies,* a term meant to indicate particular friends who shared their cleaning and polishing rags when detailed to spruce up the ship's brightwork. When two such shipmates quarrelled, they were said to have "parted brass rags"—i.e., they no longer shared their cleaning rags with each other.

Don't get your rag out, then, was a way of saying "calm down," "don't get excited," "let's not get to the point where we insist on ending the friendship and returning each other's cleaning rags."

There is an interesting parallel with a similar expression, "to lose one's rag," but the source is quite different. *To lose one's rag* is to lose one's temper, and it derives from the Icelandic (often called Old Norse) *ragna,* to curse, to swear; the *rag* in the nautical expression is also from Icelandic, but this time the source is *rogg,* shagginess, which went into Anglo-Saxon (Early English) as *ragg* to mean broken, tattered, as in the thirteenth-century term *Kentish rag* or ragstone, a rough siliceous rock that breaks into pieces that supposedly resemble rags. Ragstone was used for sharpening steel implements.
(See also *Brass; To part brass rags. Tiddley.)*

Rake

To cause to be slanted or angled; usually the inclination forward or aft from the perpendicular. Also describes the extent to which the stem and stern angle away from the ends of the keel. The early schooners that came out of Gloucester, Massachusetts, were noted for the aft rake of their masts. The word is now used to describe the inclination or slope of a wide range of everyday objects, particularly when that inclination is adjustable; as in the rake of a roof-beam, derrick, cutting face of a machine tool, and so on. From the Swedish *raka,* to project.

Rate
How does it rate?

"I am a spirit of no common rate."
—William Shakespeare (1564–1616), *A Midsummer Night's Dream,* act 3, scene 1

This phrase and its variations derive from the way in which fighting ships took precedence when getting into the line of battle. The colloquialism today emphasises quality (or lack thereof): "How does our team rate against the visitors from the city?"

Originally, the phrases that denoted the rating of warships referred solely to the size and number of their armament, not to their efficiency or quality. Seamen in the British and Australian navies are known generally as "ratings."
(See also *A.B. Rate; To be first-rate.)*

To be first-rate

When something is said to be "first-rate," it is being held up as a paradigm or model of its class; it is the best available. The phrase derives from the fact that the fighting sail of the Royal Navy were classified into "rates" according to the number of guns carried on board. Thus, a ship with 100 or more guns was a first-rate warship; a second-rater carried between 82 and 100 guns; and so on down to a sixth-rate vessel.

In 1677, Samuel Pepys, as First Secretary to the Admiralty, drew up a manning list that established the number of men to be borne according to a ship's rating (i.e., according to the number of guns she carried). This establishment is shown in the following list (figures taken from Lloyd [see bibliography]):

First Rate:	100 guns/800 men
Second Rate:	82 guns/530 men
Third Rate:	74 guns/460 men
Fourth Rate:	54 guns/280 men
Fifth Rate:	30 guns/130 men
Sixth Rate:	fewer than 30 guns/65 men

One notes immediately the enormous number of men carried on the larger vessels; it probably goes a long way toward accounting for the fact that disease was the cause of 50 percent of the navy's casualties during the French and Napoleonic Wars around the turn of the eighteenth century. About one-third of all fatalities were caused by accidents (parting rigging, breaking spars, falling from aloft, drowning, bursting guns, heavy objects such as guns running loose on deck in a gale, uncontrolled anchor cables, and so on); founderings, wrecks, fires, and explosions carried off another 10 percent; and the remainder—less than 10 percent—were those men killed in action, directly or as a result of their wounds. These figures would approximately hold for almost any period of the era of fighting sail; indeed, it is likely that the deaths from disease were much higher in times preceding the end of the eighteenth century, when medical science was (albeit very slowly) beginning to come to grips with the scourges of scurvy, yellow fever, typhus, and smallpox.

"I praised her as I rated her."
—William Shakespeare (1564–1616), *Cymbeline,* act 1, scene 4

Pepys's six classifications constituted the ships-of-the-line-of-battle, so named because of the fact that, traditionally, sailing warships entered battle in the formation known as "in line astern," or one behind the other, with the first-rate ships leading the way. Our modern battleships derive their name directly from this nomenclature, sometimes written as "line-of-battle ships."

The colloquial use of "second-rate," "third-rate," and so on follows the analogy of being inferior to the leading or first-rate ships, when entering battle in line astern. "He's not much at pitching, but he's a first-rate batter."

Similarly, seamen were rated according to their ability and experience (Ordinary Seaman, Able Seaman, Leading Seaman, and so on through to the petty officers).
(See also *A1; To be in A1 condition.* Other entries under *Rate.)*

Rattle *To rattle* someone is to disconcert, to confuse; the phrase *to be in the rattle* is sailor's slang for being in trouble with officialdom, to be run in. The "rattle" is early sailor's slang meaning to be held in irons, to be in the brig (shipboard prison). The term probably comes from the fact that being held in irons occasioned a good deal of noise whenever one moved; hence *rattle.* "She was quite rattled when I mentioned that the new secretary was also a racing car driver."

Reach-me-downs

Exactly the same as "hand-me-downs": articles of clothing handed down or acquired at second hand, as in a family with a number of children. Such clothing is sometimes ill-fitting or of poor quality, as certainly would be the case for seamen, who either made their own clothing or bought their requirements from the ship's slops chest. According to Lind (see bibliography), the expression was in use at sea early in the 1800s.

Reckoning
Dead reckoning

"It were a pity you should get your living by reckoning, sir."
—William Shakespeare (1564–1616), *Love's Labour's Lost,* act 5, scene 2

To calculate a ship's position by plotting on the chart the distance run since the last reliable navigational fix, taking into account speed, tide, current, wind, and any other factors that might have influenced forward motion through the water.

The phrase is said to have evolved from the term *ded. reckoning,* i.e., "deduced reckoning"; another suggestion is that it arose from the seaman's use of the term *dead sea,* to describe the seas shown on some maps hundreds of years ago about which little or nothing was known. For the mariner of that era, any voyage across such a sea would presumably be governed by "dead" reckoning.

In modern times, the term has both its nautical navigational meaning and a similar construction applied to an activity involving sequential steps of some kind, wherein an estimate of one's progress or performance must be made from time to time.

Red ensign

See *Red, white, and blue.*

Red, white, and blue

In the early 1600s, the English fleet was subdivided into squadrons, with a coloured flag allocated to each. The admiral's squadron wore a red flag, the vice admiral's a white, and the rear admiral's a blue. This organisation was abolished in 1864, partly because of the rapidly growing size of the squadrons, and partly because of the fact that the system had no further relevance in the age of steam warships.

The red ensign (the senior of the three) was then allocated to the merchant service, the white to the Royal Navy, and the blue to the naval auxiliary vessels and ships of the colonial navies. The red ensign (usually written as "Red Ensign") became known colloquially as the "Red Duster," the most widely seen national flag in the heyday of Britain's colonial empire.

In time of war, the phrase *the red, white and blue* became a popular catchcry in Britain and her dominions, to refer to the Allied fighting arms that had gone into battle against the Axis nations. This phrase—"the red, white, and blue"—is also a powerful national symbol in the United States, referring as it does to the Stars and Stripes, the national flag of that country.

Reef
To take in a reef

"'Reef top-sails, reef!' the master calls again."
—William Falconer (1732–1769), Scottish poet and writer, *The Shipwreck* (1762)

As a colloquialism, the expression means to retrench, to retract somewhat to reduce expenses; also to remove by force, to steal: "If we are to weather this recession, we are going to have to take in a reef or two and lay off some of our office staff."

A reefer is a close-fitting, double-breasted jacket originally worn by seamen in the late nineteenth century. (A reefer is also a common slang term for a marijuana cigarette, but it is very doubtful that an etymological connection exists between the two words.) It was also the name given to the midshipmen who had to station themselves in the tops (the platform at the head of the lower and upper masts) to help during reefing of the topsails ("tops'ls").

"We had reefed our sails in the Gulf Stream, and I thought it something serious, but an older sailor would have thought nothing of it."
—Richard Henry Dana (1815–1882), American writer and jurist, *Two Years Before the Mast* (1840)

Nautically, *to reef* means to reduce sail area by gathering up part of the sail and securing it by fitted reef points (using the well-known reef knot), or by causing the sail to be rolled around the boom or furling stay (as used in modern yachts), a procedure known as "shortening sail."

This is an important manoeuvre basic to the whole history and practice of seafaring; hence, there are many words compounded with *reef* in the seaman's lexicon. The essential element of connection between the nautical usage and the metaphor is reduction, holding, securing, being made safe.

The word is from the Middle English *riff* and the Old Norse *rif,* rib, to describe the riblike appearance of a sail with rows of reefing-bands or reef points lying across it (the mining reef and coral reef are from the same Scandinavian source, as is "midriff," the rib area between the waist and the upper chest).

Reel
To reel off

From the reel that held the ship's log line; used in measuring the ship's speed through the water. This reel was held aloft by a seaman or midshipman, the log (properly, the "log-chip" or "chip-log") was heaved astern, and the

28-second sandglass was set running. As the log line was drawn astern by the action of the water on the chip-log, the ship was said to "reel off" her knots, particularly if she was making good speed.

Figuratively, the expression means to say, write, or produce in an easy and continuous way, more or less without hesitation: "Without pausing, he began to reel off the previous week's figures for fluctuations in the price of gold." From the Anglo-Saxon *hreol,* reel, and derived from the Old Norse *hraell,* reel.
(See also *Knots.)*

Regatta A boat race; a race meeting. Derived from the traditional Venetian gondola race, which is still held annually. From the Italian *regata,* meaning strife or contention, match, struggle. The first English regatta was held at least as early as 1768.

"Remember the Birkenhead!" A cry of encouragement and inspiration given in time of great danger; it became part of the language following the loss of the *Birkenhead* and was for nearly a hundred years a rallying call throughout the British Empire. Times have changed, however, and the generation for whom this expression would have meant something is no longer with us.

The expression derives from the tragic loss of HMS *Birkenhead* in 1852, when virtually all the ship's complement lost their lives. The *Birkenhead* was carrying some 487 officers and men of the 74th Highlanders, when she struck a submerged rock off Danger Point, just out of Simonstown, South Africa, on the morning of February 26, 1852. As she sank in shark-infested water, the soldiers were drawn up in their ranks on deck, to enable the women and children on board to get away safely. The calm and discipline of the soldiers as they went to their certain deaths became a byword for courage and self-sacrifice, epitomised in English literature by the phrase *"Remember the Birkenhead!,"* used by those who want to instill the same tradition of selflessness in the ranks of soldiers or seamen under their charge. Of all those on board the *Birkenhead,* 454 officers and men were lost.
(See also *Himself; Every man for himself.)*

Rhino Sailors' slang for money; the term was once fairly common in Australian speech, but it died out early in the twentieth century. Widely used in the seventeenth century; its origin is uncertain, but it may be connected to the Eastern belief that the powdered horn of the rhinoceros increased one's sexual potency. Rhino horn therefore commanded a high price. Sailors might well be expected, by virtue of their occupation and natural proclivities, to have come into contact with this oriental belief.

Ride
To ride it out

See *Storm; To ride out the storm.*

Rig
A good rig-out

"With stays and cordage last he rigged the ship."
—Alexander Pope (1688–1744), English poet, Homer's *Odyssey* (1726)

Of obscure origin, but the related forms *rigga* and *rigge,* from the Scandinavian languages, are probably from an early English source. The word is primarily nautical in origin and meaning: to fit out a vessel with the necessary tackle so that she is ready for the sea. Related meanings, which derive from this earlier form, refer to assembling, adjusting, and so on, especially in the aircraft and construction industries.

Colloquially, a rig-out is a dressing-up for a particular occasion, a provision for the event at hand. Variations are "to rig (something) up," "a good rig up," "to rig out," and so on.

Ringleader

See *Robin; Round robin.*

Roadstead

"Curses the roadstead,
and with gale
Of early morning
lifts the sail. . . ."
—Sir Walter Scott (1771–1832), Scottish man of letters, *Rokeby* (1813)

A special nautical use of the base word *road* (from the Anglo-Saxon *rad,* road); often rendered as *roads,* as in "Fremantle Roads," which refers not to the streets of that port city but instead to the designated anchorage for shipping that lies between Fremantle Harbour and Rottnest Island. A roadstead ("the roads") is a stretch of sheltered water where ships may ride at anchor in all but very heavy weather.

Robin
Round robin

"The members of the Royal Commission sent to Sir George Grey a sort of round robin."
—*The Daily Telegraph* (English newspaper), February 24, 1886

A petition or protest written in circular form so that no particular signature heads the list, and therefore no one person can be singled out as a ringleader. From a French custom, probably from *rond ruban,* round ribbon, which was originally used by sailors when urging a formal protest or claim on their superior officers. The urger or instigator of the protest or petition was, of course, known to the others (but not to the authorities), and as a result of the shape of this "round robin" he was known as the "ringleader." Now commonly used to refer to a sporting competition in which each team plays every other team.

Robinson Crusoe

Colloquially, a "crusoe" is one who lives alone, sometimes on an uninhabited island, but always isolated from human society. From Daniel Defoe's classic tale *Robinson Crusoe.* Usually expressed in full: "He's been a bit of a Robinson Crusoe these past few months, stuck out in the diggings on Fly Flat looking for gold."
(See also *Maroon.)*

Rocks
To be on the rocks

The allusion is obvious: to be broke, short of money, no longer able to fend for oneself, as a ship that has gone on the rocks will quickly break up unless she can be floated off. Used in expressions such as "They were happy for a year or two, and then their marriage went on the rocks because of financial difficulties."
(See also *Broke; To be broke.)*

Rope

"Axes to cut, and ropes to sling the load. . . ."
—Alexander Pope (1688–1744), English poet, Homer's *Iliad* (1720)

From the Anglo-Saxon *rap,* and common to the Teutonic languages; a general term applied to all cordage greater than one inch in diameter. Until recent years, all rope and small stuff was made of hemp or cotton yarn twisted into strands, which were then again twisted and laid up into rope. Stranded wire rope is now widely used for certain purposes, such as standing rigging, some running rigging, lifting tackles, and so on.

A taste of the rope's end

"He was found out, and handsomely rope's-ended on his bare legs."
—*Scribner's Magazine,* November 1878

To flog or belabour a sailor or ship's apprentice with a short length of rope, nearly always knotted at the business end. It was a common punishment for petty misdemeanors, and frequently accompanied the bosun's or mate's orders as an additional incentive for getting the job done quickly and thoroughly. The term is sometimes used when threatening punishment, in some everyday situations where an overseer might resort to a cuff or blow (generally token) in an effort to encourage his team to greater efforts.
(See also *Cat-o'-nine-tails.)*

Money for old rope

Something for nothing. Old rope was useless to the sailor (other than for the making of oakum, used in caulking the seams of a wooden vessel), so it was sold to dealers who used it in the paper and book-binding trades. "They pay me very highly just to give them advice on exporting machinery to Southeast Asia—it's money for old rope." A variation of this expression has "money for jam"—probably of military origin.

Ropes
To know the ropes; to learn the ropes

To acquire the skills and knowledge relating to an occupation; to gradually absorb the details and information that will allow one to function efficiently in one's new environment, as in an apprenticeship or a change in job: "She'll make a very good section-manager once she gets to know the ropes."

The reference is to the fact that sailors had to learn—and quickly—the location and operation of every rope on board ship. They had to be equally proficient at handling the multitude of lifts, braces, tacks, sheets, guys, pendants, halliards, etc., that festooned the vessel, in good weather and bad and in the dark of night as well as in the daylight watches.

Most vessels of similar rig standardised their rigging layout, so that a seaman would be able to carry out his duties quickly and efficiently even if he were to find himself in another vessel. Shipboard apprentices were taught the ropes and tested on their knowledge of them, but a mistake often meant a taste of the rope's end for the lazy or forgetful tyro.

It is worth noting that a large sailing vessel has perhaps only a dozen or so ropes that are so called; some such are "bolt ropes," "foot ropes," "bell ropes," "bucket ropes," "man ropes," "yard ropes," "back ropes," and "top ropes." Otherwise, when a rope is put to use on a vessel, it becomes a "line" (such as a "clew-line") or acquires a particular name (such as "halliard" and "tack").

Rort Sailor's slang; someone who is "rorty" is bellicose, spoiling for a fight, particularly because of drink. *Rort* is common in Australian colloquial speech; it refers to a trick or a scheme, and sometimes a wild and boisterous party. Its origin is uncertain, but it may have been formed on "wrought" and "naughty." Used as in "The students at the Agriculture Department get-together were engaged in one long, drunken rort."

Rostrum A word with interesting maritime connections. It is Latin for "beak," and is cognate with *rodere,* to gnaw. Originally, a rostrum was the platform for speakers in the Roman Forum (the place of assembly for public business); it was called a "rostrum" because it was adorned with the beaks of enemy ships captured in the wars of the fourth century B.C.

"Myself will mount the rostrum in his favour."
—Joseph Addison (1672–1719), English poet, dramatist, and essayist, *Cato* (1713)

The beak—the projection built onto the prow of a vessel for the purpose of ramming an enemy warship—was cut off by the Roman victors and displayed as a trophy in the Forum, from which orations, pleadings, and the like were delivered to the public. Hence, *rostrum* today means any platform or stage used for public speaking, music, and such. (See also *Heads.)*

Rough it A nautical phrase from the eighteenth century; from the Anglo-Saxon *ruh,* surface. It has passed into widespread colloquial usage while still retaining the same meaning it originally had: to live in a relatively primitive manner, without even the ordinary comforts or conveniences. Used as in "The people on the frontier had to rough it for many years before living conditions gradually improved."

Round
To round down; to round up; to round to

In general, *to round down* means to gather in the slack of any rope that passes through blocks; to close the space between these blocks when there is no weight on the tackle. *To round down a tackle* is to overhaul it. *To round to* is to bring a sailing vessel up to the wind. Nowadays, the phrase *to round to* is usually rendered as *to round up,* so that a sailing vessel that is rounding up is one that is coming head to wind, with the object either of going off onto the other tack, or of losing sufficient way to come to anchor.

As a metaphor, *to round (up) on someone* is to turn on them, to stop them in their tracks, to bring them to a halt in their explanation or argument: "She rounded on him as soon as he walked through the door, demanding to know why he had not telephoned earlier."

The sailor's equivalent colloquialism is *to be brought up all standing,* more commonly rendered as *to be taken aback.* (See also *Aback; To be taken aback. Chock-a-block. Overhaul.)*

Rouse
To rouse in; to rouse out; to rouse up

"In rushed the rousers of the deer."
—Sir Walter Scott (1771–1832), Scottish man of letters, *Glenfinlas* (1801)

"Ridicule of scoffing and incredulous canal-boat captains and roustabouts."
—*Scribner's Magazine,* March 1880

To rouse out is the old sailing term for turning out the hands for duty or for a muster call. In rope handling, *to rouse* means to pull together; for instance, on an anchor cable or halyard, without the assistance of any mechanical aid such as a capstan.

Widely used in Australia as a colloquialism for organising, stirring up, getting things going; as in "to rouse up a meal," rouse someone from sleep or inactivity, to stir to anger, and so on. "She roused the children away from the TV set and out into the garden."

The word *rouseabout* derives from *rouse,* and describes the general handyman to be found on many Australian sheep and cattle stations, in hotels, and such. It is also a common name for wharf labourers in the United States, but the American form is *roustabout.* The origin of the word *rouse* is obscure, but it may derive from an Old French word *rouse* connected with hunting, with a reference to a hawk ruffling its feathers.

Rover

"The best men of ye cytie by thyse ryotous persones were spoyled and robbid; and by the rouers also of ye see."
—Roger Fabyan (d. 1513), English historian and sheriff of London in 1493, *Chronycle* (1516)

Rover was the name sometimes applied to what is now more commonly called a pirate, buccaneer, or freebooter. It is from the Dutch *zee-rover,* sea-robber, and is not related to *rover* as in wanderer, one who moves aimlessly about. This latter *rover* is from the Icelandic *rafa,* to wander, travel. (See also *Filibuster.)*

Royal Navy

Navy is from the Latin *naves,* ships; originally the name of the entire shipping of a nation, including warship, merchant vessels, and fishing craft. The Royal Navy proper dates from the time of the Restoration, when Charles II replaced

Cromwell in 1660 and the Admiralty Office was established under the Duke of York.

The navy as such had existed variously under the reigns of Henry VII (late fifteenth century), his son Henry VIII, Edward IV, and others, but it is only from the time of Charles II that we have a continuous history of a navy closely supported by, and identified with, the monarch.

It was in this period that Samuel Pepys established the Admiralty as an effective administrative organisation. He was most instrumental in introducing aspects such as the "Articles of War," war and peace establishments, and—perhaps of greatest importance—the growing tendency to make experience rather than influence the basis for promotion.

A hundred years later, Lord Anson (famous for his circumnavigation as Commodore George Anson in 1740–1744) added to the excellence of Pepys's administrative achievements. He tightened up and helped regularise naval discipline, resisted political influence (as had Pepys), and attempted to reform the dockyards, which were generally sinks of venality and corruption. Anson introduced uniform clothing for officers (1748), supervised the introduction of copper sheathing (1761), and expressed interest in Harrison's chronometer (1761). Of greater importance was the interest he took in the gunnery experiments carried out by Benjamin Robins between 1743 and 1750.

However, when war broke out between Britain and her American colonies in 1775, the Royal Navy had become weakened by political and financial neglect. The French Revolution and the subsequent wars of 1793–1815 destroyed the discipline of the French navy; and it was Nelson who introduced into sea warfare the ruthless and total destruction that so characterised the British navy of that period.

The peace of 1815 ushered in an era when the British Merchant Service found itself in virtual monopolistic control of the world's trade routes, opened, protected, and surveyed by the Royal Navy.

The age of steam, which ended the epoch of the sailing ship finally in the late nineteenth century, saw an enormous awareness of the importance of a nationally organised, modernised, and properly maintained navy, and it was in this period that the Naval Defence Act of 1889 completed the transition from sail to steam and laid down a settled building policy for a modern navy ready to take its place among the nations of the twentieth century.
(See also *Nautical. Navy.)*

Rudder

"Swept from the deck, and from the rudder torn. . . ."
—Alexander Pope (1688–1744), English poet, Homer's *Odyssey* (1726)

From the Anglo-Saxon *rothor,* steering oar; a word found in cognate forms in all the Teutonic tongues, and ultimately from the Latin *remus.*

The rudder is the board or plate of wood or metal hinged vertically at the stern of a boat or ship and used as a means of steering. The invention of the rudder in the thirteenth century helped bring about a period of intense development in ship design and construction methods. The word has found its way into at least one colloquial, if now dated, expression: "Who won't be ruled by the rudder must be ruled by the rock" (He who won't listen to reason must bear the consequences, like a ship that runs upon a rock if it will not answer the helm).

Rummage

"This post-haste and romage in the land. . . ."
—William Shakespeare (1564–1616), *Hamlet,* act 1, scene 1

"To rummage (sea term): To remove any goods or luggage from one place to another, especially to clear the ship's hold of any goods or lading, in order to their being handsomely stowed or placed."
—Phillips, *New World of Worlds,* cited in the *Universal Dictionary of the English Language* (1897)

This very old nautical term has found a secure place as a colloquialism in our everyday language; its maritime origin is quite unsuspected. It stems from the French *arrumage,* from *arrumer,* to stow goods in a ship's hold. Early meanings also included the moving of cargo for any reason, such as getting at a leak in the hold, or the discarding of ballast and refuse and putting in new ballast.

In modern usage, *to rummage* means to search thoroughly and actively through a place or receptacle of some kind—especially a drawer, cupboard, or the like—for some necessary item: "She began frantically to rummage through her handbag in search of her train ticket." A "rummage sale" is generally a sale of no-longer-needed clothing and other household chattels, often for the purpose of raising funds for charity; but originally a rummage sale was an auction, on the dockside, of unclaimed goods from ships' cargoes.

Run

To come down with a run

When a sail, yard, halliard, or the like is lowered smartly, or when an object is released from a height and falls quickly, sometimes getting out of control, it is said "to come down with a run."

To cut and run

To escape, to quit in a hurry; to drop whatever one was doing and to leave immediately. The *cut* is in reference to the need for a ship to cut its anchor cable (in the days of sail, a very heavy hempen rope) when danger threatened and it was necessary for the ship to leave its anchorage in the emergency.

Weighing the anchor and stowing the cable below was normally a long and tedious business. When the Spanish Armada was anchored off Calais, most of the captains cut their cables and ran out to sea in an attempt to escape when Howard, the English commander-in-chief, sent his fireships among them.

Originally, the expression derives from the practice of square-rigged ships (when at anchor in an open roadstead), furling their sails by stropping or tying them to the yards with light line instead of the heavier rope used for gaskets. When the need to get underway was urgent, as because of threatening weather or an approaching enemy, the sails could be quickly set by sending men aloft to cut the light rope-yarns. The sails would immediately hang free from their yards in readiness for instant departure. The anchor cable would, of course, either have to be cut, as previously described, with the anchor buoyed for possible future recovery, or the moorings slipped if the vessel happened not to be riding to an anchor.

Used colloquially as in "When he noticed what time it was, he told his friends in the bar that he would have to cut and run if he was to avoid a scene with his wife."
(See also *Cut; To cut along. Slip; To give one the slip.)*

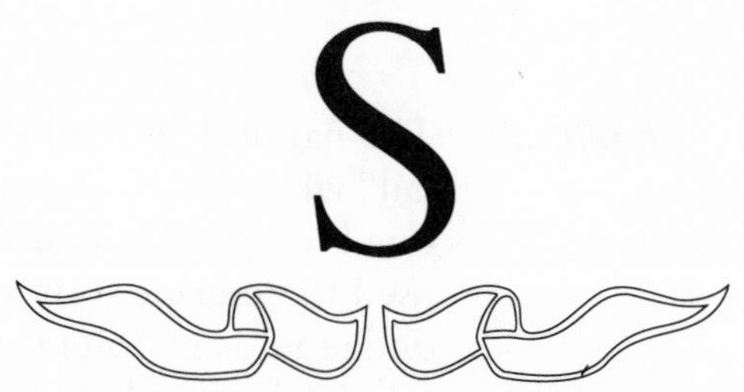

Sag Originally a Scandinavian expression, from the Swedish *sacka,* to subside. It likely came into English purely as a nautical term from the Low German, where it is found also as a nautical word.

Specifically, a ship "sags" when her weight is supported at the bow and stern (as by waves, for example) and her unsupported midships section has a tendency to settle. The word can also be used to describe a vessel's movement when she drifts; she is said to "sag away" to leeward.

"*Puritan* was sagging to leeward a good deal."
—*Field Magazine,* October 3, 1885, cited in the *Universal Dictionary of the English Language* (1897)

The everyday usage carries much the same force as the nautical meaning: to sink or bend downward because of weight or pressure, especially in the middle; to droop or hang loosely. "Her shoulders sagged from utter exhaustion after her first day as a kindergarten teacher."

Sail From the Anglo-Saxon *segl,* and found in similar forms in all the northern languages.

"We have descried . . . A portly sail of ships make hitherward."
—William Shakespeare (1564–1616), *Pericles,* act 1, scene 4

The expressions "sail ho," "a fleet of 40 sail," and so forth refer to the period when ships carried but one sail (known later as the mainsail). The word "sailor" (written "sailer" up to the fifteenth century) is relatively modern; prior to this, seafaring men were known as seamen or mariners.

The sail is, of course, one of the essential items on board a ship; hence, as with other elements characteristic of the seaman's life afloat, sails appear as a central figure in many nautical expressions.

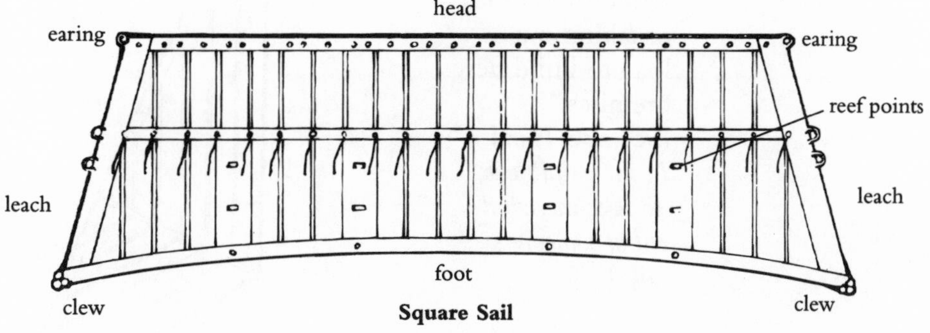

Square Sail

In full sail The nautical allusion is obvious. Colloquially, one is "in full sail" when all the details of an enterprise are in hand and one is on one's way in full stride, without hindrance. Often used to describe somebody storming out (or off) in high dudgeon, as in "She flounced out of the play rehearsal in full sail, leaving behind her a shocked silence."
(See also *Sail; To set sail.)*

To crowd on sail Nautically, to carry as much sail as possible; sometimes excessively so. Usually done to sail as fast as possible in a race, or to catch, or escape from, an enemy vessel, and—in the days of the great tea and wool clippers—to make or break records. *Crowd* is from the Anglo-Saxon *crudan,* to press, push.

Metaphorically, the terms *to crowd* or *to crowd on sail* mean to use all of one's resources, in order to go all-out for a win or an impressive display; to make every effort.
(See also *Press; To press on.)*

To hoist sail To be off, to go with all speed, to be on one's way without further ado; as a vessel that hoists sail cannot stay its departure, so metaphorically *to hoist sail* is to act decisively, without delay; to commit one's resources to whatever is engaging one at the time: "As soon as it became clear that there was no point in waiting for a taxi to come along, we decided to hoist sail and begin the long walk back into town."

To sail against the wind To oppose popular or current trends, fashions, or opinions; to swim against the tide; to be courting a setback, as does a sailing ship when headed by the wind, thereby retarding its progress: "She was sailing against the wind in her efforts to convince the tennis club to abandon the idea of taking out a loan to build new premises."
(See also *Wind; In the wind's eye, To take the wind out of someone's sails.)*

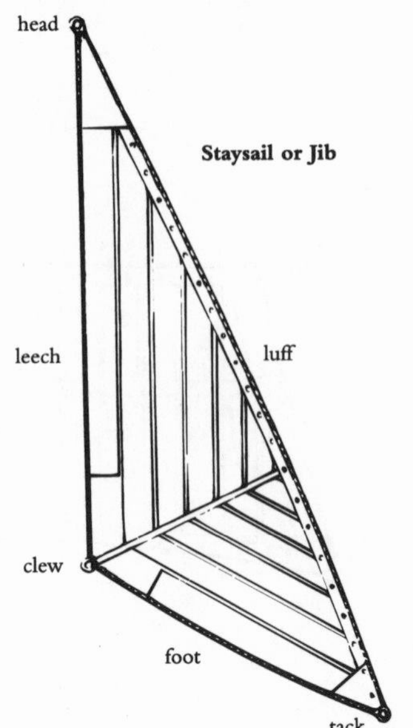

To sail before the wind As a sailing ship is held at bay by a head wind, so it is enabled to move easily and rapidly with a following wind. The colloquialism refers to the art of keeping in with one's fellows, so as to meet with success and good favour, rather than to spoil one's prospects by crossing, or falling foul of, these colleagues: "Her outstanding ability as general secretary enabled her to sail before the wind, no matter what mistakes were made by the governing board."

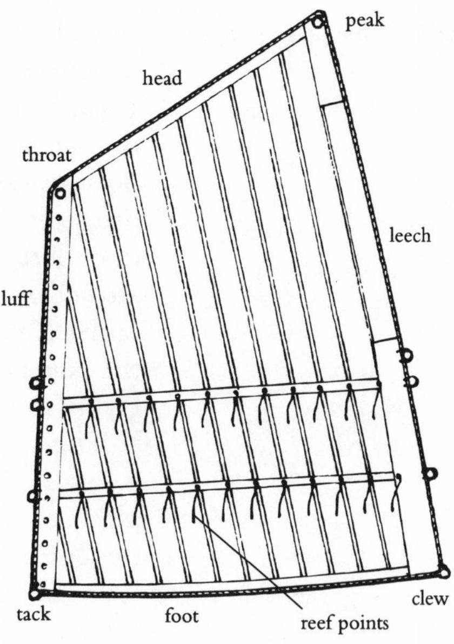

Gaff Sail

To sail close to the wind To take a chance; to go as close as possible to the brink of what public decency or the law will allow, without actually incurring penalty: "He is sailing very close to the wind with his unorthodox batting technique." The phrase derives from the frequent necessity of keeping a vessel's head pointing as high into the wind as will keep the sails still full and drawing; any higher, and the sails will spill their wind and the vessel will lose way (also as in "a bit close to the wind"). (See also *Outpoint.)*

To sail into *To sail into someone* is to forcefully attack or reproach, as in a fight or an argument: "She sailed into her husband because he had forgotten their wedding anniversary." The same is said of a person who sets about a task vigorously and with determination: he "sails into it." From the days of sailing warships, when close engagement with the enemy was necessary if the cannon were to do their work; many a vessel was caused literally to sail into its opponent.

To sail off As a sailing vessel severs all ties with the land when she sets sail and makes her departure, so a person who will have no more to do with a situation "sails off" and departs the scene: "Having dropped her bombshell about resigning as secretary, she sailed off into the five-o'clock rush." The colloquialism is not always pejorative. Eager and enthusiastic partygoers, for example, may gaily sail off into the night's festivities.

To sail under false colours In earlier days of sail, many a man-o'-war enticed an enemy ship to within cannon range by flying the flag or ensign of a nation friendly to the unsuspecting victim. At the appropriate moment, the attacker would haul down its "false colours," hoist its own, and forthwith do battle. Pirate vessels and privateers were adept at using this ruse; it has also been frequently used during the major wars of this century. The Australian warship HMAS *Sydney* was sunk by the German raider *Kormorant* off the West Australian coast in 1941, after the *Kormorant* lured *Sydney* into gun and torpedo range by flying the colours of Holland, a nonbelligerent country.

The application of the phrase to human behaviour is self-explanatory: "We discovered that the team's physiotherapist was sailing under false colours when the committee investigated his academic record."
(See also entries under *Colours. Sail; To strike sail/to strike the colours.)*

To set sail For a sailing vessel to begin a voyage, its sails must be "set" or "bent" to its yards, masts, or stays. Quite often, weather conditions would allow a ship to set a full press of sail, creating an impressive sight as it gathered way. Similarly, the idiom refers to one's beginning a journey, trip, or outing of some kind: "She put on her hat, threw some clothes into a bag, and set sail for London."
(See also *Sail; In full sail.)*

"On the 13th, at six o'clock in the morning, I sailed from Plymouth Sound."
—Captain James Cook (1728–1779), English navigator and explorer, *Second Voyage* (1777)

To strike sail/to strike the colours To acknowledge oneself beaten, to throw in the towel; also to submit, in the sense of paying respect to another: "The boxing coach was ready to strike his colours when it became clear that his protégé was being badly beaten." From the naval custom of indicating that one is defeated by lowering one's topsail halfway down the topmast; a gesture of disarming oneself. More commonly, warships showed surrender by lowering or striking their colours; today, only the flag is struck under these circumstances. Warships pay their respects to senior or foreign warships, and to various dignitaries, by dipping the ensign to half mast and then rehoisting it.
(See also *Colours; To lower one's colours.)*

To trim one's sails to the wind A sailing ship's progress through the water is brought about by the careful setting and trimming of its sails, so that the best speed can be extracted for the desired course. If the wind changes in strength or direction, the sails are trimmed accordingly. In the same way, a person who modifies or adjusts his opinions, policy, actions, etc., to suit the circumstances of the times is said to be "trimming his sails" to the (prevailing) view: "Every political candidate trims his sails to the wind of popular opinion as occasion demands; then, when he is elected, he immediately sets sail on his own course of action."

Sailing
It's all plain sailing

Another example of how landsmen have, over the years, innocently corrupted the language of sailors. The expression refers to anything that is straightforward and easy to do; there need be no hesitation about the course of action to be followed.

The expression in fact derives from the earlier phrase *plane sailing,* which is the art of determining a vessel's position on the assumption that the earth is flat and that she is therefore sailing on a plane surface.

For more than a century after the Mercator chart was introduced in 1569, shipmasters were still using plane charts for their navigation, even though the sphericity of the earth made for problems in drafting the meridians onto paper. The use of these plane charts was known as "plane sailing," often written as "plain sailing" because of the ease (i.e., the plainness) with which navigators could use the old established method.

Sailor's Disgrace

The fouled-anchor emblem of the Royal Navy, being the official seal of the Lord High Admiral of Britain, and now the personal flag of the Queen, who assumed the title of Lord High Admiral in 1964. It was adopted as the official seal at the end of the sixteenth century.

The device consists of a rope cable loosely draped around the stock, shank, and flukes of an anchor; the intention was to create a pleasing and balanced design. In practice, a fouled anchor is an abomination to seamen, being a mark of indifferent seamanship and awkward to set to rights.

Sails
To lower one's sails

To salute, to show respect to a superior, as a sailing ship does to a man-of-war by momentarily lowering her topsail. The sail would not be rehoisted until the salute had been acknowledged by the other vessel. The phrase is used colloquially in the same sense, to admit inferiority or defeat, as in an argument or some other kind of conflict: "He was compelled to lower his sails to her superior logic during their political debate."

(See also *Sail; To strike sail/to strike the colours.)*

Salmagundi

Originally a dish served at sea as a welcome change from salt meat. It consisted of slices of cured fish boiled with onions. Now a mixed dish of minced meat, anchovies, eggs, onions, and spices. From the French *salmigondis,* which in turn derives from the Italian *salami conditi,* pickled sausages.

Salt
An old salt

A long-experienced sailor, one who has been at sea a considerable time; often called a "shellback" from the limpets and barnacles that are said to have had time to grow on his back because of his long service at sea. By extension, an "old salt" in any job is someone who has accumulated vast experience and knowledge, and who has much of value to pass on: "If you need any advice on how to handle this job, go talk to Bill; he's an old salt when it comes to arranging interstate transfers."
(See also *Shellback.)*

Salvage

"... if any ship be lost on the shore, and the goods come to land ... they shall presently be delivered to the merchants, paying only a reasonable reward to those that saved and preserved them, which is entitled salvage."
—Sir William Blackstone (1723–1780), English jurist, *Commentaries on the Laws of England* (1769)

The word is Old French, and is from the Late Latin *salvus,* safe; found also in the Medieval Latin *salvagium.* Salvage is the recovery of a vessel from danger, or of a vessel or her contents from the sea bed. It is also reckoned in money terms as a proportion of the value of the ship or its cargo, based on the danger involved, the amount of labour involved, and the weather conditions at the time. The word is widely used to mean the saving of anything from fire, flood, or other danger, and is found in metaphors such as "to salvage one's fortunes"—to recoup one's losses by whatever means possible.

Salvo

A discharge of firearms, artillery, and especially ship's cannon, in regular succession; also a round of cheers, applause, or such. The term is more closely related to the armament of warships in the steam age; ships' guns in the days of sail delivered a broadside rather than a salvo. (A broadside is the simultaneous—or nearly so—discharge of all the guns along one side of the ship; a salvo is the simultaneous—or nearly so—discharge of several of these guns at once.) From the Old French *salve* and the Latin *salvere,* be in good health; hence, a salute.

"The crash reverberates like the broadside of a man-of-war through the lonely channels."
—Charles Darwin (1809–1882), British scientist and writer, *A Voyage Round the World* (1839)

Now sailors' slang for a spirited reply, a ready defence. "The bosun fired a salvo of pungent advice at the seaman who was slacking off while his mates were heaving on the anchor cable."

Scandalise

Not nautical in origin, but once very widely used by square-rig seamen. *Scandal* is from the Greek *skandalon,* a trap or snare laid out for an enemy; a stumbling block, and hence something to be avoided; that which gives offence. The word has a firm place in sailor's language, and it means to deliberately set a vessel's spars and sails in disarray, such that the yards all point in different directions and the sails hang loose in untidy folds. Scandalising the yards and sails of a ship was a sign of mourning for the death of a shipmate.

The force of this expression in nautical parlance comes from the fact that any sailor would have been deeply shocked by, and very critical of, a vessel that was so poorly disciplined as to allow her spars and sails to be stowed in such a lubberly manner. Clearly, such an occurrence was anathema to the sailor's tidy mind; so the deliberate use of such a device was accepted among seamen as an unmistakeable signal of something amiss, namely, a death on board that ship.

Scant

"They [winds] rose or scantled, as his sails would drive."

—Michael Drayton (1563–1631), English poet, *The Moon-Calf,* cited in the *Universal Dictionary of the English Language* (1897)

An old seaman's word used to describe a wind when it draws ahead of the ship, so that she can only just lay her course (i.e., sail the desired heading), with the yards braced up as sharply as possible. Yachtsmen nowadays would call this "pinching up"; the more common term from the later days of sail would be "sailing close-hauled." From the Old Norse *skamt,* short; when the wind blows progressively from ahead, it is said to "shorten."

The word is not related to *scantling,* the dimensions of timber used in ship- and boatbuilding after it has been reduced to the standard size for that type of vessel (Old Northern French *scantillon,* pattern or sample). We now use *scant* in everyday speech to mean barely sufficient, inadequate: "He paid scant regard to the niceties of good manners during his attack on the chairman of the board." Also, a small amount, a stinted supply of: "I was paid a scant ten dollars for my efforts." The element of short, confined, restricted is apparent in all these usages.

Scarf

"In the joining of the stern, where it was scarfed. . . ."

—Admiral George Anson (1697–1762), navigator and explorer, *A Voyage Round the World* (1748), the account of Anson's voyage by Richard Walter (1716–1785)

Also "scarph." Originally a nautical word, describing a method of joining the ends of two pieces of timber by tapering or bevelling them so that they fit closely together. It is a joint of great antiquity, used by early Egyptian and Phoenician boatbuilders, no doubt because they did not have access to quantities of timber of any length. Most of their boatbuilding was done with short lengths of locally available timber ingeniously joined end-for-end by scarfing. Now a widely used join in the house-building and general timber industries. From the French *ecarver,* to scarf, and also found in the Scandinavian languages, such as Swedish *skarf,* to join.

Schooner

A particular type of vessel that originated on the northeastern seaboard of North America in 1713. A schooner has two or more masts of equal height (or, if two-masted, the aftermast may be taller than the foremast);

fore-and-aft rigged on every mast, usually with jibs on the forestays, and occasionally with a square topsail on the foremast (that vessel being known as a topsail schooner).

"It was the schooner Hesperus
That sailed the wintry sea. . . ."
—Henry Wadsworth Longfellow (1807–1882), American poet, *The Wreck of the Hesperus* (1841)

Because of their rig, schooners were fast and very handy craft, requiring only a small crew compared to the full square-rigged ship of comparable size. The largest schooner ever built was the seven-masted *Thomas W. Lawson,* built in 1902 and measuring 375 feet on the waterline. Most of her running gear was handled by steam winches; consequently she carried a crew of only 16.

The word *schooner* is found in Dutch *schooner,* German *schouer,* Danish *skonnert,* and Spanish and Portuguese *escana,* testifying to the widespread use of this efficient rig. It possibly derives from the Scottish verb (still apparently in use) to *scan* or *scoon,* to skip over the water like a flat stone (compare with "to play ducks and drakes," originally a game that involved skimming flat stones across water, and used as a metaphor today in a totally different sense).

Scope
To have scope for something

Scope (from the Greek *skopos,* mark, aim) is the length of cable run out when a vessel rides to its anchor. It is the amount (approximately) by which a ship swings about its anchor; its freedom of movement, so to speak. This also exactly describes the figurative use of this phrase; *to have scope for something* is to have room to move, to have sufficient opportunity and wherewithal to carry out a particular task: "He had sufficient confidence in himself to give scope to his considerable abilities as an innovative manager."

Scout

A nautical word from the eighteenth century, referring to a boat detached from the fleet or squadron for the special duty of reconnoitering so as to obtain information about the enemy. The vessels chosen for this task were handy and fast, such as the cutter hull and rig that became popular with both smuggler and excise officer alike. The word is used widely in everyday speech; we have "scouts" in the military, the air force, sports, the film and stage industry, and so on. Used as in "See if you can scout up an entertainer for the clubroom party next Saturday." From the Middle English *scowte* and the Old French *escouter,* to listen; ultimately from the Latin *auscultare,* to listen.

"On the bordering deep
Encamp their legions, or with obscure wing
Scout, far and wide into the realm of night,
Scorning surprise. . . ."
—John Milton (1608–1674), English poet, *Paradise Lost* (1667)

Scran

Sailor's slang for food, originally ship's biscuits. A "scran-bag" was formerly used as a receptacle for the remains of a meal, but it is now used as a stowage for personal gear, such as clothing that has been left lying about. When an item is claimed by the owner, it is customary (in the modern Royal Navy) to pay a forfeit of a bar of soap for anything reclaimed.

The word probably is related to the Norwegian *skran,* lean, shrivelled, and the Old Norse *skraelna,* to shrivel; hence possibly the Anglo-Irish colloquialism "bad scran to you," as a form of curse (in the same vein as "bad cess to you").

Scrimshanker See *Scrimshaw.*

Scrimshaw

"Some of them have little boxes of dentistical-looking implements specially intended for the skrimshandering business."

—Herman Melville (1819–1891), American writer, *Moby Dick* (1851)

Also "scrimshander," "scrimshanker," "scrimshandering," "skrimshander," "skrimshanker." *Scrimshaw,* the more commonly used word, is the carving done by sailors (especially American whalers of the early nineteenth century) on the bones, teeth, and tusks of whales and walruses; shells and ivory were also popular carving media. In essence, it was a hobby to while away the time off watch. *To scrimshaw* is to make any ingenious and useful article from marine animal parts.

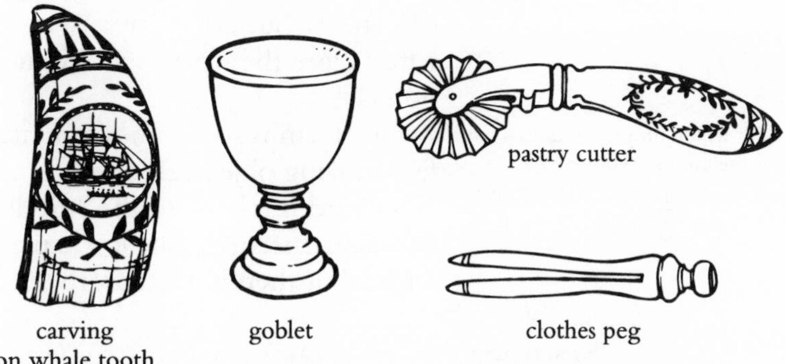

carving on whale tooth — goblet — clothes peg

"It was the army that gave us 'strafe' and 'blight' and 'napoo' and 'wind-up' and 'scrimshanker.'"

—*Saturday Review,* August 1917

The military uses *scrimshanker* as a term of abuse meaning "shirker," which no doubt is derived from the soldier's perception of what would seem to be a fairly easy existence afloat, if one has the time in which to carve and whittle.

The origin of the word is not certain, but it is likely to be connected with one Admiral Scrimshaw, who was noted for his expertise in this work.

Scrub

"We heeled her, scrubbed her bottom, and tallowed it."

—William Dampier (1652–1715), English buccaneer and explorer, *Voyages* (1697)

From the Dutch *schrubben,* to scratch, to clean with vigour. Originally a nautical word, but taken into everyday speech in the sixteenth century. One interesting usage from eighteenth-century England refers to a reprehensible person, a blackguard, someone to be avoided as a "scrub."

To scrub round *To scrub round* is to perform a task inadequately or superficially; to skimp on it. The word means, of course, literally to rub hard with a brush, broom, or cloth in order to clear away or clean. Because of the early association with the broom or brush made from sticks, reeds, twigs, straws, or the like, there may be ultimately a connection with *scrub,* meaning bush, low trees, undersized or inferior growth, as found in the Australian interior. The word is also used to mean to gather up, to look for, to try to make do with: "We'll have a scrub round to see if there are enough competent players to make up a team for the football competition."

To scrub something

Scrub is seaman's language meaning to cancel, to wipe out; from the days when messages, log readings, etc., were recorded on the slate kept by the officers for this purpose on the quarterdeck of the vessel. The phrase has passed into everyday use; "to scrub something" is to abort it, to erase it and to begin anew: "Scrub that last bit; I'll dictate a new paragraph instead"; "The shuttle launch had to be scrubbed at the last minute because of a computer malfunction."
(See also *Slate; A clean slate.)*

Scud

"Scud" is a low, fast-moving cloud, generally the forerunner of a storm, but not always. A vessel is said to scud when she runs before the storm with reduced sail or even under bare poles.

"All which time we scudded, or run before the wind very swift."
—William Dampier (1652–1715), English buccaneer and explorer, *Voyages* (1697)

The term is sometimes figuratively used to describe any fast-moving object, especially animals or aspects of weather. The word is related to the Middle English *scut,* short, short garment, hare; originally it was used to describe the running of a hare, but then it was absorbed by nautical terminology.

Scupper
To be on one's scuppers

To be at one's last resort; to be nearly scuttled; to be very close to final disaster: "He had lost his job and was already on his last scuppers when his wife decided to leave him." From the fact that when the sea is pouring in through the scuppers as much as it is pouring out, the vessel is in a parlous state.
(See also *Scuppered; To be scuppered. Scuttle-butt.)*

Scuppered
To be scuppered

To be scuppered means to be beaten down, quite defeated, even killed: "He knew that he was scuppered when the accountants moved to have him declared bankrupt." Nautically, it means to sink or founder. Scuppers are apertures cut through the sides of a vessel at deck level to allow boarding seas to drain away over the side. Clearly a vessel was in trouble when it settled to a depth such that the sea poured in, rather than out, through the scuppers. The word may be derived from *scoop,* or it may be an altered form of the Old French *escubier,* hawse-hole.
(See also *Scuttle.)*

"With all her scuppers spouting blood. . . ."
—Thomas Babington Macaulay (1800–1859), English essayist and historian, *History of England* (1848)

Scurvy A disease caused by the lack of vitamin C, brought about by an exclusive diet of salted meat, with no fresh vegetables. The symptoms are spongy flesh, swollen gums, foul breath, and extreme tiredness and debility. Death usually follows if the condition is not treated, but recovery can be remarkably quick if the sufferer is given access to fresh fruit and vegetables.

The disease was prevalent in ships that sailed the long Far Eastern routes, particularly in the sixteenth to eighteenth centuries. Captain Cook in the 1770s was one of the first Royal Navy captains to institute a regimen of antiscorbutic measures, but in fact Dr. James Lind had proved, 20 years earlier, that citrus juices—particularly the juices of lemons, oranges, and, to a lesser extent, limes—were an effective cure for scurvy. Lime juice had, by law, to be carried on all British ships, but it wasn't until the twentieth century that it was discovered that limes had only half the antiscorbutic value of lemons, and that black currants were far superior to both.

"Whatsoever man . . . be scurvy or scabbed. . . ."
—Leviticus 21:18–20

It is interesting to note that as long ago as 551, Brendan the Navigator, the Irish monk, is said to have set sail on one of his legendary voyages of discovery with a supply of the roots of blue sea holly, which he believed would safeguard the crew against scurvy.

It was for a long time believed that scurvy was due to the endless use of salt meat aboard ship, but Anson's circumnavigation of 1744 proved this to be a fallacy. When he crossed the Pacific in the *Centurion,* he issued no salt meat at all to the men; instead, the ship's company lived on the livestock that Anson had taken on board before leaving Mexico, and an abundance of fish was caught daily. In addition, the wet season allowed Anson to issue the unusually generous allowance of five pints of quite fresh water daily to every man on board. Nevertheless, during this crossing scurvy claimed the lives of a dozen men each day.

On the *Gloucester,* which accompanied the *Centurion* for most of the crossing, only 77 men and boys were alive when she foundered; the rest of a crew of more than 400 had been taken by scurvy. It is significant that in the whole of Anson's four-year circumnavigation, only four men were lost because of enemy action; virtually all other deaths—over 1,300 men belonging to Anson's company of six ships—were due to disease, mainly scurvy. Half the shipwrecks in history, writes Professor Lloyd (see bibliography), have been due to crews enfeebled by scurvy.

The word has found its way into our everyday language: we speak of "a scurvy trick," to mean low, mean, contemptible behaviour; "a scurvy lad," to mean someone who, in a jocular sense, is a bit of a villain, one who behaves in a shabby manner. "It was a scurvy thing to do, to persuade the old lady to sign a form that she could barely read, let alone understand." From the Anglo-Saxon *scurf,* scaly, scabby, but influenced by the French *scorbut,* scurvy, and perhaps deriving from the Russian *scrobot,* to scratch. (See also *Limey.)*

Scuttle See *Scuttle-butt.*

Scuttle-butt A shipboard "scuttle" (from the Spanish *escotilla,* a hatchway), as distinct from the coal scuttle, a word of different origin, is a hole or formed aperture in the topsides of a vessel. To scuttle a ship is deliberately to hole it so that it will sink (such as the scuttling by the Germans of their High Seas Fleet in Scapa Flow, 1919, to avoid surrender to the British). A "butt" is a cask.

"We hoysed out our boat, and took up some of them; as also a small hatch, or scuttle rather, belonging to some bark."
—William Dampier (1652–1715), English buccaneer and explorer, *Voyages* (1697)

Sailing ships carried their water in large casks, and a long voyage demanded that drinking water be sparingly consumed. The crew obtained their water from a cask provided daily, but to prevent too much being used, a section of a stave was sawn out from the cask so that no more than half a butt of water was available each day. The butt was thus "scuttled."

The term *scuttle-butt* quickly came to mean the shipboard gossip, news, griping, and so forth that would be passed around as the watch gathered from time to time at the water cask. The colloquialism has come to mean gossip generally: "The latest scuttle-butt is that the boss's wife has threatened to leave him."

An exact analogy is the "furphy," coined by Australian soldiers to mean a latrine rumour, so named because of the soldiers' habit of passing on inside, if unreliable, information while at the latrines. Joseph Furphy was the manufacturer who supplied the army with water tanks and containers for sanitary use in the early twentieth century. He has unwittingly lent his name to a now-hallowed pastime in the Australian army. (See also *Scuppered; To be scuppered.)*

Sea

To be all at sea

"This time backers were sadly at sea in their selection."
—*The Globe* (English periodical), September 2, 1885

In the same way that a vessel that has lost its bearings could be anywhere on the high seas, so a person who is "all at sea" is one who is wide of the mark, in a state of error or uncertainty, puzzled or bewildered: "Can I help you? You seem to be all at sea this morning."

To undergo a sea change

"Doth suffer a sea-change. . . ."
—William Shakespeare (1564–1616), *The Tempest,* act 1, scene 2

Not of nautical origin, but included here to indicate how thoroughly the sea has permeated the metaphors of our language. A "sea change" is a complete or radical transformation.

Sea-legs
To get one's sea-legs

"It was Martin's turn . . . to hear poor Mark Tapley . . . getting his sea-legs on the *Screw*."
—Charles Dickens (1812–1870), English novelist, *Martin Chuzzlewit* (1844)

The allusion is clear: to have or get one's sea-legs is to be a good sailor, to be able to stand up to the ship's motion without getting seasick. Similarly, to adapt oneself to new conditions or a new environment, such as in employment, is to gain one's sea-legs: "You have exactly two weeks in which to find your sea-legs as branch accountant; after that we expect results."

Seas
The high seas

The open sea, especially that part of the sea beyond a country's declared territorial limit, forming a free highway to the shipping of all nations. The limit used to be defined by the utmost range of a cannon shot, generally accepted as three miles. However, in recent years this limit has been challenged by many countries with a seaboard, with some claiming a territorial limit of up to 200 miles. International maritime conferences have so far failed to settle the issue.

Colloquially, *to be on the high seas* is used as a description of someone who is behaving in a high-handed and cavalier fashion, as if he considered himself beyond the reach of proper authority; like a buccaneer.

To be half seas over

Sailor's slang for someone who is well on the way to getting drunk. The phrase describes a vessel being swept by breaking seas as she lies stranded on a reef or a leeward shore; in this condition, she is clearly unable to take any action to ease her situation.

The force of the colloquialism derives from the fact that a sailor affected by drink is incapable of carrying out his duty, such as steering a steady course. In the sixteenth century, the phrase meant simply to be halfway across the sea; the transition to the metaphor is clear.
(See also *Shot; To be half shot. Sheets; Three sheets in the wind.)*

Seize

"The man pulled off his clothes, and walked up to the grating. The quarter-masters seized him up."
—Captain Frederick Marryat (1792–1848), English naval captain and novelist, *Peter Simple* (1834)

Nautically, *to seize* means to bind together, or to join a rope's end to its own standing part to form an eye. There are many varieties of seizing, according to method of forming and function to be served. Earliest uses refer to shipboard activity. The overall general sense of grasping, taking possession, lashing together (as well as becoming jammed) subsists in the literal usages of the word in everyday language. From the Frankish Latin *sacire,* to put into possession; the nautical sense is from the Dutch *seizen,* to secure.

Sell
To sell down the river

An expression from the old slaving days; it means to betray, to cheat, to defraud. The chief source of African slaves was for 350 years the West African coast between the River Volta and Mount Cameroon. (Slaves were known to seamen as "blackbirds"; hence the term *blackbirding* to mean slave-trading, especially in Australian Pacific waters in the nineteenth century, ostensibly called "labour recruiting" until it was put down by the Royal Navy in the 1880s.) Slaves were delivered from the hinterland to the coast either by being force-marched through the forest or by being carried downriver on local craft. Slaver ships often went upriver to take on a cargo of slaves.

Another source is the fact that slave owners in the southern states of America frequently got rid of unsatisfactory slaves by selling them to the cotton and sugar plantations of Louisiana that lay farther down the river (i.e., down the Mississippi), where conditions were generally far worse than in the states of the upper Mississippi.

The expression perhaps also owes something to the fact that a short-handed vessel lying in dock would usually secure its complement of crew through the activities of the crimpers. Most of the world's commercial ports of the eighteenth and nineteenth centuries lay on large rivers or estuaries (e.g., London, Shanghai, Rio de Janeiro, and Adelaide). When the shanghaied seaman woke from his alcohol- or drug-induced haze, the ship was usually well on its way down the river to the sea, to begin its voyage. It was by then too late for the seaman to do anything about it; he had been sold down the river. "The gang found that their captured leader had sold them all down the river to the police."

(See also *Blood money. Shanghai.)*

Serang
Head serang

A colloquialism once well-known in Australia and the commonwealth countries, meaning "chief" or "boss" (corresponding to another Australian idiom, "chief cook and bottle washer"). Originally an Anglo-Indian term, ultimately from the Persian *sarhang,* leader or captain of a crew of Lascars on board a local vessel. Used metaphorically in phrases such as "He was head serang in the mathematics department for quite some time."

Serendipity

An unusual word that means a lucky discovery made while looking for something else; the ability to make unexpected and happy discoveries.

It comes from the old name for Sri Lanka—Serendib or Serendip—from the Arabic *Sarandib,* which in turn is from the Hindi *Silan;* the island was named by the ancient Arabic seamen who traded in that region.

The place name appears again in the English translation of a Persian fairy tale called "The Three Princes of

Serendip." In 1754, Horace Walpole coined the term *serendipity* from the title of that story, the heroes of which, he wrote in a letter to a friend, "were always making discoveries, by accidents or sagacity, of things they were not in quest of. . . ." Walpole's happy coinage has become a permanent part of our language. Included here because of its original association with seamen.

Serve
To serve out; To serve one out

Ultimately from the Latin *servus,* slave. The expression *to serve out* is first found in the nautical usage "to serve out grog"; thence to the boxing ring with "to serve one out," to defeat one's opponent. As a metaphor, it means to give a strong rebuke, to hand out a tongue-lashing, to cause someone to be the victim of retribution: "It would serve him out if his tax returns were closely queried this year." Also rendered by *to serve one right,* as in "His wife left him and it serves him right; he was an alcoholic and a compulsive gambler."

Served
To be well served

To serve has two nautical meanings: one is to wind spun yarn tightly and closely around a rope that has been wrapped with a canvas sleeve for protection against water rot; the other is to work the ship's guns (the "great guns," as they were called). The gun crew is said to "serve" a gun as they work rapidly through the process of priming, wadding, loading, heaving, pointing, and firing. A gun is well served or not, as the case may be.

Colloquially, the phrase means to be treated or dealt with in a proper and satisfying manner, to be given good service, as in "He was well served by his ancient but reliable Land Rover on the long trip into the interior."
(See also *Serve; To serve out.)*

Shake
To shake a cloth in the wind

A sailor's indication that a man is slightly intoxicated but not yet hopelessly drunk.
(See also *Sheets; Three sheets in the wind.)*

Shakes
A brace of shakes; in two shakes

When a vessel is steered too close to the wind, its sails shiver or shake; thus, *a brace of shakes* is the seaman's way of saying that something is happening as quickly as it takes for a sail to shiver twice—which is very quickly indeed. The more common expression among landsmen is *two shakes:* "Hang on, I'll be there in two shakes."
(See also *Shakes; No great shakes.)*

No great shakes

"I had my hands full and my head too, just then when he wrote Marino Faliero, so it can be no great shakes."

—George Gordon Byron (1788–1824), English poet, *To Murray,* cited in the *Universal Dictionary of the English Language* (1897)

Shakes are the staves of a cask after it has been taken to pieces. As a seaman's well-being depended upon the integrity of the ship's casks and their contents, a disassembled cask was of little value to him. Hence, attributively, *no great shakes* meant of no use, of little importance. "He was said to be a very good pitcher, but so far what I've seen of him has been no great shakes." (See also *Stave; To stave in.)*

Shanghai

To abduct a sailor by force, generally with the help of drink or drugs, so as to enlist him aboard a ship other than his own. Particularly common in the nineteenth century on American vessels when crew numbers had to be made up, especially when the fierce reputation of many captains and their bucko mates for ferocity made normal recruitment unlikely. Shanghaied sailors were delivered to the ships by "crimps," who ensnared their otherwise unwilling crew with women, drink, and often drugs, and who were paid by the ship's captain for every man shipped aboard.

The term was widely known in the United States, but its origin is obscure; it may derive from the phrase *to ship him to Shanghai,* i.e., to send him on a long voyage; or it may stem from the Australian word *shanghai,* known by every boy in that country to mean a catapult or "ging," similar in form and use to the much older slingshot. In this sense, unfortunate seamen were "catapulted" off to sea as soon as they were made insensible. However, it is more likely that this Australian slang word for catapult derived from the older nautical usage, as various Australian ports, such as Melbourne, Adelaide, Sydney, and Hobart, were important and well-known shipping centres for merchant sail of many nationalities in the nineteenth century.

To shanghai, in the colloquial sense, means to steal or capture, often by surreptitious means. "We managed to shanghai a couple of cases of beer from the coolroom before it was locked up for the weekend."
(See also *Bucko. Sell; To sell down the river.)*

Shanty

Also "chantey." From the French *chanter,* and the Latin *cantare,* to sing, especially songs sung on board to lighten the labour of working the ship, as in heaving the anchor or hauling on sheets and braces. These songs, usually simple but melodious tunes with vigorous lyrics, had definite rhythms that made it easier for the crew to stamp and go, to pull together.

By 1875, the advent of steam-driven machinery saw the demise of the sea shanty on board ship, and it survives now only in popular folklore, as in "Blow the Man Down,"

"Shenandoah," "Bound for the Rio Grande," and many others equally famous.

A good shantyman was a valued member of the crew because he could be relied upon to keep a shanty going in time of hard work, such as swaying up a spar or yard to the masthead. Singing these shanties, and dancing to them, was a popular pastime for the off-watch crew.

Shape
To shape up

The complete colloquialism is "to shape up or ship out." *To shape,* in nautical language, is to select a course for the ship to sail; *to shape a course* is common parlance among seamen. Figuratively, *to shape up* is to stick to the course, to keep up to expectations. Failure to do so invites the demand to ship out, to quit, to leave the job to someone better qualified. "The coach told the new recruit that if he wanted to remain on the team he was going to have to shape up or ship out." From the Old English *scieppan,* create, shape.

Shark

"The sharks in your profession are always alert and on the scent."
—Robert Southey (1774–1843), English poet and essayist, *Letters,* cited in the *Universal Dictionary of the English Language* (1897)

From the German *schurke,* the name given to a person who battens on to someone else, one who gulls his companion. The word was used by seamen as a nautical nickname for the fish that we now call a shark, their intention being to describe how the shark behaves very much like certain kinds of sharp-dealing landsmen that they knew; a rake, a rogue.

Sheer
To sheer away; to sheer off

To sheer is to deviate or stray off course in an irregular manner; this might happen because of difficulties with the steering gear, or because of a negligent or inexperienced helmsman. *To sheer off* is a deliberate manoeuvre, in which the vessel is suddenly moved away at an angle to its original course to avoid a collision or some obstacle.

The word is from the German *scheren,* to depart, and is not to be confused with the word as used in "sheer nonsense" or "a sheer slope"; this latter usage is from the Old English *scir,* clear, pure, complete. Metaphorically, the terms *to sheer off* and *to sheer away* mean suddenly to change one's direction of movement, or thrust of argument, because of some perceived obstacle or impediment: "He sheered away from the subject of money as soon as his wife entered the room."

Sheet

From the Anglo-Saxon *sceata,* napkin, winding sheet, and with the additional sense of the foot (or "skirt") of a sail. Thence applied to the rope that was sewn round the border of the sail and leading out from the lower corners for the purposes of controlling the set and shape of the sailcloth. (See also other entries under *Sheet.)*

A sheet in the wind's eye The early stages of being drunk. *In the wind's eye* is to be directly opposed to the wind, i.e., to have a headwind. (See also *Sheets; Three sheets in the wind.)*

That was my sheet anchor The sheet anchor is an additional anchor carried for security in case the bower anchor should fail to hold the ship. Nowadays the bower and sheet anchors are of the same weight, but in earlier times the sheet anchor was the heaviest anchor carried aboard. It was lashed in such a manner that it could be "shot," or let go immediately, when needed in an emergency; the word *sheet* here is a corruption of "shoot" or "shot" and is not related to the sheet of a sail.

"This saying they make their shoot anchor."
—Thomas Cranmer (1489–1556), English cleric, *Answer to Gardiner,* cited in the *Universal Dictionary of the English Language* (1897)

The term *sheet anchor* is used as a synonym for security in a general sense. It is one's best hope, one's last refuge; to lose it is to be quite done for. "We were sorry to see her leave the firm; she was an excellent worker and was often our sheet anchor at busy times."
(See also *Anchor; One's best bower anchor.* Other entries under *Sheet.)*

To sheet home the blame To attach the blame to some particular person or cause for an event. A sail is "sheeted home" by hauling on the rope that controls its shape and setting; this rope is called the "sheet." The attachment of blame to the guilty is analogous to the fact that the sheet is ultimately responsible for the behaviour of the sail. "By carefully sifting through the bank records, we were able to sheet home the blame for the firm's insolvency to the chief accountant."
(See also other entries under *Sheet.)*

Sheets
Three sheets in the wind To be very drunk. The sheet is the line (rope or chain) attached to the clew or lower corner of a square sail, or to the aftermost lower corner of a fore-and-aft sail. It controls the extent to which the sail is permitted to capture the wind. If the sheet is let go so that the sail flaps or flags out of control, the sheet is said to be "in the wind," and the vessel will describe a very erratic course.

To have a sheet in the wind is a nautical expression for being a little tipsy; thus the phrase *three sheets in the wind* is to be quite out of control, thoroughly inebriated. (The phrase in America is usually rendered "three sheets *to* the wind.") "By the time we got him out of the pub, he was already three sheets in the wind and in no fit condition to report for work."

Shellback An old sailor, often renowned for his ability to spin well-embroidered yarns of his experiences at sea; an old salt who has been at sea long enough for limpets or barnacles to have grown on his back. The term now carries an element of affection and admiration for such a seaman's vast knowledge of seamanship, and for the fact that he had much to teach the younger sailor in his chosen profession.

The term is still largely nautical, but it is sometimes loosely applied to anyone who has accumulated a large store of knowledge and experience that is ready to be passed on.

(See also *Salt; An old salt.)*

Shifty A shifty person is one who is evasive, unreliable, deceitful, furtive. The phrase is from the name *shifter,* the cook's mate in the old sailing navy. His main job was to shift and wash the salt meat that was stowed in casks in the ship's hold; the meat then had to be steeped in fresh water to remove the salt that it had acquired during its long immersion in brine. No doubt the sailors mistrusted the shifter's devotion to duty, and perhaps they had good reason to, for the residual salt content of their victuals was still at an unhealthily high level. He was, they felt, unreliable; hence "shifty": "I don't like the look of the new doorman; he's got shifty eyes."

Ship From the Anglo-Saxon *scip* (pronounced "ship"), connected with other Teutonic words such as Dutch *schip,* German *schiff,* Old Norse *skip.* The Italian *schifo* is from the Teutonic influence.

"Ships are but boards, sailors but men."
—William Shakespeare (1564–1616), *The Merchant of Venice,* act 1, scene 3

A ship today is generally regarded any large, oceangoing vessel; and in the days of sail any vessel that was propelled by wind was called—loosely—a ship. The seaman, however, understood the term *ship* to mean a specific kind of vessel: strictly, one with a bowsprit and at least three masts, with each mast made up of three sections: a lower mast, a topmast above that, and a topgallant mast surmounting both. Furthermore, the vessel had to be square-rigged on all masts.

Four- and five-masted ships were also built in the late nineteenth century, but by this time it was unusual to see a full ship-rigged vessel. The more common rig incorporated fore-and-aft rig on one or more of the aftermasts with square sails on the remainder. Such a combination required a smaller crew and was therefore cheaper to maintain.

The three-masted ship was common in the eighteenth century, and a number of four-masted ships appeared in the following century. At the beginning of the twentieth century, the only five-masted ship-rigged vessel ever built took to the sea: the mighty *Preussen,* of German registration.

Sailing vessels came to be classified according to the number of masts they carried and the way in which each mast was rigged (i.e., square, fore-and-aft, or a combination of each). Thus, the late eighteenth- and nineteenth-century seaman would have used the following terms:

Brig: Two-masted, square-rigged on both, with crossjack (square sail on lower mainmast, pronounced "cro-jak") and spanker (fore-and-aft sail) both set on the aftermost mast.

Brigantine: Exactly as a brig, except that it never carried the crossjack (main course).

Hermaphrodite brig: Two-masted, square-rigged on the foremast and fore-and-aft rigged on the aftermast (i.e., on the mainmast).

Barque (also "bark"): Three-masted, square-rigged on the fore and main, and fore-and-aft rigged on the aftermost mast (i.e., on the mizzen). Four- and five-masted barques (i.e., fore-and-aft rigged on the aftermost mast only) became very common in the late nineteenth and early twentieth centuries as an economy measure in the struggle against steam.

Barquentine (also "barkentine"): Three-masted, square-rigged on the foremast, and fore-and-aft rigged on the main and mizzen (the two aftermost masts). This rig was much more efficient to windward, and required fewer crew; thus, four- , five- , and six-masted barquentines became common (i.e., square-rigged on the foremost mast only).

Jackass-barque: A three-masted barque with the addition of a fore-and-aft sail on the lower mainmast. A four-masted jackass-barque was square-rigged on the two foremost masts, and fore-and-aft rigged on the two aftermost masts.

Ship: Three-masted, each mast in three sections, square-rigged on all, with a bowsprit. Four-masted ships were also built, but only one five-masted ship was ever launched (the *Preussen).*

Schooner: From the Dutch *schooner,* found in other seafaring tongues, and probably deriving from the old Scottish verb *to scoon,* to skip over water like a flat stone. The basic type is a two-masted vessel, fore-and-aft rigged on both, with the foremast shorter than the mainmast, or (a modern development) both masts of equal height. The schooner originally carried square topsails on the fore topmast, but the jib-headed foresail soon replaced the square sail. A few topsail schooners can still be found in various parts of the world.

Schooners of three or more masts had each mast of equal height; a number of them were built with three, four, five, and six masts. The biggest schooner ever built was the massive, seven-masted *Thomas W. Lawson;* launched in the 1890s, she carried only 16 crew, and was fitted with steam winches. She was lost in a storm in 1907, with only one survivor.

A double topsail schooner carried square sails on two masts (generally the fore and main): the term *topsail schooner* is applied to the schooner that carries a square sail on the foremast only.

Modern rigs include:

Schooner: Generally only two- or three-masted, fore-and-aft rigged, occasionally with square topsails.

Ketch (originally "catch"): Two-masted, fore-and-aft sails, with the foremast (the main) being taller than the mizzen, and with the mizzen stepped forward of the rudder post.

Yawl: Exactly as for the ketch, except that the mizzen is stepped aft of the rudder head.

Sloop: One mast only, fore-and-aft rigged, flying one headsail.

Cutter: As for the sloop, except that it flies two headsails, and the mast is usually stepped a little further aft to accommodate this. Often rigged with a bowsprit to take the foremost headsail.

These five main rigs are further delineated by the shape of their driving sails: *bermuda* (also called "jib-headed," "marconi," or "leg-o'-mutton"), the triangular sail characterised by the jib or headsail; and *gaff,* a four-sided sail with its upper side held aloft by a spar to which the sail is attached. This spar is in turn hoisted on the mast and is controlled by its own running rigging.

Thus, a ketch may be gaff-rigged or bermuda-rigged, on one or both masts. The gaff rig has definite advantages in off-the-wind sailing, whereas the bermuda rig cannot be surpassed for close-hauled sailing. Important yacht races, such as the America's Cup contest, are contested by bermuda rigs; cruising sailors have shown a more or less equal preference for the marconi rig and the gaff rig.

Illustrations of historical and modern rigs follow on pages 286–290.

Brig

Brigantine

Hermaphrodite Brig

Snow Brig

Barque (Bark)

Barquentine

Jackass-Barque (Bark)

Ship

Two-Masted Fore and Aft Schooner

Three-Masted Fore and Aft Schooner

Three-Masted Topsail Schooner

Double Topsail (or Two Topsail) Schooner

Two-Masted Topsail Schooner

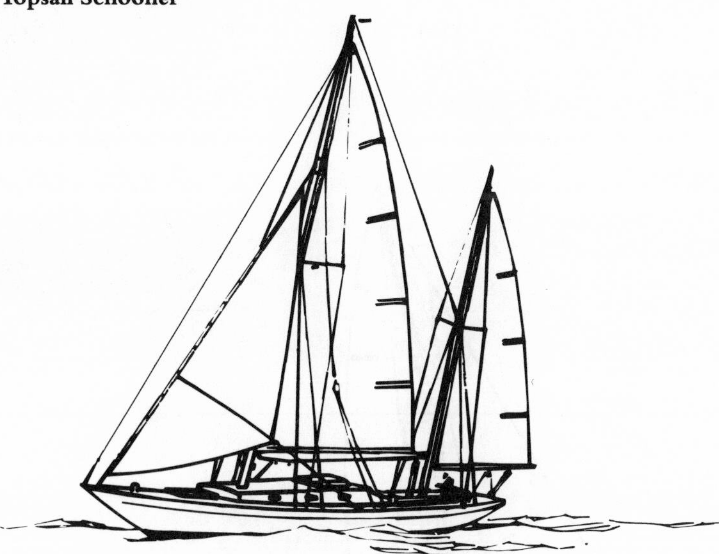

Ketch (Bermudan Rig)

Ketch (Gaff Rig)

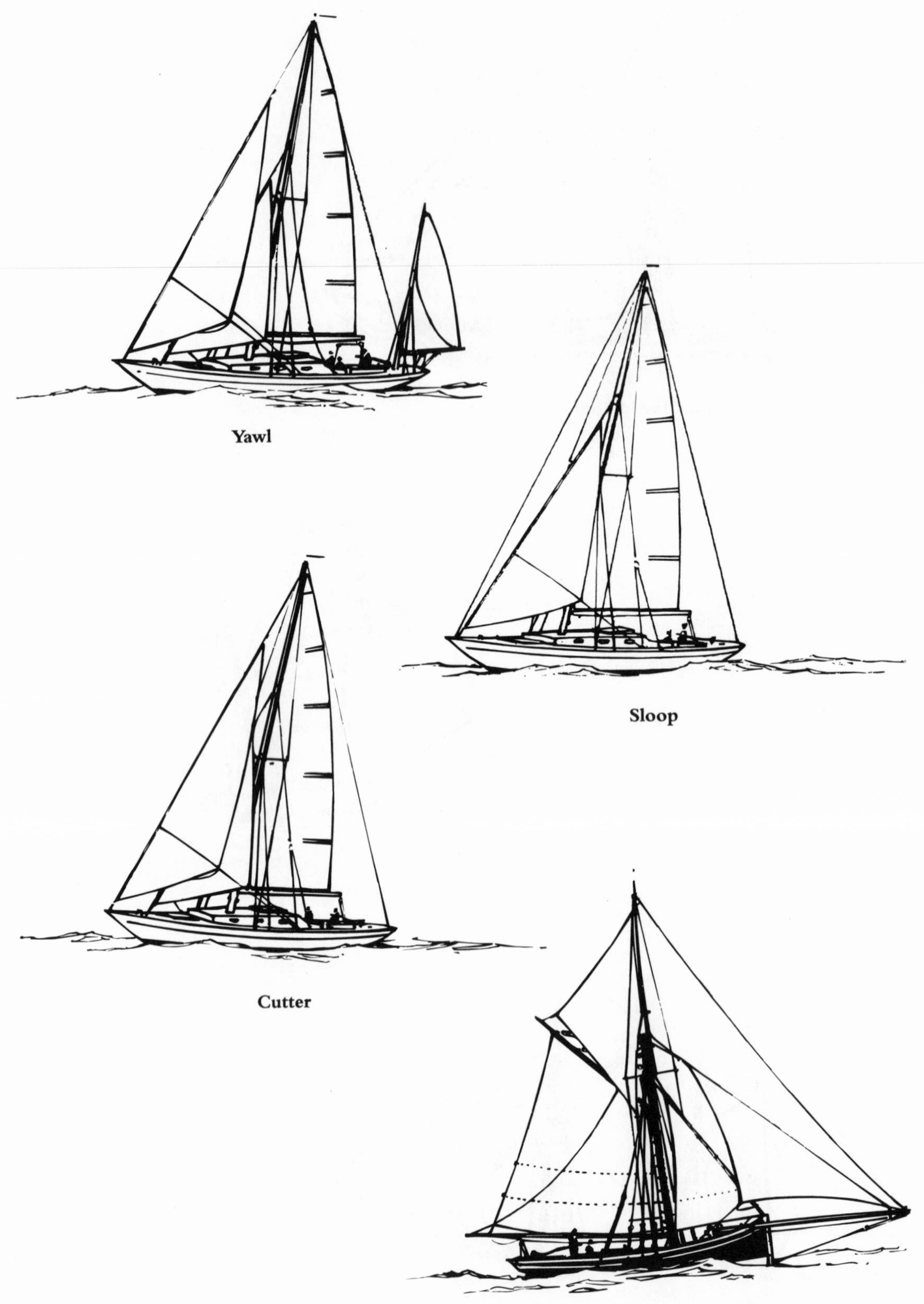

Yawl

Sloop

Cutter

Gaff (Cutter with Bowsprit)

Don't give up the ship Don't surrender, don't give in or give up; keep on trying, fighting, persisting; hold on. To lose or surrender one's ship is a most serious occurrence; virtually all maritime nations conduct a court-martial to determine the reasons for the loss and, if appropriate, where the blame is to be sheeted home.

The expression was made famous during the War of 1812. In a battle off Boston on June 1, 1813, the *Chesapeake,* under the command of Captain James Lawrence of the U.S. Navy, was reduced to a shambles by HMS *Shannon.* Lawrence was mortally wounded in the action, and, as he was carried below, he is said to have uttered repeatedly, "Don't give up the ship." In fact, the *Chesapeake* was captured and taken back to England as a prize.

The Battle of Lake Erie was fought later that year, on September 13. The American commander, Oliver Hazard Perry, was forced to abandon his stricken flagship, the *Lawrence,* but transferred his battle flag to the *Niagara.* On this flag were emblazoned Lawrence's dying words, "Don't give up the ship." Perry's action (he was victorious in the battle) has associated the phrase more with him than with anyone else.

Spoil the ship for a ha'porth of tar Pitch, or tar, was one of the materials needed for caulking the seams of a wooden sailing vessel to make it watertight. The origin of the phrase "spoil the ship . . ." seemingly comes from the fact that if the ship's timbers were insufficiently payed *(not* "paid") with pitch, or if a small length of seam were overlooked as being of no consequence, not worth the effort of applying just a little bit more tar (a ha'porth, a halfpenny's worth), then inevitably water must find its way into the hull. At the least the neglect would make life uncomfortable; at the worst, it could perhaps lead to disaster.

However, not so; the phrase dates from shepherds' dialect: *ship* is a rendering of *sheep.* The reference is to the practice, common even in Shakespeare's time, of daubing a sheep's injuries or cuts with tar to protect the animal from infection.

Modern-day usage of the colloquialism carries the same warning: by skimping or neglecting a detail, the whole enterprise is put at risk: "By refusing to have his thesis typed professionally, he was spoiling the ship for a ha'porth of tar—it was unlikely that his supervisor would be willing to accept the final draft."

To jump ship To desert or leave a ship without proper authorisation. Colloquially, to quit, to abandon an enterprise, to leave without forewarning: "Things were going badly in the insurance business; his first impulse was to jump ship and head for another city."

To leave a sinking ship The phrase is of obvious nautical origin and meaning: the seaman will abandon his vessel only when it is clear that nothing else can be done to save it and he must look out for himself. So—metaphorically—does one abandon an untenable position, as in the losing side of an argument, or a commercial enterprise that is foundering or facing bankruptcy: "He felt that unless the team found a new playing-coach they were doomed to failure, but he was reluctant to leave a sinking ship so early in the season."

To run a tight ship *To run a tight ship* is to enforce shipboard discipline with great vigour and thoroughness. The early methods of supplying men to make up the crew of a ship usually meant that many of the hands knew nothing whatsoever about ship-handling; indeed, it was not unknown for a new crew member to stagger on deck the morning after being press-ganged into service and gaze upon the ocean for the very first time in his life. Consequently, the ship's officers would set about teaching their new hands the meaning of duty—often with blows from a knotted rope or a rattan cane to get them moving quicker. A captain who ran a tight ship was held in high esteem by the authorities, and in great respect and often some dread by the crew.

Colloquially, the expression means much the same thing, except that it is applied to any group effort that requires discipline and cooperation from each member of the group. A principal could be said to run a tight ship where it was evident that he exercised his authority in demanding, and getting, total adherence from his staff to matters of school policy concerning punctuality, yard duty, lesson plans, and the like. The expression is applicable only where a person, or a corporate body, is responsible for exercising authority and the making of decisions: "He prided himself on being concerned with the welfare of his employees and on running a tight ship."

The word *tight* is a variation of the earlier "thight," which is from the Old Norse *thettr,* tight, solid, staunch. (See also *Bucko.)*

To ship someone off To send someone on her way, to send her packing, to get rid of her without undue ceremony: "The new engineer was keen to put her ideas into practice, so we shipped her off to the gold diggings to give her her chance." From the fact that *to ship* something was to load it as cargo on a vessel bound for other parts. The verb *to ship* is in widespread use in all forms of commerce and industry. It stems from the Old English *scip,* a ship.

To ship water Nautically, to take in water over the side of the vessel, as when waves break over it. Figuratively, also to take in water in any way, as a motor car might leak rain through its door seals: "My new underwater camera began to ship water on our first dive."

To take ship To embark; to go aboard preparatory to taking a sea voyage. Loosely, as a metaphor, the expression means to begin, to set off on a journey, either in the sense of putting plans for an enterprise into motion, or in the sense of undertaking some travel, usually—but not necessarily—by sea.

When my ship comes home/in An allusion to the fact that merchants frequently financed voyages to foreign ports, in the hope that when the ships returned to their home port, the merchants would make enormous profits from the sale of their rich cargoes. The practice was widespread among the members of the centuries-old Hanseatic League, and of course in the spice trade to the Far East. The voyage of the *Argosy,* the tale of Dick Whittington, and Shakespeare's play *The Merchant of Venice* all have plots that incorporate this kind of venture. Colloquially, the phrase refers to an expectation, justifiable or not, that one's luck will change and good fortune will attend one's chosen endeavours: "We'll buy a big house in the country when my ship comes in."

Shipmates A companion in some enterprise. From the obvious nautical meaning: one who serves with another in the same vessel.

The conditions of shipboard life demanded that each man be tolerant of his fellows, moderate in his behaviour, and reluctant to take selfish advantage of the weak. Rarely did seamen attain these giddy heights of saintly behaviour, but they always, on the whole, in their own inarticulate way, tried to do their best, and certainly valued these qualities in their fellow voyagers. It was considered one of the highest accolades to call a man "shipmate"; the term implied trust (one of the worst crimes that a seaman could commit—other than murder—was to steal from his fellows), a shared suffering, a common bond of the sea, and an interdependence of each on the other in their daily tasks.

Ships

Ships in the night Perhaps nautical in origin, but its poetic ring makes this seem unlikely; more likely to be used by stage sailors, as was the imprecation "shiver my timbers," which no seaman himself ever used. The phrase *ships that pass in the night* means chance acquaintances encountered only briefly. Henry Wadsworth Longfellow used the expression in his 1874 *Theologians Tale:*

> Ships that pass in the night
> and speak to each other in passing
> Only a signal shown
> and a distant voice in the darkness;
> So on the oceans of life
> we pass and speak one another,
> Only a look and a voice;
> then darkness again and a silence.

Shipshape
All shipshape and Bristol fashion

To have things well organised, in proper order, ready for instant use. The reference is to the methodical way in which a ship and her rigging were equipped, organised, and handled. Such a ship and her crew were said to be "shipshape."

It was necessary for a standardised system of organisation to be adopted, because seamen and officers served in a wide variety of vessels in the course of their careers; in war and in bad weather, the crew had to know instinctively where each item of gear should come to hand.

> "Keep everything ship-shape, for I must go."
> —Alfred, Lord Tennyson (1809–1892), English poet, *Enoch Arden* (1864)

Bristol fashion refers to the days when Bristol was England's major west coast port, and its shipping had to be maintained in proper good order because the city had no docks and ships were thus left high and dry at low tide. Vessels using the port, therefore, had to be well built and properly maintained to withstand the stresses of taking the ground.

"She was very well organised, with her desk and files always shipshape and Bristol fashion."

Shonky

Originally sailors' slang for a mean messmate, one who will drink with his fellows but who will avoid paying his round. Now an established colloquialism in Australian and British speech (often spelled "shonkie"), meaning of dubious integrity or honesty: "He wanted to sell me a video machine in the pub yesterday, but he seemed a bit shonky to me so I passed it up"; unreliable, especially mechanically: "My old Land Rover is getting a bit shonky these days."

Shore up

From the Dutch *schoar,* a prop, and found in the Anglo-Saxon *scorian,* to project. A shore is a prop or stanchion fixed under a ship's side or bottom, to support her while she is on the stocks or aground. It is also a stout timber used to back up a bulkhead in a ship when excessive pressure is applied to it from the other side, as with a flooded compartment.

Used colloquially to convey the same sense, as in "The premier strove desperately to shore up the faltering agreement that the two political parties had foolishly committed themselves to."

Short
To be brought up short

A vessel is "brought up short" when it is caused to stop suddenly by letting go an anchor with too much way or forward motion on the ship. The phrase also describes the result when a ship pitches while at anchor and the cable tautens to such an extent that it holds the bows down at the top of the pitch. In both cases, another common term is *to snub.* The essential element is unexpectedness, curtness.

As a colloquialism, the expression means to stop or deal with someone in an abrupt and summary manner, or to be so dealt with oneself; to be jolted, to be stopped suddenly: "The heckler's sharp retort brought the speaker up short: for a moment he could think of nothing to say."
(See also *Snub.)*

Short rations

A reduced issue of food during a long voyage; brought about by a variety of factors. The most common were the difficulty of keeping food fresh for any length of time, and the outright dishonesty and venality of provisioning firms ashore and, very often, ships' pursers afloat, many of whom connived with each other to provide short weight and inferior quality to the luckless seaman. The usual stratagem adopted in the Royal Navy when the men were to be put on short rations was to issue food for four men, then to be divided among six, a system known as "six-upon-four"; also called "bare Navy."

Used colloquially in exactly the same sense: to be given, usually through reasons of exigency, a reduced supply of victuals: "The fishing party found themselves on short rations; they had run out of Emu Bitter and were now down to light lager."

From the Latin *ratio,* proportion, allowance of provisions. Hence, to be short, to be lacking, to have insufficient of; to discover an inconvenient lack of something, such as money: "He intended taking her to the Policemen's Other Ball, but he found himself short of cash."

Shot

From the Anglo-Saxon *sceot, scot, gesceot,* shot, shoot, and related to other Teutonic languages, such as the Old Norse *skot,* missile. The same word also carries the meaning of contribution or portion, as in "to pay one's shot" (this usage is not, of course, nautical, and from which is directly derived "to get off scot-free").

A long shot A guess, decision, attempt, or the like, based on long odds and full of risks, unlikely to be right or to succeed but still worth trying. From the firing of a ship's gun at extreme range and hoping to score a hit: "Entering my new horse for the Melbourne Cup was a long shot, but it certainly paid off."

A telling shot A shot that counts, one that does the job; from the Anglo-Saxon *tellan,* to count, to tell.

The first record of naval guns goes back to 1336. These weapons were often rather crude affairs made of cast bronze or wrought iron. Only much later, in the sixteenth century, did cast iron replace wrought iron and, ultimately, bronze. Because of the uncertain accuracy of cannon construction, the unreliability of powder, and the dubious conformity to calibre of the cannonball, it was always a cause for considerable satisfaction whenever a ball struck its intended target.

Colloquially, a telling shot is a remark or a retort that neatly wraps up an argument in the speaker's favour; a reply that leaves the other side lost for words: "His parting comment, that the councillor was guilty of an undisclosed conflict of interest, was the most telling shot of all."

Never say die while there's a shot in the locker Don't give up while there is still some hope left. From the days of fighting sail, when only a few rounds of shot (cannonballs) left in the ammunition locker might still—with luck—be enough to win the day.

To be half shot To be nearly drunk; in a somewhat wider sense, to be almost exhausted, almost spent. The phrase probably comes from the term *half-musket-shot,* when a musket's maximum effective range was some 200 yards. British naval gunners preferred to close at half-musket range (i.e., 100 yards); they were accustomed to use this range as their yardstick, so that when they opened fire their shot would have the maximum effect on enemy vessels at close range.

By a curious inversion of meaning, the phrase came to represent the "halfway-thereness" of exhaustion, likened to the halving, as it were, of the distance between enemy vessels before the destruction began: "By the time we got him out of the pub and on his way home, he was already half shot, but that was nothing compared to what his wife would say."

To have (or not have) a shot in the locker "A shot in the locker" is money left unspent after a run ashore. To have no shot in the locker is to be quite out of food, drink, and money; to have no resources left. *Shot* is the name given to everything that was fired out of a naval gun except bombs or shells that were filled with explosive. The locker was the sailor's stowage place for his personal gear, and in this phrase parallels the magazine in the hold where the vessel's shot and powder were stored. Colloquially, the expression would be used as in "I've still got one last shot left in my locker and I'll use it to dislodge the prime minister."

Shove off From the Anglo-Saxon *scufan,* to shove, and common in other Teutonic languages (e.g., Gothic *afskiuban,* to shove off). Nautically, it means to push clear of, as in a pulling boat or small sailing boat being pushed away by hand (or by boat hook) from a wharf or larger vessel. Colloquially, *to shove off* is to leave, to get going, to start off or away, all usually with a sense of force, immediacy, or urgency: "When the party degenerated into a brawl, we could see that it was high time to shove off home."

Sick bay Originally an area or compartment in the vessel reserved for the treatment of injury or illness. The equipment and personnel provided might range from merely a medicine chest and the sometimes dubious skills of the captain, to a fully equipped room with facilities for surgery, attended by properly qualified medical officers. The earliest sick bay was simply a small, little-used area of the lower deck, without adequate ventilation, accommodation, or sanitation arrangements. It is probable that as many ill men died from the combination of noise, smell, foul air, and general gloom in the sick bay as from any other condition.

A sick bay is found ashore as well as afloat; it is much smaller than a hospital, and is often called an "infirmary." The origin is, of course, nautical; men in the sick bay were on the sick list. From the Anglo-Saxon *seoc,* sick, and Latin *batare,* to gape—not directly related to bay as in geography.

Sign
To sign on When a seaman joined a naval ship, he signed his name (or as often made his mark) in the ship's muster book. On this basis he drew his daily provisions during the voyage, and when the ship returned to its home port he was given his pay, for which he signed. When he signed on, the seaman bound himself to the customs and usages of the sea; notably, to the "Thirty-Six Articles of War."

In the merchant service, the seaman signed simply the "Articles," which were the conditions of service he agreed to undertake. They were also signed by the master of the vessel, and they constituted a legal contract binding on both sides.

The "Ship's Articles" specified the rates of pay, scale of provisions, daily hours of work, and—in the days of the Cape Horners—the extremes of latitude beyond which a seaman was not obliged to serve. Discipline on board ship was also set out and governed by the Articles. In a general sense, *to sign on* is to offer oneself for hire, to commit oneself to employment, usually ratified by the signing of a contract between the two parties: "He liked the look of the place and was keen to sign on as the new branch manager."

The "Articles of War," which on a Royal Navy vessel were read out by the captain to the crew at each Sunday service (if the captain chose to "rig church"), laid down both the rules of conduct for seamen and the punishments that could be visited upon them if they transgressed those rules.

The first attempt to codify naval conduct came with the "Black Book of the Admiralty," issued in 1336 and based on the laws of Oleron, which was a system of maritime law enacted by Eleanor of Aquitaine in 1152, and possibly owing something to the earlier Rhodian Law of the Mediterranean. However, many naval captains had already devised their own systems of shipboard punishment; so, to give some uniformity to naval practice, the English government issued the "Articles of War" in 1653, which were then incorporated in the Naval Discipline Act of 1661.

The Articles devoted much effort to spelling out what constituted a crime on any of the English navy vessels and the punishment that could be awarded for each crime. At least one third of these Articles prescribed the death penalty as a proper and lawful punishment.

The comparable regulations in the United States were known as the "Articles for the Government of the Navy." In May 1951, however, Congress introduced the Uniform Code of Military Justice, which now applies to all U.S. armed forces administered by the Department of Defense. By contrast, in Britain, the Army Act of 1955 omitted the "Articles of War," although they are still retained in the Naval Discipline Act of 1956.
(See also *Articles; Ship's Articles.)*

Signals
To get one's signals crossed

The first record of a system of communication by flags at sea was in 1753; this method utilised five different flags. By 1857 an International Code of Signals had been introduced, and there was general agreement among the maritime nations to adopt it by the end of the century. Many attempts were made in the intervening years to establish a workable system and to make it acceptable to the warships and merchant ships of the world.

It is easy to understand, therefore, how it would often happen that in the heat of battle, or in an exchange between vessels of different nationalities, mistakes could occur in the fitting of the flags in their correct sequence to the hoist—thus, literally to have one's signals crossed is to have them arranged in the wrong order, with the inevitable confusion or delay in understanding on the part of the receiver.

"Mark that the signal-gun be duly fired,
To tell us when the hour of stay's expired."
—George Gordon Byron (1788–1824), English poet, *The Corsair* (1814)

Colloquially, the phrase means to misunderstand someone's intentions, to read the situation wrongly; the emphasis here is on the receiver rather than the sender. "He obviously got his signals crossed; the girl wasn't one bit interested in his attentions."

To make signals of distress

Flags were a very early means of signalling between ships at sea; prior to that, other signals used were smoke or flames, and gunfire. More modern methods of signalling include Morse Code and direct voice communication by radio.

Internationally agreed signals of distress include flares, making smoke, hand signals (semaphore) if within close enough range, and radio and telegraph codes such as "SOS," "CQD," and "Mayday." Another widely accepted method of indicating distress, that help is needed, is to fly one's flag of nationality upside down at the masthead or at some other convenient height.

As a metaphor, to make signals of distress means to make signs, gestures, hand movements, sounds, etc.—in fact anything that will attract attention—so as to convey the fact that assistance is needed. The help required may be moral or material.

(See also *Flag; To nail one's flag to the mast.)*

Sink

"A load would sink a navy. . . ."
—William Shakespeare (1564–1616), *Henry VIII,* act 3, scene 2

From the Anglo-Saxon *sincan,* and common to the Teutonic languages. Another of those words that are basic (some would say essential) to nautical experience. A number of figures of speech derive from the nautical usage, for example, "to sink the ship," "to sink our differences," "to sink or swim." "For the next six months we're going to sink our differences and work together on the project."

Skids
To be on the skids

The skids, or skid-booms, are the beams that support the deck on which the ship's boats are stowed; frequently a vessel's spare spars were used as support or skids for the boats. They were usually kept on the waist deck, with the boats lashed on top of them. Gradually, methods were evolved of lowering the boats (especially as lifeboats) over the ship's side into the sea by sliding them along the skids to the ship's side; these skids are now known as davits.

Colloquially, *to be on the skids* means to be going down in the world, deteriorating rapidly, to be in the process of a downfall; as in "Skid Row." Probably derived from the word *ski* (Old Norse *skith,* snow shoe, also a short length of wood). Used as in "Ever since his wife and children left him he has been on the skids with a drinking problem."

Skipper

Not itself of nautical origin, but included here because of its widespread use in maritime affairs. It is from the Dutch *schipper,* itself from *schip,* ship; the "skipper" variation is first found in the sport of curling, widely played in Scotland and Canada. In this sense the word meant captain.

"And the skipper had taken his little daughter,
To bear him company. . . ."
—Henry Wadsworth Longfellow (1807–1882), American poet, *The Wreck of the Hesperus* (1841)

Metaphorically, the word is freely used to describe the leader of many kinds of group enterprises; loosely, also the name for the master or captain of a ship, especially a small vessel such as a shrimper or a crayfishing boat. More accurately, a "skipper" is one who commands a fishing boat, such as a trawler or drifter; he is not a captain. By the same token, the master of the *Queen Elizabeth II* is not a skipper; neither is qualified to supplant the other.

Skull and crossbones

The well-known representation of a human skull above two crossed bones, usually on a black background, said to have been used on pirates' flags. The crossbones are two human thigh bones, and the skull, of course, is the age-old emblem of mortality. Now used as a warning sign, as on a bottle of poison or weed killer.

This flag was intended to terrify the pirates' chosen victims, and it seems to have been eminently successful in this; the literature of the era abounds with accounts of the wanton brutality and cruelty of the "brethren of the coast," and it is little wonder that fat, sluggish merchant ships submitted immediately and meekly to a pirate captain's demand that it heave-to and receive boarders.

In any case, it was as likely as not that the pirates would assault the merchantmen anyway, butchering the crew, raping any female passengers who had the ill fortune to be there, and then throwing everyone overboard to the sharks. It was not unknown for a pirate captain to herd any survivors below decks, secure the hatches, and set fire to the wretched vessel; on one occasion, the vicious ex-privateer Charles Gibbs (who was later caught by Lieutenant Commander Lawrence Kearney, U.S.N., and hanged) burned an entire merchant crew to death by this means.
(See also *Jolly Roger.)*

Sky pilot The sailor's word for the ship's chaplain when carried aboard. A ship is the religious parish of her captain, whether a clergyman is carried or not, and responsibility for the conduct of religious services lies with the captain. He may, of course, co-opt the help of the ship's chaplain or a clergyman passenger. From the fact that a pilot was a person well qualified to guide a vessel through his own particular area; today there are channel pilots, river pilots, harbour pilots, and others. Colloquially, a sky pilot is any clergyman.
(See also *Pilot.)*

Skylark
To skylark about To fool around, to amuse oneself in a light-hearted way, to be merry and to indulge in mild horseplay. Originally nautical, from the custom of boys who went aloft to tend to sails and rigging, frolicking about while still on the yards or shrouds, and almost certainly only in mild weather conditions. One example of skylarking was to return to the deck from aloft by sliding down the backstays, instead of coming down the ratlines on the shrouds by way of the lubber's hole in the crosstrees.

Skylark is from the Old Norse *sky,* shade or shadow, and *lark* is an altered form of an English dialect word *lake,* sport (the word *sky* originally meant cloud; the sense of *sky* meaning the heavens developed later). "The children were so excited at the prospect of the approaching Christmas holidays that they drove their teacher mad with their continual skylarking about in the classroom."

Skyscraper Originally a nautical term for a light-weather sail, set high above the royal sails in very fine weather. It was triangular in shape and was designed to obtain the utmost advantage of every breath of wind. The name was later, in the twentieth century, applied to very tall buildings, particularly those in North American cities.

Slack-jawed "Jaw" is the distance between corresponding points on adjacent strands of a rope. A hard-laid rope will show a shorter jaw than a softer-laid rope. When a rope has been much used and the lay or strands have become slack, the distance between corresponding points will have increased, and the rope is then said to be "slack-jawed" or "long-jawed." It is tempting to conjecture that the metaphor—to be slack-jawed with surprise, to be taken aback, gaping in bewilderment—owes something to the nautical term.

Slant A "slant" in seaman's language is a tack, a direction of movement at an angle to the wind, usually into the wind rather than with it. Wind that is unfavourable but not foul is said to be a "slant wind." The main idea is one of obliqueness, as in a vessel having to proceed indirectly or at an angle to its destination because of unfavourable winds. Used as a metaphor in phrases such as "to get a new slant on things"—that is, to see matters in a different light. In this sense, slant is from the very much older *aslant,* which derives from the Danish *slente* and Swedish *slinta,* to glide, to slip obliquely. *Slant* and *aslant* are both used today in quite similar ways.

"*Lenore* again got away, but the others were catching slants on their own account and keeping inside the handicaps."
—*Field Magazine,* September 4, 1886

Slate
A clean slate

A slate was kept on deck, on which were recorded the courses and distances run during the period of a watch. At the end of the watch, this information was recorded in the deck-log and the slate was then wiped clean so that it was ready for use by the officer keeping the next watch. The phrase has come to mean that past actions and occurrences are to be forgotten and that a new start can be made, i.e., the slate has been wiped clean: "She said that if he was prepared to apologise for his recent behaviour, she would wipe the slate clean and forget the whole sorry episode." (See also *Log. Scrub; To scrub something. Wash-out.)*

Slew A nautical word meaning to turn something on its own axis; to cause to swing round or to swerve awkwardly. Also *slewed,* seaman's slang for drunk. The origin of the word is unknown. It is in wide usage in everyday speech: "When the car hit the oily patch, it slewed across to the other side and slammed into the side of the shop."

Slip From the Anglo-Saxon *slipor,* slippery.

To give one the slip *To slip* is to release the inboard end of mooring lines securing a ship to the bollards or mooring cleats on shore. It was sometimes necessary for a vessel to be able to clear its berth immediately if it were exposed to untoward weather; to do so, the lines were slipped from the bitts inboard. If at anchor and slipping was necessary, the anchor cable was buoyed before letting it slip through the hawse-pipe, so that anchor and cable could be recovered at a later date when conditions were more favourable.

In the metaphorical sense, "to give one the slip" is to steal away unobserved, undetected, so as to elude pursuit: "The bank robber gave the pursuing policeman the slip by disappearing into a large crowd of shoppers."

(See also *Run; To cut and run.)*

To let slip *To slip,* or *to let slip,* is to release the inboard ends of the mooring lines that secure a ship to the bollards or mooring cleats on shore, or to the mooring buoy. This is often done by using a slip rope, the end of which is passed through the ring of the mooring buoy and brought back on board. The ship is then easily freed from her mooring when the rope is let go from inboard and hauled back through the mooring ring.

As an expression, *to let slip* is to say or reveal something quickly but unintentionally: "He let slip that his wife had been criticising me for my talkativeness"; also to release something quickly and efficiently (as in Shakespeare's "... let slip the dogs of war"—*Julius Caesar* III.i). The element common to all these expressions ("to give the slip," "to slip away," etc.) is that of swiftness, speed without fuss.

To slip off/away *To slip off* is to move away quietly, without fuss and bother, so as to give little if any notice of one's departure. From the fact that a vessel could effect a sudden and efficient departure by slipping her cable after having buoyed the anchor, and running to open sea, as in a bad storm while anchored near the shore.

(See also other entries under *Slip.)*

Slops An old name for a loose garment (from Old English *slype, slyp,* and *sloppe,* breeches). In the Royal Navy, *slops* has always meant the articles of clothing, towels, blankets, and such sold from the ship's store, which is known as the "slop-shop," "slop-room," or "slopschest." This clothing was kept by the master of the ship for sale to the crew, since many of the seamen had inadequate or inapproriate clothing when they embarked on a voyage.

Originally, slop clothing referred only to the baggy trousers universally worn by seamen; as their original clothing wore out, their shipboard purchases of slops gradually developed into a sort of unofficial uniform. The system was open to much abuse by dishonest captains and pursers (who pocketed a naval commission and, no doubt, some of the profits of their business). It wasn't until 1857 that an official uniform for seamen was introduced into the navy.

"He had nothing upon him but a pair of slops, and upon his body a goat skin."
—Sir Philip Sidney (1554–1586), English poet, *Arcadia* (1590)

Ashore, *slops* means any general rubbish, such as food scraps or no-longer-serviceable clothing. *Sloppy* is a derivative, also in wide use: "The slops from the restaurant were later sold to the local pig farmers"; "His work is very sloppy indeed; no tradesman could possibly employ him." (See also *Navy blue.)*

Slush fund Also "slush money"; a fund of money for use in political campaigning, as for the production of propaganda, posters, news releases, and the like. The term has gained some notoriety because a slush fund is usually kept secret, out of the public gaze; in twentieth-century politics, the amounts can be very large, leaving many people to wonder about the origin of these monies, and whether they are used for the purposes of bribery, corruption, or other unsavoury ends.

The origin of the term itself, and its meaning, is perfectly innocuous. "Slush" was the fat collected from meat after it had been boiled in the coppers of naval ships. This slush was one of the perquisites of the ship's cook; he usually sold it to the purser, who made it into candles (the "pusser's dip," a long-lasting candle made by repeatedly dipping the central core or wick into the fat and allowing it to congeal).

Slush was also the name given to the grease (usually mixed with linseed oil, tallow soap, and any remaining fat) used for rubbing down masts, spars, and rigging to help preserve them against water-rot. Hence the name for partly melted snow, and for fat, grease, and slops in general that are discarded from the kitchen.

The transition in meaning from an accepted practice in the sailing navy to what has become a questionable practice in present-day politics is a curious one, and bears witness to the pervasive nature of nautical language and customs. The connection is the fact that the refuse—the slush—collected by the "slushy" (the ship's cook) was distasteful, repulsive, to be kept apart, away, hidden (in the sense of securely stowed); hence the secret and somewhat abhorrent nature of political or commercial slush funds, the operators of which do not generally want its existence to be made known or seen. "It was not widely known that the party kept a slush fund for financing propaganda against its political opponents."

Probably from the Norwegian *sluss,* mud, mire. (See also *Kickback.)*

Small-boat names It is interesting that a number of the best-known names of small boats are from Eastern tongues. Some of these are as follows:

Cutter: A small, decked vessel with a bowsprit and one mast, originally with a gaff mainsail and square topsail, and two headsails; nowadays fore-and-aft rigged throughout; from the Indian Malabar coast *catur* and the Sanskrit *chatura,* swift.

Dinghy: Originally a small, open rowing boat used in rivers; now sometimes partly decked and frequently equipped with mainsail and jib; from the Hindi *dengi* or *dingi,* small boat.

Launch: Usually the largest ship's boat of a sailing man-of-war, with mast and sails for short independent cruising. Larger pulling launches were later developed in the steam battleship era. Now the generic name for a small power boat carried as a tender in larger yachts. From the Malay *lancharan.*

The English language is familiar with other exotic boat names, such as the "junk" (Portuguese *junco,* Malay *adjong);* the "sampan" (Chinese *san-pan,* three-board); the "catamaran" (South Indian Tamil *katta,* tie, and *maram,* wood; a small navigable raft); and the "kayak" (Eskimo *oomiak,* man's boat).

Smart money The term used in the old days (seventeenth century) of the sailing navy to describe a pension awarded for wounds acquired on active service. It was issued on a sliding scale according to rank and the extent of the wound. The term refers to the fact that compensation is based on the severity of the wound and the degree of pain (the "smarting") it caused.

Nowadays the expression is a colloquialism that alludes to the knowing way in which informed persons make a prediction or lay a bet, often in opposition to others who are influenced by general opinion: "The smart money was on *Australia II* in the seventh race, because of the inherent advantage she had with her winged keel."

Smasher The name given by sailors to the carronade, a very short, light carriage gun, named from the Carron Iron Founding and Shipping Company in Scotland, where it was invented. These guns, which were in use from about 1785 to 1815, fired a very heavy ball at very close range, and could do considerable damage to the wooden warships of the period.

Colloquially, in British and Australian usage, a smasher is an extremely attractive person, usually female, whose appearance and charms are thought to be devastating.

Smokescreen
To lay a smokescreen

A device of machinery-powered navies of the nineteenth century. A thick cloud of dense funnel smoke is made to screen one's movements from the enemy. The most common means of doing this was by reducing the amount of air supplied to the combustion chambers of the engines, and simultaneously spraying in cold fuel oil. The result was a thick, heavy smoke of oil that was only partly burnt; it lay on the surface of the sea and took a long time to dissipate. Modern naval vessels usually make smoke by chemical means.

Colloquially, *to lay (put up) a smokescreen* is to take steps to conceal one's basic motives from one's opponents or rivals, or from the public at large; any device used to conceal the truth: "His energetic involvement in the union committee's work was simply a smokescreen for his amorous designs on the new secretary."

Smoko A rest from work; a morning or afternoon teabreak, during which a smoke could be enjoyed—a term very widely used in Britain, Australia, and New Zealand. From the practice of forbidding general smoking in sailing ships, and instead restricting it to prescribed areas at specific times. The place where smoking was permitted was usually the galley or the fo'c'sle, in the evening. Sailors would gather for their smoko when they had been told by one of the mates that the smoking lamp had been lit. This nautical custom is now a time-honoured practice in, for example, the building trades in Australia.
(See also *Tailor made.)*

Smuggle

"And I had the greatest reason to believe that not a single article was smuggled by any of our people."

—Captain James Cook (1728–1779), English navigator and explorer, *First Voyage* (1771)

From the Low German *smuggeln,* the act of importing or exporting goods secretly to avoid the payment of duty. Smuggling has a very old history of association with the sea, because of the fact that for thousands of years the sea was by far the main highway of trade between countries. The word is now applied to any act of bringing or taking goods from one place to another surreptitiously.

Snob

"That which we call a snob, by any other name would still be snobbish."
—William Makepeace Thackeray (1811–1863), English novelist, *The Book of Snobs* (1847)

Originally a shoemaker or shoe repairer on board ship, in the eighteenth century. The transition of meaning between that of cobbler and that of someone who affects airs of social importance and exclusiveness is quite obscure. This latter sense—that of a social upstart—is a mid-nineteenth-century development.

Snore
To snore along

To be sailing on a comfortable reach, with a fair and steady wind, making good progress. Used loosely to describe easy and comfortable progress, growth, development, etc.: "His project—to adapt bananas to growing in salt water—was snoring along quite comfortably."
(See also *Bone; To have a bone in her teeth.*)

Snottie

Snottie is naval slang for a midshipman, an apprentice officer. In the early days of fighting sail, midshipmen went to sea at a very early age, often as youngsters barely newly breeched, and their nickname is said to come from their habit of wiping their noses on their sleeves. Tradition has it that Nelson ordered three buttons to be sewn on the sleeves of midshipmen to prevent this unseemly practice.

To be snotty is to be angry, querulous, easily irritated; from the fact that the extreme youth of the nautical snottie made him susceptible to temper and tears—until the unerring hand of naval discipline showed him the value of accepting all things to do with nautical life: "He was very snotty with the foreman for having put in an adverse report on his ability as a charge hand."

Snotty

See *Snottie.*

Snub

From the Old Norse *snubba,* to check or rebuke; essentially to shorten, as in the nautical usage to suddenly stop a rope or cable from running out any further by taking extra turns around a bollard, etc., or by applying a cable stopper or some other means of braking its movement. A vessel snubs when she is brought up short by her anchor while pitching in a seaway.

Metaphorically, when we snub someone we give a sudden check or restraint to an assumed acquaintanceship or friendship; the disdain and contempt expressed in the snub puts a sudden end to further social intercourse: "He asked her for the next dance, but she snubbed him with a curt refusal."

Snug

Found in nautical expressions such as "to make all snug," "to snug down," meaning to be properly secured, fixed, all in order, the whole ship prepared to meet a gale, especially

"We snugged up for the night. . . ."
—*Field Magazine,* December 9, 1885

by reducing sail. Derived from the Swedish *snygg* and Danish *snyg,* tidy; the Dutch *snugger,* sprightly, neatly; and of more recent influence from the Middle Dutch *snuggher,* smart, shipshape. Widely used in everyday speech as "snug," "snugly," "snugness," and others, to mean comfortable, cosy, compact, well fitting, as in "a snug cottage," "a snug fortune," and so on.

So long The sailor's farewell: "goodbye till we meet again." The expression was an integral part of the sailor's vocabulary; Captain Frank Bullen ends his *The Cruise of the Cachalot* (1910) with it. Now a common part of the landlubber's language: "So long; I'll see you when I come back this way next month."

Sod's law The sailor's name for the assertion that unfortunate things always happen at the worst time and in the worst place (the landsman recognises this as a variant of Murphy's Law); sometimes known as the Law of Imbuggerance. Also celebrated in "Sod's Opera," which is an impromptu ship's concert usually highly libelous of authority.

The phrase almost certainly stems from the seaman's ingrained distaste for things unnatural. The word is from *Sodom,* the ancient biblical city near the Dead Sea, destroyed by fire from heaven because of the wicked and unnatural practices of its inhabitants. *Sod* is an abbreviation for *sodomy,* and—very curiously—seamen have an abhorrence of this practice. In the days of the sailing navy, it was an offence punishable by hanging; the men themselves were as likely to exact retribution from the guilty person as were the authorities.

I say "curiously" because it is well established that prolonged and enforced isolation in an all-male society, cut off from access to females, usually encourages homosexual activity on a scale far beyond the norm for ordinary society; confinement in prison is one such example. Yet seamen never generally indulged in sodomy; there were no doubt a few cases from time to time, but given the close quarters of their living conditions, the long periods of all-male company, and the often lengthy periods of sea-keeping between ports, it is perhaps surprising that seamen, at least in the days of sail, weren't more inclined to homosexual practices.

Probably the open nature of the living quarters in the fo'c'sle mitigated against this. It must also be remembered that the sailor of bygone days was an extraordinarily conventional, traditional, God-fearing man, generally of straitlaced principles and beliefs. His language might have been fierce to the ear, but for the seaman it was just that—only words. Hence the force of the expression *sod's law;* it represents a strong exclamation of annoyance or disgust.

SOS The internationally agreed distress call made by a ship requiring assistance; it was adopted in 1908. These three letters were chosen because in Morse Code they were easy to read and transmit: three dots, three dashes, three dots. These letters, contrary to popular belief, do not stand for "save our souls" or "save our ship." The expression now means any call for help, as in "Alan Bond sent out an SOS to the Australian public in 1983 for help in providing new sails for his America's Cup challenge yacht."
(See also *CQD. Mayday. Morse Code.)*

Sound
To sound somebody out

"His Holiness, however, on being sounded on the subject by the Spanish Ambassador in Rome, declined."
—*The Evening Standard* (English newspaper), October 3, 1885

To sound, from the ancient Sanskrit *sond,* messenger, is to determine the depth of water beneath the vessel's keel, using either the hand lead line or, in more recent times, electronic devices, such as sonar. *To sound somebody out* implies that one is going to plumb his or her depths, as it were, to determine what he or she thinks of a certain matter; to obtain an opinion, often so as to solicit approval or cooperation. "We sounded out the club secretary on the advisability of running a sweepstake to raise funds for the children's Christmas party."
(See also *Fathom; To fathom something.)*

Span
Spick and span

"In the same doings, to make a spick-and-span new world."
—Sir Walter Scott (1771–1832), *Redgauntlet* (1824)

Of nautical origin, meaning quite new, entirely new, of recent manufacture. In the days of wooden sailing ships, a "spic" was a nail or spike, and a "span" was a chip of wood just struck from a length of timber. A "spick and span" new ship was therefore one in which every nail and chip was new, as from being freshly built. Colloquially, to be all neat, clean, bright, and tidy, exactly as in brand new: "She took great pride in keeping her room in spick-and-span condition."

From Old Norse *span,* chip, and Swedish *spik,* nail, spike. Other versions are "span-new," "bran-span-new," and "bran-spanking-new," which were once very common expressions in Australia and England.

Spanish English seamen dealt in a very derogatory fashion with the Dutch, as the result of the Anglo-Dutch wars in the seventeenth century. They treated the Spanish almost equally severely in their coining of phrases that reflect the hostility that once marked relations between England and Spain,

> "My father dear he is not here;
> he seeks the Spanish main."
> —Richard Harris Barham (1788–1845), English cleric and novelist, *The Ingoldsby Legends* (1840)

warfare at sea as both nations strove to control the world's trade routes.

Some examples of these expressions are:

Spanish reef: A method of reefing topsails by simply lowering the yard; considered very slovenly by British seamen.
Spanish worm: A nail concealed in a piece of wood.
To walk Spanish: To walk on tiptoe, by being lifted and pushed by a more powerful person, as in frogmarching; from the way pirates treated their captives on the Spanish Main.

(See also *Dutch. Mare; To ride the Spanish mare.)*

Spanker See *Spanking.*

Spanking
To be spanking along

Spanking means brisk, lively. The "spanker" is the fore-and-aft sail set on a gaff on the mizzenmast of a three-masted vessel, or on the aftermost mast of a vessel with four or more masts, such as a four-masted barque (or "bark") or the five-masted full-rigged ship, the remarkable *Preussen.* Vessels with one or two masts do not carry a spanker as such.

This sail was set principally to take advantage of a following wind; it proved to be so useful in this regard, and also as an aid to steering, that it replaced entirely the mizzen

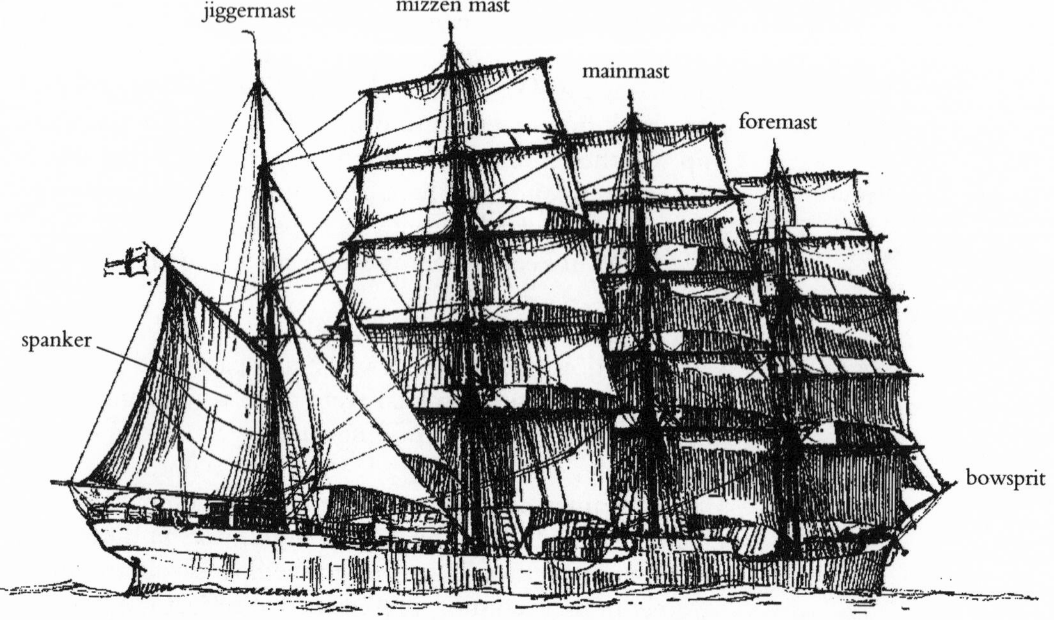

A Four-masted Barque (Bark)

"If you are not mine by entreaty, there are four spanking greys ready harnessed in Cropland Park, here, that shall whisk us to town in a minute."

—George Colman (1762–1836), English dramatist, *Poor Gentleman,* cited in the *Universal Dictionary of the English Language* (1897)

course (the lowest square sail once set on the mizzen mast, corresponding to the mainsail on the mainmast).

Hence, the phrase *to be spanking along* is, both nautically and colloquially, to be moving at a brisk and lively pace, with all stops out. A wind producing this turn of events is known as a "spanking breeze" or a "spanker." From its imitative relationship with a resonant slap; but also cognate with the Scottish *spang,* to move rapidly, and also possibly the Portuguese *espancar,* to strike.
(See also *Booming; To boom along.)*

Spar

The general term for a rounded length of timber on board ship, such as a yard, gaff, boom, or mast. Now used to refer to any principal lateral member of an engineering framework, as in the components of a derrick, or the wing of an aeroplane. From the Middle English *sparre,* and ultimately the Icelandic *sperra,* rafter.

Spick
Spick and span

See *Span; Spick and span.*

Spike
To spike someone's guns

From the Latin *spica,* ear of corn, and thence the pointed nail which was originally a nautical implement, long nails being once produced only for the construction of ships. *To spike a gun* is to drive a big nail heavily into the touch-hole of the gun, thus preventing the powder from being fired. The earlier and now obsolete term for this was the French *accloy,* to prick, to spike. A gun would be spiked if it was evident that the enemy was going to gain control of it, such as when a crew might be forced to abandon a vessel in the face of a superior force.

"... which they received with a great deal of indifference, except hatchets and spike-nails."

—Captain James Cook (1728–1779), English navigator and explorer, *Second Voyage* (1777)

Colloquially, *to spike someone's guns* is to render that person's plans useless or abortive; to frustrate the scheme that he or she has been preparing: "He planned to disrupt the meeting with some outrageous accusations, but we spiked his guns by holding it on a different night without telling him of the change."

Spinnaker

A very large, somewhat balloon-shaped, three-cornered sail set forward of the mast, usually with a boom to the windward side, and employed when the wind is aft of the beam. Handling a spinnaker requires a good deal of skill, but the effort is worth it: the sail is a powerful one in light to moderate breezes. Early spinnakers tended to gyrate wildly when running before a freshening breeze, but sailmakers have introduced designs that have overcome this problem.

The name is from the yacht *Sphinx,* which first introduced this sail to yachting during a race in the Solent in the 1870s.

"Both hauled up spinnakers as they crossed the line."
—*Field Magazine,* October 3, 1885

The crew of this boat called the sail a "sphinxer," and the word has undergone the usual process of linguistic corruption to become *spinnaker.* It is also likely that the modern form has been influenced by *spanker,* a fore-and-aft sail with boom and gaff, and set on the mizzenmast of a large sailing vessel.

Spirit
To spirit away

Originally a phrase in nautical usage, to mean the abduction of young boys in England for transportation to the West Indies plantations, where they were put to work as slaves. The reference was to the fact that they were taken in secret, as though they had been supernaturally removed.

The expression is used as a metaphor carrying much the same ground-sense: to carry away or remove something or someone secretly and suddenly, as if by magic: "The organiser of the car rally left the building by the back door and was spirited away before the disgruntled drivers and navigators could accost him."
(See also *Kidnap.*)

Spithead nightingale

The British sailor's nickname for the boatswain's mates (pronounced "boe-sun," often spelled "bosun" in nautical literature); from the fact that the mates have the duty of piping all orders to the crew with calls on their pipes. *Spithead pheasant* is seaman's slang for a kipper.
(See also *Pipe; To pipe down.*)

Spruce
To be spruced up

Spruce means to be smart in dress or appearance; to be trim, neat, dapper. It is from the Old French *pruce,* and German *Preussen,* Prussia, and was originally used as a description of Prussian leather, from which particularly neat and smart-looking jerkins were made. The word has come to us via the seamen of the Hanseatic League, a merchant trading confederation of North German towns that led to the growth of an enormously powerful maritime trade monopoly that spanned the years 1240 to about 1600, and which included major ports in sea-trading nations around the world.

"Now my spruce companions. . . ."
—William Shakespeare (1564–1616), *The Taming of the Shrew,* act 4, scene 1

Other commodities introduced to the English-speaking world by the Hanse merchants were "spruce beer" (made from the leaves of the spruce tree) and "spruce board" (from the tree, named after Prussia). Used in such expressions as "He was told to spruce himself up for the meeting."

Squeegee

The familiar rubber-edged "broom" used for sweeping water from windows, vehicle windscreens, and the like, after they have been washed. Originally a nautical word, with the variation "squilgee"; it referred to the swab used for washing and cleaning the decks, and is a corruption of "squeege," which itself is a colloquialism for "squeeze."

Stand From the Anglo-Saxon *standan,* and common to the Teutonic languages; derived from the Latin *stare,* to stay, to be at, and the Sanskrit *stha,* to be at. Found in a number of originally nautical expressions, which in turn have become metaphors of everyday speech.

To be at a stand To be puzzled, unsure, not knowing what to do next; derived from the phrase *to be brought up all standing.* (See also *Standing; To be brought up all standing.)*

To stand by A common expression, as in "Stand by for further instructions," "Stand by for the weather report"; to wait in a state of readiness, be ready to give assistance, if needed. From the Anglo-Saxon *stanan,* with similar cognates found in other Teutonic tongues.

"Now, brother Richard, will you stand by us?"
—William Shakespeare (1564–1616), *Henry VI, Part 3,* act 4, scene 1

A very common word in nautical language; found also in nautical expressions such as "to stand in," "standing block," "to stand off and on," "to stand on," "to stand up," and others. It is interesting that a "standby"—which is now a supporter, an adherent, something kept in readiness, a fall-back—was originally an attendant ship, a smaller vessel that stood by and kept in company with a larger vessel, to act as messenger, escort, signal repeater, and the like.

To stand off

"Such behaviour frights away friendship, and makes it stand off in dislike and aversion."
—Jeremy Collier (1650–1726), *On Friendship,* cited in the *Universal Dictionary of the English Language* (1897)

Nautically, *to stand off* means to keep clear, stay at a distance. A vessel stands off the land when she raises it and then keeps her distance from it, sometimes sailing away from it. In everyday speech, *to stand off* is to keep apart, at a distance; to come no nearer: "She was always inclined to stand off from the crowd whenever she attended a social function." (See also *Off and on. Stand; To stand by.)*

To stand on A vessel *stands on* when she continues on course toward the land, or toward any other destination. Colloquially, *to stand on* means to stick to ceremony ("to stand on ceremony"), to insist on things being done properly, to be determined; not to deviate, as a vessel does not deviate when she maintains her set course.
(See also *Off and on.)*

Standby See *Stand; To stand by* for a discussion of the background of this expression.

Standing
To be brought up all standing

A vessel is *brought up all standing* when she is forced to lose way suddenly because her sails have been put aback by a sudden change of wind. Also said of a person who has been so taken by surprise that she is at a loss to know what to do to recover her equilibrium: "He was brought up all standing when his young son asked him where babies came from."

Stand-offish From the nautical term *to stand off* (to keep away from the shore or from another vessel). When a ship nears the land but wishes to wait for clearer conditions, or for a pilot, she will sail alternately toward and away from her destination until she is able to proceed safely; that is, she will stand "off and on."

The expression is applied colloquially to people: *to be stand-offish* is to be unfriendly, unsociable, snobbish, in the sense of deliberately keeping away from one's fellows: "The neighbours were rather stand-offish when we first moved into our new house."
(See also *Off and on.)*

Start From the Anglo-Saxon *styrtan,* to move with a bound. There were two main usages on board ship. In the first usage, to ease a sheet or rope is to "start" it, and when a cask is opened or a ship's plank has worked loose, each is said to have "started." The second usage refers to the practice, once widespread in the sailing navy, of hitting or "starting" the crew with canes or rope ends to get them moving smartly at their work.

This method of encouraging alacrity among the men was not eradicated by law until the early nineteenth century, and even then it lasted for a long time after that on the American Cape Horn clippers. The phrase is found in many applications to do with movement of the person, especially movement associated with surprise, an involuntary jerk as in alarm, and so on.

"You must look to see another plank in the State-vessel start ere long."
—Robert Southey (1774–1843), English poet and essayist, *Letters,* cited in the *Universal Dictionary of the English Language* (1897)

Staunch
To be a staunch supporter Sometimes as "stanch." From the Old French *estanche,* watertight. Found in metaphors such as "staunch supporter"—one who is firm, steadfast in principle: "She was a staunch supporter of the party, regardless of its dismal performance in the political arena." Also "to staunch (or stanch) the flow"; to prevent, to stop the flow.

"Build me straight, O worthy Master, Staunch and strong, a goodly vessel."
—Henry Wadsworth Longfellow (1807–1882), American poet, *The Building of the Ship,* cited in the *Universal Dictionary of the English Language* (1897)

Stave A back-formation from the plural of *staff,* which is from the Anglo-Saxon *staef.*
(See also other entries under *Stave.)*

To stave in *To stave in* something is to break it up. Specifically, it means to break in the planking of a vessel to sink her, or to drive in the head of a cask, especially if it contains spirits, to prevent the crew getting at it in the case of

"The feared disorders that might ensue thereof have been an occasion that divers times all the wine in the city hath been staved."
—George Sandys (1578–1644), English poet and traveler, *Travels* (1615)

shipwreck (otherwise the men would become unmanageable). A boat is stove in, a cask is staved in. Staves are the component "planks" of a cask after it has been dismantled or knocked down.
(See also *Knock; To knock down.)*

To stave off

To stave off is to keep the boat's side away from a jetty or some floating object by thrusting with a pole, boathook, or some similar implement. The intention is to prevent collision. As a metaphor, the expression carries the same meaning: to keep off or ward off, by force or evasion or some other means, some undesired event: "We staved off bankruptcy by selling every asset that we possessed." *Stave* here is related to *staff,* from the Old English *staef,* stick or pole.
(See also *Stave; To stave in.)*

Steady as she goes

The order given to the steersman, when sailing a particular course, to keep that course. Loosely applied as a colloquialism to a person engaged in performing any activity that requires some forethought and concentration.

Steam

From the Anglo-Saxon *steam,* vapour, fumes; "steam-boat" is recorded from 1787.

Full steam ahead

With vigour; to go ahead unchecked, without faltering; as in a business decision being made after considering all the problems and obstacles: "The firm's building programme was going full steam ahead, despite financial setbacks from the recession." From the age of steam, ushered in by *Sirius,* the first ship to cross the Atlantic from Britain to America in 1838. Nautically, the expression means to get up a full head of steam in the boilers and to deliver maximum power to the propeller shaft.

"He steamed into the station at the usual speed."
—*The Daily Chronicle* (English newspaper), October 19, 1885

To be steamed up

To be excited or angry over something; to experience the sensation of having a full pressure of emotion in the head or heart, as it were. From the days when steam replaced sail; a steamship that had a full working pressure ("head") of steam in its boilers, available for immediate delivery to the propulsion machinery, was said to be "steamed up."

To blow off steam; to let off steam

Colloquially, to give vent to anger, to work off one's feelings or energy, in the same way that steam pressure is released from the cylinder or boiler of a steam engine: "The children had a great time letting off steam at the Christmas party." It is difficult to judge whether it was the steam railroad locomotive or the early steam-powered vessels that first gave rise to this expression; logic suggests that

"Moving east on a north-easterly track, a little south of steamer-lanes."
—*St. James's Gazette* (English periodical), April 6, 1887

the land-based vehicle probably deserves the honours here, although it is certainly true that in the heyday of steamship travel, the wail of the ship's hooter or siren was a common-enough sound in the port cities of the world.

To get up steam To summon energy for a special, concerted effort; to call on all of one's reserves. From the heyday of the steam engine, which, more than any other invention, gave rise to the Industrial Revolution. The phrase is essentially a nautical one, although the operation, of course, is not originally nautical. *To get up steam* is to charge the boilers with a full load of wood, coal, or other fuel until the maximum pressure of steam is available for delivery to the propeller shaft.

Steer
To steer clear Ultimately from the Icelandic *styre,* to guide, and found in similar forms in most of the Scandinavian and Germanic languages. Nautically, the phrase means to avoid some known danger, such as a reef. Colloquially, it carries the same force: to adopt some course of action that will enable one to avoid something undesirable: "If you want to steer clear of trouble, don't get married."

To steer a safe course See *Course; To chart a safe course.*

Stem
From stem to stern The stem of a vessel is the upright timber at the bow into which the side timbers (or planks, or plates) are worked. The stern is the after-most or rearmost section of the vessel. A ship is affected "stem to stern" when, for example, she is hit by a heavy sea and the resulting crash is felt the whole length of the hull. A "stem-to-stern" search for contraband (drugs, for example) would involve examining every nook and cranny within the ship, from one end of the vessel to the other.

Similarly, the use of the phrase as a metaphor implies the wholeness or totality of the effects of some event upon a person; for example, the phrase *to be shaken stem to stern* is to be thoroughly agitated or disturbed by something: "She was shaken stem to stern by an official letter requesting that she explain certain anomalies in her last tax return."

"... armed the stemme and beake-head of the ship with sharpe tines and piles of brass."
—Philemon Holland (1552–1637), English scholar, *Pliny* (1601)

Stern
A stern aspect Related to *steer,* from the Old Norse *stjorn,* steering. The stern of a vessel is its hind- or aftermost part, the external rear section of a ship's hull. It is usually a quite bluff conclusion to a vessel's lines, and this abruptness of appearance is reflected in the phrase *a stern aspect,* meaning an angry or at least unfriendly and forbidding face or

appearance: "Heathcliffe's house in *Wuthering Heights* presents a very stern aspect to the Yorkshire weather."
(See also *Starboard* in appendix 2.)

Stevedore From the Spanish *estivador, estivzar,* to stow a cargo. A stevedore is a docker employed in the working of cargo in the holds of a merchant ship when she is being loaded or unloaded in port. Known by this name in America (also called a "longshoreman" in that country), but commonly called "wharfies" or "lumpers" in Australia.
(See also *Longshoreman. Lumper. Rouse.)*

Stinkpot Originally an earthenware pot filled with gunpowder and other combustible materials, and fitted with a fuse. They were used against an enemy vessel when attempts were being made to board it. The fuse of the stinkpot was lit and the whole apparatus thrown onto the deck of the enemy vessel, where the noise, flame, and thick acrid smoke created such confusion that the raiding party was able to rush aboard and overcome the enemy. Stinkpots were commonly used in the eighteenth and nineteenth centuries.

The term is loosely used nowadays to describe any piece of machinery that gives off an offensive odour; in particular, among the yachting fraternity, a "stinkpot" is any vessel that carries a motor, especially a diesel engine or a two-stroke outboard. *Stinkpot* is also a colloquialism for a person who smells strongly and badly, like a fisherman just returned from a successful fishing trip.

Stitch
Every stitch she can carry

The maximum amount of sail ("stitch") that a vessel can carry in the prevailing weather conditions at the time. An old nautical expression, still applied to sailing craft, and used colloquially as an exhortation to greater effort in some enterprise.

Stocks
To be on the stocks

The stocks (always plural) are the structure on which the ship and her launching cradle are built; naturally, the stocks slope down in the direction of launching. *To be on the stocks,* nautically speaking, is to be under construction, in preparation.

"Farewell; you know I have other business upon the stocks."
—John Dryden (1631–1700), English poet and playwright, *Love Triumphant* (1694)

As a metaphor, to have something "on the stocks" is to be partway through a project, to have unfinished business in hand: "The government has announced that a new plan for expanding the car industry is now on the stocks."
(See also *Beam; To be on one's beam ends. Hard; Hard up. High; High and dry.)*

Stop

"I'll stop my ears against the mermaid's song."
—William Shakespeare (1564–1616), *The Comedy of Errors,* act 3, scene 2

From the Anglo-Saxon *stoppian,* to plug up, and derived from the Latin *stuppare,* to plug up. The etymological development of the word points to it being an early nautical loan word from the Dutch *stoppen* and the Low German *stopfen.*

The current nautical meaning is to plug a leak in a seam or joint, and to lightly tie up a sail or awning with light line. All the meanings of *stop* and its compounds spring naturally from the ground-sense, as in "stopgap," for example: "We put him in as number three batsman, but it was only a stopgap measure to wear out their fast bowlers."

Stopper
To put a stopper on things

A stopper is a short length of rope or chain, firmly secured at one end, used as a temporary measure to take the strain off a cable that is under tension; as in "anchor-stopper," "deck-stopper," "sheet-stopper." Colloquially, a stopper is anything that puts a stop to something, for example, a sudden rainstorm spoiling a barbecue party. "Her decision to get the house redecorated put a stopper on his plans for a fishing trip up the coast with his friends."

Storm
To ride out the storm

A ship can usually lie more or less comfortably in severe weather by selecting just sufficient engine power to maintain steerage, or by setting small, very strong sails that will enable her to lie to the wind and waves without excessive rolling or leeway. Sometimes a sea anchor, a small and very strongly built drogue, will enable a vessel to lie-to in relative comfort and safety. It is generally otherwise very dangerous for a vessel to try to ride out a storm by lying to an anchor, because extreme weather conditions will cause most anchors to drag, or possibly the cable to part. For this reason, prudent mariners always put to sea if a gale is in the offing and there is no protected anchorage nearby.

Colloquially, *to ride out a storm* is to take the buffets and blows of a situation, to endure without damage; as in a marital conflict, overspending the family budget, and so on: "The company director refused to resign; he was determined to ride out the storm that had arisen over his recent share market dealings."

Stow it

"On Wednesday we had finished the stowage of the hold."
—Captain James Cook (1728–1779), English navigator and explorer, *Third Voyage* (1784)

Sailors' slang for shut up, stop it. From the maritime usage, to arrange goods compactly in a ship's hold or between decks; more generally, to put away, stop, as in "stow the hammocks," or "stow that talk." From the Dutch *stouwen,* to pack or press in.
(See also *Pipe; To pipe down.)*

Stowaway A comparatively recent term from the nautical world; a stowaway is a person who hides himself or herself on board a vessel in the hope of either escaping from the country undetected, or of getting a free ride to the ship's next port. It would seem that most stowaway attempts are unsuccessful; there are not many places on board a ship today where a person could comfortably and safely keep hidden from the crew at all times and in all weathers.

"The people who make stowaways of themselves are usually of the most hopeless sort."
—*The Daily Telegraph* (English newspaper), September 5, 1885

Perhaps the only really successful cases are those that depend upon some member of the crew for food, water, and shelter. Stowaways who are caught are either confined to a locked cabin or put to work on board ship, usually without pay; in virtually all cases, they are handed over to the police at the next port of call.

The term now applies to stowing away on any kind of transport. (There are a few recorded instances of individuals hiding themselves in the wheel bays of jet liners; some have died by falling out, others perished from the extreme cold, and some died from being crushed by the wheel-retracting mechanism.)

A stowaway in the colloquial sense is a person (or animal, bird, and so on) getting a free ride or free benefits of some sort: "When we finally arrived at the picnic spot in the hills, we found that our dog had sneaked into the car as an uninvited stowaway."

Straggler The old-time description of a deserting seaman, one who has had "R" for "Run" put alongside his name on his ship's muster-roll. Civilians-at-large were paid a reward, plus conduct money, for reporting him to the authorities, and the seaman himself was charged with "straggling," the equivalent of desertion. Nowadays the word means simply one who falls behind, who fails to keep up with others; also to wander about, ramble: "The last straggler in the city-to-beach marathon crossed the finish line just before sunset." From a Middle English combination of *stray* and *draggle (drag + le).*

Straits
To be in dire straits

"The strikes continue, and the people are in great straits."
—*The Weekly Echo* (English periodical), September 5, 1885

A strait is a narrow passage of water connecting two large bodies of water, as in lakes, bays, or seas (e.g., the Straits of Gibraltar connect the Mediterranean and the North Atlantic). *Dire* is from the Latin *dirus,* danger. The phrase means to be in a position attended by great fear or danger, as a sailing vessel would often find herself in great difficulty or danger if unable to navigate or manoeuvre through a narrow passage of water because of adverse wind or tide. The original spelling was "streights," as applied to the

Mediterranean: "Without their specialist forward player, the team found itself in dire straits in the final quarter of the game."

Stranded
To be stranded

"A whale, with a tongue seventeen feet long and seven feet broad, had been stranded near Aberdeen."

—Thomas Babington Macaulay (1800–1859), English essayist and historian, *History of England* (1848)

"Then came shallow water where both canoes and hopes were well-nigh stranded."

—*Scribner's Magazine,* August 1887

A vessel is "stranded" when she is driven ashore, or onto a shoal, by bad weather; she is then in a helpless—and sometimes hopeless—position. The term comes from the old name *strand* for land bordering the sea or other water; the Strand in London was so named because it once occupied an extent of the shore of the River Thames. *To be stranded* in the metaphorical sense is to be abandoned, as by a friend, or as when one hasn't the fare to catch the last bus home. From the Anglo-Saxon *strand,* and the Old Norse *strond,* border, coast. "She found herself stranded in Massillon, Ohio, after the wedding because of the bus strike."
(See also *High; High and dry.)*

Strap

Originally a nautical word, as a dialectical variation of *strop.*
(See also *Strop. Stroppy; To be stroppy.)*

Stream
To go against the stream

A stream is a body of water flowing in a channel or bed, as a river or creek; it is also a steady, definable current in a river or ocean (e.g., the Gulf Stream in the Caribbean Sea). Hence *to go against the stream* is, figuratively, to oppose public opinion, to go against whatever is the prevailing practice or mode of thought; as the Flat Earth believers go against the stream of generally accepted thinking concerning the sphericity of the earth.
(See also *Tide; To stem the tide.)*

Stretch
To stretch out

To stretch out was to sail close-hauled while crowding on every stitch of sail possible; hence the sailor's slang *to stretch off the land,* meaning a short nap. This derives from the old sailing days when the crew of a ship tacking along a coast could relax their attention a little when the vessel was stretching on the seaward leg. "Stretch out" was also the order given by the officer in charge of a pulling boat when he wanted his men to put every effort into their work; to put their backs into it.

Loosely, *to stretch out* is to draw out or extend oneself to one's full length or extent, as in "to stretch oneself out on the ground"; also to extend or force beyond the usual limits, to strain: "His accounts of his fishing exploits were apt to stretch the facts." From the Anglo-Saxon *streccan,* strong, vigorous.
(See also *Back; To put one's back into it. Stretcher.)*

Stretcher Originally a piece of wood fixed sideways across the bottom of a pulling boat against which the rowers could brace their feet; also a short length of wood used for spreading apart the corners of each end of a hammock when it was being used. The modern sense of the word—a light folding bed, such as a camp stretcher or first-aid stretcher—derives from the nautical ground-sense of hauling taut, or of drawing out or extending oneself, as in rowing.
(See also *Stretch; To stretch out.)*

"... was insensible for a short time, and had to be brought back on a stretcher to the enclosure."
—*Field Magazine,* September 4, 1886

Strike
Strike me dead! An exclamation of surprise, dismay; an oath. Sailors' slang for thin, wishy-washy beer. From the Anglo-Saxon *strican,* to go, to advance swiftly; to strike in both the physical sense and in the sense of industrial unrest. In nautical use, the term *to strike* means to surrender, indicated by the lowering (or "striking") of a warship's colours; *to strike sail* is to lower sail, usually the topsail, in saluting other ranking warships.
(See also *Sail; To strike sail/to strike the colours.)*

Strop A piece of rope spliced into a circular wreath, used to surround the body of a block so that it can be suspended; also to form a sling for heavy articles that must be hoisted. Another usage refers to the oiled leather strap on which one sharpened a straight razor.

Strop is the older form of *strap;* from the Anglo-Saxon *strop* and the Latin *struppus,* garland, thong.
(See also *Strap. Stroppy; To be stroppy.)*

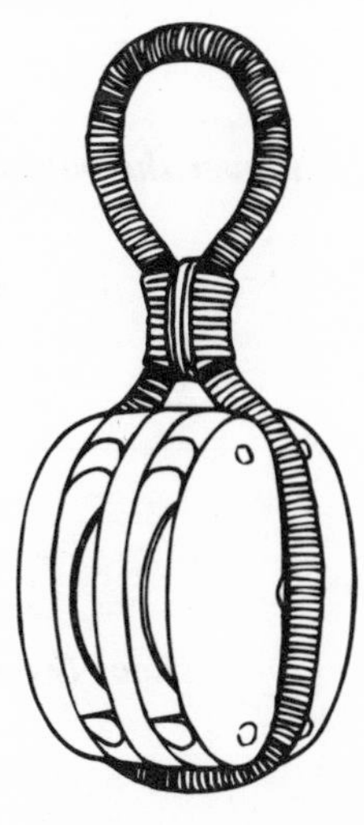

"Stropping a razor seems a very simple affair."
—*Field Magazine,* March 19, 1887

Stroppy
To be stroppy A sailor's way of saying that someone has become irritable, angry, or upset at something. The usage probably derives from the fact that a strop, in its many forms, is generally used as a reinforcement for the shell of a block, or a length of rope worked into a continuous sling for hoisting heavy gear. Strops generally are required to take considerable strain, and a person said to be "stroppy" is one who is feeling the adverse effects of some situation beyond his or her immediate control, such as weather, romance, work, and such.
(See also *Strop.)*

Stuff A word that has enjoyed a remarkably wide sense-development. Originally it meant "tow" (pronounced "toe"), the fibre of flax, hemp, or jute, prepared for spinning. This sense is still preserved in the nautical term *small stuff,* meaning any yarn, cord, or line less than one inch in circumference; and in *stuff,* meaning a composition of materials used to smear or pay the sides and bottom on a ship as a protection against worm. The mixture usually included turpentine, varnish, tar, oils, and various other ingredients. The stuffing-box of a propeller shaft (or piston rod on a steam engine) is an adjustable gland containing (originally) teased-out oakum which, when compressed by the gland nut, provided a reasonably watertight or steamtight fit or joint.

"We are such stuff as dreams are made on."
—William Shakespeare (1564–1616), *The Tempest,* act 4, scene 1

The word now refers simply to the material of which anything is made. In the leather and fabric industries, *stuff* has a particular meaning, but in everyday usage the meaning varies widely, often being determined only by context: "Bring me that stuff that's lying on the table." From the Old French *estoffer,* to provide, and ultimately from the Latin *stuppa,* tow.

Sun
The sun over the yardarm

Of obvious nautical origin, but still frequently used by landsmen to indicate that it is time for a morning drink. The saying derives from the assumption that in northern latitudes the sun would show above the foreyard of a ship by 1100 hours (an hour before noon). In many ships this time coincided approximately with the forenoon "standeasy," when many officers would slip below for their first drink of the day.
(See also *Bay; Over the bay. Hawse; To freshen the hawse.)*

To shoot the sun

An expression well-known to seamen, meaning to take an altitude (a vertical angle) of the sun with a sextant, a navigational instrument invented for that purpose. *Shoot* is from the need to aim the sextant's eyepiece or telescope at the sun, suitably protected by shaded lenses by means of a simple system of reflecting mirrors.

Sundowner

Originally a slang name for a bullying officer in a ship, from the practice of many sailing-ship masters' giving shore leave to their crew only up to the time of sunset; any seaman returning to his ship after sundown could count on a severe dressing-down from the officer of the watch. In the former British colonies of Africa and Asia, a sundowner is an alcoholic drink traditionally taken at sundown.

In Australia in the nineteenth and early twentieth centuries, a sundowner was a swagman, a tramp who, when traveling from one farm to another seeking work, generally made it

his business to arrive at the homestead too late to begin a job but just in time to claim rations for the evening meal; traditionally, this was never refused. The practice was naturally an unpopular one with the landowner, but the conventions of the outback required that the sundowner be given some food and lodgings for the night, even if only in the shed (barn). The word is also used occasionally in this way in the United States.
(See also *Bucko.)*

Supercargo Earlier as *supracargo,* from the Spanish *sobrecargo,* literally overcargo. In fact, the English form is an abbreviation and inversion of *cargo superintendent,* who as a representative of the ship's owner traveled on board the vessel and handled the commercial business in connection with the cargo during the voyage. As a nautical term, it has now become almost obsolete. In everyday speech, *supercargo* refers to anyone who is an addition—usually unneeded—to a group, team, or project; the same as a supernumerary.

Superstitions Possibly no body of men has harboured as many superstitions as have sailors. Perhaps the dreadful conditions that pertained to their calling made it necessary for the seaman to wrap himself round with a multiplicity of talismans to ward off evil. Some of the better-known sailors' superstitions are listed here; it is interesting to note the religious content of many of these beliefs.

"Superstition is the weakness of the human mind; it is inherent in that mind; it has always been, and always will be."
—Frederick the Great (1712–1786), Letter to Voltaire, September 13, 1766

Albatross: Sailors believed that the souls of their departed comrades inhabited that graceful bird of the Southern Ocean, the albatross; hence, to kill one was considered a crime, and the wretch who did so was subject to fearful penalties. Coleridge's *The Rime of the Ancient Mariner* is a graphic account of what happened to a sailor who, in ignorance, shot an albatross with his crossbow.

Apparitions: To sight the *Flying Dutchman* would result in shipwreck at least, death at worst. St. Elmo's Fire, the curious fireball of lightning that is well-known to mariners, was sometimes seen as a benevolent warning of perils to come; at other times it was an omen of death for a particular person.

Bucket: To lose a bucket over the side was considered little less than a calamity. It will be remembered that "silly buckets" are mentioned in Coleridge's *Rime of the Ancient Mariner;* the word *silly* meant blessed, from the German *selig,* happy, blessed.

Castor and Pollux: Two stars in the constellation Gemini; of great interest to early sailors because, according to myth, they were the twin sons of Zeus. They joined Jason in his quest for the Golden Fleece; during this expedition, a violent storm beset the ship, whereupon two flames were seen to play around the heads of the twin brothers and the storm abated at once. Because of this incident, great faith was placed in the power of the twins to protect sailors at sea, and the flames, also called St. Elmo's Fire, are still widely known by sailors as Castor and Pollux. Seamen would pray to the twins during a storm, and navigators revered them for clearing the Hellespont and the neighbouring seas of pirates.

Departure: Friday is still widely held to be an ill-omened day of departure, because of the fact that Jesus' crucifixion took place on a Friday.

"Superstition brings the gods into even the smallest matters.
—Livy, *History of Rome*, cited in H. L. Mencken's *Dictionary of Quotations* (1942)

Drowning: A belief well-known into the twentieth century was that possession of the caul of a newborn child was an infallible protection against death by drowning. Seamen frequently advertised in newspapers for cauls and were prepared to pay considerable sums of money for them. It is interesting that men who spent their lives at sea, frequently in the most perilous conditions, were remarkable—at least in the days of sail—for their inability to swim.

Flowers: Sailors have for hundreds of years abhorred the carrying of flowers on board ship; they believed that flowers were destined to form a funeral wreath. Even twentieth-century submariners were firm on this point.

Launching: The custom of breaking a bottle of wine or champagne across the bows of a vessel about to be launched derives from the much earlier practice of pouring wine on the ship's deck and onto the surface of the sea as a libation to the gods of the ocean, so that they would "Bless this ship and all who sail in her," to use the modern-day ceremonial form.

Ringing glass: No one must allow an empty glass to ring at a mess table, for it sounds the knell of some unfortunate sailor who, it is said, will die by drowning. If the glass is immediately stopped from ringing, however, the assembled sailors in the mess can breathe more easily: the devil will take two soldiers instead.

St. Elmo's Fire: The well-known phenomenon whereby electrical charges from the atmosphere are attracted to the masts, yards, and rigging of a ship at sea during a storm. The effect is also observed ashore around spires, chimney stacks, and so on. The phenomenon is named after St. Erasmus, a fourth-century Syrian bishop who came to be regarded as the patron saint of seamen. His name was corrupted to "St. Ermo," and thence to "St. Elmo," and the electrical discharge is attributed to him.

This phenomenon is known by some 50 different names, one of which is "Corposanto," the body of Christ. Old-time sailors believed that it was a bad omen; in particular, they believed that if the light from St. Elmo's Fire fell upon a man's face, he would die within 24 hours. Other seamen regarded it as a favourable omen, indicating in particular the end of stormy weather.

Whistling: Every sailor knows that to whistle on board ship is to court disaster: a strong wind at least, a gale at worst. A woman whistling on board ship, even today, hardly bears thinking about.

Women: Curiously enough, seamen have never been happy with women on board ship, believing that their very presence brought on gales and other bad weather; a woman whistling on the vessel was an abomination. At the same time, though, it was believed that a naked woman could calm the storm-tossed sea; hence the fact that so many figureheads of vessels throughout the ages have shown a woman with bared breasts. (It must also be remembered that sailors, for all their brutality of background and employment in the past, were an oddly conservative and even sensitive group of people; their language might often have been vicious and depraved, yet their behaviour in the main, especially around women, was typically reserved and even decorous.)

Swab

"One of the forecastle men took a swab and swabbed up the blood."

—James Owen Hannay (1865–1950), English cleric and novelist, *Singleton Fontenoy,* cited in the *Universal Dictionary of the English Language* (1897)

Originally a large mop used on shipboard for cleaning decks. In the old navy, swabbing down was done before hands were piped to breakfast, at which time the decks were scoured and holystoned until they were white. Colloquially, a swab is a friendly epithet for a companion or fellow; it is also sometimes used to describe a contemptible or useless person. Probably from the Dutch *zwabber,* a swabber, the drudge or menial of a ship.

Swarm

Originally nautical in the sense of meaning to climb ("The seamen swarmed up the rigging of the enemy ship"); a word much loved by writers of maritime fiction, but also used legitimately in the days of sail. It meant then, and still does, to climb by clasping with the hands, arms, and legs and thereby drawing oneself up (e.g., swarming up a pole, tree, rope, etc.). The word is almost certainly a special sense of *swarm* as in bees, from the Anglo-Saxon *swearm;* found also in the northern languages, such as Icelandic *svarmr,* tumult. When excited children swarm around Mickey Mouse, they are demonstrating both senses of the word's meaning.

Swashbuckler

A noisy display of bravado, of braggadocio. From the tapping or clanging upon their bucklers as swordplayers or fencers engaged each other in practice or in combat. (A "buckler" was a small, round shield, usually made from hardened leather, with a round boss or knob at the centre; it made a very satisfactory noise when hit with some object.) The noise produced is directly analogous to the fearsome display put on by otherwise harmless animals, such as the bearded or frilled lizard, or the blowfish; that is, it is all show, a bluff, full of nothing.

"A ruffian is the same with a swaggerer, so called, because endeavouring to make that side to swag or weigh down, whereon he ingageth. The same also with swashbuckler, from swashing or making a noise on bucklers."

—Thomas Fuller (1606–1661), English divine, *The Worthies of England* (1662)

Originally the term described a ruffian or bragging ne'er-do-well, and was widely used in literature dealing with pirates. Privateers and the like who carried out their often-illegal pursuits in a colourful and vigorous manner were said to be swashbuckling by nature. *Swash* is from the imitative sound of the blow; *buckler* is from the French *bouclier,* a boss, shield, also found in Chaucerian Middle English as *bokeler.* Today its usage is just as colourful, but less disparaging.

Sweep
To make a clean sweep

When a man-o'-war went into action, the crew cleared the decks of unwanted gear, including the movable bulkheads (walls) that formed the divisions between various cabins and spaces on the gun decks. To do so was *to make a clean sweep.* Also, if a broadside of shot wreaked enough havoc on the enemy's decks, so as to kill or injure a large number of the crew working there, the guns were said to have made *a clean sweep.*

"The waves o'ertake them in their serious play, and every hour sweeps multitudes away."

—William Cowper (1731–1800), English jurist and essayist, *Retirement* (1782)

"Cutting the fome, by the blew seas they swepe."

—Henry Howard Surrey (?1517–1547), English poet, Virgil's *Aeneid* (1557)

The expression has found its way into a number of usages, some associated with gaming (gambling at the table), horseracing, and so on. Colloquially, *to make a clean sweep* is to dispose completely of anything; to get rid of materials, methods, or staff that are regarded as obsolete or redundant; to get rid of entirely: "By the end of the week, the new manager had made a clean sweep of all the lazy and inefficient people in his department."

There is a story, probably apocryphal, that the Dutch admiral Marten Tromp hoisted a broom to his masthead after a victory over the British in the English Channel in 1652; if true, his meaning is obvious. From the Middle English *swepe,* to sweep.

(See also *Deck; To clear the deck.)*

Sweet Fanny Adams

A common saying with an interesting background; still in use in Britain, Australia, and New Zealand.

In 1867, Fanny Adams, a child of about eight, was murdered in Hertfordshire, England (the location is sometimes given as Hampshire), and her body systematically dismembered. The case made headlines in the newspapers. Tinned meat had only just recently been introduced into the Royal Navy, and sailors rather gruesomely likened the new rations to the body of the child. *Fanny Adams* became the navy's slang name for tinned meat; the *sweet* was simply reminiscent of the child's innocence. A "Fanny" was also a mess tin, from the fact that the containers in which the meat was packed were used as mess utensils throughout the Royal Navy.

The phrase *sweet Fanny Adams,* often just *sweet F.A.,* became synonymous for anything that was worthless, anything that added up to being very little or next to nothing, echoing the naval seaman's opinion of his tinned rations. Seamen then turned the expression, in particular *S.F.A.* and *sweet F.A.,* into a far more pungent epithet of contempt.

(See also *Harriet Lane.)*

Swipes

"He's only a little swipey, you know."

—Charles Dickens (1812–1876), English novelist, *Martin Chuzzlewit* (1844)

Drinks; often the leftover portions to be found in glasses after a party or other gathering. Originally, thin beer on board ship, sometimes called "purser's swipes" and also often known as "small beer," which is a rather poor, washy beer. From the Norwegian *skvip,* thin beer. To be "swipey" is to be drunk.

Swivel

"The gun is placed on the top, where there is an iron socket for the gun to rest in, and a swivel to turn the muzzle any way."

—William Dampier (1652–1715), English buccaneer and explorer, *Voyages* (1697)

Originally nautical, a fourteenth-century usage; from the Anglo-Saxon *swifan,* to revolve. Applied to guns mounted on pegs or pivots that allowed the weapons to be swivelled to cover a large field of fire (the word is related to *sweep).* Nowadays, any fastening device that allows the thing fastened to turn round freely on it.

T

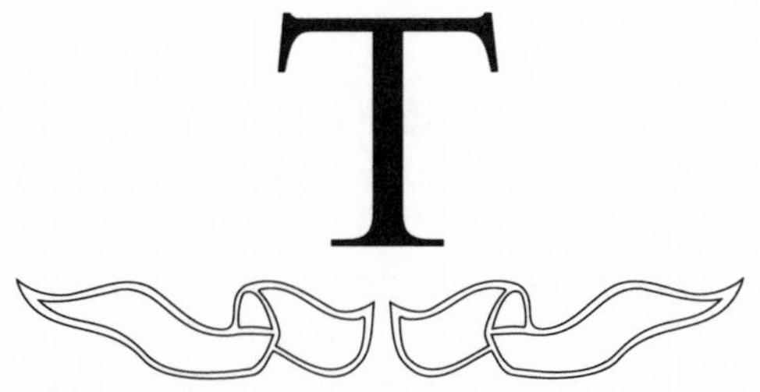

Tack As a noun, food, especially hard tack (ship's biscuit) and soft tack (ship's bread). Probably abbreviated from *tackle,* which is found in the Low German *takel,* rope; earlier, the word meant equipment in general, that which can be laid hold of (to take); then in a wide variety of senses, including that of food or a meal.

"When they change tacks they throw the vessel up into the wind, ease off the sheet, and bring the heel or tack-end of the yard to the other end of the boat, and the sheet in like manner."
—Captain James Cook (1728–1779), English navigator and explorer, *Second Voyage* (1777)

Used as a verb, *tack* means fastening. It is from the Old North French *taque,* which is a reduplication of *tache,* to hold together (whence the English word *attach).* To tack in sewing and to change tack (direction) on a vessel both derive from the original sense of to fasten.
(See also *Tack; Hard tack.)*

Hard tack Hard tack was originally ship's biscuit: very coarse, hard bread, invariably infested with weevils. Together with salted meat, ship's biscuit was the staple item in the seaman's diet. With meat almost always tough and putrescent, and bread that defied the generally poor teeth of most sailors, the term *hard tack* came to mean food that was unappetising and unpalatable.

Ship's biscuit often outlasted the lifespan of many of the ships it was intended to serve. There are records indicating that biscuit had been issued to seamen 40 years after its original baking. By contrast, "soft tack" was ship's bread baked on board; it was relatively fresh and infinitely more palatable. Hard tack today is any food that doesn't measure up to standard, such perhaps as the iron rations issued to combat soldiers. "The cook's on holiday, so it'll be hard tack for a while until she comes back."

To be on the right (or wrong) tack To take the correct (or wrong) course of action; to have a correct (or false) understanding of a matter. A tack is the course of a ship when tacking or sailing to windward. The allusion is to the direction in which a person's effort or understanding is being bent, but the point of the phrase lies in the fact that a tack is a vessel's zigzag course steered when sailing to windward. The colloquialism emphasises the fact that some matters are best resolved by an indirect rather than a direct approach: "If you want him to help you with your homework, you should try another tack."

To change tack When a sailing ship is proceeding to windward, she can gain ground only by sailing a zigzag course, at an angle to the wind. The vessel must then come about on the opposite tack if she is eventually to reach her destination upwind.

Similarly, when one changes one's approach in an argument and perhaps abandons one angle of attack (or defence) for another, then one is said to "change tack." "When he saw that he was getting nowhere with his plea for a complete review of the firm's accounting system, he changed tack and began inquiring into its marketing policy."

Tackle
To tackle something

"If a wight [man], who hated trade,
The sails and tackle for a vessel bought,
Madman or fool he might be justly thought."
—Francis, Horace's *Satires,* cited in the *Universal Dictionary of the English Language* (1897)

Ultimately from Old German *taken,* to lay hold of. In the colloquial sense, *tackle* means to grapple with, to come to grips with, to approach with a view to settling the matter. More immediately, the phrase derives from shipboard tackle (pronounced "tay-kel"), which is an arrangement of blocks by which the power exerted on a rope (effort) is multiplied in order to lift or move a heavy load. There are many varieties of tackle, all of them using rope or cordage of some kind, and a vessel's deck gear with its attendant ropes is often loosely called "tackle." Similarly, we have "fishing tackle."

Tailor made

Cigarettes made in a factory. This was the sailor's derisory description of the tinned tobacco that was introduced to replace the leaf tobacco that each seaman had learned to roll and cure aboard ship. Because smoking was restricted to certain times and places, most seamen preferred to chew their tobacco; consequently, they made their individual issues up into a *perique* (usually corrupted to "prick"), a one-pound pack of rolled, bound, and cured tobacco leaf. *(Perique* was the French name for a rich-flavoured tobacco grown in Louisiana.) The expression *tailor made* was once in wide circulation, particularly following both world wars, but the generally improved standard of living since the war years has made the commercially produced cigarette so common and readily available that the "roll-your-own" type is more the exception than the rule.
(See also *Smoko.)*

Tally
To tally on, along

Tally is sailor's slang for a name, any seaman's name: "What's your tally?" It is also the count taken of the number of packages, bales, casks, and so forth loaded on a vessel or unloaded from it. The order "tally on," "tally along," is given when more men are needed to clap on to a

"The sailors hauled the whip-line on board, and when the tally board, on which the directions for the method of procedure are printed in English on one side and French on the other, was received, the captain attempted by the light of a lantern to read them."

—*Scribner's Magazine,* January 1880

rope, fall, cable, or some other burden that needs extra concerted effort applied so as to move it where desired.

Found in colloquialisms in these forms to mean the same thing: to help out, to give a hand. Derived from the French *tailler,* to cut, when keeping a tally of goods, animals, etc., was done by scoring or marking a stick or board with horizontal scratches and then splitting it vertically. One half was kept by each party to the transaction, and both were compared in the event of disputes about totals (this is the origin of the expression *to keep score,* as in many games that accrue runs, hits, goals, and the like).

Tampon Nowadays a plug or dressing of cotton or similar material used to plug or staunch the flow of blood from a wound; also a sanitary device for absorbing the menstrual flow. Of nautical origin, unlikely though it might seem; from the French *tompion, tampion,* a wooden plug or stopper placed in the muzzle of a cannon, when not in use, to keep out seawater. The English word *tap,* as in "bath-tap," is also cognate with this French word.

Tango Not of nautical origin, but introduced to the Western world by sailors. The tango is a dance for couples, with many varied steps, figures, and poses; it originated from Cuba and found its way into South America by mariners who were engaged in the jerked beef trade to the Antilles in the Caribbean.

(See also *Jerked beef.*)

Tarpaulin Tarpaulin (originally "tarpawling") is canvas treated with tar or other waterproofing materials. In the old days of sail, seamen made their clothing from this material, which gave rise to the popular name for sailors in the North Counties of England, where they were known as "Tarry Breeks." *Breeks* is a dialect form of *breeches,* that is, britches or trousers of any kind, from the Old English *brec,* Icelandic *braekr,* and related to the Latin *bracae,* breeches. *Tarry* is probably derived from the even older name of *Jack Tar* for a British seaman.

"Every tarpawling, if he gets but to be lieutenant of a press smack, is called captain."

—Daniel Defoe (?1660–1731), English author, *Captain Singleton* (1720)

The etymology is interesting: *tar* is from Middle English *terre,* related to tree; *paul* is Middle English *palyoun,* canopy, and Old English *paill,* covering, from whence derives our modern *pall* (for example, as in "pallbearer" at a funeral); and *-in* is a variant of *-ing,* a common suffix for forming the present participle of verbs. The sense is of an awning held up by an adjacent tree.

Tarpaulin muster

A tarpaulin muster was a collection or whip-round among the crew for some charitable purpose. The money would be collected in a piece of tarpaulin.
(See also *Tarpaulin.*)

Tarred
Tarred and feathered

A punishment that involves being stripped to the skin, painted with tar, and then rolled in feathers. It is first recorded as being applied as a punishment at sea in the *Laws of Richard Coeur de Lion, Third Crusade* (1189): "A robber convicted of theft shall be shorn like a hired fighter, and boiling tar shall be poured over his head, and feathers from a pillow shall be shaken out over his head." This form of retribution against wrongdoers is still practised in some primitive communities today (one wonders how the victim survives the burns to his body). Once known as "painting the lion," an old nautical term of much the same meaning.

"Tarred and feathered and carried on a cart
By the women of Marblehead. . . ."
—J. G. Whittier (1807–1892), American poet, *Skipper Ireson's Ride* (1857)

The practice was not unknown in America, as noted by Francis Gros in *A Classical Dictionary of the Vulgar Tongue* (1785): "Tarring and feathering: a punishment lately inflicted by the good people of Boston on any person convicted, or suspected, of loyalty."

Tattoo

There are two meanings, each from quite different parts of the world. One is from the Dutch *taptoe,* which was the beating of the drum at night to recall soldiers to their barracks, associated with the warning to public houses to "put their taps to," i.e., to shut the taps of their ale casks. *Tattoo* is still a military expression in the British and Australian armed services. The term *taps,* as in "to play (or beat) taps," is the equivalent term in the armed services of the United States.

"Perhaps, however, the most beautiful of all was that of the New Zealanders, who were generally tattooed in curved or spiral lines."
—Lubbock, *Origin of Civilisation,* cited in the *Universal Dictionary of the English Language* (1897)

The other meaning of *tattoo* is the well-known indelible marking or etching made on the human body, to whatever design is desired. It is from the Polynesian *tatan,* mark, and was described by Captain James Cook in his journal of July 1764, during his first voyage of circumnavigation. The custom of tattooing became very popular with sailors, and indeed for a long time was solely associated with seafarers, especially those in the Royal Navy.

Taunt
All-a-taunto

From the French *autant,* as much; an old expression to mean very tall masts and narrow sails; to be under full sail with all rigging in use. This was the common rig for North European ships; British sailing ships used shorter masts and wider sails. Not to be confused with *taunt,* to scold or provoke, which is of a different origin.

"Her enormous taunt spars are made very apparent, but of course the fore-shortening takes off the length of hull."
—*Field Magazine,* June 4, 1887

Taut
A taut ship

Taut (ultimately from the Old English *togen,* drawn, and connected to *tight)* to the seaman means very efficient, smart, as in "a taut hand" or "a taut ship." "He's a stern disciplinarian"; "The ship is smart and well disciplined." The colloquial application is obvious: somebody who stands no nonsense in his business, his office, or other personal undertakings, is said to "run a taut (or tight) ship."

Tea-clipper

The "clipper" was a type of very fast sailing ship introduced in the early 1800s (notably the Baltimore clipper), which reached the height of beauty and efficiency in the mid-nineteenth century. They were characterised by a long, low, and moderately narrow hull, a sharply raked stem, and an overhanging stern. As a three-masted square rig, the clipper was probably the finest ship that the age of sail ever produced.

The discovery of gold in California in 1848 and in eastern Australia in 1850, and the opening of the China-England tea trade to foreign vessels, gave the impetus to the development of beautiful American clippers such as *Flying Cloud, Lightning,* and *Champion of the Seas,* and the equally impressive and successful British clippers such as *Taiping, Ariel,* and of course the *Cutty Sark,* now preserved in Greenwich as the only survivor of the British type.

The China tea trade was a very profitable one, and several clippers were built specifically for this trade. Each

Tea-clipper

year the ships loading in the Chinese tea ports, principally Foochow, would join in the race to be the first to get home to London, where the first arrivals always commanded the highest prices. The most famous of these races occurred in 1866, when the *Fiery Cross, Ariel, Taeping, Serica,* and *Taitsing* all left Foochow within a three-day period, at the end of May. Three months and one week later, after a voyage of some 16,000 miles across the world's oceans, the *Taeping* and *Ariel* docked in London within half an hour of each other, the *Serica* arrived two hours later, and the *Fiery Cross* and *Taitsing* reached London two days later—altogether an astonishing display of navigation and seamanship.

The tea-clippers died out soon after the Suez canal was opened in 1869; for a while they engaged in the wool trade from Australia, but they were soon found to be too small and labour-intensive for this type of cargo.

The term *clipper* came about because these ships could "clip" or cut short the passage-making times of the fast packet ships of the day (the word is from Middle English *klippa,* to shear, and is found in the Scandinavian tongues, e.g., the Old Norse *klippa,* imitative of a sharp, thin sound). The name was also applied in the mid-twentieth century to the flying-boats that crossed the Atlantic on scheduled flights.

Tell
To tell off

To tell off is to detail each man in a watch to some particular duty or position in the ship. The essential sense is to enumerate, to mention one thing after another, to separate each individual person from the whole or group and to assign to each one a particular task. When the watch was mustered, or at some other convenient time in the ship's routine, each man would be "told off" by the officer of the watch, usually one of the ship's mates. Colloquially, *to tell off* is to scold, to rebuke severely, to itemise one after another the victim's flaws and faults; hence, *to be told off.* "When he returns from his fishing trip I intend to tell him off for not taking the children with him."
(See also *Told; All told.)*

Telltale

Originally, the compass (sometimes called the "overhead compass" or "hanging compass") hanging face downward from the beams in the captain's cabin, so as to show him the direction of the ship's head (its compass course) without the need to go on deck. Nowadays the word *telltale* on board ship is used generally to indicate any mechanical contrivance that repeats or reproduces useful information. It is also the word for the lengths of ribbon, wool, etc., attached to the shrouds of a sailboat to indicate airflow. Colloquially, a "telltale" is something that reveals or discloses, or betrays what is not intended to be known, as in "a telltale blush."

There she blows!

The time-honoured call of the lookout in a whaling ship when a whale was sighted. Used loosely as a colloquialism whenever something being searched for has been sighted; as, for example, during a rabbit-shooting trip.

Thwart
To thwart; to be thwarted

"The Indians made us exceedingly comfortable by arranging blankets on the bottom of the boats, with the thwarts well covered with wraps for a back."
—*Scribner's Magazine,* August 1877

From the Icelandic *thvert,* across, transverse. To *thwart* somebody is to prevent him (often by any means and sometimes to his surprise) from carrying out his intentions; to be thwarted often arouses indignation or anger. The phrase derives from the fact that a thwart is a wooden plank set transversely across a small boat to act as a seat for oarsmen. By extension, a thwart cuts across the direction of movement; hence the metaphor of blocking or opposing a person's plans: "Her plans to go out for the evening were thwarted by her father's refusal to lend her the family car."

Tick
To get something on tick

Colloquially, to get something on credit, to owe for what one buys. *Tick* is a seventeenth-century clipped form of *ticket,* which itself was the ordinary term for the written acknowledgement of a debt; to live on credit was called "living on ticket" or "on tick." The expression derives from the seaman's practice of obtaining goods for himself and his family on the strength of his pay-ticket or advice note. Samuel Pepys refers to this practice in a diary entry for October 1666.

Perhaps the sailor's greatest grievance in the sailing navy was the fact that he was rarely paid his wages on time. Often he was owed back pay for two years or more, and if he was pressed into another vessel he lost his claim, because his wage was paid only on his original vessel, the one to which he had been drafted. If he deserted out of sheer economic necessity—or indeed for any other reason—his name on the ship's muster book was marked "R" for "Run," and he automatically forfeited all monies due him.

Finding the money to pay the fleet's wages was a perennial difficulty. For a long time the Navy Board tried to overcome the problem by issuing a promissory note, or ticket, which could be cashed only by presentation at the Pay Office in London. Naturally, this was an impossibility for many of the seamen, and there grew up in the ports a black market in the cashing of tickets, usually at a horrendous discount of up to 25 and sometimes even 33 percent. Even then, these tickets were occasionally

"I shall contrive to have a quarter before-hand, and never let family tick more for victuals, cloathes, or rent."
—Richard Steele (1672–1720), English dramatist, *Correspondence* (1787)

dishonoured at the London Pay Office because of the shortage of funds.

Pepys (quoted in Lloyd; see bibliography) notes, in August 1667, that lack of pay "... makes them mad, they being as good men as were ever in the world, and would readily serve the king, were they but paid." Hence the phrase *payment on tick,* which derives from this old practice of paying seamen with a promissory note in lieu of cash. "She sent her child down to the corner store to buy some butter on tick."
(See also *Pay; To pay off.*)

Ticket
To get one's ticket; to lose one's ticket

To get one's ticket meant to become a qualified mate or master in the merchant navy; to get one's certificate of competency after passing the appropriate examinations. There are various kinds of tickets, based on the degree of qualification and experience required, and promotion to a higher rank depended upon the officer having first passed the examination and gaining the ticket for that rank. *To lose one's ticket* was to have it withdrawn as a result of incompetence, such as putting the vessel in hazard.

"She's not the ticket, you see."
—William Makepeace Thackeray (1811–1863), English novelist, *The Newcomes* (1855)

Colloquially, *to get one's ticket* is to get a discharge, as from a firm, the army, or another group; also in *that's the ticket*—that's the correct, right, or proper thing to have or do.

Tiddley
To be tiddley; tiddled up

Also "tiddly." The seaman's word for smart, neat; said of ship's gear, personal appearance, clothes, and the like. Still widely used, both ashore and afloat; also with a secondary meaning of being tipsy, slightly drunk. Almost certainly from the sailor's deliberate pronunciation of *tidily* in three syllables, as "ti-di-ly," with the "tid" being pronounced as in "bid." The sailor refers to his "tiddley suit" (smartest going-ashore uniform), "tiddley bull" (ceremony and protocol), a "tiddley ship," "tiddley haircut," and so on.

Tiddly

See *Tiddley.*

Tiddy-oggies

The sailor's name for meat pasties; a small flat meat pie, oval in shape, and known as a "Cornish pastie" ashore. This writer has never seen an explanation of how this term came to see the light of day.

Tide

"I have important business
The tide whereof is now."
—William Shakespeare (1564–1616), *Troilus and Cressida,* act 5, scene 1

From the Old English *tid,* time, season; related to our word *time* and the Modern German *zeit,* time. Because the tide is a very important element in seafaring, there are many metaphors built around the term.

Against the tide

"A tide-like darkness overwhelms
The fields that round us lie. . . ."

—Henry Wadsworth Longfellow (1807–1882), American poet, *Birds of Passage,* cited in the *Universal Dictionary of the English Language* (1897)

The reference is obvious. A vessel sailing with the tide against her might or might not make headway, depending upon other conditions such as wind, the state of the sea, etc. As a metaphor, the expression means to go against public feeling, to be opposed to the generality of thought and opinion: "He was swimming against the tide in his efforts to get the public interested in his political agenda."
(See also *Tide; To stem the tide.)*

Lose not a tide

To lose not a tide is to waste no time, to set off at once on the appointed task or business. The connection is with the tides of the ocean, and the importance to the seaman of utilising these tides to his best advantage.

The tide has turned; the tide will turn

As the ocean tides undergo their diurnal ebb and flow, so can man expect that his own personal fortunes will improve (turn) for the better, given time. Shakespeare writes in *Julius Caesar* (act 4, scene 3):

> There is a tide in the affairs of men,
> Which, taken at the flood, leads on to fortune.

Tide of feeling; tide of opinion

The growth and swelling of public opinion on some matter is likened to the diurnal rise (and subsequent ebb) of the tide of the sea. Particularly apt is the sense suggested by the irresistible, overwhelming surge of the tide's flood: "The tide of public opinion swung very strongly in favour of lowering personal taxes."

To miss the tide

Of obvious nautical origin and meaning; colloquially, *to miss the tide* is to fail to grasp an opportunity; to be too late; to miss the bus: "If you don't apply for a place in that motor mechanics course soon, you are going to miss the tide."

To stem the tide

To stem the tide is to hold one's own against adversity: "She was determined to stem the tide of public opinion by continuing to insist that the only policy that merited any attention was one that included concern for the environment."

The phrase derives from a vessel's being able to make little, or only slight, headway against a contrary current or tidal stream, perhaps as a deliberate manoeuvre while standing on and off, waiting to pick up her pilot, or for some other purpose in which she had to remain more or less stationary.

The stem is the foremost member of the bow of a vessel. The phrase *to breast the tide* carries exactly the same metaphorical force. Not to be confused with the other

English word *stem,* which is from the Old Norse *stemma,* to check, hinder, prevent, as in stemming the flow of blood. (See also *Current; To swim against the current. Stream; To go against the stream.)*

To swim with the tide Of obvious nautical origin and meaning. Colloquially, to take the line of least resistance, to go with the crowd, to agree with general opinion.

To tide over "Tiding over" was the technique used by sailing vessels in their attempts to make progress against a foul wind (a foul wind is a head wind, one that prevents easy or safe progress). It was a method of working the tides, which involved anchoring during the contrary set of the tide, then weighing anchor at high water and beating to windward, thereby utilising the fair tide in making progress in the desired direction. The process was repeated for as long as was necessary.

Figuratively, *to tide over* or *to tide over a difficulty* means to persevere with patience to surmount a difficulty; to get by: "My father gave me a hundred dollars which, he said, should tide me over while I was looking for a job."

"Decent artisans, who are in need of help to tide them over a period of temporary distress."

—*Daily Telegraph* (English newspaper), February 24, 1886

In American usage, the colloquialism is sometimes corrupted to *tie over,* but the meaning is exactly the same.

Tides

To work double tides To work extra hard, with all one's might; to do two days' work in one, by working the two sessions of slack water that occur in each 24-hour period. From the days when work on the underwater hull of a vessel could be carried out only by beaching or careening at high tide, then taking every advantage of low tide to get the work done.

Tide-waiter

Sometimes called a "tidesman"; a customs officer who boards ships entering port to ensure that the customs regulations are observed. So named because he was forced to wait ashore until the tide served, so that the customs vessel (usually called a "revenue cutter") could sail out to meet the incoming ships. Figuratively, a tide-waiter is one who waits to see the trend of events before deciding to take action; he tests the tide of opinion, as it were, before venturing forth.

"From the nobleman who held the white staff and the great seal, down to the humblest tide-waiter and gauger, what would now be called gross corruption was practised without disguise and without reproach."

—Thomas Babington Macaulay (1800–1859), English essayist and historian, *History of England* (1848)

Tidings

Bad tidings; good tidings *Tidings* is ultimately from *tide,* generally used in the plural; it means happening, news, information. The words *time* and *tide* are in fact related to each other, and the expression—used figuratively—refers to the fact that time, like the tide, is a flow, as of events. Tidings is the flow

"Tidings do I bring, and lucky joys
And golden times, and happy news of price."
—William Shakespeare (1564–1616), *Henry IV, Part 2,* act 5, scene 3

or onset of news or happenings that reaches us in the normal course of events, welcome or unwelcome as that news may be: "We could see from the expression on his face that he had nothing but bad tidings for us."
(See also entries under *Tide.)*

Tidy *To be in tide* is to be in season, to be timely, as in eventide and springtide. To do things at their proper time or season is to ensure that they are done in an orderly manner, in the same way that the tides ebb and flow in a regular rhythm; hence, by association, the word *tidy* came to mean methodical, neatly done, well arranged. The connection with ocean tides is obvious; *tidy* is an adverbial formation from *tide.*
(See also *Tide.)*

A tidy sum A satisfactory amount of money, sufficient for a specific purpose or for the future generally. The phrase is not nautical in origin, but it owes its force to man's age-old relationship with the sea.
(See also *Tidy.)*

Tier Originally nautical, to mean a row, rank, or range of things; now with the sense of each row rising one behind or above another, as of seats in an amphitheatre or guns in a man-o'-war ship. The earliest usage of the word was applied to guns and oars (as in an ancient galley, such as a bireme or a trireme). We speak of a tier of casks in a wine cellar. The word may be from the Old French *tire,* sequence, but it is also likely that the English word owes something to the French *tire,* shooting; Sir Walter Raleigh, in *A Report of the Truth of the Fight about the Isles of the Azores* (1591), refers to ". . . three tire of ordinance on a side, and eleven pieces in every tire. . . ."

"They bring nothing else but jars of wine, and they stow one tier on the top of another so artificially, that we could hardly do the like without breaking them."
—William Dampier (1652–1715), English buccaneer and explorer, *Voyages* (1697)

Tiger The well-known nickname given to (usually) boys or young men by their elders, often as a mark of the enthusiasm that the young have displayed in some enterprise or their effort in some task. A colloquialism common in the countries of the British Commonwealth, and still used in England, Australia, and New Zealand, for example.

From the days when ship's captains employed their own native stewards from Eastern ports; these men usually wore a distinctive striped cloth, hence giving rise to their nickname *tiger.* In England of earlier times, the servant who rode out with his master was called a "tiger," as were pageboys, as in these lines from Richard Harris Barham's *The Ingoldsby Legends* (1840):

> Tiger Tim was clean of limb
> His boots were polished, his jacket was trim. . . .

We might say that so-and-so is a "tiger for punishment," indicating that that person is very enthusiastic about some activity or other and does not mind the setbacks that sometimes occur as a result.

Tight As in secure, unbroached; from the earlier nautical word *thight,* and the Old Norse *thettr,* both meaning watertight, solid, staunch. *Tight* is also the sailor's slang term for being drunk, and is very commonly used ashore: "By the end of the party he was as tight as a tick and we had to carry him out to the car."

Timbers
Shiver me timbers! Timbers are the ribs or frames of a wooden vessel; they give a ship its shape and strength. The planks for the deck and hull are then fastened to these timbers. As a nautical expression, it carries very little credibility, though it conveys the sense of shock or surprise one might experience when a ship strikes a rock or other obstacle such that her timbers shiver. The phrase is rather too theatrical an expression to have been used by practising seamen.

It is the sort of mild oath that was popular in sea stories written for children; for example, in *Treasure Island* by Robert Louis Stevenson, Long John Silver greets Jim Hawkins: " 'So,' said he, 'here's Jim Hawkins, shiver my timbers! dropped in, like, eh? Well, come, I take that friendly.' " A page later, Long John uses the expression "shiver my sides!" Stevenson had a lifelong interest in the sea, but it is doubtful that he ever mastered the language of sailors.

It should be remembered that in nineteenth-century England there was a tremendous upsurge of interest in, and admiration of, the British seaman who had done so much to contribute to the country's political and commercial preeminence in world affairs over the preceding 400 years. This adulation was reflected in the popular literature, the stage, and the music halls of the period; anything that remotely smacked of Jack Tar was cause for celebration. It is quite likely that *shiver my/me timbers* is a product of this period; it may even be that Stevenson himself coined the phrase. Certainly, one does not encounter it in the literature of the sea or in the speech of practising seamen.

Time
To serve one's time

From the early days when young men joined the British navy with a view to becoming naval officers. Their rank was next below that of sublieutenant, but originally they were petty officers under the immediate command of the bosun (boatswain). Many of these young men went to sea as a captain's servant, and after three years' service they were rated as midshipmen. Following another three years' sea-time service, they were eligible to sit for their lieutenant's examination; hence the origin of the expression *to serve one's time:* to put in the period of duty and service that qualified one for the next promotional examination.

Colloquially, to put in the necessary time in a place or position, as in an apprenticeship or probationary period. A "time-server" is one who puts in this necessary time for the sake of salary, retirement benefits, or such; one who waits for this to happen.

"He is a good time-server that improves the present for God's glory and his own salvation."
—Thomas Fuller (1608–1661), English preacher, *The Holy State and the Profane State* (1642)

Perhaps one of the best-known examples of time-serving was the sixteenth-century Vicar of Bray, who managed to retain his position in his Berkshire parish despite the religious upheavals that marked the reigns of Henry VIII, Edward VI, Mary, and Elizabeth I, all of which occurred during the vicar's lifetime. This gentleman is commemorated in the song named after him.

Tit
Useless as a fish's tit

The expression explains itself. Widely used by sailors to mean useless, fatuous, being of no merit or service whatsoever—yet another example of the vigour of the nautical metaphor. The phrase has long since been adopted by landsmen, to retain the original and obvious meaning.

Toe the line

To submit to discipline or regulations, to come into line with the rest. From the fact that when the captain of a naval ship had his crew mustered for inspection (called "beating to divisions"), the ship's company lined the quarterdeck, the gangways, and the forecastle, with each group of men lined up along the deck, where their officers made them stand upright, keep in order, and "toe the line" (stand in a straight line along the appointed seams in the deck). Beating to divisions was an important ceremony, charged with tradition and discipline; toeing the line was an important element of that discipline.

The expression is widely used in everyday speech and conveys the same sort of meaning: to conform, to behave according to the rules: "He quickly found that he couldn't do as he liked when he joined the new firm—they made him toe the line from his first day onward."

Toggle

"The yard ropes were fixed to the yard by a toggle in the running noose of the latter."

—Captain Frederick Marryat (1792–1848), English naval captain and novelist, *Frank Mildmay* (1829)

Originally a nautical word meaning a cross-bar, usually short, made of wood or metal and used for fastening or securing a link in a chain, a loop in a rope, or some other such (for example, a duffle coat is fastened by small wooden toggles). From the Middle English *takel,* gear.

Togs

"Look at his togs, superfine cloth and the heavy swell cut."

—Charles Dickens (1812–1870), English novelist, *Oliver Twist* (1838)

Slang for clothes in general, and also for clothing for a particular purpose, such as football togs and swimming togs. Originally a Scandinavian word for seamen's clothing, but it may in fact derive from the Latin *toga,* a robe, or from the Dutch *tuig,* trappings.

Told
All told; to be told off

A very common expression meaning in all, in sum, in total. *To tell off* was for seamen to be sent off or detailed —to particular jobs or duties. When this had been done for the whole watch, all the men were said to be "told off." Today, *to be told off* means to be scolded or rebuked, probably from the fact that when seamen were told off to their tasks, the orders were given by mates or officers who frequently were hard-driving, irascible men, determined often to cow and subdue the crew by any means possible.
(See also *Bucko. Tell; To tell off.)*

Tombola

The nautical name for "housie-housie," or what has come to be called "bingo," a gambling game in which players put markers on a card of numbered squares according to the numbers drawn and announced by a caller. From the Italian *tombolare,* to tumble, fall upside down.

Ton

Once the same word as "tun," *ton* is from Middle English and now means a unit of weight. Originally *tun* referred to a large wine container, a cask; it was a measure of capacity, holding 2 pipes, or 4 hogsheads, or 252 old wine gallons. *Tun* became the unit of a ship's lading in the fourteenth century and was, naturally, the space occupied by a cask (a tun) of wine. Nowadays, for the purposes of registered tonnage, it is a space of 100 cubic feet; for the purposes of freight, it is usually the space of 40 cubic feet. *Tonnage* is also originally a nautical term.

Top
To blow one's top

To become very angry, to lose one's temper. There are at least two suggestions as to the origin of this term. One is that it is from the early days of oil-wells in the United States, when gas and oil were struck during the drilling process and the (frequently) unexpected eruption caused the derrick or drill-rig to blow or collapse. The other refers to the blowing-out of a topsail, and its subsequent loss, during a storm.

This second suggested origin is the one to be preferred, simply because of the enormously widespread nature of nautical metaphor and the equally sparse availability of the oil-well metaphor. Furthermore, the possessive pronoun "his" refers more obviously to the ship's captain than it does to any particular person logically connected with a drilling rig (note the curious nautical distinction between "she" the ship and "he" the captain or master, or "old man": *she* was invoked when a ship's performance was referred to; *he* was used when the seaman spoke of ship management).

Used colloquially as in "She blew her top when he arrived home late from the office party."

Top up; topped up; topping up

The element "top" occurs in many nautical words, such as "top" (a masthead platform); "topgallant mast" (the uppermost mast of a complete, three-piece mast); "topgallant sail" (the square sail set on the topgallant mast); "topmast" (the middle section of a three-piece mast); "topmen" (seamen who worked on the upper masts and their yards); "topsail" (pronounced "tops'l," the sail set on the topsail yard); and so on.

"Topping up" is the act of raising the end of a spar (yard, boom, etc.) by means of a topping lift, a tackle rigged for that purpose; the spar would then said to be "topped up" (raised as high as it needed to be). The expression *to top up* came ashore to mean to fill up something that was partly empty—a drink glass, a container for fuel or water, and so forth. When full, the receptacle is said to be "topped up" or "topped off": "We made certain that all our water and petrol cans were topped up before we set off across the desert toward the distant oasis." From the Anglo-Saxon *top,* summit, a word found in cognate forms in other Teutonic languages (for example, German *zopf,* Old Norse *toppr).*

"All . . . topped their booms for home."
—*Field Magazine,* September 4, 1886

Top drawer

Anything that is "top drawer" is of the best quality, the finest available. The origin of this expression dates from the practice of carrying the ship's papers always and only in the topmost drawer of the desk in the captain's study or the vessel's chart room. Thus, if it were ever necessary to abandon ship, the captain or one of his officers would instantly and automatically know where to retrieve these important documents, because of their being kept only in that one place.

Used colloquially in expressions such as "He's only an average batter, but as a pitcher he is absolutely top drawer."

Top-hamper

Top-weight; any weight carried above the upper deck. In the days of sail, this included upper rigging, spars, tackle, topsails, and all other gear aloft; in any vessel, the fittings, furniture, and tackle that are above the upper deck. Loosely, *top-hamper* refers to anything that might make for awkwardness, such as cumbersome headgear worn in a strong wind.

Tornado An English corruption of the Spanish *tronada,* from the Latin, *tonare,* to thunder, and the Sanskrit *tan,* to resound. One of the elements of the Spanish word is *tornar,* to turn, which is descriptive of the violent, thunderous whirlwind that occurs over land and sea in moderately low latitudes. Its winds are capable of wreaking great havoc. The word came into English through the days of privateering and piracy by the Spanish in the Caribbean.
(See also *Cannibal.)*

Tot
A tot of rum A tot is a measure of rum, the ration issued to ratings of the Royal Navy. Probably from an Old English word *tot,* small child, also *totter,* and found in Old Norse as *tuttr,* a nickname for a dwarf. The word may have been applied to the measure of rum because of its effects upon the drinker.

The traditional issue of rum to seamen was (erroneously) known as "Nelson's Blood," because seamen believed that Lord Nelson's body had been pickled in rum to transport it back to England after the Battle of Trafalgar; however, the spirit used was brandy, not rum.

Brandy was the spirit originally issued to men, along with beer to replace the shipboard water that was usually badly tainted and often putrid (beer kept for longer periods than water). Then in 1655, Jamaica was captured by the British, and Jamaica rum soon supplanted brandy because it was cheaper, easier to obtain and improved with age. By 1731, it became an official issue to seamen, the daily half-pint being divided into a morning tot and an evening tot, both as neat spirit.

In 1740, Admiral Vernon, on the West Indies station, became alarmed at the degree of drunkenness that resulted from this twice-daily imbibing of neat spirits, and he instituted a diluted issue of a quart (two pints) of water to half a pint of rum (a proportion of four to one, known at that time as "four-water rum"). By this means did Admiral Vernon unwittingly bequeath his nickname "Old Grogram" to the vast range of alcoholic beverages drunk today, euphemistically known as "grog."

By the mid-1800s, the Admiralty was still concerned about the incidence of drunkenness in the fleet, and in 1850 various measures were adopted to curb these excesses. One of these was that the rum ration was reduced to one-eighth of a pint. The rum issue had become part of the official daily routine, marked by the pipe "Up spirits" in the forenoon watch. However, by 1969 the British Ministry of Defence decided that the daily issue of rum had become an anachronism in a navy that was ever more dependent on modern technology; accordingly, it was decreed that rum would no longer be issued to seamen of the Royal Navy, as of August 1, 1970. On July 31 of that year, Royal Navy ships in various ports around the world staged funeral ceremonies to mark the passing of their beloved "Nelson's Blood."

Rum has not yet completely disappeared from shipboard life; spirits are available in messes to certain ranks, and the traditional order to "splice the mainbrace" is still made on special occasions.

(See also *Grog. Mainbrace; To splice the mainbrace. Nelson's Blood. Up spirits!)*

Touch
To touch at

"And the next day we touched at Sidon."
—Acts 27:3

To stop briefly at a port or harbour, to take on or discharge passengers, for example. Probably from the physical fact of coming into contact with the land, either by being alongside at the wharf, or by means of the anchor or mooring buoy. Used widely as part of the language in the travel industry, especially to apply to intermediate stops between the point of origin and destination: "The cruise ship will touch at Samoa and Hawaii on its journey across the Pacific."

To touch off an argument

Cannon were fired by applying a spark or flame (usually from a slow fuse called a "slowmatch" in the days of the sailing navies) to the vent or touch hole in the breech of the cannon. This ignited the powder cartridge and the hot gases of the explosion drove the ball up the barrel. The metaphor *to touch off an argument* implies that—as in a cannon—the conditions are ripe for a disagreement; all it needs is the necessary spark, often an ill-chosen remark: "His comment about the influence of the church in national politics touched off a bitter argument with his mother-in-law."

Touch and go

To *touch and go* is to run a vessel aground but to refloat her almost immediately; it is to graze the bottom very slightly, in such a way as not to cause any serious damage or even check the vessel's progress through the water. An originally nautical term, which now means metaphorically a narrow escape, something that was precarious and risky; also something that almost didn't quite come off, as a celebration party or the like: "It was touch and go whether they would catch the plane in time to begin their overseas holiday."

Tow
To take, have in tow

Tow is from the Old English *togian,* to pull by force; *to tow* is to pull or drag by force, using rope, chain, or some other means. It was not uncommon in the days of sail for one vessel to tow another disabled vessel, although it must have been a laborious process having to rely on wind power alone. The old name for the rope used for towing was *tew.*

As an expression, the phrase means to have someone in one's charge, or under one's influence, usually expressing a sense of movement, with one person following—or being drawn by—another person, as in somebody leading another person through a crowd; to take charge of, to be responsible for: "He seems to have taken most of his wife's relatives in tow."

Train oil

See *Trane oil.*

Trane oil

"A kind of cloth which they weaue [weave], and sell to the merchants of Norwaie, together with their butter, fish, either salted or dried, and their traine-oile. . . ."
—Raphael Holinshed (d. ?1580), translator and historian, *Chronicles* (1577)

Also "train oil." A former term for whale or seal oil, obtained by boiling the blubber of these animals. From the Dutch *traan,* literally "to tear," probably in reference to the fact that the blubber is torn off in strips. The adoption of a Dutch word for this product is due to the activity of this nation in very early whale-fishery in European waters. The oil, of course, is in no way connected with railroad trains.

Another name for train oil is "case oil," a term widely used by American whalers in the eighteenth and nineteenth centuries. It was so named because the finest sperm oil came from a cavity in the top of the sperm whale's head known as the "case." This cavity held about 500 gallons of oil, which was also known as a "Heidelberg tun" (referring to its volume).

Tobias Smollett (1721–1771), in his novel *Roderick Random* (1748), writes of the ". . . butter served out by the gill, that tasted like train oil thickened with salt."

Trice
To do something in a trice

"To trice up" is the operation of hauling and lashing to make something more secure, as, for example, in lashing a seaman to the gratings in preparation for a flogging. *Trice* means to tie up, to make fast smartly and without waste of time, in a seamanlike manner. Hence, *to do something in a trice* is to do it in an instant, as a knowledgeable and experienced seaman would. From the verb *trice,* related to the Dutch *trijsen,* to hoist. The old verb *trice* meant at one pull, at one haul; to pluck or snatch; hence the modern usage implying immediacy: "Within a trice she snatched the money up from the bar, thrust it into her pocket, and got through the door before anyone knew what was happening."

"In a trice the turnpike men
Their gates wide open threw."
—William Cowper (1731–1800), English poet, *John Gilpin* (1782)

Trick
To do a trick

"... And all I ask is a merry yarn
from a laughing fellow rover,
And quiet sleep and a sweet dream
when the long trick's over."

—John Masefield (1878–1967), English poet laureate, "Sea Fever," from *Salt-Water Ballads* (1902)

A "trick" was the spell of duty done by the helmsman at the wheel or tiller. A "regular trick" varied in time between half an hour and one hour, depending on the size of the crew and the prevailing weather conditions. The ability to steer was a prime requisite for a seaman (an able-bodied seaman was one who could "hand, reef, and steer"), and a skillful trick at the wheel was something to be admired.

Colloquially, one who pulls off a delicate task with skill and perhaps daring is said to have done, or to have pulled, a "neat trick": "She pulled a neat trick on her bothersome supervisor by phoning his wife and pretending to be an angry creditor."

Trim
To be in good trim

Trim is the word used to describe the state of the yards and sail; when in good trim, the ship's gear is so arranged such that she can make the best of the wind available. *Trim* also describes the difference between the draught of a vessel fore and aft, to indicate the degree to which she is deeper in the water at the head or at the stern. *To trim* is to distribute weight so that the boat rides in the water to the best advantage.

"Where lies the land to which
yon ship must go?
Festively she puts forth
in trim array. . . ."

—William Wordsworth (1770–1850), English poet, *Sonnets* (1807)

Widely used as a metaphor, taken from the original nautical use "to trim the ship," "to be in fighting trim," etc. The overall application of the word is to smartness of appearance, good condition or order, or manner; to modify: "He kept himself in good trim by playing squash twice a week."

From the Anglo-Saxon *trymman,* to arrange, make firm. (See also *Keel; To be on an even keel.)*

Trimaran

A type of vessel with a central hull and twin floats, one on either side. The form is a development of the catamaran, and the name is from *tri,* three, and the Tamil word *maram,* wood, log.
(See also *Catamaran.)*

Trip

"Trips to Ireland are inexpensive
and by no means difficult."

—*The Daily Chronicle* (English newspaper), May 25, 1885

"We could not trip the bower
anchor with all the purchase we
could make."

—Captain James Cook (1728–1779), English navigator and explorer, *First Voyage* (1771)

Originally a nautical word when used to refer to a journey. *Trip* is an early seafaring word for a leg, which is the distance a vessel sails on a tack. A "day tripper" is one who goes on an outing for the day, usually by ferry, steamer, or pleasure boat; the term is used mostly in England. A "trial trip" is a journey or voyage made by the builders of a vessel prior to handing it over to the owners. The phrase *to trip the anchor* means to break it out of the ground by turning it over with a tripping line attached to one of the anchor's flukes. From the Old French *triper,* to dance, skip; thence to the Anglo-Saxon *treppan,* to tread.

Truck A common word in Modern English for a vehicle of a certain type. The word was also used as long ago as the eighteenth century to describe a vehicle. Originally a truck was a small wooden wheel; it still survives in nautical terminology as the word for the wooden disk to be found at the masthead of sailing ships; hence the expression *from truck to keelson* (i.e., from top to bottom). From the earlier *truckle,* originally a grooved wheel, such as the sheave (pronounced "shiv") of a pulley; found in the term *trundle* (e.g., a trundle-bed) and the expression *to truckle under.* Not related to *truck* as in barter, swap, exchange; this is from the French *troquer,* to barter, exchange.

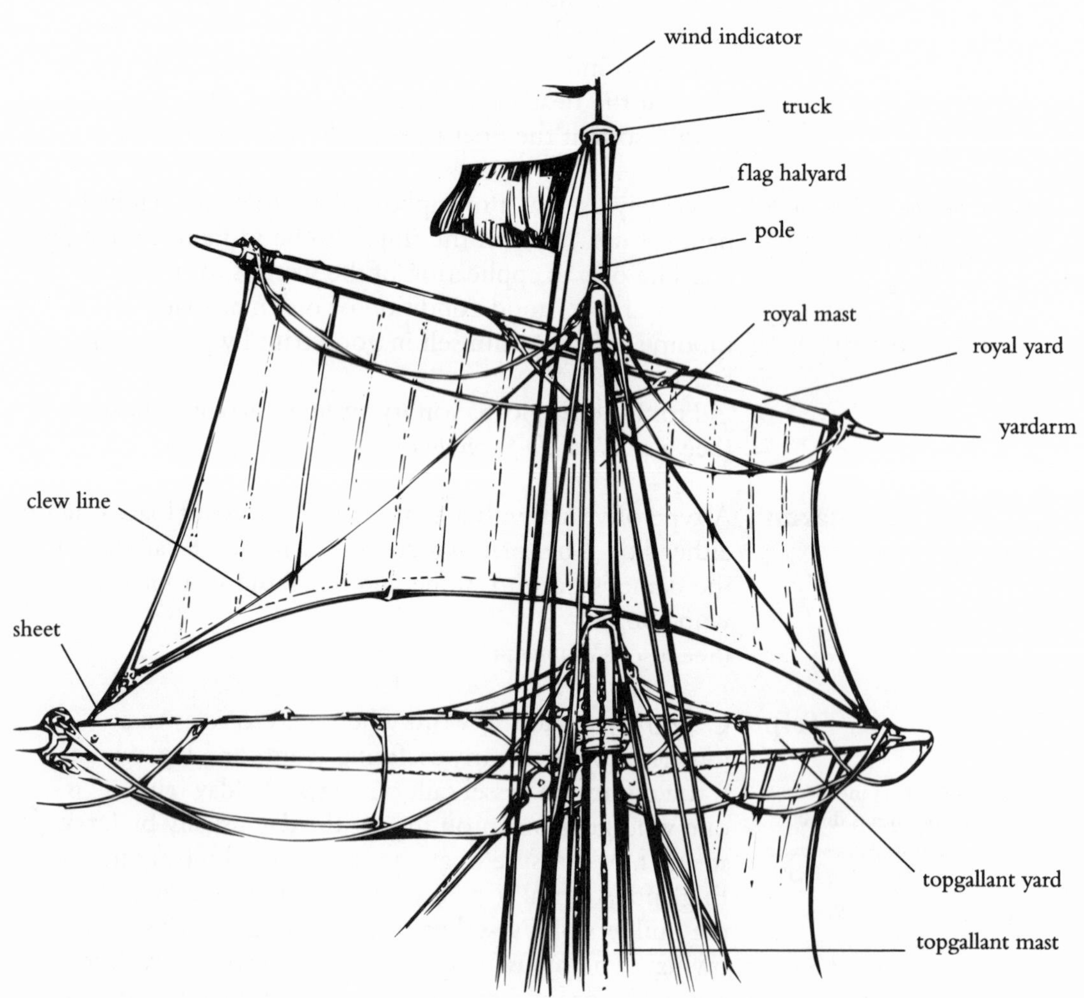

True blue A well-known expression in the English-speaking world; as a colloquialism, it is a testament to someone's faithfulness, unswerving loyalty, and honesty.

The term came to be applied to the seamen of the Royal Navy, who felt (rightly enough) that their willingness to endure the natural hazards of the sea and the rigours and dangers of battle, all of which were a part of the seaman's daily life afloat, was a sufficient measure of their unwavering loyalty to crown and country. In this they were, of course, absolutely right. Basil Lubbock, in his book *The Blackwall Frigates* (1924), tells an interesting anecdote concerning an encounter between the monarch and one of his sailors:

> On one occasion King George was inspecting the embarkation of some cavalry before a large number of spectators, when a jolly tar, who was described as "three sheets in the wind and a-brimful of loyalty," forced his way to the side of the king and held out a quart mug full of porter. Then after "tongueing his quid, unshipping his skyscraper and hitching up his canvas" [i.e., spitting out his chew of tobacco, removing his hat, and hitching up his trousers] he expressed the hope that His Majesty would not refuse a drink with a "true blue"... whereby they toasted the army and the navy.

The origin of the term stems from the reputation that the city of Coventry had long enjoyed for the quality and fastness of its dyeing. For hundreds of years, the people of this city had been at the forefront of the wool trade and in particular were renowned for their skill in producing dyes that were both fast and consistent in colour. "Coventry Blue" was one of the best-known of these dyes.

Hence, any individual who exhibited these same qualities—of steadfastness and trueness—could be called a "true blue." To many people, the seamen of the king's navy were a prime example of true-blue qualities.

Try
To try; to try out

To try was the old seafaring term that described the attempt by a sailing vessel, during a severe storm, to remain in the trough of the waves by reducing sail; sometimes done under bare poles; to ride or lie a-try; hence the origin of the trysail, a sail of much reduced size used by sailing vessels (especially small craft) in place of the mainsail during a storm. *To try back* means to veer or change direction slightly.

The expression *to try out* is from the days of whaling (which itself goes back into antiquity). Whale oil was obtained from the blubber by boiling it in the "try-works,"

"The wylde corne, beinge in shape and greatnesse lyke to the good, if they be mengled [mingled] with great difficultie wyll be tryed out."

—Sir Thomas Elyot (?1499–1546), English scholar, *Boke Named the Governour* (1531)

"The fire seven times tried this: Seven times tried that judgment is."

—William Shakespeare (1564–1616), *The Merchant of Venice,* act 2, scene 9

a very large iron pot set in brickwork on board the vessel; this process was known as "trying out the oil." The try-pot was set going by a wood fire, and then maintained with pieces of blubber from which the oil had already been extracted. The resulting overall stench on such a whaling ship was peculiar to the industry and quite permanent.

The metaphor *to try out* derives from the whaling usage; it means to test, to experiment, to compete, as for a position; to make an attempt or endeavour: "She was determined to try out for a place on the athletics team."

From the French *trier,* to sift or sort, to separate the good from the bad; to test, to prove.
(See also *Trane oil.)*

Trying
A trying time

A colloquialism meaning a testing time, when one may be annoyed, irritated, distressed; where one's patience is put to the test or one's mettle is proved. "The wedding reception at the hall turned out to be a trying time: the food was cold, the drinks were warm, and the speeches were interminable."

From the nautical manoeuvre "to lie a-try," which meant to lie-to in heavy weather, usually under reduced sail and sometimes under bare poles; also known as "trying." Sails specifically developed for lying-to under these conditions were called "trysails" (pronounced "tri-s'ls").
(See also *Try; To try, to try out.)*

Turkeys

Sailor's slang for the Royal Marine Light Infantry, before they became known more simply as the Royal Marines; from the fact that they wore red tunics as part of their uniform.
(See also *Bullocks. Grabbies. Jollies. Pongo.)*

Turn

From the Anglo-Saxon *turnian* and the Latin *tornare,* to turn or work with the wheel, and the Latin *tornus,* lathe.

To bring up with a round turn

Nautically, *to bring up with a round turn* is to check suddenly the movement of a line by throwing a turn of it around a cleat or belaying pin. Colloquially, the expression means to cause to stop suddenly, as with a jolt: "Our alert chairman brought the speaker, who had launched into a tirade of personal abuse, up with a round turn."
(See also *Lee; To bring by the lee.)*

To take a turn

To turn in seaman's language is to pass a rope around any yard, cleat, bollard, or similar fitting, generally to secure the rope or in preparation for some other action with it. The sense of there and back, around, or back and forth is expressed in the seaman's phrase *to take a turn on deck,* that is, to go up for some fresh air and a bit of exercise. Used in exactly the same way as a colloquialism in general speech, but not to be confused with turn as in order, rotation, proper sequence, etc., which of course is not nautical in origin.

To turn turtle

"We had not steamed two miles from that berg when it split in three portions with thunderous sounds and every portion turned turtle."

—*The Daily Telegraph* (English newspaper), February 28, 1887

To turn completely over, upside down. Originally said of a vessel that had turned right over, from the fact that a turtle, when turned over on its back, is quite helpless. As a metaphor, *to turn turtle* means exactly the same thing. "The drama production turned turtle when the leading lady broke her leg during the final rehearsal."

Turn and turn about

The same as "hot bunking": the use of the same bunk for sleeping by seamen in opposite watches; practised only in vessels that offered restricted accommodations, such as submarines. The shoregoing version of hot bunking is known as "Box and Cox," from the nineteenth-century farce *Box and Cox* by J. M. Morton (1811–1891), in which the deceitful lodging-house landlady Mrs. Bouncer lets the same room to two men, Box and Cox, who unknown to each other occupy it alternately. One of the two is out at work all day, the other all night; each man pays full rates for the room. The play was very successfully produced in 1847.

Hence the colloquial usage meaning one after the other, each taking his turn: "It was a very long journey to the eastern seaboard, and they drove the car turn and turn about."

Sailing ships of the nineteenth century provided sufficient space in the fo'c'sle for the men's bunks, although it was always cramped, dirty, and usually damp. Of course, in the Royal Navy of an earlier period, each man had his regulation 14 inches of space in which to sling his hammock from the beams of the lower deck.

Turn it up!

In Britain and some of the Commonwealth countries, a colloquialism for "Stop it!" or "Shut up!" From the nautical expression *to turn up,* which means to secure any rope to a cleat or bollard by simply taking several turns around it (but not the same as a "turn-up"). The transition to the metaphor is clear: to secure, hold fast, to prevent, or put a stop to: "We were tired of his constant criticism of our performance and told him that if he didn't turn it up he would be dumped from the team." In America, the phrase means to work harder, to be more enthusiastic about whatever is attempted.

Curiously, the British and the American usages are at odds with one another; if we liken the element *it* to power (as in an electric current), the Britisher using this phrase wants someone to switch it off, whereas the American wants it increased.

Turnout
A good turnout

"... there was a good turn-out of members."

—*Field Magazine,* October 8, 1885

"The morning commences with the watch on deck 'turning to' at daybreak and washing down, scrubbing, and swabbing the decks."

—Richard Henry Dana (1815–1882), American writer and jurist, *Two Years Before the Mast* (1840)

A "turnout" is a showing, a gathering, the result of some organising of events, such as a party or a celebration of some kind. The colloquialism stems from the order to sailors to "turn-in" to their bunks at the end of their watch, then to "turn-out" at the beginning of their work period, and to "turn-to" at their appointed tasks.

The turnout was the total complement of men available and fit enough for watch-duty. Hence the modern-day meaning of a "good turnout," which refers to a gathering somewhat larger, more pleasing, or more impressive than had been expected.
(See also *Turn-up.)*

Turn-up

The expression *to be turned up* meant to be "turned out": roused out of the fo'c'sl and sent up on deck to bear a hand or do some job or other. The phrase is still met with in some literature; Captain Marryat, for example, speaks of the midshipmen—the apprenticed boys—being turned up for their duties on deck.

More loosely, a turn-up is a showing; for example, a good turn-up at a party would be a sufficiently large number of people to help celebrate whatever it was they were gathered to celebrate.
(See also *Turnout.)*

Twaddle

"The penny cockney bookseller, pouring endless volumes of sentimental twaddle. . . ."

—William Makepeace Thackeray (1811–1863), English novelist, *English Humourists* (1851)

Sailor's slang from the early nineteenth century, meaning trivial, feeble, or tedious talk or writing; to prate or prattle on. Today the word still means to speak nonsense, to carry on in a foolish manner: "I could never get used to my uncle's twaddle about life on his tea plantation in India before Independence."

Twiddle

A twiddling line is a light line (up to about one inch in circumference) made fast at one end, with the other end passed round the uppermost spoke of the ship's wheel; such a line eased the helmsman's arm when steering. In moderate weather, a twiddling line could be attached to either side of the wheel; this is also common practice with modern tiller steering.

The current meaning of the word is to turn round and round, especially with the fingers, as in "to twiddle one's thumbs"; to be idle, or to play with something in an idle manner, probably from the fact that the twiddling line enabled the helmsman to enjoy periods of comparative idleness: "We had to sit in the waiting room and twiddle our thumbs while Father tried to sort out the very complicated arrangements for booking reservations."

U

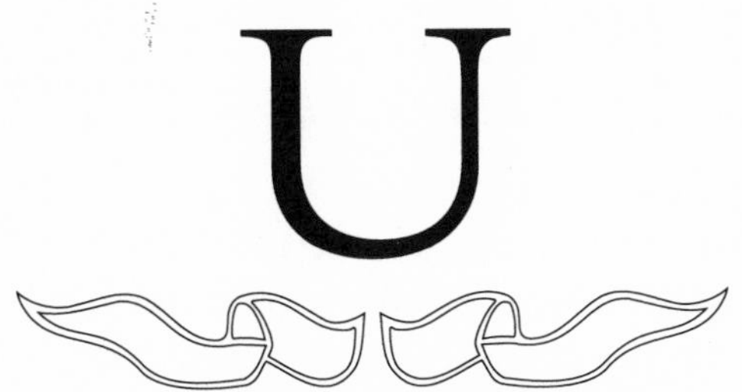

Under
To go under The allusion is obvious. As a ship is lost and ruined if she sinks (goes under), so is a person or firm ruined if overwhelmed by debt, catastrophe, or the like: "Many a firm went under in the recession of the early '90s."

Undermanned To be short-handed; said of a vessel that does not have a sufficient number of men to form a full complement of crew. By extension, any corporate effort can be undermanned if it lacks the required number of people to run it properly—as in a team game, a business office, and so on.

Unstayed To become unhinged; to be confused, nonplussed, at a loss; to lose one's equilibrium. A "stay" is the rope (earlier manila, for hundreds of years; now generally plough steel wire, or some other steel) used to support a mast—obviously an essential piece of rigging (stays are called "standing rigging"). A sailing ship engaged in battle would try to destroy the enemy's shrouds, the festoon of stays that reach up around each mast; the object was to bring the masts down and thereby render the vessel unmanoeuverable.

The colloquial usage reflects the awfulness of such an event, as in a stage actor forgetting his lines at a crucial moment—he becomes unstayed (along, probably, with everyone else onstage with him at the time).
(See also *Mainstay; To be one's mainstay.)*

Up spirits! The pipe or bosun's call for the daily issue of rum in a warship. At six bells in the forenoon watch the call was made, and the issue of rum was commenced to the Captain of the Hold, a petty officer, the Officer of the Day, and other ratings. These men drew off the required quantity of neat spirit from a tapped cask in the spirit room, and then spent some time mixing it with the correct quantity of water in the rum tub. Exactly at noon, eight bells were struck and the rum issue to each man commenced.
(See also *Grog. Tot; A tot of rum.)*

V

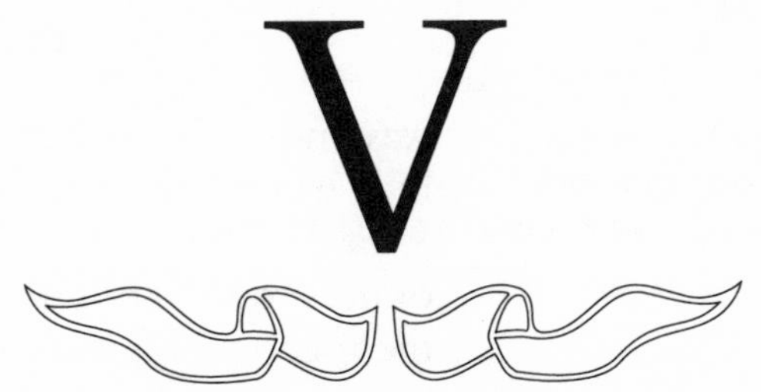

Van
To be in the van

"Sir Roger, you shall have the van."
—Francis Beaumont (1584–1616) and John Fletcher (1579–1625), English dramatists, *The Scornful Lady* (1610)

The word *van* is from the French *avant,* in front; the vanguard is the foremost division or the leading part of a force, applied first to the fleet at sea (from the Old French *avant-garde,* the guard coming before all others). From the beginning of the seventeenth century onwards, fleets of British warships were organised for battle into three divisions: van, centre, and rear, flying the White Ensign, the Red Ensign, and the Blue Ensign, respectively.

Metaphorically, the expression *to be in the van* means to be in front, at the head of; to be seen to be leading, as in "That secondary school is always in the van with innovative ideas in education."

Vanguard

See *Van; To be in the van.*

Veer
To veer away; to veer off

"The wind veered, the rain ceased."
—*The Daily Chronicle* (English newspaper), January 4, 1888

"Veering about one hundred and fifty fathoms of cable, the ship was happily brought up."
—Captain James Cook (1728–1779), English navigator and explorer, *First Voyage* (1771)

To veer, in the sense of turning or shifting to another direction, as does the wind. From the Latin *vertere,* to turn; but the nautical usage, to slacken or let out (as in "veer the anchor chain") is from the early Dutch *vieren,* to let out. Colloquially, when one veers away from something, one is shifting direction, as is a ship when it veers in its course: "He veered away from the group when he saw his ex-wife chatting with them."
(See also *Sheer; To sheer away, to sheer off.*)

Victuals

"There remained in company only our own squadron and our two victuallers."
—Admiral George Anson (1697–1762), English naval commander and explorer, *A Voyage Round the World* (1748), by Richard Walter, Anson's chaplain on HMS *Centurion*

The old name for food, provisions; from the Latin *victualia,* provisions. The term has long been linked with maritime history, since the days of exploratory voyages beyond sight of land, when the provisioning and storing of food on board ship became a matter of considerable importance. Victualling ships were always required to supply a fleet when it was likely to be at sea for a lengthy period.

The Victualling Board of the Royal Navy, in its various forms over a long period of time, was responsible for the purchase, preservation, and distribution to ships of food, slops, and other provisioning requirements. The official on board ship whose task was to issue rations to the seamen

"To see that the crew properly victual themselves."
—*Field Magazine,* December 24, 1887

was known as the purser (ultimately from the Greek *byrsa,* hide or leather, a bag or container, hence a purse).

In distributing these victuals, pursers reckoned on 14 ounces to the pound and pocketed the difference themselves. This sort of corruption and gross dishonesty became enormously widespread throughout landbound officialdom in the navy, and it wasn't until the beginning of the nineteenth century that the serving seaman was dealt with more honestly in the matter of his rations.
(See also *Slops.)*

Vogue
To be in vogue; to be the vogue

"The vogue of the hansom in Paris was transient."
—*The Daily Telegraph* (English newspaper), March 15, 1886

From the French *voguer,* to be carried forward on the water by oar or by sail, or to move with the tide or the current. When something is "in vogue," or "is the vogue" (usually fashion, or some expression in speech), it is copied by those who wish to be thought up-to-date. The phrase is no longer in vogue with seamen today.

Voyage

"All nations have interknowledge of one another, by voyage into foreign parts, or strangers that come to them."
—Francis Bacon (1561–1626), English jurist and writer, cited in the *Universal Dictionary of the English Language* (1897)

A sea journey from one port to another; a crew's voyage consists of a round trip from the ship's home port. The word is French, from the Latin *viaticum,* provision for a journey, from *viare,* to travel, and in turn from *via,* way. In medieval times, the word in English was applicable to any journey; then, as Britain established herself as a seafaring nation, it came to mean only a journey by sea.

W

Waft

"But soft, who wafts us yonder?"
—William Shakespeare (1564–1616), *The Comedy of Errors,* act 2, scene 2

A now obsolete nautical term, meaning to convey merchant shipping, to provide protection to such a convoy. Merchant ships in time of war were *wafted* from place to place by *wafters,* what today we would call escort vessels. The word was widely used in this sense in early nautical literature, but now it means to bear or carry through the air or over the water, as in "The sound of singing was wafted on the gentle breeze"; to bear or carry lightly, as in "He wafted her away from the noisy throng." From the Dutch *wahten,* to watch, guard; found in the Middle English *waughter,* armed escort vessel.

Waister

"The waist of a ship of this kind is an hollow space of about five feet in depth, contained between the elevations of the quarterdeck and the forecastle, and having the upper deck for its base or platform."
—William Falconer (1732–1769), English seaman and lexicographer, *The Shipwreck* (1762)

The term *waister,* sometimes *waster,* referred to a seaman (or a number of them) employed in the waist of a ship for various duties. (The ship's "waist" was the area of the upper deck between the forecastle and the quarterdeck.) They did not have to work on the masts or yards, and in fact had little to do beyond swabbing the decks or hauling in ropes. Waisters were untrained or incompetent seamen, often landsmen of uncertain intellect who found it impossible to comprehend and master the rudiments of seamanship. Rated seamen usually regarded waisters with a certain contempt, and the term *waster,* from the Latin *vastae,* to waste or destroy, owes some of its meaning to the originally nautical word *waister.*
(See also *Idler.)*

Wake
In the wake of

"In a storm they will hover close under the ship's stern, in the wake of the ship (as 'tis called) or the smoothness which the ship's passing has made on the sea."
—William Dampier (1652–1715), English buccaneer and explorer, *Voyages* (1697)

A wake is the track left by a ship or other object moving through the water; from the Icelandic *vok,* a hole in the ice. To be "in the wake of" is to follow behind, literally and figuratively: "The children set off in the wake of their mother as she stormed into the manager's office." The expression *in the wake of the storm* simply refers to the aftermath; both literally and figuratively, that which follows.

To set off in someone's wake

See *Wake; In the wake of.*

Walk
Walk the plank

See *Plank; Walk the plank.*

Wallop

A resounding blow; to beat vigorously. Claimed by one contemporary authority (Lind; see bibliography) to originate from the fact of one Admiral Wallop having destroyed a number of French ports during the reign of Henry VIII. However, this seems unlikely; very few proper nouns were adopted by seamen for the naming of things or events (among the very few that come to mind are the Nelson touch and the Bentinck sail). Rather, the word *wallop* derives from the Middle English *walop,* and is closely related to the French *galoper,* to gallop.

Warp

To warp is to move a vessel from one mooring to another by heaving on a rope, called a "warp" or "transporting line," which is secured to some fixed point, such as an anchor, a buoy, or a mooring position on shore. The word also describes the laying out of rigging in rigging lofts in the days of sail, for the purpose of measuring it and cutting it to length. In this case the rigging was said to be "warped" before it was cut.

All these senses of straight lines being deflected are embedded in current usage: to bend or twist out of shape. This idea of distortion, bending, etc., is originally nautical, and is common to the Scandinavian languages: "She had such a warped sense of humour that no one ever understood her jokes." From the Anglo-Saxon *weorpan,* to throw.

Wash-out

Colloquially, a fiasco, a failure, a nonstarter; also to cancel, to disregard; from the times when naval signal messages were taken down on a slate, which was wiped or washed clean when the message had been dealt with. The metaphor is in wide use in everyday language: "I tried to make my living as a writer, but it was a wash-out."

Waster

See *Waister.*

Watch
To keep watch

"Watchman, what of the night?"
—Isaiah 21:11

"I must to the watch."
—William Shakespeare (1564–1616), *Othello,* act 2, scene 3

To keep watch means to be aware of, to stay alert in order to notice possible danger and the like, to look out for someone or something, to be on the watch for: "The staff were always keeping watch for shoplifters, especially during the busy periods at the end of the year."

One of the duties of the watch was to maintain a sharp lookout for other vessels and the attendant hazards of the sea, particularly when close to land. So important was this duty that the name for it has impressed itself upon the language of landsmen. Thus, *to keep watch* is to keep an eye out, to be vigilant, to be on the alert. The motto of Frederick the Great (1712–1786) was *Toujours en vedette:* "Always on the watch."

Watches One of the basic routines of all shipboard activity. A watch is the length of time during which part of the crew is on duty, usually for a period of four hours, except at the time of the evening meal, when the dog watches are only two hours long to allow each of the two watch-keeping groups (traditionally called the "starboard watch" and the "port watch") to have their evening meal at approximately the same time.

The passage of time in each watch is marked by a stroke on the ship's bell every half-hour, so that eight bells signals the end of each watch. When reporting the time, sailors refer to it as so many "bells"; thus, half past three is seven bells, five minutes to one is five minutes to two bells, and so on.

"Had your watch been good, This sudden mischief never would have fallen."
—William Shakespeare (1564–1616), *Henry VI,* Part I, act 2, scene 1

The shipboard watch-keeping system of 24 hours begins at midnight, and is broken up into seven shifts of work for the men (in the Royal Navy, the new day began at noon). Furthermore, the 24-hour clock is used; this precedent, which the other armed services later adopted, was set many years ago. The watches and times are as follows:

0000–0400: Middle Watch (graveyard watch)
0400–0800: Morning Watch
0800–1200: Forenoon Watch
1200–1600: Afternoon Watch
1600–1800: First Dog Watch
1800–2000: Last Dog Watch
2000–2400: First Watch

The purpose of having each of the two dog watches of two hours' duration is to produce an uneven number of watches in the 24-hour period—traditionally, seven—so that watch-keepers do not have to keep the same watches every day.

The origin of the name *dog watch* is obscure; one suggestion is that they were so called because they were curtailed: this is too ingenious by half. The phrase might be related to "dog-sleep," an old term meaning feigned sleep, or light and fitful sleep that is easily interrupted, such as when one of the crew on watch is having a nap. Another possibility is that it is a corruption of "dodge watch"—i.e., by this means the crew are able to dodge being on duty at the same time every day.
(See also *Watch; To keep watch.)*

Water
High water mark *High water* (often called "high tide") is the highest level reached during one tidal oscillation; it is also the highest elevation reached by water, as in a river. Hence, the high water mark is the mark (often indicated by flotsam and jetsam) showing the highest level reached by the water, as in a flood or particularly high tide. Colloquially, it is the highest point of anything, or reached by some agent or some event; for example, the best season of achievement by a sporting team.

To back water To row backward in order to reverse or slow a boat's motion; hence, colloquially, to go easy, to retrace one's steps, to retreat: "He was forced to back water when questioned closely by the fisheries inspector about the number of rock lobster he had actually caught."

To be in deep water From two sources, both to do with the sea: to be in water over one's depth; and to experience the conditions that pertain to deep-water, offshore voyaging—ocean swell, developed weather systems, and the absence of the protection offered by the proximity of land. Colloquially, it means to be in difficulties; to be over one's head, as it were: "He found himself in deep water when he took on the job of managing the ailing firm."

To hold water (or to not hold water) To a seaman, anything that can hold water can also, by definition, keep water out, but a watertight hull was never said to be one that could actually hold water. Of course, any vessel or container that leaks is one that won't hold water, as in the all-important water cask kept on board all sailing ships. As a figure of speech, *to hold water* means tenable, correct, possible, valid: "His claims to be the owner of that horse will not hold water."

To keep one's head above water The nautical allusion is obvious. As a figure of speech, it means to avoid insolvency, to escape being overwhelmed by one's task or commitments: "She kept her head above water by calling in a receiver for her business and slowly trading her way out of the financial difficulties."

Waterlogged Said of a vessel so flooded and saturated with water that she barely manages to stay afloat. Anything that is so soaked or filled with water as to be heavy or unmanageable is said to be "waterlogged"; for example, waterlogged ground or timber that is saturated to capacity. The earliest nautical use referred to the loglike inertia of a ship partly full of water; it is interesting to note that a mid-eighteenth-century writer uses the term "water-lodged."

Waters
To be in smooth waters

To have no present anxieties; to be in a situation where one's troubles are a thing of the past. The nautical derivation is obvious.

(See also *Sailing; It's all plain sailing. Water; To be in deep water.*)

To be in treacherous waters

"The annihilating waters roar
Above what they have done. . . ."
—George Gordon Byron (1788–1824), English poet, *Heaven and Earth* (1818)

To find oneself in grave difficulties; to be in a position of some danger. Literally, a vessel caught in an area of reefs, strong tides, and a full wind would be in treacherous waters—for example, in the Arafura Sea between New Guinea and the coast of northern Australia. As a metaphor, it means to be out of one's depth in, say, the world of finance; or to be led into an argument or debate on a subject about which one knows little or nothing.

To fish in troubled waters

To take advantage of a troubled situation, such as political unrest, domestic unrest, and so on, for the purpose of personal gain. The derivation is from the fishing fleet rather than from the merchant or fighting navies: "During the war, the electronics company was fishing in troubled waters by selling communications equipment to both sides of the dispute."

(See also *Oil; To pour oil on troubled waters.*)

To pour oil on troubled waters

See *Oil; To pour oil on troubled waters.*

Wave
"A Life on the Ocean Wave"

A song of music-hall fame, which tells of the romance and adventure to be found afloat. The reality is, of course, another matter. Not an expression that any seaman would ever have used; in this regard, it is similar to "shiver me timbers," as both are spuriously nautical.

Waves
To make waves

"By the salt wave of the Mediterranean. . . ."
—William Shakespeare (1564–1616), *Love's Labour's Lost,* act 5, scene 1

Colloquially, to cause a disturbance, to upset existing standards or notions: "He delighted in making waves at the weekly directors' meetings by questioning the board closely—it gave him an air of self-importance."

From the physical fact that water is displaced, so as to form waves, when a vessel moves ahead under power (either by sail, steam, or any other means). In this sense, the water's usual state of rest is disturbed for a time.

Way

"A very great multitude spread their garments in the way."
—Matthew 21:8

An ancient word, from the Sanskrit *vah,* to carry, later assimilated into the Latin *via,* way. Not originally used nautically, but included here because some of its special senses have found their place in the seaman's vocabulary and thence into colloquial usage.

In way of

"Way" is the vessel's motion through the water. Literally, the phrase means "in that direction," "in that manner." The

"What my tongue can do in the way of flattery. . . ."
—William Shakespeare (1564–1616), *Coriolanus,* act 3, scene 2

metaphorical usage is very similar: "by this example," "as if to say." "By way of showing the apprentice how potentially dangerous the new machine could be, the foreman threw a wooden box into the chute, and within seconds it was matchwood."

To be underway

A ship is "underway" when she is in motion, making headway or sternway. *To lose way* is to lose speed and *to gather way* is to pick up speed. The term *under weigh* applies to the vessel at the moment when she has just broken her anchor out of the bottom and she herself is still stationary in the water; she is then said to be "underway" (note the different spellings) when she begins moving through the water. Often (but incorrectly) spelled "under weigh" when referring to motion.

Figuratively, an enterprise is said to be "under way" when it is set into motion, in progress, afloat: "Her plans are well under way for setting up a child-care centre for working mothers."

To gather way

To increase slowly in speed after getting underway; as a vessel works up to her normal cruising speed, she is said to be "gathering way." Similarly for any movement or enterprise that is set into some deliberate motion: "The enthusiasm of the audience gathered way and the players were spurred on to give their best performance in years."

To give way

"Spanish and Egyptian gave way a little. . . ."
—*The Daily Telegraph* (English newspaper), October 5, 1883

"Give way" is the order, given to the crew of a pulling boat, to cease pulling (rowing) on one side so that the oars on the other side can turn the boat suddenly, as required. Colloquially, the expression means to break down, to yield, to withdraw or retreat: "He was forced to give way to her compelling argument for better conditions for his employees." It is also implied in the expressions *gangway* and *make way,* in the sense of "clear a path or lane."

To lose way

The expression *to lose way* means to lose speed when sailing; the exact opposite of *to gather way.*

To make way

The expression means exactly the same as *Gangway!,* in the sense of to allow to pass, to stand aside and leave room, to give up or retire in favour of some other person: "The crowd drew back to make way for the ambulance men." (See also *Gangway; To make gangway.)*

Wear
To wear it

To wear a vessel is to put it onto the other tack by putting its stern through the wind, exactly as in a gybe, or jibe (the usual and safer method is to put the bow through the

"We were obliged in the afternoon to wear ship."
—Admiral George Anson (1697–1762), English naval commander, *A Voyage Round the World* (1748), by Richard Walter, Anson's chaplain on HMS *Centurion*

wind). This action is known as "wearing ship" (in the past tense, a ship is "wore," not "worn"). The word may be the sailor's corruption of the nautical term *to veer,* from the Medieval French *virer,* to turn about. *Veer* is to let out rope (as in "Veer the cable!") and to turn (as in "The wind began to veer to the north"). However, the expression *to wear ship* is older than *to veer ship.*

The colloquialism is usually expressed as a negative: to not wear it, as in "I wouldn't ask for a raise yet if I were you: the boss wouldn't wear it." Used in this fashion, it means to not tolerate something, to not stand for it, to not believe; to be unpersuaded and unmoved, as is a sailing ship that, for whatever reason, fails to wear round onto the opposite tack, thereby putting itself in possible danger.

Weather

From the Anglo-Saxon *weder,* common in all the Teutonic tongues in similar forms, and ultimately from the Sanskrit *vata,* wind.

A fair weather sailor; a fair weather friend

"I would throw a dozen of such fair-weather gentlemen as you are."
—H. Brooke, *Fool of Quality,* cited in the *Universal Dictionary of the English Language* (1897)

The allusion is to persons who profess friendship when it suits their own purposes to do so, in the same way that some yachtsmen go sailing only when the weather is clear and settled: "As soon as he found himself seriously short of money, all his fair weather friends deserted him."

To be under the weather

To feel unwell, out of sorts, either as a result of illness or, less often, untoward weather. Literally, it means to be in the path of bad weather, made worse perhaps by the possibility of having a lee shore. It is also a colloquialism for being inebriated.

The phrase has an obvious connection with *mal-de-mer;* sailors are traditionally lightly contemptuous of landsmen who succumb to seasickness, which is the visible symptom of being under the influence of the weather (although it is worth noting that Lord Nelson himself freely admitted to being seasick for a day or two whenever he went to sea): "I am feeling somewhat under the weather today because of the flu I picked up on that camping trip last week."

To keep the weather of

"Whilst *Arethusa* was on this (port) tack, *Neptune* hove round again and weathered her, thus becoming leading vessel again."
—*Field Magazine,* September 4, 1886

To get round, to get the better of; to overcome, to have the upper hand. From the fact that a ship to windward of another (i.e. having the weather gage) is in a position of advantage.

To make heavy weather

To make a task seem unduly laborious, by approaching it in an ill-prepared manner; to exaggerate the difficulty of a job by reason of one's inexpertness. The reference is to the

labouring motion of a ship in rough seas, when forward movement (progress) is difficult, if not sometimes impossible, to achieve: "The new mechanic said that he'd finish the job in half an hour, but it was obvious that he was making heavy weather of it." *Making heavy weather of it* also means to be so drunk that one staggers, as if on board a ship at sea.
(See also *Weather; To weather the storm.)*

To weather the storm

"Many a rough sea had he weathered in her. . . ."
—Alfred, Lord Tennyson (1809–1892), English poet, *Enoch Arden* (1864)

"We have been tugging a great while against the stream, and have almost weathered our point; a stretch or two more will do the work."
—Joseph Addison (1672–1719), English poet, dramatist, and essayist, *Todd,* cited in the *Universal Dictionary of the English Language* (1897)

When a vessel has come through heavy weather or storms, and has done so more or less safely, it is said to have *weathered it,* or *weathered the storm.* The allusion is to the obvious relationship between going to sea and the necessity for the ship to be built to withstand very trying conditions. *To go to weather* is to sail or steam into the storm so as to maintain steerage and thus avoid being broached. This would be done only if it were not possible to outdistance the area of influence of the storm.

Similarly, one is said to have *weathered the storm* if one has safely come through trying and difficult times: "I knew that I was going to catch a lot of criticism from my wife for not coming home in time for the children's party, but I weathered the storm by pleading illness."
(See also *Weather; To make heavy weather.)*

Weather-beaten

"Weather-beaten old seamen who had risen from being cabin-boys to be admirals."
—Thomas Babington Macaulay (1800–1859), English essayist and historian, *History of England* (1848)

To be lined in the face; to have rough, dry skin; to appear as if one had been thoroughly exposed to the elements for a long time, as seamen are. Much used in describing workers who have spent their lives out of doors, as in "The old gardener's weather-beaten face screwed up in thought at my question about possible rain."

Weather-eye
To keep a weather-eye open

Metaphorically, to have one's wits about one, to keep a good lookout, to be on guard. From the fact that seamen always kept a close watch on the wind, sea, and sky so as to be prepared for squalls, etc., that would come from the weather side of the vessel: "You should always keep a weather-eye open for any possible difficulties that might lie ahead."

Wend

"Unaccompanied, great voyages to wend. . . ."
—Henry Howard Surrey (?1517–1547), English poet, Virgil's *Aeneid* (1557)

An old seafaring term meaning to go from one tack to the other. From the Old English *wendan,* to pursue one's way, which meaning is still retained in everyday usage: "We watched the children wend their way down the path to the pool in the playground."

Wet
To be wet; to be all wet

Sailor's slang for "stupid"; *to be as wet as a scrubber* means to be extremely stupid, a scrubber being one of the menials on board ship, a loblolly. The phrase is widely used in British

colloquial speech, and is also commonly used in Australia and New Zealand. *He is pretty wet* means "he is fairly stupid," and *Don't talk wet* means "don't talk such nonsense, don't be silly." "He boasts a lot about his mountaineering exploits, but it's just a lot of wet talk—he's never climbed a ladder, let alone a decent hill." From the Anglo-Saxon *waet,* wet.
(See also *Loblolly.)*

Whack
To get one's whack

"Whack" was the regular daily supply of provisions to the seaman, the amount of which was determined by regulations. Colloquially, *to get one's whack* was to make sure that one got what one wanted or, at the very least, got what one deserved; also *a whack up,* to divide up, to share the spoils. Used as in "Did you get your whack from the share-out of the club's lotto win last night?"

"This young bachelor had taken his share (what he called his whack) of pleasure."
—William Makepeace Thackeray (1811–1863), English novelist, *A Shabby Genteel Story* (1840)

Landlubbers will be interested to know that it wasn't until 1907 that knives and forks ("port and starboard oars") became official issue in Royal Navy messes; for hundreds of years prior to that date, only spoons were provided by the Admiralty.
(See also *Whacked.)*

Whacked

Originally, "whack" was the serving-out of the cooked food in each mess in the days of sail in the British navy. Nowadays a quite well-known colloquialism in British and Australian usage, to mean exhausted or defeated: "I am quite whacked from all that work on the squash court." Derived from the fact that one's whack was the exact amount, the limit, beyond which there was no more (in this sense, the squash player has used up all her energy—there is nothing left). American usage is similar, with the added meaning of crazy, often seen in the form "whacky," "wacky," or "wacko."
(See also *Whack; To get one's whack.)*

Wheel
The man at the wheel

The wheel, sometimes called the "helm," was probably first adapted by the Dutch. The earliest method of steering a vessel was by a steering oar clamped or pivoted over the right side of the vessel close to the stern (hence the term *starboard,* which is a corruption of *steer-board,* from the Old English *steor,* steering, and *bord,* side).

For hundreds of years before the introduction of the wheel, the ship's rudder was controlled by the tiller, a long bar by which the rudder was moved from side to side as required. In early vessels, the stern sections (the after-castle and the poop deck) had become so tall that the helmsman had to be located well below deck level, such that he no longer was able to see anything pertaining to the behaviour of the ship.

One method of bringing the helmsman back to the level of the upper deck was to intall a whipstaff, which was essentially a vertical lever that pivoted about its own fulcrum. The upper end of the whipstaff was held by the steersman, while the lower end was simply yoked around the forward end of the tiller. Side-to-side movement of the whipstaff produced a corresponding and opposite horizontal movement of the tiller. This system lasted about 250 years, until the introduction of the wheel.

Clearly, the skill of the helmsman, especially in time of battle or bad weather, was of paramount importance; upon him depended the safety of the vessel and all aboard her. Every seaman was required to do his trick at the wheel (an able-bodied seaman was one who could "hand, reef, and steer"), but in times of danger only experienced and capable men were placed at the wheel.

Similarly, in a colloquial sense "the man at the wheel" is the person who has charge of some particular enterprise, of whatever nature; upon his or her shoulders sits the responsibility for the final outcome, such as the manager of a commercial firm or the leader of a political party.

Whip
To whip something up

A whip is a small tackle (block and pulley arrangement) used for light tasks; usually comprising a single rope rove through a single block, and used for hoisting, pulling, and the like. Combinations can be made so as to exert more power, as in a double whip, whip-upon-whip, and such.

"The whip passes rapidly toward the wreck, and arriving there the sailors make fast the tail-block in accordance with the directions on the tally-board, and show a signal to the shore."
—*Scribner's Magazine,* January 1880

To whip up was literally the act of hoisting quickly and without delay; hence the colloquial usage meaning to create or organise quickly and efficiently: "She whipped —up a reception committee for the unexpected arrival of the foreign dignitary"; "He whipped up a batch of cookies when he saw that the children had eaten all the cake."

Whipping

A method of preventing a rope end from fraying, by taking a series of turns around it with yarn, twine, or other small line. The ends of the whipping are usually secured by knotting or tucking them under the turns. The most usual forms of whipping used at sea are common whipping, sailmaker's whipping, and West Country whipping. From the Dutch *wippen,* to shake or to wag, and found in other Teutonic languages. The nautical use is from the fact that the ends of the reef-points used for furling the sails would whip and thrum against the fabric of the sail itself, thereby fraying their ends. The word has the same literal meaning in everyday speech: a binding or winding of cord about something.

Whistle
To whistle for it

"Your fame is secure, let the critics go whistle."
—William Shenstone (1714–1763), English poet, *The Poet and the Dunce,* cited in the *Universal Dictionary of the English Language* (1897)

Sailors once believed that, when a ship was becalmed, a wind could be raised by whistling for it; no doubt if one spent long enough at it, a wind would eventually blow anyway. In time (as an illustration of the perversity of some nautical expressions), the phrase came to mean just the opposite; nowadays the popular superstition holds that whistling will abate the wind. *You can whistle for it* now means that, try as you might, whatever it is you're after, you won't get it.
(See also *Wind; To whistle up a wind.)*

White ensign See *Red, white, and blue.*

Wildfire A very old nautical name for a mixture of flammable materials, the whole of which caught fire very easily. It was also extremely difficult to extinguish. Naturally, such a substance found early favour with the progressive maritime nations of the world, who used it widely in their sea battles.

The word is found in colloquial figures such as "The news of the president's arrest spread like wildfire."
(See also *Greek fire.)*

Wind

"Storming her world with sorrow's wind and rain. . . ."
—William Shakespeare (1564–1616), *Complaint of a Lover,* cited in the *Universal Dictionary of the English Language* (1897)

From the Anglo-Saxon *wind;* the word is traced back through the Teutonic languages to the Latin *ventus,* and ultimately to the Sanskrit *vata.* The wind, of course, is the *sine qua non* of the sailor's life in sail; its importance is reflected in the many nautical expressions that have found a secure place in our everyday speech.

According to classical mythology, the winds of the north, south, east, and west (respectively Boreas, Notus, Eurus, and Zephyrus) were ruled by Aeolus, who kept them in a cave. Aeolus gave Ulysses a bag containing all the dangerous and unfavourable winds, such as storms and tempests, so that he might complete his journey without being delayed. However, his crew opened the bag, thinking that it contained treasure; all the hurtful winds escaped and a terrible storm at once arose and drove the boat back to the island of Aeolus.

A bit close to the wind See *Sail; To sail close to the wind.*

A capful of wind Legend says that Eric, king of Sweden, could command evil spirits to send wind from the direction in which he pointed his cap; for this he was called "Windy Cap." The Laplanders used to sell winds—or protection therefrom—to mariners, and it is recorded that as recently as 1814 a woman named Bessie Millie of Pomona, in the Orkneys, was selling favourable winds to sailors for a small fee. The three witches in Shakespeare's *Macbeth* boast of their power to direct the winds.

Modern usage refers to winds that are favourable and of just the right strength to ensure a fast but safe voyage. Colloquially, "a capful of wind" is the amount of effort that will be just enough to secure the desired result—not too much and not too little.

Betwixt wind and water Nautically, means on or close to the line of immersion on a ship's hull. This area is alternately wet or dry, according to the motion of the ship and the waves; consequently, it is the most dangerous place for a ship to be holed. The reference is to finding oneself in an awkward or potentially dangerous situation and having thereby to make a decision as to one's course of action.

The emphasis here is on the danger inherent in the situation: "She was betwixt wind and water as to whether she should accept the promise of promotion by her boss, or apply for a much better position in a rival company."
(See also *Devil; Between the devil and the deep blue sea, The devil to pay.)*

In the teeth of the wind/gale Meaning with the wind dead against one, dead against one's teeth; to be directly opposed all the way. Metaphorically, to be opposed to the general current of opinion.
(See also *Wind; In the wind's eye.)*

In the wind's eye Nautically, to be directly opposed by the wind, to be headed; colloquially, to be opposed to general opinion, as "to sail against the wind."
(See also *Wind; In the teeth of the wind/gale.)*

To be windy See *Wind; To have the wind up.*

To eat the wind An old-time sailing term meaning to overhaul another vessel, to overtake her, especially when both are sailing on the wind (that is, into the wind) and the faster vessel passes close to windward, thus giving what yachtsmen call "bad air" to the slower vessel. A tactic much approved of in yacht racing circles, and one that can count for everything in important races, such as the America's Cup series.
(See also *Wind; To take the wind out of someone's sails.)*

To have the wind of To be on the alert for, to keep a strict watch on, as a seaman constantly monitors the speed and direction of the wind:

"My son and I will have the wind of you."
—William Shakespeare (1564–1616), *Titus Andronicus,* act 4, scene 2

"She thinks that she has outsmarted me in my ambition to be appointed company secretary, but I have the wind of her—I know exactly what she is planning to do."

To have the wind up

To take fright (often expressed as "to be windy"), to be alarmed; from the sense that when a wind blew up at sea, the seaman could be certain of a hectic and trying time. Used as in "He got the wind up when he saw how close we were to the edge of the cliff."

The mariner over the centuries has accumulated a vast weather lore, including the ability to foretell the weather by the sky's appearance, changes in wind direction, cloud formations, variations of atmospheric pressure, sea swells, and so on. He often expressed this knowledge in jingles or short rhymes, some of which have passed into everyday speech. Among the best known are:

Mackerel skies and mares' tails
Make tall ships carry short sails

If woolly fleeces deck the heavenly way
Be sure no rain will mar a summer's day

Red sky in the morning, sailor take warning
Red sky at night, sailor's delight

To raise the wind

Nautically, parallel to the expression *to whistle up a wind.* Colloquially, the phrase *to raise the wind* means to raise the necessary funds for some particular purpose, to get the wherewithal; as a wind—which traditionally is summoned by whistling on board ship—provides the necessaries and essentials for any voyage under sail.
(See also *Wind; To whistle up a wind.)*

To see how the wind blows

See *Wind; To see which way the wind blows.*

To see which way the wind blows

"Indications are not wanting to show which way the wind blows."
—*Field Magazine,* October 17, 1885

To establish the state of affairs, what the position is, how things are going on or are likely to turn out, to see what the outcome of some matter will be, to judge its tendency. From the seaman's lifelong habit of checking the wind for its strength and direction; upon both depend the outcome of his endeavours. Used as in "He telephoned the boss's secretary to see which way the wind was blowing concerning his request for a transfer."

To take the wind out of someone's sails

In the days of sail, the only sure way of causing an opponent's vessel to slow down—short of ramming her or sinking her by gunfire—was to sail as close to her as possible on her windward side, thereby blanketing her sails and depriving her of the wind. The tactic is much used and highly thought of in yacht racing.

The colloquial application is similar; it refers to the act of stealing one's thunder, often by utilising that person's methods or information and forestalling him or her with a judicious and often surprising reversal: "She was about to tell her brother about her secret engagement when he completely took the wind out of her sails by saying that he already knew of it."

To whistle up a wind To entertain false hopes, such as in trying to borrow money for a spree or run ashore. From the sailors' superstition that a wind could be raised by whistling for it; the meaning has long since been reversed, so that "whistling up a wind" will produce nothing: "If he thinks that I am going to take him back after what he has done to me, he is whistling up the wind."

Whistling on board ship is still abhorred by many sailors. One of the reasons for this is that whistling could be confused with the calls of the bosun's pipes. The only exceptions to this rule were the cook and his assistant; they were encouraged to whistle (but not too loudly) because when they were doing so the crew could be fairly sure that their provisions weren't being surreptitiously eaten in the galley.

It is worth noting that sailors, when endeavouring to whistle up a wind, always faced in the direction from which they wished it to come. When they saw a "catspaw," or ruffle of wind on the surface of the sea, they would rub the ship's backstay (as though fondling a cat) and whistle all the more to induce the wind to come to the ship.
(See also *Whistle; To whistle for it.)*

Windjammer The name by which square-rigged vessels were known, especially by landsmen. It was not used until steam superseded sail, and even then rarely by sailors.

Windward
To get to windward of

"We weyed and turned to the windwards."
—Richard Hakluyt (?1552–1616), English cleric and maritime historian, *Principall Navigations, Voiages, and Discoveries of the English Nation* (1589)

Means to be upwind of an object, as a ship would endeavour to be downwind (i.e., to windward) of a hazard such as a shoal, rocks, and so on; in this position the vessel can safely steer clear of the danger. Used as in "He heard about the group's secret plan to topple the chairman from his post, and he got to windward of them by alerting the board to the possibility of trouble."

Woodser
Doing a Jimmy Woodser

Recorded as an expression from the merchant marine; it means a solitary drinker, and the phrase is possibly based on the habits of a person named Jimmy Woods. The phrase is fairly common, especially in Australian idiomatic speech; it also refers to the alcoholic drink consumed alone: "I'm drinking with Jimmy Woods" would be understood to mean "I'm drinking by myself, thanks."

Word
Pass the word

To relay an order or summons. In the normal course of events, an officer in a man-o'-war could order his next subordinate, for instance, to get or fetch the surgeon; that order would usually be rendered as "pass the word for the surgeon" down the chain of command.

Used for the same purpose in everyday speech, except, of course, no sense of hierarchy is implied. Frequently used in a crowd, where a direct request might go unheard; as in a political party's headquarters on polling day, when the candidate, amid all the hubbub, might wish to speak with her agent.

Work

A word widely used in the sailor's vocabulary. A vessel is said to "work" when her timbers are being strained by her labouring in a heavy sea. *To work to windward* is to beat or tack (both, of course, being points of sailing to windward); it also means to get a vessel underway in a contrary wind.

"I never did anything worth doing by accident, nor did any of my inventions come by accident; they came by work."

—Thomas Alva Edison (1847–1931), quoted in H. L. Mencken's *Dictionary of Quotations* (1942)

Working is found in such expressions as "working her timbers"; "working strain" (the maximum load that can be borne by any working gear); and "working up." The phrase *to be worked up* describes the state of the vessel when she has been brought to her highest pitch of efficiency, when every member of her crew and every item of gear are working or performing as intended.

It is tempting to speculate that the colloquialisms "to be worked up," "to be working toward," and the like derive from the nautical usage. This is quite possible, because the verb *to work,* from the Anglo-Saxon *wyrcan,* in all its applications, has been in seafaring use for a very long time.

Worse things happen at sea!

A well-known expression, used in the British Commonwealth countries but virtually unknown in American speech. It means just what it says: things may seem pretty bad at the moment, but there is some consolation in the knowledge that things are usually worse at sea. From the fact that sailors have only their ship and each other to turn to for help when they are in dire peril. If their vessel is in danger of foundering in a storm or of being driven ashore and wrecked in a gale, the margin of succour available to the seamen is very slim indeed. More freely translated, the expression means "count your blessings": "Don't get too upset about the dent in your new car—worse things happen at sea."

Wrinkle A smart way of doing something; sometimes also the sailor's smart way of dodging doing something. Probably from the sailor's everyday familiarity with the behaviour of sailcloth, rope, etc., and the wrinkles that were literally part of the nature of these items. From the Anglo-Saxon *wrincle,* and in the sense described here it is probably related to *wrench,* which is from the Anglo-Saxon *wrenc.*

Y

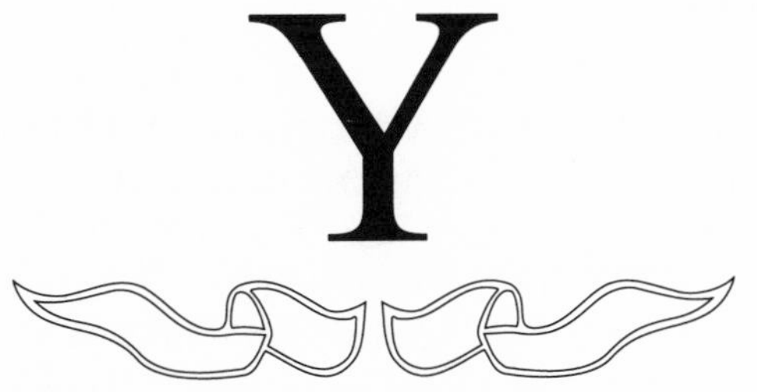

Yacht Included here because of its established place in our language. From the Dutch *jacht, jagt,* and *jagtschip;* and compounded on *jagen,* to hunt, to hurry.

Originally a yacht was a Dutch vessel of state, speedy and easy to handle, used for carrying very important people. In 1660 the Dutch East India Company presented Charles II with a yacht as a pleasure boat, named the *Mary,* and from that time the word has remained in the language to mean "any vessel propelled by either sail or power, and not plying for hire."

Yachts were at first utilised by the Dutch navy as revenue cutters and despatch boats, because they were very fast and handy. For some time they were employed by wealthy Dutch owners in re-creating famous battles, sham fights, and water parades and reviews.

"I sailed this morning with his Majesty in one of his Yatchts [sic]."
—John Evelyn (1620–1706), English diarist and at one time a member of the court of Charles II, *Diary* (1641–1706)

However, they did not use their yachts for racing; this first took place in England. Soon after Charles II was presented with his yacht by the Dutch, other such vessels were built in England on exactly the same lines as Charles II's vessel *Mary.* By 1661 there were four of these craft in England. In October of that year, the king challenged his brother, the Duke of York, to a race for a purse of £100. The king lost the Greenwich-to-Gravesend morning match, but won the return passage in the afternoon. Thus was yacht racing born, only one year after the type had been introduced into England.

The sport quickly grew. In 1851 the Royal Yacht Squadron offered a trophy known as the "100-Guinea Cup" (more affectionately as "The Auld Mug"), for a race around the Isle of Wight. The 170-ton schooner *America,* representing the New York Yacht Club, soundly defeated a fleet of 15 British yachts. (One story has it that Queen Victoria, watching the event and perhaps miffed at the fact that the sole American entry had won, stonily enquired as to which vessel had come in second; "Madam," said her aide, "there is no second.") Since then, the cup, known for decades as the "America's Cup," remained with the

Americans until 1983, despite some 23 challenges from international syndicates costing untold millions of dollars.

On September 26, 1983, the 12-metre *Australia II,* skippered by John Bertrand, created a world sensation by defeating Dennis Conner in the American *Liberty* by 41 seconds in the last of the seven match races, to win the series 4 to 3. Four years later, in 1987, Conner regained the cup in waters off Fremantle, Western Australia, sailing under the auspices of the San Diego Yacht Club in California.

In 1992 Buddy Melges in *America* beat the Italian syndicate 4 to 1 in a Cup series that saw the introduction of a new type of yacht, known as the International America's Cup Class, thus relegating the old and well-tried 12-metre class to obscurity.

F. Scott Fitzgerald, American novelist and short-story writer (1896–1940), once commented that he "entertained on a cruising trip that was so much fun I had to sink my yacht to make my guests go home."

Yardarm
To clear one's yardarm

The yardarm is each end of the yard of a square-rigged vessel. Most of a ship's flag signals were hoisted from these positions, and when the disciplinary code on board included punishment of death by hanging, it was always the yardarm from which the condemned man was hanged.

"His imagination was full of sails, yard-arms, and rudders."
—Thomas Babington Macaulay (1800–1859), English essayist and historian, *History of England* (1848)

In battle, ships would maneouvre close to one another so that boarding parties could swarm over to the other vessel for hand-to-hand combat; a common device was to station some men on the yards so that the enemy's yardarms could be secured to one's own by a lashing, grapnel hooks, and the like, to prevent the vessels from drifting apart again. Inevitably, the chaos and confusion of close-quarters fighting like this led to a great deal of damage on, and entanglement between, the opposing vessels. If one wanted, for whatever reason, to break apart from the other vessel, then all the lashings, grapnels, etc., would have to be cut and cleared away; hence the term, "to clear one's yardarms," meaning to get clear, to disentangle.

As a metaphor, it means to sort out one's argument or disagreement with another person, to put matters right, to clear up the mess and—it is hoped—be absolved of blame: "He wanted to clear his yardarms by confessing all his petty crimes to the police."

The sun over the yardarm

See *Sun; The sun over the yardarm*.

Yarn
To spin a yarn

To tell a story. From the sailor's habit of telling stories and reminiscing to pass the time while engaged in deckwork such as teasing pieces of old rope into short lengths of

"[He] who has yarned aforetime 'On the Fo'k'sle Head' and 'Round the Galley Fire.'"

—*The Daily Telegraph* (English newspaper), December 29, 1885

oakum, or working up rope-yarn into more serviceable small stuff. Spun yarn had a variety of uses on board a wind-driven vessel, such as stropping sails to enable them to be hoisted while still bundled (furled), or for a variety of kinds of seizing, serving, and the like.

The metaphor is from the idea of stretching, teasing out, putting to good use, and so on: "He began to spin a yarn to his wife to account for his late arrival home."

Youngster Originally a nautical usage, to refer to the midshipmen (the "young gentlemen") who messed in the after cockpit on the orlop deck, a nonfighting deck immediately above the hold, and consequently one that was dingy, damp, and very small, beset by foul odours from the bilge, rotting rope, spilled gin and beer, and the lingering odours of fried food. The other occupants of this mess were the master's mates, the surgeon's mates, and the captain's clerk, most of whom were known as "oldsters."

Professor Lloyd (see bibliography) points out that the *Sea Grammar* (1627) of Captain John Smith (the same John Smith who founded the colony of Virginia) defines the sailor as "the older man who hoists the sails and the younker is the younger man called foremast man to take in top sails etc." Captain Smyth, in his *Sailor's Word Book* of some two centuries later, gives both terms, *youngster* and *younker,* and defines them as referring to "a volunteer of the first-class, and a general epithet for a stripling in the service." An English formation influenced by the Dutch *yonker* and *yong heer,* young sir.
(See also *Oldster.)*

Bibliography

The following is a selected list of books that deal with topics covered by this volume. A brief commentary is attached to each one to indicate its importance as a reference for this text. A list of dictionaries consulted for etymologies and historical citations (where appropriate) appears at the end of the bibliography.

Selected Sources

Admiralty Manual of Seamanship. Volumes 1–3. London, 1972.

The widely respected basic textbook of seamanship used by officers and sailors in the Royal Navy. Focuses, naturally, on modern warships, but the sections dealing with general seamanship in each volume are absorbing. Excellent black-and-white illustrations and line drawings.

Chapman, Charles F. *Piloting, Seamanship and Small Boat Handling*. 53d ed. New York: Motor Boating and Sailing, 1967.

Long recognised as the "bible of boating," this book covers virtually every aspect of going to sea. Rather conservative, but perhaps this is one of its many strengths.

Clarkson, Henry. *The Yachtsman's A–Z*. Newton Abbot, England: David & Charles, 1979.

A basic encyclopedia of sailing for the less experienced sailor; covers most areas, and is well illustrated with bold line drawings.

Dana, Richard Henry. *Two Years Before the Mast*. Reprint ed. London: Heron Books, 1968.

First published in 1840, Dana's book quickly was recognised as one of the masterpieces of the sea. It is an account of a two-year trading voyage around the Horn from Boston to California, and paints a particularly vivid picture of what life at sea was like for a merchant seaman in an American fo'c'sle.

Falconer, William. *An Universal Dictionary of the Marine*. Reprint ed. Newton Abbot, England: David & Charles, 1970.

After Smyth (1867), perhaps the best of the early dictionaries of nautical terms.

Gaby, Captain James. *Mate in Sail.* Artarmon, New South Wales: Antipodean, 1974.

A warm and personable account of a deepwaterman's experiences in square riggers, covering a lifetime of service at sea. Extremely interesting for its account of the seaman's day-to-day life. Particularly well illustrated with photographs and marine paintings.

Garrett, Richard. *The British Sailor.* London: Wayland, 1974.

An introductory survey of what it was like to have been a sailor in the British Royal Navy, from the twelfth century to modern times. A necessarily brief examination, but entertainingly written and well illustrated.

Greenhill, Basil. *The Merchant Schooners.* Revised ed. New York: A. M. Kelley, 1968.

Deals with the history of the British merchant schooners and with life and conditions on board. Of great interest to the social historian; long regarded as the standard work on this particular subject.

Hakluyt, Richard. *Voyages and Documents.* Janet Hampden, ed. London: Oxford University Press, 1958.

First published in 1589 as *Principall Navigations, Voiages, and Discoveries of the English Nation,* Hakluyt's book has become the prose epic of maritime history. Of great importance to the social and linguistic historian for the scores of original accounts of sixteenth-century voyages and travels.

Hampshire, A. Cecil. *Just an Old Navy Custom.* London: William Kimber, 1979.

An important book for the maritime historian. The author explores the meanings and origins of a great many of the nautical terms and expressions that have become part of our everyday language.

Harland, John. *Seamanship in the Age of Sail: An Account of the Sailing Man-of-War, 1600–1860.* London: Conway Maritime Press, 1984.

A work of astonishing scholarship. This book examines and explains how sailing ships were handled in the old days, covering every evolution and eventuality from setting of the sails, weighing anchor, reefing, steering, managing a vessel in a storm, heaving to, and many other aspects. Profusely illustrated by Mark Myers, with line drawings that bring the text to life.

Kemp, Peter. *The British Sailor: A Social History of the Lower Deck.* London: Dent, 1970.

A social history of the day-to-day living conditions of the British sailor from Tudor times to the twentieth century, discussed in a clear and always interesting manner.

Kemp, Peter, ed. *The Oxford Companion to Ships and the Sea.* London: Oxford University Press, 1976.

An excellent compendium of maritime lore. The book is a lively historical survey of man and ship, with a preponderance of focus on sail and the rich language of the sea. An important reference work.

Landstrom, Bjorn. *The Ship: A Survey of the History of the Ship from the Primitive Raft to the Nuclear-Powered Submarine.* Michael Phillips, transl. London: Allen & Unwin, 1961.

Perhaps the best general survey of ship types available today. Examines the history of humankind's association with the sea from prehistoric times to the modern day; magnificently illustrated.

Lewis, Michael. *A Social History of the Navy, 1793–1815.* London: Allen & Unwin, 1960.

A very detailed and well-documented account of the officers and men who fought in the wars of the late eighteenth and early nineteenth centuries (the French Revolutionary War and the Napoleonic War). Perhaps the best study available of a particular period in Britain's naval history.

Lind, Lew. *Sea Jargon.* Sydney, Australia, 1982.

A compact collection of the words and phrases that form such an essential part of nautical language. It is, as the author says, a "Dictionary of the Unwritten Language of the Sea."

Lloyd, Christopher. *The British Seaman 1200–1860: A Social Survey.* London: Collins, 1968.

One of the best contemporary studies of the life of the British sailor, from 1200 to 1860. The author has conducted some fascinating research into the problems associated with manning the Crown's ships in time of war, and the result is both erudite and extremely readable.

The Lore of Ships. New York: Crescent, 1975.

A large-format survey of ships from early sail to the modern warship. The illustrations are detailed, informative, and attractive. The sections on mechanical propulsion and twentieth-century shipbuilding will not be of great interest to sail enthusiasts, but the sections devoted to the days of sail are magnificently presented.

Marryat, Frederick. *Mr. Midshipman Easy.* Reprint ed. London: J. M. Dent, 1959.

First published in 1836, the novel is a series of naval adventures that offers to the present-day historian a very interesting and revealing—if highly romanticised—account of life in the Royal Navy of the nineteenth century.

Masefield, John. *Sea Life in Nelson's Time.* Reprint ed. London: Conway Maritime Press, 1971.

An interesting and enthusiastically written account of the Nelson age, and useful as an introduction to naval history. Masefield, like Smollett before him, had the great advantage of having had sea experience; toward the end of the nineteenth century, at the age of 15, he had rounded the Horn in a square-rigger.

Morton, Henry. *The Wind Commands: Sailors and Sailing Ships in the Pacific.* Reprint ed. University of Queensland Press, 1980.

A scholarly, highly readable, and fascinating treatise on sailors and sailing ships in the South Pacific. Covers some four centuries of maritime experience in this great ocean. Many photographs and line drawings.

O'Brian, Patrick. The "Jack Aubrey" novels. London: Collins.

Master and Commander (1970)
Post Captain (1972)
HMS Surprise (1973)
The Mauritius Command (1977)
Desolation Island (1978)
The Fortunes of War (1979)
The Surgeon's Mate (1980)
The Ionian Mission (1981)
Treason's Harbour (1983)
The Far Side of the World (1984)
The Reverse of the Medal (1986)
The Letter of Marque (1988)
The Thirteen-Gun Salute (1989)
The Nutmeg of Consolation (1992)
Clarissa Oakes (1993)

A series of novels, founded on detailed research, tracing the life and career of Jack Aubrey in the Royal Navy of the Nelson era. Each is an amazingly accurate recreation of British naval life of that period; certainly it is the wittiest and most erudite fiction available dealing with this subject.

Rogers, John G. *Origins of Sea Terms.* 2d ed. Mystic, Connecticut: Mystic Seaport Museum, 1985.
Defines a wide range of terms associated with seafaring and offers a brief summary of the etymology of most of the words listed. An interesting innovation is that the author has provided a citation reference for each entry, a useful device for readers who might want to explore further a particular source.

Sleightholme, J. D. *A.B.C. for Yachtsmen.* London: Adlard Coles, 1965.
An interesting compendium of sailing as it applies to the small-boat sailor. Arranged in dictionary format, with brief but adequate definitions and explanations, and well illustrated with many line drawings.

Smollett, Tobias. *The Adventures of Roderick Random.* Oxford, England: Oxford University Press, 1981.
Written in 1748, this novel is of particular interest to maritime scholars because it contains a first-hand account of life on the gundeck of a British man-o'-war.

Smyth, W. H. *The Sailor's Word Book.* London: Blackie and Son, 1867.
The most comprehensive dictionary of nautical terms available to the student of Britain's sailing navy. It is the natural successor to Falconer, and surpasses it in both scope and scholarship.

Warner, Oliver. *The British Navy: A Concise History.* London: Thames and Hudson, 1975.
A very useful but necessarily condensed history of the Royal Navy from earliest times to the nuclear age. With copious illustrations, many of which do not appear in other standard histories.

Whitlock, Peter C. et al. *The Country Life Book of Nautical Terms under Sail.* London: Hamlyn, 1978.
One of the very best compendiums of nautical lore produced since World War II. Copiously illustrated; covers virtually every facet of sail. An essential reference for the serious student.

Dictionaries Consulted

Brewer, E. C., ed. *Brewer's Dictionary of Phrase and Fable.* London: Cassell,1981.

Delbridge, A., ed. *The Macquarie Dictionary.* St. Leonards, Victoria: Macquarie Library, 1981.

Funk, Wilfred John. *Word Origins and Their Romantic Stories.* Reprint ed. New York: Bell, 1978.

Hunter, Robert. *Universal Dictionary of the English Language.* New York: Collier, 1897.

Little, William; H. W. Fowler; and J. Coulson. *The Shorter Oxford English Dictionary on Historical Principles.* Oxford, England: Clarendon, 1962.

McAdam, E. L., Jr. and G. Milne. *Dictionary, Samuel Johnson (1755): A Modern Selection.* London, 1982.

Murray, J. H. et al., ed. *Oxford English Dictionary.* Oxford, England, 1970.

Partridge, Eric. *Origins: A Short Etymological Dictionary of Modern English.* New York: Greenwich House, 1983.

Webster's New Twentieth Century Dictionary of the English Language. Unabridged, 2d ed. Cleveland and New York: World Publishing Company, 1965.

Weekley, Ernest. *An Etymological Dictionary of Modern English.* Reprint ed. New York: Dover, 1967.

Appendix 1
Nautical Prepositions

This appendix contains a list of words, with brief etymologies and definitions, that form the prepositional phrases so peculiar to nautical language. Certainly many other such examples occur in everyday speech, such as *above, ablaze,* and *abound,* but the specialised language of the sea contains by far more of them than does the jargon related to any other profession.

The reason for this is the need for economy of language at sea. For many shipboard evolutions, the sailor in command needs to make himself or herself understood, and needs to have action undertaken, in the shortest possible time; hence the development of these almost epithetical phrases.

The most common formation is that of a preposition preceding, and linked with, a noun. Some half-dozen of these combinations have not yet become homogenous words, in that the preposition is still separated from its stem by a hyphen. This is one of the curious accidents of linguistic morphology, and given the conservative nature of maritime terminology it is likely that they will remain this way (although note that *a-weigh* is acceptable also as *aweigh).*

A

Aback Middle English *abak,* Old English *on,* preposition + Old English *baec,* noun, back. Said of a square-rigged vessel when the wind suddenly shifts onto the foreward surface of its sails.

Abaft Middle English *abaft,* Middle English *a,* preposition + Middle English *baft,* from Old English *baeftan,* adjective, behind. Farther aft—nearer the stern—relative to some other object or position.

Abeam Old English *on,* preposition + Middle English *beem* from Old English *beam,* noun, tree, piece of wood. At right angles to the fore-and-aft line of the vessel; directly opposite the middle part of the ship.
(See also *Abreast* in this appendix.)

Aboard Old English *on,* preposition + Old English *bord,* noun, border, side. Into or within a vessel; also, alongside; to fall foul of another vessel.

About Middle English, from Old English *abutan,* variant of *onbutan,* Old English *on,* preposition, + *butan,* noun, outside of. To tack; to go from one tack to the other, to turn the vessel's head through the wind (to come about, go about, ready about, about ship).

Abox Old English *on,* preposition + *box,* noun, shrub or small tree of genus *Buxus.* To lay the fore-yards of a square-rigged vessel square to the foremast in order to heave-to; or to brace them aback to the wind so that the bows can be cast off in the required direction.

Abreast Old English *on,* preposition + Middle English *brest,* from Old English *breost,* noun + verb, swelling, to swell. Side by side, parallel to; the position of being opposite to—at right angles to—another ship, mark, or place.
(See also *Abeam* in this appendix.)

Abroad Middle English *a broad,* adverb, from Old English *on,* preposition + Old English *brad,* adjective, wide, broad. Out to sea, as in "The wind is getting abroad the night"—bad weather is coming.

A-burton Old English *on,* preposition + *burton,* probable variant of *Breton,* native of Brittany, early fishermen and whalers. A method of stowing casks in the hold, athwartships, in line with the deck beams.

A-cockbill Old English *on,* preposition + Middle English *cok,* from Old English *cocc,* verb, to turn to one side, + Old English *bill,* noun, sword. Originally *a-cockbell;* describes the position of an anchor as it hangs by its ring at the bows ready for letting go.

Adrift Old English *on,* preposition + Middle English *drift,* verb, act of driving, from Old English *drifan,* verb, drive. To float at random; to cast adrift, to abandon to the sea.

Afloat Old English *on,* preposition + Middle English *flotien,* verb, from Old English *flotian,* verb, to float, to rest on the surface of a liquid. The condition of a vessel when she is wholly supported by the water and clear of the ground.

Afore Middle English *aforne,* adverb, from Old English *onforan,* Old English *on,* preposition + *foran,* in front, before. An old sailing ship term meaning forward, or forward of.

Aground Old English *on,* preposition + Middle English/Old English *grund,* noun, bottom, ground. Said of a vessel when she is resting on the bottom, by purpose or by accident.

Ahead Old English *on,* preposition + Middle English *heved,* noun, from Old English *heafod,* noun, head, upper part of the human body. In front of the ship, in the direction toward which her stem is directed.

Ahoy From *a,* interjection + Middle English *hoy,* interjection. The standard hail or cry to a ship or boat to attract attention.

A-hull Old English *on,* preposition + Middle English *hul,* noun, from Old English *hulu,* noun, frame and covering of a ship. To ride out heavy weather at sea under bare poles, with the vessel's helm a-lee (i.e., tiller to leeward), so as to force the bows up to windward.

A-lee Old English *on,* preposition + Middle English *lee,* noun, from Old English *hleo,* noun, shelter. Position of the helm when it is pushed down to the lee side of the ship (away from the wind), so as to bring the bows up into the wind in readiness for tacking.

Aloft Middle English *aloft,* from Old English *on,* preposition + Old English *loft,* noun, air. Up in the masthead, or anywhere about the upper yards and rigging.

Aloof Old English *on,* preposition + Middle English *luf, lufe, loofe,* noun, windward side. An old sailing ship term meaning at a distance, off to windward; also, to keep sailing as close to the wind as possible.

Alow Old English *on,* preposition + Middle English *losd, lokd, lah,* adjective, from Old Norse *lagr,* adjective, flat, lying down. Below, the opposite to aloft; on or near the deck.

Amain Old English *on,* preposition + Middle English *meyn,* from Old English *maegen,* noun, strength, power. An old seafaring word meaning now, immediately; as in preparing to anchor, "Let go amain."

Amidships Old English *amiddan,* preposition, from Old English *on,* preposition + *middan,* adjective, + Middle English *ship,* from Old English *scip,* noun, ship, vessel, boat. In the middle of the ship; usually a helm order, as in "midships," meaning "align the helm and rudder with the keel."

Apeak Old English *on,* preposition + North England dialect *pike,* noun, hilltop, from French *pigue,* foot soldier's weapon. The position of an anchor just before it has been broken out of the ground, with the bows of the vessel directly above it.

Aport Old English *on,* preposition + Latin *porta,* door, gate. From the fact that ships, from earliest days, hung the steering oar from the right-hand side of the stern—hence "starboard"—and when coming alongside a wharf, dock, or pier for loading and unloading, it was necessary to range up with the left-hand side of the vessel. Any entrance doors or ports were cut into this side—thus *portside.* Toward the port side of a vessel; also a steering order, as in "Helm's aport."

Ashore Old English *on,* preposition + Middle English *schore,* from Dutch *schoor,* boundary between land and sea. Aground, on the land. A ship runs ashore when she strikes the land proper, and aground when she strikes a bank, rock, or the like not connected with the shore.

A-stay Old English *on,* preposition + Middle English *steye,* noun, from Old English *staeg,* noun, support. Old-time terminology for the condition of the anchor cable when it is in line with the fore stay.

Astern Old English *on,* preposition + Middle English *steorne,* rudder. Behind the ship, backwards, in direction and in movement.

Athwart Old English *on,* preposition + Middle English *thwert,* adverb, across, transverse. Across, from one side to the other; also, across the line of a ship's course.

A-trip Old English *on,* preposition + Middle English *trippe,* verb, from Old French *tripper,* verb, to strike with the feet. Said of an anchor when it has just broken out of the ground and is hanging by the cable.

Awash Old English *on,* preposition + Middle English *waschen,* verb, from Old English *waescan,* verb, to wash, to apply water. Said of an object that is almost completely submerged, as a ship lying very low in the water, or a rock or bank being exposed on a falling tide.

A-weather Old English *on,* preposition + Middle English and Old English *weder,* noun, the state of the atmosphere. To the windward side, upwind; the opposite of a-lee.

A-weigh Also "aweigh." Old English *on,* preposition + Middle English *weghe,* verb, from Old English *wegan,* verb, to carry, to weigh. When the anchor has just been lifted from the seabed and the vessel has way on. This is just past the point of the anchor being a-trip. Frequently misspelled as "anchors a-way."

Appendix 2
Changed Spellings and Corrupted Word Forms

This appendix presents a representative but not exhaustive list of words that have changed their forms over the centuries, usually by way of abbreviation (or, as the linguistic terminology has it, through the process of corruption). The reasons for this happening are not hard to find. Language is a living entity, and as such is subject to constant change (less than a hundred years ago "ain't" was a perfectly proper part of the vocabulary of well-educated persons).

Seamen in the early days of sail were, by and large, an illiterate mass, the very dregs of society. The brutal treatment dealt out to them by the press gangs and the conditions of naval service, and by a social system that believed in a rigid division of class, did nothing to encourage a sensitivity toward language as a subtle means of communication. The exigencies of life at sea required that most verbal intercourse be reduced to a series of orders that could be readily understood by everyone in an emergency; hence the abbreviated form.

Finally, the crews of sailing ships, both naval and merchant service, were generally a polyglot mixture, especially in peacetime. The pronunciation of many of our common nautical terms today is the end result of a score or more different languages' having made their contribution in the expressing of a particular phrase.

B

Boatswain See *Bosun* in this appendix.

Bosun The shortened form of *boatswain.* Always pronounced "bosun," and frequently spelled as such; also as "bos'n." The bosun is the warrant officer responsible for handling the ship's crew and for the ship's general maintenance; he was also the ship's executioner. In spite of the title, the bosun does not normally have jurisdiction over the ship's boats.
(See also *Coxswain* in this appendix.)

Bowline Always pronounced "boe-lin." Originally a line attached to each leech (edge) of a square sail, and led as far forward into the bows as possible. Its purpose was to hold the weather leech of a close-hauled sail as taut as possible, to enable the ship to sail close to the wind.

Oddly enough, the name of this line did not derive from the fact that it was led into the bows of the ship. The word is older than *bow* (as in ship's bow), and differs in pronunciation; its derivation is the Old French *bouline,* and in Italian, Portuguese, and Spanish as *bolina,* with an ultimate relationship to the Latin *bolis,* a sounding line. A square-rigged ship is said to "sail on a bowline" when she is sailing as close to the wind as possible.

We remember the bowline today as perhaps the most useful knot ever devised by the seaman; of course, it takes its name from the manner in which the original bowline was attached to the leech-bridle of the sail. The bowline is a knot that can never slip or jam.

Bowsprit Pronounced "boe-sprit," never "bow" as in "how." Called "botsprit" in earlier days, from the Middle English *bouspret,* literally a bow-sprout, a sprouting of a tree from the bow (Old English *spreot,* a pole, a spear). The bowsprit is the spar that projects forward over the stem to stay the foremast and to carry triangular sails (staysails or jibs) on the various stays that lead down from the foremast.

In the early days, a sail, called a "spritsail," was set from the bowsprit to aid the steering and handling of the vessel. Sometimes another sail, called a "spritsail topsail," was stepped perpendicularly on the end of the bowsprit. The bowsprit is the final development of a very early foremast that was set up and stayed with extreme forward rake. This mast inclined ever-closer to the stem as ships grew bigger and seamen sought for ways to balance the rig.

Bulwark A combination of "bole" (from the Old Norse *bolr,* tree, plank) and "work."
(See also *Bulwark* in the main body of this book.)

Bummaree A corruption of *bottomry,* which is a mortgage raised on a vessel by a master who is out of touch with the owners and who needs to raise money for repairs or to continue the voyage. The mortgage is based on the ship's bottom, i.e., in a whole and general sense, the hull. *Bummaree* is also the term applied to fish salesmen or partners in fish markets, particularly in the Billingsgate markets. It is said that the word is a version of the French *bonne maree,* good fresh fish, *maree* being a French term for all kinds of fresh fish. Sometimes used as a colloquialism for a habitual loafer or tramp.

C

Capstan Sometimes written as "capstern" as late as the early 1800s; from the Provençal *cabestan,* and deriving from the Latin *capistrare,* to fasten with a rope. A capstan is an apparatus that enables the anchor, heavy yards, and the like to be raised by hand. It is a type of winch, the gearing of which is obtained by inserting capstan bars into sockets in the drumhead and putting a gang of seamen to work heaving round the capstan barrel, which is set on a spindle through to the next deck below.

Carrick bend A quick means of joining two ropes or hawsers, such that the join lies relatively bunched, so that when it is required to go round the barrel of a capstan it does not get jammed between the whelps or slats on the barrel, as a flat join such as the reef knot would. The name is a corruption of *carrack,* the type of trading vessel prevalent in northern and southern Europe between the fourteenth and seventeenth centuries. The carrack was the forerunner of the three-masted, square-rigged ship that dominated naval architecture until the mid-nineteenth century.

Carvel Carvel-built, with planks fitting edge to edge, and the seams then caulked with oakum and payed (not "paid") with pitch. Authorities differ markedly as to whether this word is a corruption of "caravel" or not. A caravel was a relatively small trading vessel in the Mediterranean between the fourteenth and seventeenth centuries. Typically, it was a three-masted vessel, used especially by the Spanish and the Portuguese. Columbus's flagship, the *Santa Maria,* was a larger caravel of some 95 feet in length. If these vessels were built on the edge-planking principle (and for that length of hull they would have been), then it is likely that the ship-type lent its name, caravel, to the method of construction, carvel.

Channel The chain-wales; broad, thick planks set on-edge horizontally into the side of the ship. They are used to spread the shrouds outwards and thus give them a wider base; the channels also keep the standing rigging (shrouds and so forth) away from the gunnel (the gunwale). When heaving the lead, the seaman whose duty this was stood in the fore-channels on the weather side to make his cast. (See also *Gunnel* in this appendix.)

Coxswain Pronounced "coxun"; from an earlier form, *cockswain.* The coxswain was the helmsman of a ship's boat. Originally, all boats carried on board a ship were known as "cockboats," or "cocks"; hence the origin of the term. *Swain* was originally a male servant, especially that of a knight; from the Old Norse *sveinn,* boy, boy servant, whence we get our *swine* and *swineherd.* Thus, a cockswain was a servant of a boat; interestingly enough, in the typical nautical fashion of inversion, the cockswain (or coxswain) was in fact the designated master of the ship's boat, rather than its servant. *Bosun* is formed on exactly the same principles.

Crojack Sometimes spelled "crossjack." The lower yard on the mizzen mast of a square-rigged ship. In some sailing ships, a sail called the "crossjack" (crojack) used to be set on this yard.

D

Deepsea Always pronounced "dipsy" when referring to the deepsea lead and line, used for sounding waters up to 200 fathoms, sometimes more. The lead weighed 25 to 30 pounds and the line was marked with knots or pieces of cloth or leather at regular intervals. The hand-lead and line were used in channels and harbours; the lead for this line weighed 7 to 10 pounds and the line was 25 fathoms long. The lead used in all these sounding devices had a recess in its base which was filled with tallow so that specimens of the bottom could be brought up when taking soundings.

E

Euphroe Variously spelled "euvro," "uphro," or "uphroe." An oblong block, usually of ash, up to 30 inches in length and 2 to 5 inches in diameter, containing a number of holes through it at equal distances. There are no sheaves in the holes. A groove runs round the edge of the wood, and the block is attached to a rope that is tightly secured in the groove. Also commonly called a "crowfoot block" or a "deadeye"—*dead* because it has no moving parts such as a sheave and pin, and also because the traditional deadeye used for attaching the shrouds to the chainplates has three holes piercing it in such a way that the block vaguely resembles a human skull. This block or euphroe accepts the lines that support the awning sometimes spread as a protection against the sun.

The word is from the Dutch *juffrouw,* perhaps earlier *jung frau,* which means maiden. Why the Dutch word for maiden should provide the origin for the name of this kind of wooden block is obscure. It is worth remembering, though, that seamen have never been guilty of undue delicacy in their naming of parts (note the "arse" of a block; "cut splice," which is a more refined version of the original word; and "contline," a barely disguised rendition of the earlier—and earthier—term). Hence, it is suggested here that the early sailors gave the euphroe its present name because of their appreciation of those aspects of young women that they found most attractive. This is not to malign maidens or mariners; it is simply to refer to what is already well established in the history of seafaring: that sailors, when they go ashore after long periods at sea, usually seek solace in liquor and women.

F

Forecastle Always pronounced "foke-sill" (and usually spelled "fo'c'sle"), from a foreshortening of *forecastle,* which is the space in the bows where the crew had their living quarters.

For hundreds of years, this was where the men were housed: generally cramped, damp, foul-smelling, and infested with cockroaches and other pests. Bedbugs were the common lot of seamen. The forecastle took its name from the fact that in the old fighting ships a castle—a raised, fortified platform—was built up over the bows, from which the ship's archers could attack an enemy vessel. As the methods of warfare changed, so the forecastle disappeared, but its name remained to signify the place where the ship's hands live, whether it is in the bows, as of old, or in a deckhouse on the foredeck.

Furl To gather in a square sail, roll it up, and secure it with gaskets (ties of light line) to the yard, boom, or mast. Authorities differ on the origin of this word: it came from either the French *ferler,* or from the Spanish *fardo* and Arabic *fardah,* package, with an intermediate Middle English word *farthell,* to roll up the sails (i.e., to furl them). In fact, *farthell* appears regularly in the older literature of the sea, and it may well be the progenitor of *furl.*

Futtock A corruption of *foot hook,* found in a number of places on board a square-rigged sailing ship. A futtock is a bent timber in the lower part of a ship's compound (laid up) frame; usually known as futtock timbers. The name refers to the "foot" of the timber and the shape of the piece.

The futtock hoop or futtock band is an iron band around the upper end of the lower mast, with eye-bolts let into it to take the lower ends of the futtock shrouds. These futtock shrouds are attached at their upper end to the futtock plate, which is an iron plate encircling the top (the platform across the head of the lower mast, used for spreading the mast's rigging).

Sometimes the futtock shrouds are anchored at their lower end, not by the futtock band, but by the catharpins (or catharpings). In this setup, the futtock shrouds terminate at iron staves lashed to the upper ends of the lower mast shrouds, and the catharpins brace the two staves towards each other, thus keeping taut the futtock shrouds and the lower mast shrouds.

G

Garboard Sometimes called the "garboard strake" or—in ships of iron or steel construction—the "garboard plate." The garboard strake is the first plank laid along a vessel's bottom immediately each side of the keel. This plank is rabbeted or let into the keel and the stem and sternpost. From the Dutch *gaarboord, gadaren,* to gather, and *boord,* board, which translated into English as "gathering board," and thence became shortened to "garboard."

Garnet A tackle (always pronounced "tay-kle") is composed of a single block and a double block, with a hook on the lower block, used for hoisting goods into and out of the ship. Also attached to the clews (or clues) of the courses (the lowest square sails) on a square-rigged ship, by means of which the clews are hauled aloft to the yards for furling. Altered from an earlier English form of the French *garaut,* fall-tackle.

Gauntlet Pronounced "gantlet" in Australia and Great Britain, "gontlet" in the United States. Familiar to us in the phrase "to run the gauntlet." A corruption of *gantlope,* from the Swedish *gatloppe,* a gate run, and written as "gantlope" or "gauntlope." The spelling "gauntlet" is due to a confused etymology with "gauntlet," a glove (from the Old French *gantelet,* diminutive of *gant,* a glove).
(See also *Gauntlet* in the main body of this book.)

Gunnel Gunwale, the uppermost run of planking (or strake) on the ship's side; the uppermost edge of the bulwarks. A "wale" is one of a number of strong, thicker-than-usual planks extending the entire length of a ship's side at different heights. Their purpose is to provide protection against rubbing and crushing (hence the "rubbing strake" found on vessels of all sizes today). Most sailing vessels had a main-wale, a chain-wale, and a channel-wale. The gunwale was so named because it was possible to mount a small swivel cannon on it in a battle.
(See also *Channel* in this appendix.)

H

Halliard Often "halyard," occasionally "haulyard." From an earlier "halier," "hallyer," that which hales or hauls, and influenced by "yard." A halliard is a rope or tackle used to hoist or lower a sail, yard, or gaff (except that the fore, main, and mizzen yards were controlled by jeers, a system of chain tackles much stronger than rope halliards).

Harpoon A whaling spear with a single, razor-sharp barb and a three-foot (about one metre) socketed shank into which a wooden shaft was fitted. The harpoon was attached to the whale-line, which fastened the whale to the whaleboat. Thus, the harpooner was sometimes called the "whale fastener." From the Dutch *harpoen,* and the French *harpon, harper,* to grapple; the sixteenth-century English equivalent was "harping-iron."

Hussif A corruption of the word *housewife.* Hussif is a sailor's kit for making repairs to clothing; it contained needles and thread of various kinds. *Hussy* is in turn a corruption of "hussif." From the Middle English *huswif,* housewife.

J

Jaunty The sailor's slang name for the master-of-arms in a British warship. It is derived from the French *gendarme,* which in turn is a back-formation from *gens d'armes,* men at arms. The jaunty, sometimes written "jonty," was responsible for the maintenance of shipboard rules and regulations.

K

Keelson Sometimes "kelson"; an internal keel mounted over the floor timbers (or ribs or frames), immediately above the main keel. Its function is to provide additional structural strengthening.

The etymology is curious. *Keel* is from the Old Norse *kjolr* through the Middle English *kele,* whereas the Dutch and German *kiel* are taken from the Middle English word, which is a reversal of the usual traffic in the nautical terminology of that era. But *keelson* itself seems to be of Scandinavian origin, as is the German equivalent *kielschwein,* literally "keel-pig," "keel-swine." The use of animal names is very common in nautical language, but the connection here is obscure.

Kevel Sometimes called a "kennet" by old-time seamen. A large, sturdy cleat fixed to the ship's side and used for belaying (tying off) large ropes. Kevel-heads are the ends of a vessel's top timbers (frames) projected above the level of the gunwale and similarly used for belaying ropes. From the Old North French *cheville,* peg, ankle, and ultimately from the Latin *clavicula,* the diminutive of *clavis,* key (hence "clavichord," the musical instrument, and "clavicle," the human collarbone).

L

Lanyard From the Middle English *lanyer* and the earlier French *laniere,* rope, with the suffix "yard" added. Sometimes spelled "laniard" or "lanierd." In general, a lanyard is any short piece of line fastened to an object in order to secure it or to act as a handle. The short, redoubled lengths of lines that secure the shrouds to the dead-eyes are also called lanyards.

Larboard See *Starboard, Larboard* in this appendix.

Larbolins See *Starbolins* in this appendix.

M

Marline A two-stranded, light line, generally used for seizing strops onto blocks. *To marl* (or *marle)* is to preserve a rope's end, or the lower end of a shroud or stay, by worming and parcelling: the rope is covered by winding a strip of canvas around it, which in turn is secured by repeated turns of marline drawn taut and secured at each turn by a marling hitch (a hitch still used today in securing a doused sail to its boom). From the Dutch *marren,* to bind (whence we derive our word *moor),* and *lijn,* line. The sailor's marline spike is from the same source.

O

Orlop The orlop deck is the lowest deck in a ship, situated over the beams of the hold. This is an excellent example of the process of language corruption—or change, at least—at work. *Orlop* is from the Dutch *overloop,* a running over, hence a covering, from *overloopen,* to overrun, to spread over. Initially it was anglicised to "over-lop."

In merchant ships, the orlop deck forms the floors of the cargo holds. In the days of sail, it carried the anchor cables, the powder magazines, the principal storerooms, and the cabins of junior officers. Smollett gives a brilliant description of what living conditions were like on the orlop deck of a man-o'-war in the eighteenth century, in his *The Adventures of Roderick Random.*

P

Parbuckle A nautical term with certain applications in other occupations. A parbuckle is a means of hauling up, or lowering, a cask or other cylindrical object where it is not possible to use a hoist such as a tackle; it worked by securing the middle of a rope to a bollard, bitt, or some inboard fixture, passing both halves under and over the object and hauling up on both ends. This method of cask handling is commonly used by brewery workers and others. Earlier "parbuncle" and "parbunkel"; its origin is unknown, but perhaps it is connected with "buckle," from the Old French *boucle,* cheek, or strap of helmet, and derived from the Latin diminutive *buccula,* mouth. Found in the expression *to buckle to,* to get down to hard work.

Parrel A sliding ring or collar of rope, beaded rollers, or such, which confines the yard or the jaws of a gaff to the mast. The parrel permits movement of the spar up and down the mast. From a corruption of *apparel,* that which is worn.

R

Rabbet The deep groove or channel cut into a timber so as to receive the edge of a plank. The keel is rabbeted to take the garboard strakes, and the stem and sternpost are similarly rabbeted to accept the ends of the planks of the hull. Originally a verb, from the word *rebate,* a cut, groove, or recess made on the edge or surface of a board or the like.

Ratline Pronounced "rat-lin," and often written as "ratling," which is closer to its origin. A ratline is a series of rope steps up the shrouds of a mast, 15 to 16 inches apart, by which seamen could go aloft. The word is from the Middle English *radelyng,* which in turn derives from a dialectical *raddle,* to intertwine, as in making a fence by interweaving pliant twigs or the like. The current term *ratline* is folk etymology, a type of pseudo-learned modification of a linguistic form, as "Welsh rarebit" is a folk etymology for the earlier, and correct, form, "rabbit." *To rattle down the shrouds* is to prepare ratlines.

Roband Also variously "roving," "robben," "robbin," or "rope-band"; small lengths of line passed through the eyelet holes at the head of a sail to attach it to its yard or jackstay. A version of an earlier form, "rope-band," which derives from the Old Norse *ra,* sailyard, and the Old English *band,* ligature, binding; *band* is found as such in most of the Teutonic languages.

Rowlock Always pronounced "rollock" and often spelled in this fashion. A rowlock is the U-shaped space cut into a boat's gunwale to accommodate the shaft of the oar. The metal U-shaped swivel that is mounted on the gunwales is not a rowlock but, properly, a "crutch." One of the earliest and simplest devices for providing a fulcrum for the oar was the thole pin, either singly or in pairs. The pin sat in a hole in the gunwale and the oar pivoted against it.

S

Starboard, Larboard Two basic terms of seafaring. Starboard is the right-hand side of a vessel as viewed from aft looking forward. The word is a corruption of the Anglo-Saxon *steorbord,* steer board, which was a board or oar hung over the right-hand side of the vessel and used for steering, before the invention of the hanging rudder. It is likely that the right-hand side of the vessel was chosen because the vast majority of men were right-handed, and such a position allowed the steersman to face ahead occasionally, while controlling the steering board with his right hand, more comfortably than if the board were hung over the left-hand side of the ship.

The left-hand side was known as the larboard, from the Middle English *ladeborde,* loading side (note the Modern English *laden,* as in "heavily laden"). This was a logical development, because a vessel with its steering gear hanging over the right-hand side could conveniently come alongside for loading cargo only by presenting its left-hand side to the wharf; hence *larboard.*

Centuries earlier, the Anglo-Saxons called this left-hand side the *baecbord* or *beckboard,* because it was the side that lay behind the steersman (at his back). The two terms *starboard* and *larboard* often created a great deal of confusion because of their sound-alike names; in an emergency, steering orders have to be perfectly clear and unambiguous. The larboard (loading side) gradually came to be called the port side (officially, this occurred in 1844) because the loading port was necessarily on this side, opposite to that of the steering oar.

It is agreed convention amongst all maritime nations of the world that the starboard side is the focal point from which derive the Rules of the Road (the *International Regulations for Preventing Collision at Sea),* which lay down the conditions under which one ship must give way to another. For example, two vessels that are approaching each other head on must each alter course to starboard so that they pass each other port side to port side.

In the older navy, the starboard side of a ship used to be the side reserved for the captain; he used the starboard ladder when going ashore or returning. At these times he was *piped the side* by a ceremonial call made on a boatswain's pipe or whistle, dating from the days when important visitors were hoisted in and out of a ship in a bosun's chair at the end of a yardarm whip. The notes of the call were the orders by which the men manning the bosun's chair knew when to hoist and when to lower. If the captain wished to avoid ceremony, he left and reentered by the port side. The starboard side of the poop deck or quarterdeck was usually reserved for him when he came on deck for exercise, and his cabin was usually on the starboard side. The starboard side of a cross-tree or spreader is the point from which certain important flags are flown.

Starbolins Sometimes written "starbowlines," but always pronounced as in "boe-lin." An old but once very common term for the men of the starboard watch. A ship's crew was divided into two watches, port and starboard, with each watch alternating their periods of duty; for hundreds of years, this was four hours on and four hours off. The port watch was known as the "larbolins," from *larboard,* the ancient name for the loading side of a vessel (i.e., the port side). (See also *Bowline* in this appendix.)

Studding sail Always pronounced, and sometimes spelled "stuns'l." The earliest form of the word is the Scottish *stoytene-sale,* from the Dutch *stooten,* to push, to urge. The Middle English term for sail was *bonnet.* In the twelfth century the Old French word for sail was *estouin,* and it is likely that the present *stuns'l* or *stunsel* represents a diminutive of this, and that *studding sail* is a meaningless elaboration. At one time these were known as "scudding sails," *scud* being then a nautical word. A stuns'l was an additional sail set in fine weather when the wind was abaft the beam; they were set on booms that were run out from the yards of the square sails. They were introduced in the early 1500s.

T

Tackle Pronounced "tay-kle" by sailors, even today. A tackle (from the Middle English *take,* gear, and related to our modern *take)* is a purchase system in which two or more blocks are used to multiply the power exerted on a rope. There are many different kinds of tackle on board a large sailing ship; their basic purpose is to lift and move heavy objects, and to add greater purchase to various stays and other items of rigging.

Topgallant Pronounced "t'gallant"; *gallant* is from an earlier *garland.* A topgallant mast is the third mast stepped above the deck of a square-rigger. First was stepped the lower mast, then the topmast, followed by the topgallant mast. Originally ships carried single-pole masts; such a pole mast had a garland around it near the top to help support the mast's stays (shrouds) and the second yard that gradually evolved. The garland would have been a tightly worked collar of rope, and the mast above this garland was known as the "top-garland mast"; hence, "t'gallant."

Transom A Middle English word, from the Latin *transtrum,* transverse, a cross-bar. The diminutive *transtillum* goes through *trastillum,* whence comes the Old French *trestel* and the Middle English *trestle.* A transom is one of the beams fastened across the stern post, strengthening the stern and giving it shape. The word is loosely used to describe a flat or slightly curved stern on a boat or ship. *Trestle* is found in *trestle-trees,* which are two strong pieces of timber placed fore and aft at the head of a mast to support the cross-trees and the foot of the mast next above.

Treenails Pronounced "trennels" and occasionally written as such. A treenail is a cylindrical wooden pin used to secure a ship's planks to its frames. They swell with moisture when the ship is afloat, thus making a firm fitting. When made of sound, dry oak, they were considered superior to metal fixings of any kind.

Trestle See *Transom* in this appendix.

Appendix 3
Nautical Terms Related to Human Anatomy

This list contains a wide sampling of nautical terms that were derived from parts of the human anatomy.

The nature of the seaman's life on board ship brought him into close—usually always uncomfortably close—physical contact with his fellows, living and messing as they did in the cramped, gloomy, foul-smelling, and always damp gundeck or fo'c'sle. Furthermore, to a very large extent each man owed his personal safety and well-being to the physical skill and strength of his watch-mates. Necessarily, each depended on the other when handling sails and gear in a roaring gale, when an improperly belayed halliard or poorly spliced line could come apart in a moment and fling a man from high aloft to the deck or into the wastes of the sea.

Throughout the ages, the sailor has entertained a keen concern for his physical well-being, for the very good reason that he was always—without exception, until the postwar era of the twentieth century—extremely badly treated by the ship's owners, and by the captain and deck officers. His food was execrable, his living conditions often bordered on the subhuman, and his pay was pitiful. On top of this, the captain—for centuries "master under God" and, in the early days of sail, officially sanctioned with the power of life and death over every man under his command—at worst drove the crew into sullen despair with his disregard for their needs and rights, and at best showed only a cursory interest in their welfare, usually as a result of a cap-in-hand approach by an apologetic delegation from the fo'c'sle.

Thus, the seaman was forced to take considerable interest in his day-to-day physical existence. He was generally always hungry and severely undernourished. His clothing was of poor quality and seriously inadequate; many a seaman rounded the Horn in winter without the kind of protective clothing that today's suburbanite would consider essential for a trip to the supermarket on a rainy day.

He signed on for voyages that often encompassed both the Southern Ocean in winter and the doldrums in summer; he was preyed on by crimps, prostitutes, bootleggers, and the bailiff; and his meagre pay, usually only won at the cost of his health, condemned him to the same dreary round, since he was virtually unemployable in any other market.

His pleasures were few: liquor ashore, raddled tarts who meant nothing to him in some sleazy port, and the tobacco that he chewed and smoked—usually to excess—aboard ship. His rations were of the poorest quality, and sometimes in the smallest quantity, that a profit-hungry owner could provide. He was subject to physical abuse and direct assault from officers whose right it was to enforce discipline with the rope's end, cane, knuckle-duster, and belaying pin.

The seaman's daily existence was always an intensely physical one, centering inevitably about his own bodily functions and his utter dependence on his ability to do his job, both for his own safety and that of his shipmates. Little wonder, then, that so much of the shipboard gear that he worked with was named after things with which he was most familiar: his own body.

A

Arm As in yardarm, the outer part of a yard.

Arse Situated at the choke end of a wooden block; the immediate area from which the fall (the hauling part of the rope) issues.

B

Bearding The process of removing timber from a vessel's hull to modify or improve its lines.

Belly The bulging part of a sail where it captures the wind; it encompasses the bunt of a sail (the middle sections); also, the main body of a trawl net used in fishing.

Bite A word that describes the action of an anchor when its fluke is firmly embedded in the seafloor; the anchor is then said to "bite."

Body As in "body plan," a drawing showing the midship section of a vessel, done during its design stages. Also "body hoops," which hold the various parts of a made-up mast together (these hoops were known as "wooldings" in the old days, from the several turns of rope wound tightly and closely around the mast to reinforce it). The body of a sail is its general midsection.

Bosom As in "bosom piece," a short length of angle-bar fitted within the angle of another similar piece of bar for added strength. Also, to join two other angle bars by inside lapping.

Breast The opposite end of the block to that through which the fall of the rope runs (the loose end of a tackle, upon which the seaman hauls). The word is found in many other compounds: breast anchor, breast band, breast hooks, breast rope, and others.

Breech The old name for the external angle of a knee timber. Also, that part of a block opposite the swallow; the rope enters the block at the swallow side and exits from the breech side (more specifically, the rope enters the choke at the swallow and exits as the fall from the arse of the breech). Sailors were nothing if not specific.

Brow The gangway-planks located between the ship and the shore, usually equipped with rollers at the shore end to allow for the rise and fall of the ship with the tide; called a "ramp" on ferries, landing craft, and such. Properly, a gangway is the narrow platform that traverses the waist of the ship in a fore-and-aft direction, connecting the quarterdeck to the forecastle.

Buttocks The convex part of a vessel under the stern, where the hull rounds down to the sternpost.

C

Cheeks Large upward-curving timbers in the bows; also flat timbers or iron plates bolted on either side of the mast-head to form a support for the heel of the mast above it; and the side pieces of a block, usually of wood, but nowadays often metal or high-impact plastic. Also the old name for the vertical side-pieces of the old-fashioned wooden gun carriage.

Choke Used as a verb, as in "to choke the luff": to jam a tackle by slipping the fall immediately under the rope where it enters the block. This jams the sheave and holds it tight. A pull on the fall (the hauling part) releases the sheave. The choke is opposite the swallow.

Contline The acceptable name today for the spiral hollows that lie between the strands of a laid-up rope. The earlier name, of closely similar spelling, was a very earthy and perhaps indelicate reference to the appearance of these rounded grooves.

Crotch An angled timber mounted at the end of the keel, where the hull becomes narrow.

Cut splice Two ropes spliced together to form an eye, not end-to-end as in a short slice, but overlapping so that the end of one rope is spliced into the body of the other. The result presented a shape for which seaman had a crude name.

E

Earring A small rope used to lash the upper corners of a square sail to its yard.

Elbow When a vessel lies at two bow anchors, an elbow is formed in each of her cables when the vessel is swung through 360 degrees by wind or tide.

Eyebrow An alternative name for a rigol, which is the curved ledge fitted just above the portholes on the outside of the hull, so as to prevent water running down the side and entering the opening.

Eyes The parts of a ship near the hawse-holes, in the bows; derived from an old Eastern and Mediterranean custom of painting an eye on each bow so that the vessel could "see" her way safely through the water. *Eye* is also the name given to the loop that is spliced or whipped at the end of a rope or wire (as in "eye splice").

F

Face piece A timber fastened to the knee that joins the stem to the keel; a strengthening timber.

Foot The lower end of a mast; also the lower edge of a sail. A vessel is said to "foot it" through the water when she is making her course at a good speed.

Forelock A small iron wedge or pin driven through a hole or slot at the end of a sheave-pin to prevent it from working out.

G

Grow Said of the anchor cable, to refer to the direction in which it leads from the vessel to the anchor. When weighing anchor, the bridge will frequently ask the officer at the bows, "How does the cable grow?"

Gut A narrow strait of water between two headlands, two opposing coasts, or the like.

H

Hair As in "hair-bracket," a small, shaped timber or plate used to connect two or more parts of a ship. Certain brackets were known as "knees" when they joined the deck beams to the ship's frames.

Hand Any member of a ship's crew. Also, as a verb, the act of furling the sails to the yards of a square-rigged ship.

Head The front or forepart of a vessel, including the bows; the upper part of many items of gear on board ship, as in masthead, head ledge, head sheets, and so on. The head of a sail is its upper edge, if a square sail, or its upper corner, if a triangular sail.

Heart A type of deadeye but with only one hole in it; shaped rather like a heart and used for setting up the stays in a square-rigged ship.

Heel The junction of the after end of the keel and the lower end of the stern post; also the lower end of a mast. *To heel* is to lean over to port or starboard, as a vessel does because of wind pressure, heavy seas, or shifting cargo. (Careless writers will call this "keeling over," which it most definitely is not; a ship can never be said to "keel over.")

J

Jaws The inner end of a boom or gaff, with a prong fitted so as to embrace the mast, usually with a parrel to prevent the jaw from lifting away.

K

Knee An angled piece of timber used to connect the ship's beams with her sides or frames. Such knees were generally massive affairs, as they carried the full weight of the beams and decking above. The best kinds of knees were those shaped from the natural bends and angles of the oak tree.

Knuckle The sharp angle in the frame of a wooden vessel; also the name given to a sharply bent stem on a modern yacht, as in the 12-metre class.

L

Leg A short rope that spreads out into three or more parts, usually for stretching taut the weather leech of a sail (as in a bowline), or supporting an awning (as in a crowfoot). Also the run or distance made on a single tack by a sailing vessel (often called a "board," probably from the days when the ship's course and direction were plotted on the traverse board. A peg was inserted into a hole on the compass rose on this board every half hour to indicate speed and direction, and at the end of the watch the course made good was calculated from the position of the eight pegs).

N

Navel Used in "navel line," a rope or tackle running from the masthead to the truss or parrel (the point of suspension and pivot) of a yard, to enable the yard to be maintained in a proper relationship with its parrel. The "navel pipe" is a stout pipe that leads from the forecastle deck to the cable lockers below, through which the chain cable would pass during anchoring operations. The purpose of the pipe is to feed the chain directly into the chain locker, thus avoiding possible kinking of the chain links.

P

Palm A strip of leather, rawhide, or the like, with a metal cup or disc let into it. The whole is worn on the hand with the metal cup located at the palm or ball of the thumb. It is used as a thimble to force the sailmaker's needles through heavy canvas when making or repairing sails. Also the face of the fluke of the Admiralty pattern anchor, known as the "fisherman's anchor."

Paunch A thick mat made of interwoven strands of rope, used in the rigging and the yards as a protection against chafing and rubbing when, for example, the ship is rolling heavily. Their shape and consistency suggest that other well-known paunch, the protuberant belly of the person who has led the good life.

R

Rib A frame or timber upon which the vessel's outer skin is fixed.

S

Shank The shaft that forms the main part of an anchor. It connects the anchor ring to the arms and meets the arms at the crown.

Shoulder As in "shoulder block," a large single block almost square at the arse or lower end and sloping in towards the sheave (pronounced "shiv") at the top. A ship cutting her way boldly through the water is said to "shoulder" the seas aside.

Skin The outside plates or planking of a vessel after it has been fastened to the frames.

Sole A piece of timber attached to the foot of the rudder to reinforce it and to bring it into line with the false keel. Also the name given to the decking ("floor") in a yacht's cabin.

Span A small line with its middle (or its ends) fastened to a stay with blocks or thimbles fitted at the free ends (or in the middle, respectively) to act as a fairlead or a purchase for other ropes. Also, the distance between the port and starboard fixings of the lower ends of the mainmast shrouds, as measured over the masthead, is known as the "span" of the rigging.

Swallow The space between the sheave (or pulley, in landlubber's terms) and the shell of a block—i.e., the encompassing pieces, called the "cheek pieces." The swallow is the opening or entrance through which the line runs; opposite to the swallow is the choke.

T

Throat The inboard end of a gaff where it fits against the mast; also the upper foremost corner of a four-sided fore-and-aft sail.

A throat halliard hoists the jaws of a gaff and the throat of a sail. Throat seizings hold a thimble or other fitting in place during splicing, or while turning in a deadeye, heart, or block with a strop.

Thumb knot Another name for an overhand knot (the granny knot); sometimes used to prevent the end of a line running out (unreeving) through a block, but a figure-of-eight knot is preferable because it will not jam tight. A thumb-cleat is a small cleat with only one horn (a cleat with two horns is sometimes called a "staghorn cleat").

Toe As in "toe-straps"; a strap running along each side of a dinghy used for hooking the feet under when leaning outboard to balance a heeling small boat. Also, a toe-link in an anchor chain, similar in shape to a claw.

Tongue Sometimes called a "tumbler"; a block of wood pivoted in the jaws of a gaff so that the gaff will slide up and down the mast more easily.

W

Waist The part of a vessel that lies between the quarterdeck and the forecastle; in earlier sailing ships, the waist was located between the foremast and the mainmast.

Whisker As in "whisker boom," the wooden or iron spar that projects from the cat-head on either side of the bow to spread the stays of the jib-boom. A "whisker pole" is a modern development, to enable a foresail to be borne out on the opposite side to the mainsail when running before the wind.

Appendix 4
Nautical Terms
Derived from the Land

Many of the words that refer to shipboard gear and to parts of the ship itself reflect the seaman's earlier life before he went to sea. This appendix organises a reasonably extensive collection of these words under three headings: Domestic Environment, General Environment, and Animal Environment

This demarcation is quite arbitrary. It is merely one way of looking at the fascinating manner in which the nautical environment is described by the seaman largely in terms of the known and the homely.

As ships evolved into increasingly complex structures, with modified spars, extra sails, improved rigging practices, and different techniques for handling, new names had to be found for all these things. Generally the sailor gave a name to a thing according to its purpose or location (mainstay, foremast, amidships), but very often he named things and places for what they reminded him of or looked like (knee, breast, acorn, house, butterfly).

These words are now all part of the lore of the sea, but they remind us of the strong ties that the seaman of yesteryear felt for his hearth and home.

Domestic Environment

Most of these words are derived from common household items. A number of others are related to matters that might be a normal part of household life, customs, and conversation.

A

Apostles The two large, sturdy bollards or bitts securely fixed to the main deck in the bows, around which the anchor cables were belayed.

Apparel All the equipment of the sailing ship that is removable; a term very similar in meaning to *furniture*.
(See also *Furniture* in this appendix.)

Apron A stiffening piece located on the inside of the stem immediately above the forward end of the keel.

B

Balcony Another name for the stern gallery found on vessels of the sixteenth to eighteenth centuries. They were very ornate, with much glazing and gingerbread work. Structurally the balcony was one of the weakest points in a vessel's hull.

Bed The general term for the base or foundation provided for a heavy object such as an engine; also the timbers used to keep the bilges of casks away from the bottom when they were stowed in the hold; also the shaped piece or pieces that accept the anchor when it is to be secured on deck.

Benches The seats in the stern of a ship's boat, where the captain, officers, and other important guests traditionally sat; also known as the "stern sheets."

Bibbs Pieces of timber bolted to the hounds of a mast of a square-rigged vessel to support the trestle-trees at the masthead.

Bible The small block of sandstone that was used for scraping and scouring the deck each morning on a man-o'-war. So named because the sailor had to get down on his knees to do the job. Also commonly known as a "holystone"; the allusion is obvious.
(See also *Prayerbook* in this appendix.)

Bolster Rounded pieces of wood placed on top of the trestle-trees at the head of each of the two lower mast sections (i.e., at the head of the lower mast and the topmast) to prevent the rigging from chafing on the sharp edges of the trestle-trees.

Bonnet Additional canvas laced to the foot of a sail to increase its area, for the purpose of gathering extra wind. In the early days of seafaring, the grommets at the bottom of the sail and the top of the bonnet were usually lettered A.M.G.P. repeatedly, in this order. Not only did this ensure that bonnet and sail were matched at the correct grommet, but it was also a mnemonic for the sailors as they laced the bonnet on: "Ave Maria, gratia plena" (Hail Mary, full of grace)—a sort of recitation of the rosary as the crew gave thanks for fair winds.

Boot topping A band of paint around the hull at the water-level line, covering that area generally known as being "between wind and water." It demarcates the bottom antifouling from the topside paint.

Bosun's chair A plank seat used for sending a man aloft. A short plank is enclosed in a bridle, which itself is usually—and preferably—secured with bowline hitches. A temporary bosun's chair can quickly and safely be fashioned from a bowline itself.

C

Cap The wooden baulk that holds the foot (or heel) of an upper mast against the top (or head) of a lower mast. Cap shrouds are additional shrouds found usually only in gaff-rigged yachts.

Ceiling An inner skin of planking attached to the inside of the frames and running the entire length of the hull; i.e., the internal planking. The seaman's use of *floor* and *ceiling* is quite different from the landlubber's.
(See also *Floor* in this appendix.)

Cheese down A method of coiling the end of a fall or halliard into tight coils lying flat on the deck, with the end of the rope in the centre. The end result is called a "cheese."

Chimney The flue taking the smoke from the galley to above deck.

Clew, clue The two lower corners of a square sail, and the lower after-most corner of a fore-and-aft sail. Also the lanyards by which a hammock is slung from hooks in a deck beam. The word is derived from an Old English term *cleowen,* ball of thread, and is still used in some parts of northern England in this sense.

Clothe, to To provide a ship with its sails and running rigging.

Clothed Said of a vessel that has all her working sails set.

Club The boom set at the foot of a staysail, such as a jib; also the name for the manoeuvre of drifting with the current or tidal stream with the anchor down. *To club haul* is to tack a square-rigged vessel in a confined situation with the anchor down but not touching the sea bed, in case of emergency.

Coat A canvas cover used to protect a sail that has been stowed on its boom. Also a hood fitted to where the bowsprit, mast, or rudder post pierce the deck; originally fashioned out of canvas, but now made from rubber.

Collar An eye worked into the end or middle of a shroud or stay and then looped over the masthead, whereby it holds the mast secure.

Comb cleat A wooden fitting, usually semicircular, with holes cut in the curved edge to accept ropes, to keep them apart and prevent them from fouling each other.

Comb the cat A reference to the practice of the boatswain's mate of running his fingers through the thongs of a cat-o'-nine-tails after each stroke during the flogging of a seaman. After several strokes, the tails tended to become matted with blood; by combing them apart, the bosun's mate who was inflicting the punishment in fact prevented the seaman from being more seriously injured by each subsequent stroke.

Come home The action of the anchor when it breaks free of the ground and comes toward the ship, as the cable is hauled in.

Cot A shipboard bed made of canvas; it was stretched around a wooden frame and slung like a hammock from the deck beams. It had a mattress laid in the bottom. Cots preceded the introduction of permanent berths in cabins.

Cradle A sliding carriage for hauling a vessel up a slipway; similarly, a framework that supports a ship while she is being built.

Crib Small, permanent berths in the packet ships of the nineteenth century; now any sleeping berth in a small sailing vessel.

Crutch A plate fitted in the stern of a wooden vessel to bring together the ends of stringers and other longitudinal members. Also a supporting trestle used in yachts to take the weight of the main boom off the topping lift, when the boom is not in use. Also the correct name for what is widely but wrongly called a "rowlock" (pronounced "rollock"): a Y- or U-shaped metal fitting in the gunwale of a pulling boat, to form the fulcrum for an oar, and usually secured by a lanyard fixed to a stringer.

Cuckold's knot A seized eye in a rope, made with crossing turns.

D

Dagger The timbers that support the shoring pieces of a vessel while it is on the ways, preparatory to being launched. A dagger board is a drop keel that can be raised or lowered in its trunk or case.

Devil The outermost seam in a ship's planked decking; source of the expression "Between the devil and the deep blue sea." Also the name given to the seam closest to the keel, the garboard seam; source of the expression "The devil to pay and no pitch hot." Both seams are extremely awkward to get at with caulking tools; hence the name. (See also terms under *Devil* in the main body of this book.)

Dress ship, to To decorate a ship with flags on an occasion of celebration; *to be dressed overall* is to display flags from stem to stern by way of each masthead.

E

Eking A piece of timber used to lengthen another piece of timber, such as a beam; also an old term for the moulding or carving on a quarter-gallery. From a very old word, *to eke,* which means to lengthen, extend, or add on to. From this comes the term *nickname,* a corruption of "an eke-name," which was the additional name given to someone as another means of identification and differentiation in the days before the general use of surnames.

F

Fiddle An edging or ridge fitted to tables, ledges, or such to prevent objects sliding off in a seaway.

Fiddle-block Two blocks, one above the other, made as a single unit, with the lower block smaller than the upper block; the shape resembled that of a violin or fiddle.

Floor Not, as the name might suggest, a flat and horizontal surface, but instead the vertical plates in the bottom of a vessel joining the frames from bilge to bilge.

Furniture All the gear on a ship, everything except the basic hull, but excluding items such as fuel, paint, foodstuffs, and the like. (See also *Apparel* in this appendix.)

G

Gingerbread The gilded carving and scrollwork that decorated the hulls of large ships, especially merchantmen, between the fifteenth and eighteenth centuries. To damage the captain's ornamented carving gave rise to the expression "To take some of the gilt off the gingerbread"—to reduce its value, as in spoiling a story by revealing the outcome.

H

Home The situation of an object when it is in its proper place or doing its proper job. Used as in hauling a sail home until it is setting correctly, or in securing the anchor when it is freed from the ground and hauled to the ship; the anchor is then said to "come home."

Hood A cover screening a hatch or companionway from the wind or weather.

Hood end The extreme end of a plank where it is fastened to the stem or the transom. The hood end is located in the rabbets.

House, to To make secure. For example, in bad weather the guns of a man-o'-war were housed by running them back toward the centreline of the vessel and securing them firmly with lashings.

House line Light hempen line, often white, usually three-strand and laid up left-handed.

Husband More properly, "ship's husband"; the cargo owner's legal representative on board ship with the power to handle all the financial transactions to do with crew, freight, repairs, harbour dues, and the like.

Hussif A corruption of *housewife*. A sailor's needle-and-thread kit that he used for making repairs to his clothing; *hussy* is a corruption of *hussif*.

J

Jewel block A block found at the outer ends of a yard, through which is rove the halliard of a studding sail.

K

Knittles Often written as "nettles"; small line of two or three strands laid up hard by hand, and most often used for slinging the hammock from the deck beam. Also often used as a seizing, because of its strength. The word is related to the verb *to knit*.

L

Lady's ladder The sailor's derisory term for shrouds that have had the ratlines set too close together. The usual practice was to set them 15 to 16 inches apart.

M

Marry To prepare the ends of two ropes for splicing together, by interweaving the strands so that those of one end meet those of the other end in an orderly and alternating fashion. Also, to place two ropes alongside each other so that they can be hauled on at the same time.

O

Onion The smallest fraction of a knot (an expression of speed); a term used on the clipper ships from the mid-nineteenth century onward.

P

Paternoster The wooden framing that held the tubes of a chain pump in position from the deck to the hold.

Pigtail A braid of hair hanging down the back of the head; for a long time, the familiar adornment of many females, and in the mid-twnetieth century increasingly popular with certain males. Once the seaman's preferred method of dressing his hair, particularly in the eighteenth century and later; often known as a "queue." A great deal of trouble had to be taken over the tying of pigtails, and close friends who did this for each other were known as "tiemates." Later, when pigtails went out of fashion, close chums were known as "raggies," from the fact that they shared each other's cleaning rags.
(See also *Brass. To part brass rags* in the main body of this book.)

Pillow A block of timber supporting the inner end of the bowsprit.

Pinch To sail so close to the wind as to luff the sail, thus causing it to flutter at the leading edge and thereby lose much of its drive; sometimes necessary, as when fetching (sailing to) a mark that is not too distant.

Prayerbook The smaller holystones used for scrubbing in awkward places where the larger holystone could not be used.
(See also *Bible* in this appendix.)

Puddening A band of plaited rope placed around a yard to keep it in position in case of damage. Any thick matting made of yarns, oakum, or such, used where there was danger of chafing.

Q

Quilting Woven strands of rope wrapped around jars and bottles to protect them from damage in the hold, or wherever else they might be kept; also the name given to the heavy paunch matting attached to the hull of a wooden vessel as a protection against ice floes.

S

Satchel A fishing industry term; the trawlerman's name for the trawl net.

Saucer The iron bearing in which the capstan spindle turns.

Scandalise, to An old term meaning deliberately to set a vessel's sails and yards in disarray, out of square, as a mark of mourning for the dead. Such a slipshod method of furling, harbour-stowing, or the like, would be immediately noticed and remarked upon by any sailor; hence the very obviousness of the action as meaningful.

Shelf A strong timber fastened to the inside of a vessel's frames to act as a support for the deck beams.

Shoe A triangular wooden board sometimes fixed to the fluke of an anchor to increase its holding power in the sea bed; also a protecting block for the anchor flukes when the anchor is housed on its bed. The word is sometimes also used to describe a false keel.

Shroud The side-stays of a mast or a bowsprit. The shrouds pass from the masthead to the side of the vessel, as far outboard as they can be located; they support the mast from each side.

Sill The framing, or inner lining, of a square port cut into the hull; also the bottom step of the ship's entrance to a dry dock.

Snub, to To cause a cable or rope to be suddenly checked while it is running out, as around a bitt; also, the sharp jerk that a pitching vessel's anchor gives to its anchor cable as the cable is drawn taut suddenly by the vessel's movements.

Spectacles An iron fitting attached to the clew of a sail, having three or four rings formed in it to take the bolt ropes, sheets, and other controlling lines. Also called a "spectacle clew" or "spectacle iron."

Step The mast step; a built-up pad or pillow located on the keelson for the purpose of accepting the heel of the mast. If the mast is stepped on deck, it is generally housed in a tabernacle, and the deck at that point is strengthened or reinforced to take the thrust of the mast.

Suit A vessel's complete set of working sails appropriate for the weather conditions. Most vessels would have a suit for each of mild, moderate, and stormy weather conditions.

T

Table, to To reinforce the hem of a sail by turning the edge over on itself and sewing it down. Reef bands and buntline bands are added as tablings to provide extra strength where it is needed.

Thimble A metal ring or lining for an eye; usually grooved to accept the rope or wire that is having an eye turned into it.

V

Viol block A large block, somewhat in the shape of a viol, used when heaving up the anchor.

W

Wear, to *To wear ship* is to put the vessel onto the opposite tack by putting the stern through the wind; a complicated manoeuvre in a square-rigged ship, but easily enough handled in a modern yacht, in which latter case it is known as a "gybe."

Wishbone A double spar, as a gaff, sometimes used in two-masted vessels. Each element of the spar consists of part of a natural sail curve, so that the sail enclosed between the arms of this spar takes up its correct shape when the vessel is on either tack. Not as widely used today as it was formerly.

General Environment

The words in this list are connected with the ordinary run of life encountered outside the home, including the farmyard, the village, and the larger community. It is interesting to note that a significant proportion of these terms reflect the importance of the horse in English society in the heyday of sail.

A

Acorn The small, heart-shaped or often acorn-shaped thimble or button of wood that sat on top of the windvane spindle at the masthead. Its purpose was to prevent the windvane from being blown off its own spindle.

Apple-cheek The old name for the bluff, very full and rounded bows common on sailing ships until the introduction of the hollow clipper bow of the early nineteenth century; applied particularly to Dutch vessels.

B

Bagpipe the mizzen To slow a vessel down by swinging the mizzen gaff boom across to the weather rigging, thus opposing the wind.

Belfry The protective canopy built over the ship's bell in the early days of sail; located on the foredeck between the foremast and the mainmast.

Bridge The raised structure, usually at midships, from which the vessel is conned; usually enclosed from the weather. The term is one from the age of steam, and derives from the days of the paddle steamer, when a platform was built to span or bridge the deck from the housing on one paddle wheel to the housing on the other. Sailing ships do not have a bridge; the equivalent would be the quarterdeck.

Bridle A wire or rope span, secured at both ends and controlled from its centre by another rope; also a mooring line arranged in the same manner between the ship and her mooring.

Buckler Large wooden plugs that are fitted into the hawse holes to prevent the sea getting in. *Buckler* is the old word for the small shield worn on the arm; hence the term *swashbuckling,* shield tapping, the blustering, swaggering behaviour adopted in certain early stage plays.

C

Castle The name given to the built-up platforms that were erected over the bow and stern of a vessel to provide a position from which archers and spearmen could attack an enemy ship. They were known as the forecastle and sterncastle respectively, but as methods of warfare changed over the centuries, these high, castellated platforms gradually disappeared. The present-day fo'c'sle is a linguistic remnant of the early forecastle.

Clamp A timber fitted fore-and-aft horizontally between a ship's frames, usually to act as a bearer for a beam.

Clump The heavy concrete slab to which a mooring chain is attached. Also, a large, heavy wooden block used for a variety of different purposes on board ship. They were more substantially built than the usual range of blocks, hence the name.

Coach A compartment near the stern of a large man-o'-war sailing ship, generally used as the captain's quarters.

Coach whipping A decorative or protective braiding worked as a whipping around some object, such as a bell-rope or handrail.

Cocked hat A term in navigation to describe the small triangle that results when three lines of position fail to meet at one point.

Compass rose The two concentric graduated compass cords or rings printed on a chart, the outer showing true north (i.e., geographical north), and the inner showing magnetic north (i.e., the direction to which a magnetic needle points as a result of being influenced by the earth's own magnetic field). The compass rose was introduced into mariners' charts in the early nineteenth century.

Crippled A rope or wire is said to be "crippled" when its lays have been disturbed by twisting or kinking. Because the strength of a rope resides in the frictional resistance between its tightly compacted fibres, yarns, and strands, any twisting, knotting, or kinking that disturbs this resistance weakens the rope at that point.

Crowd *To crowd,* or *crowd on,* is to set every stitch of canvas possible, in order to make the greatest speed.

Crown The point where the shank meets the curved arms of the anchor; also the topmost part of a block.

Crupper chain A short chain that secures the heel of the jib-boom to the head of the bowsprit; derived from the leather strap that passes from a saddle, or other harness gear, around the base of a horse's tail to prevent the saddle from slipping forward.

D

Driver Another name for the gaff sail on the mizzen mast; also known as the "spanker."

Drumhead The barrel or upper part of the capstan. In it are located the sockets for the capstan bars by which the capstan is turned.

Drummer's plait A type of plait in which the bight of the line is passed through each preceding loop; similar to chain looping.

E

Escutcheon The area on the ship's stern where her name and port of registry are shown. In its ground-sense, an escutcheon is a shield on which a coat of arms is displayed.

F

Fife rail An iron or wooden rail fitted round the base of a mast just above deck level, for carrying the belaying pins to which the falls, halliards, and such are belayed. A fife is also a small, shrill-toned musical intrument resembling a flute.

G

Gallows A support, of either metal or timber, to take the boom when the mainsail is lowered. The gallows frame is usually permanently mounted over the stern; known also as a "boom crutch."

Garland A rope collar fixed to a mast and used for supporting certain standing rigging; this is the origin of the term *topgallant* (mast and sail).

Gutter-way A channel on the outer edge of the deck; a waterway. Also "gutter-ledge," a reinforcing timber in a hatch cover.

Gypsy The notched wheel fitted to a windlass and adapted for accepting chain.

H

Harness cask A large cask, often kept on deck, from which the daily rations of salt beef or salt pork were issued. Salt beef was given the slang name *salt horse;* hence the name of the cask. Many a seaman in the early sailing ships claimed that he had found a horseshoe or nail in his rations.

Holiday A gap left unintentionally in the painting or varnishing of a ship; also, similarly, a gap in the caulking of a seam.

I

Irish pendant A pendant is a rope used for reefing, attaching blocks, and the like. An "Irish pendant" is the sailor's derisory name for odd bits of frayed rope, twine, and so forth left hanging about the rigging.

J

Jew's harp shackle A lyre-shaped shackle for joining the anchor cable to the anchor ring. Its shape permitted an additonal cable to be bent to the anchor.

Jury rig A temporary makeshift to bring a disabled vessel to safety; the usual components are a jury mast, jury sail, and jury rudder. The phrase is an old nautical witticism dating back to at least the sixteenth century, when the idea of "jury" was rather similar to the idea of whimsical fate or fortune. The synonymous French term is *mat de fortune,* mast of fortune or luck.

K

King plank The centre plank of a plank-decked vessel, with joggles cut into it to receive the ends of the remaining deck planks.

Knight heads The heavy timbers that rise above the stem to support the bowsprit, which is secured between them. In the early days of sail, these vertical timbers were often carved into a likeness of a human face, hence the name.

M

Manger A small space right up in the bows of a sailing ship, immediately by the hawsepipes. This space was bounded by a manger-board, the purpose of which was to prevent water from running back along the deck should it enter through the hawsepipes.

Martingale Part of the stays that prevent the bowsprit (or, in some ships, the jib-boom that extended beyond the end of the bowsprit) from being lifted by the various stays that carry the jibs. The martingale ran from the end of the jib-boom to the bottom of the dolphin striker and thence to each bow. A martingale is also the strap that passes from the nose band on a horse's harness, between its forelegs, to the girth, to keep the animal from rearing.

Messenger An endless rope, lighter than the anchor cable, passed around the capstan for a number of turns, and used to haul in the anchor cable when it is too heavy to be accepted by the capstan. The endless messenger is nipped at intervals to the cable, and the nippers are cast off as the cable is stowed below.
(See also *Nipper* in the main body of this book.)

N

Nave line A small tackle rigged from the masthead and secured to the parrel to keep it parallel to the yard when it is being hoisted or lowered. In the ground-sense, the nave is the main part of a church, extending from the principal entrance to the altar.

Ninepin block A wooden block shaped rather like a ninepin or a skittle, but with flattened sides.

P

Parcel *To parcel* a rope is to cover it in a spiral fashion with strips of tarred canvas after worming the grooves of the rope with light line. The canvas is then bound or served tightly with strong line. The whole is to protect the rope from water rot.

Partners The timber framework that reinforces the opening cut into the deck where the mast, capstan, pump housing, and such pass through.

R

Rack As in "pin rack," a wooden or iron frame for holding belaying pins; usually larger than a fife rail. "Racking" is a means of joining two eyes, bights, or the like together, with lashing hauled taut.

Riders An additional frame bolted to the main frames to strengthen the ship's hull. Also, timbers inserted between the keelson and the beams of the orlop deck above to provide greater support when the hull has been weakened by stranding or other accident.

Rose knot A type of decorative knot worked into a rope's end. A "rose lashing" is a method of securing the eye of a rope to a spar; the interweaving of the lashing is said to resemble a rose.

Rung The lowest timber in a ship's built-up frame.

Runner A rope used to increase the mechanical power of a tackle. Also, the two shifting backstays led from the masthead to each quarter of the vessel; they support the mast when the wind is abaft the beam. The lee runner is set free and the weather runner is set up, both being attended to at the same time as the vessel gybes or tacks.

S

Saddle A block of wood secured to a spar and used as a location and support for another spar; for example, the jib-boom is secured to the bowsprit by a saddle.

Sampson post A strong timber stepped on the keelson, used as a support for the deck beams; also a similar baulk of timber through-mounted on the fore-deck for taking any towing or anchoring strain.

A Scarborough warning Seamen's expression meaning to let go something without warning, such as a cargo lift and a boat's falls. From an incident in 1557 when Scarborough Castle was stormed by Stafford; any men found in the vicinity by Stafford's soldiers were hanged forthwith, without benefit of trial, on suspicion of robbery. Hence, a Scarborough warning is no warning at all.

Scotchman A protective covering placed over standing rigging to prevent chafing; usually of stiff hide, timber battens, or similar material. The term may be the seaman's way of referring to the Scot's alleged habit of jealously protecting his belongings and money.

Scroll The ornamental moulding often found at a vessel's stem in place of a figurehead.

Sea lawyer A know-all in the crew; one who knows all his rights but admits few of his responsibilities.

Shamrock knot A knot tied so that three loops are left standing equidistant about the centre; often used for attaching temporary stays and shrouds to a jury mast.

Shot garland The timbers or planks with cavities worked into them for holding the ship's roundshot in ready piles at each gun. Often arranged around a hatch opening; hence the name "garland."

Sister blocks A single shell containing two sheaves, one set above the other. The shell is grooved for stropping and seizing.

Soldier's wind The name given by seamen to the wind when it is blowing from a-beam, to a vessel that is on course. Thus, no sail-handling is needed, nor any great skill required in steering; even a soldier ("sodger") could do it.

Spoke The hand grip of a steering wheel (i.e., of the Dutch wheel).

Spur A baulk of timber used as a prop to support a vessel under construction; it is located at the turn of the bilge.

Star knot A knot with fivefold symmetry, worked into the end of a rope.

Stirrup Short ropes with eyes in the ends, attached to the yard so that the foot-rope is rove through the eye of the stirrup.

T

Tabernacle A step or housing built on deck with the after-side left open, so that a mast can be stepped and hinged, and lowered for bridges. In the ground-sense, a tabernacle is the portable sanctuary carried by the Jews in their wanderings out of Egypt. It is also an enclosure, similar to a cabinet, placed on the altar for the consecrated Hosts.

Tree A general name for a wooden beam that is used as part of a vessel's fittings, as in "chess-trees" and "trestle-trees."

Trot A multiple mooring for small craft. A long, heavy chain is laid down on the sea bed, securely anchored at intervals. Numerous individual rising chains are attached with mooring buoys at their head, to give a long line of moorings in a comparatively small area.

Truss The rope or chain that secures a lower yard to the mast. Lower yards are not hoisted or lowered, hence the truss. Upper yards are held in to the mast by a parrel, which thus allows the yard to slide up and down when needed. *To truss* is to bind, to support, or to strengthen, as a fowl is trussed before cooking, or a truss is built to support a roof.

Turk's head An ornamental knot worked into the end of a rope as a stopper knot or decoration, which resembles a turban in appearance.

W

Waif-pole The tall pole that is thrust into the carcass of a newly killed whale, with the mark of the whale-boat crew that killed it.

Well A space in the bottom of a ship, usually the lowest portion, into which the bilge water drains. The well is usually enclosed and houses the pumping gear.

Whip A light tackle used for lifting or moving relatively small objects. A single whip consists of a rope passing through a fixed block.

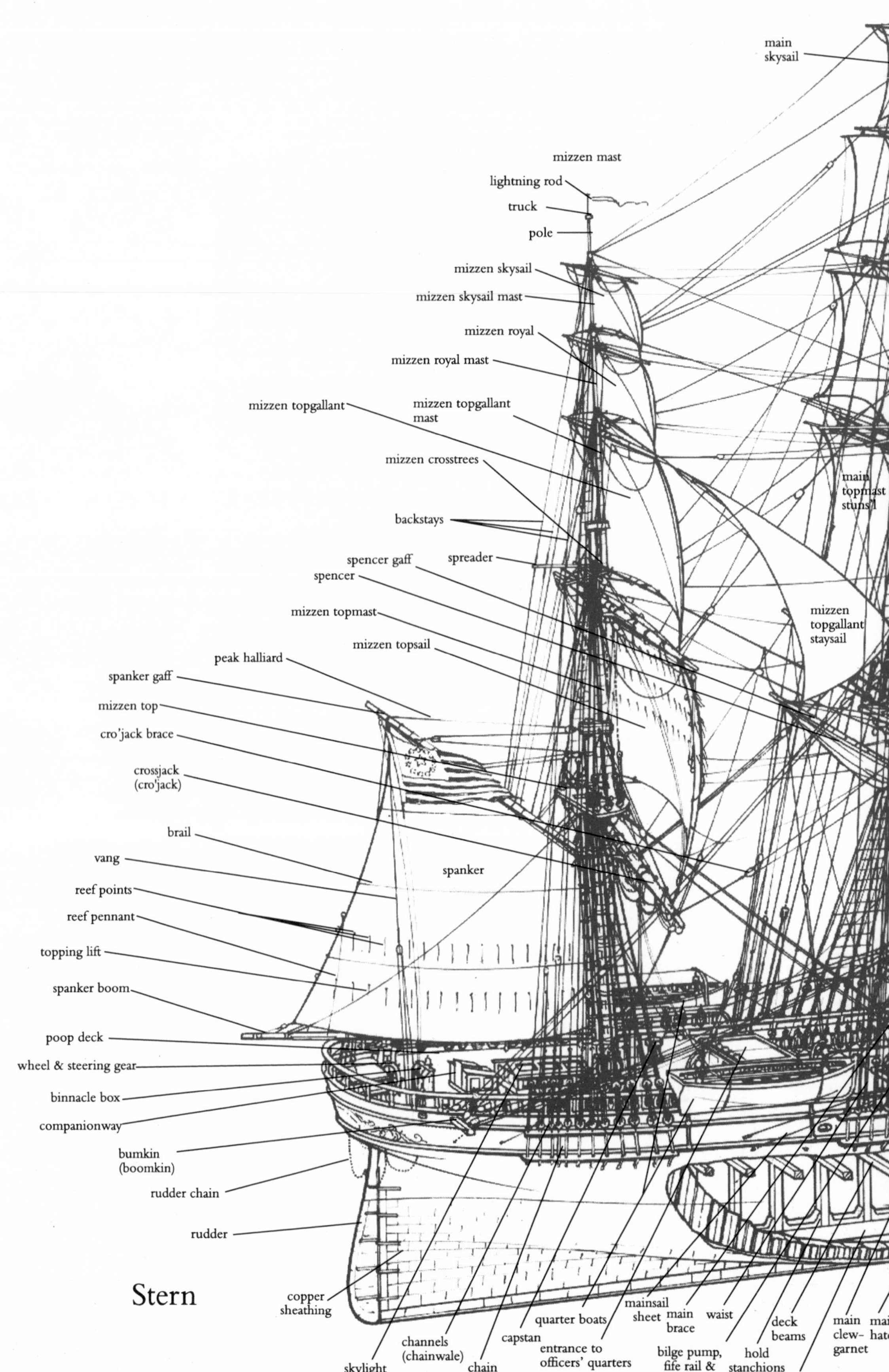

main skysail
mizzen mast
lightning rod
truck
pole
mizzen skysail
mizzen skysail mast
mizzen royal
mizzen royal mast
mizzen topgallant
mizzen topgallant mast
mizzen crosstrees
main topmast stuns'l
backstays
spreader
spencer gaff
spencer
mizzen topmast
mizzen topgallant staysail
mizzen topsail
peak halliard
spanker gaff
mizzen top
cro'jack brace
crossjack (cro'jack)
brail
vang
spanker
reef points
reef pennant
topping lift
spanker boom
poop deck
wheel & steering gear
binnacle box
companionway
bumkin (boomkin)
rudder chain
rudder
Stern
copper sheathing
skylight
channels (chainwale)
chain plate
capstan
quarter boats
entrance to officers' quarters
mainsail sheet
main brace
bilge pump, fire rail & bitts
waist
hold stanchions
deck beams
keelson
main clew-garnet
main hatch